WORKING WITH SPSS (PASW STATISTICS)

COMMON UNIVARIATE ANALYSES (with SPSS Menu Sequence)

Frequency Analysis (used to produce counts and proportions of cases falling into each response category for categorical variables)

Analyze > Descriptive Statistics > Frequencies

Descriptive Statistics (used to produce summary statistics for continuous variables)

Analyze > Descriptive Statistics > Descriptives

Chi-square Goodness-of-fit Test (used to compare sample proportions against an external standard)

Analyze > Nonparametric Tests > Legacy Dialogs > Chi-square

One-Sample T-test (used to compare a sample mean against an external standard)

Analyze > Compare Means > One-Sample T Test

COMMON MULTIVARIATE ANALYSES (with SPSS Menu Sequence)

Cross Tabulation (used to examine the joint distribution of two categorical variables)

Analyze > Descriptive Statistics > Crosstabs

Independent Samples *T*-test for Means (used to test for differences across two groups on a continuous variable)

Analyze > Compare Means > Independent-Samples T Test

Paired Sample *T*-test for Means (used to test for differences across two continuous variables provided by a single sample)

Analyze > Compare Means > Paired-Samples T Test

Pearson Product-moment Correlation Coefficient (used to assess the degree of association between two continuous variables)

Analyze > Correlate > Bivariate

Regression Analysis (used to test the relationship between one or more continuous or categorical predictor variables and a continuous outcome variable)

Analyze > Regression > Linear

Working with SPSS (PASW Statistics)

PREPARING A DATA SOURCE FOR ANALYSIS IN SPSS

Step One. Open the SPSS (or PASW) program. A dialog box titled "Open an Existing Data Source" should appear. If not, follow this menu sequence: *File > Open > Data...*

Step Two. If you recently have used the data file, it should be an option in the dialog box window. Otherwise, select "more files." In the "Open Data" dialog box, start by selecting the type of file in which the data are saved (e.g., SPSS datafile [.sav], Excel file [.xls or .xlsx], text file [.txt]) using the "Files of type:" option. Then find the data file, wherever you have stored it ("Look in" Desktop, Document, a flash drive, etc.), using the directories in the "Open Data" dialog box. Select the file and click "Open."

[Different versions of the Avery Fitness Center (AFC) data file are available under the names "AFC_MR_2012.sav" (SPSS data file) and "AFC_MR_2012.xls" (Excel). The AFC survey and codebook are available in chapter 11 of MR 2012.]

- Opening an SPSS data file takes you immediately to the working data file to begin analyses.
- Opening an Excel file opens another dialog box, "Opening Excel Data Source." If the Excel file contains variable names in the first row, click the box for "Read variable names from the first row of data" and then click "OK." SPSS will convert the Excel file (with variable names) into an SPSS data file and you are ready to begin analyses. If the Excel file does NOT contain variable names, make certain the box for "Read variable names from the first row of data" is not checked and click "OK." SPSS will convert the Excel file into an SPSS data file; you will need to add variable names to the "Name" column on the "Variable View" tab.

Step Three. Working from the "Variable View" tab, select the correct variable "type" (usually "numeric" unless a variable contains letters rather than numbers) for each variable. This is also a good time to insert a label for each variable (if necessary; sometimes it's easier just to work with a short, descriptive variable name than to work with longer variable labels—by default, SPSS uses variable names, but if you provide a label, it will use the label instead of the variable name). It is often very helpful to define value labels for some or all of the variables using the "values" column. Working from your codebook, click the cell corresponding to a variable for which you want to add labels and then click the "..." button that appears. A dialog box opens and you can insert a value (for example, "1") and a label that corresponds to that value (for example, "male" for the variable GENDER in the AFC codebook; see chapter 11 of *MR 2012*); click the "add" button to add this value label (and repeat this process for the other values associated with that particular variable). Once you have added value labels to some or all variables, you can also define any special codes that you've used to represent missing values using the "missing" column. (If you've simply left blanks for missing information, you don't need to do anything.)

Step Four. Save the data file as an SPSS data file using the menu sequence: *File > Save as...* Provide a file name, choose a destination folder, make certain that you have selected "PASW Statistics (*.sav)" in the "Save as type:" option, and click "Save."

OVER →

CourseMate

Engaging. Trackable. Affordable.

CourseMate brings course concepts to life with interactive learning, study, and exam preparation tools that support MR.

INCLUDES:
Integrated eBook, **teaching and learning tools,** and **Engagement Tracker**, a first-of-its-kind tool that monitors student engagement in the course.

ON THE WEB

MR
Are you in?

ONLINE RESOURCES INCLUDED!

FOR INSTRUCTORS:
- First Day of Class Instructions
- Custom Options through 4LTR+ Program
- Instructor's Manual
- Test Bank
- PowerPoint® Slides
- Instructor Prep Cards
- Engagement Tracker

FOR STUDENTS:
- Interactive eBook
- Auto-Graded Quizzes
- Flashcards
- Games: Crossword Puzzles & Beat the Clock
- PowerPoint® Slides
- eLectures

Students sign in at **www.cengagebrain.com**

SOUTH-WESTERN
CENGAGE Learning™

MR

Thomas J. Brown, Tracy Suter

Executive VP/Publisher: Jonathan Hulbert

Vice President of Editorial, Business: Jack W. Calhoun

Publisher: Erin Joyner

Director, 4LTR Press: Neil Marquardt

Acquisitions Editor: Mike Roche

Developmental Editor: Elizabeth Lowry

Editorial Assistant: Megan Fischer

Marketing Manager: Gretchen Swann

Product Development Manager: Steven Joos

Associate Content Project Manager: Jana Lewis

Media Editor: John Rich

Manufacturing Planner: Ron Montgomery

Senior Marketing Communications Manager: Jim Overly

Production Service: Manoj Kumar, MPS Limited, a Macmillan Company

Senior Art Director: Stacy Jenkins-Shirley

Internal Designer: KeDesign, Mason, OH

Cover Designer: KeDesign, Mason, OH

Cover Image: © Veer

Rights Acquisitions Specialist: Deanna Ettinger

Photo Researcher: Terri Miller/E-Visual Communications, Inc.

Text Researcher: Nancy Kincade, PreMedia Global, Ltd.

Library of Congress Control Number: 2011931418

ISBN-13: 978-1-111-53240-6

ISBN-10: 1-111-53240-0

Student Edition ISBN 13: 978-1-111-53238-3

Student Edition ISBN 10: 1-111-53238-9

South-Western
5191 Natorp Boulevard
Mason, OH 45040
USA

Cengage Learning products are represented in Canada by Nelson Education, Ltd.

For your course and learning solutions, visit **www.cengage.com**

Purchase any of our products at your local college store or at our preferred online store **www.cengagebrain.com**

Printed in the United States of America
1 2 3 4 5 6 7 15 14 13 12 11

MR

BROWN / SUTER

Brief Contents

Contents

© MARTIN BARRAUD/ICONICA/GETTY IMAGES

© CHAD MCDERMOTT/SHUTTERSTOCK.COM

© ISTOCKPHOTO.COM/WDSTOCK

© ISTOCKPHOTO.COM/DNY59

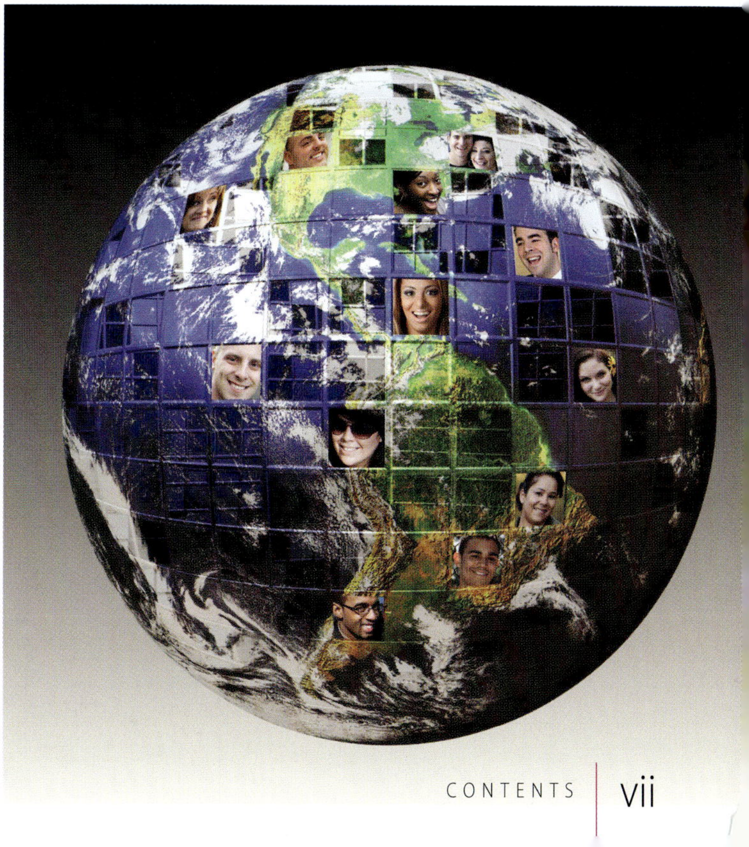

Andersen Ross/Getty Images

REVIEW!

HE DID

MR puts a multitude of study aids at your fingertips. After reading the chapters, check out these resources for further help:

- **Chapter In Review Cards** in the back of the Student Edition provide students all of the pertinent information for each chapter, along with **Qualtrics & SPSS Cards**, providing quick tips on how to use these engaging programs.

- **Online Printable Flashcards** give you additional ways to check your comprehension of key Marketing Research concepts.

- Other great tools to help you review include **interactive games, PowerPoint® slides, and auto-graded quizzes.**

Go to CourseMate for MR to find plenty of resources to help you *Review!* Access at www.cengagebrain.com.

Andersen Ross/Getty Images

SPEAK UP!

THEY DID

MR was built on a simple principle: to create a new teaching and learning solution that reflects the way today's faculty and students teach and learn. Through conversations, focus groups, surveys, and interviews, we collected data that drove the creation of the version of **MR** that you are using today.

But it doesn't stop there – in order to make **MR** an even better learning experience, we'd like you to SPEAK UP and tell us how **MR** works for you.

What do you like about it? What would you change? Do you have additional ideas that would help us build a better product for next year's students?

***Speak Up!* Go to CourseMate for MR. Access at www.cengagebrain.com.**

Industry Advisory Panel

We are indebted to the following individuals who served on our Industry Advisory Panel and provided feedback on the contents of the book during its development. They graciously donated their expertise and time to help us deliver a book that is relevant, accurate, and covers the most important issues. They offered terrific ideas and objective critique; any remaining errors in the book are our own.

Karen Ba
StrataVerve Intelligence Online
Minneapolis, Minnesota

James Breeze
Chief Experience Officer
Objective Technology Pty Ltd
Sydney, Australia

DiAnn Brown
Adjunct Professor
Business Communications
Spears School of Business
Oklahoma State University
Stillwater, Oklahoma

Patrick Glaser
Director of Research Standards
Marketing Research Association
Glastonbury, Connecticut

Andrew Kennelly
Market Research Director
EmSense Corporation
San Francisco, California

Scott Keplinger
VP Customer Insight & Retention
Aviva USA
Des Moines, Iowa

Paul Metz
Senior Vice President
C&R Research Services, Inc.
Chicago, Illinois

Sara Pitterle
Director of Institutional Effectiveness
Nicolet Area Technical College
Summit Lake, Wisconsin

Michael Render
Primary Consultant
RVA Market Research and Consulting
Tulsa, Oklahoma

1 Marketing Research:
From Data to Information to Action

© RICHARD LEVINE/ALAMY

POLL QUESTION:

Almost everyone is a consumer of marketing research.

STRONGLY DISAGREE 1 ○ 2 ○ 3 ○ 4 ○ 5 ○ STRONGLY AGREE

Learning Objectives

1. Define marketing research.
2. Discuss different kinds of organizations that conduct marketing research.
3. List three reasons for studying marketing research.
4. Discuss why researchers should care about marketing research ethics.

INTRODUCTION

Marketing research is a much broader and more common activity than most people realize. You've probably completed surveys on paper, online, or over the telephone, but there is much more to marketing research than just asking consumers how they think or feel about a product or an ad. Consider Best Buy's in-store recycling program: Consumers can drop off their old electronics at any Best Buy store in the United States. On some items, such as TVs and computer monitors, the company usually charges a $10 fee but gives the consumer a $10 gift card in exchange.

The Best Buy recycling program may be good for the planet, but what does it have to do with marketing research? The company carefully tracks usage of the gift cards to see whether the recycling program is bringing new customers to the store. And they get a glimpse of the behavioral patterns of these customers in terms of what they purchase with the gift card, a great example of observational research.[1]

This chapter introduces the broad role of marketing research within an organization. In addition, we identify different types of companies that conduct marketing research and discuss three important reasons that business students should develop a working knowledge of marketing research. We end the chapter with a discussion of marketing research ethics.

FAST FACT:

IN THE FIRST QUARTER OF 2010, **53%** OF U.S. HOUSEHOLDS HAD **HDTVs**.

THE PROBLEM: MARKETERS NEED INFORMATION

Regardless of the types of products or services offered, all organizations share a common problem: They need information in order to accomplish their goals effectively. Different organizations need different kinds of information, and the information they need can be gathered in many different ways. Services marketers use the results of marketing research studies to determine how satisfied their customers are. Politicians use marketing research to plan campaign strategies. Churches use marketing research to determine when to hold services. The point is that marketing research is an essential activity that can take many forms, but its basic functions are (1) to gather data and (2) transform the data into useful information that managers can use to make decisions.

Data → **Information** → **Action**

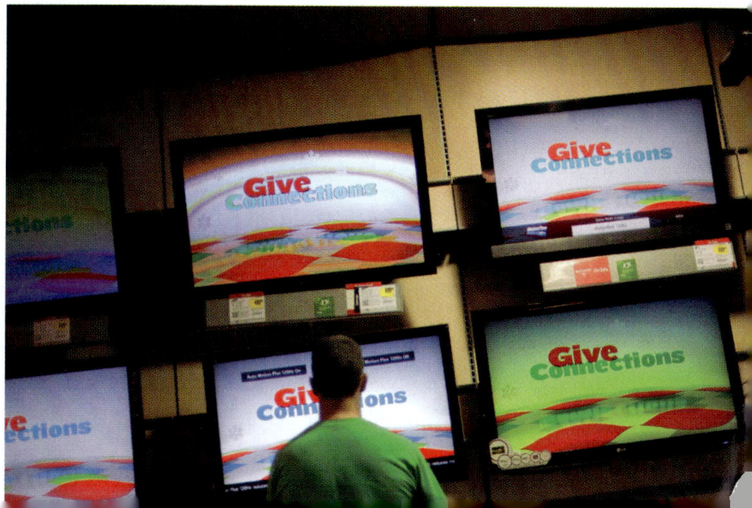

The task of marketing is to create exchanges with customers that satisfy the needs of both the customer and the marketer. In their attempts to create satisfying exchanges with customers, marketing managers generally focus their efforts on the four P's—namely, the product or service, its price, its placement or the channels in which it is distributed, and its promotion or communications mix. Many factors in the marketing environment affect the success of the marketing effort. These factors include other social actors (competitors, suppliers, governmental agencies, customers themselves, and so on) and societal trends in the external environment (economic, political and legal, social, natural, technological, and competitive trends; see Exhibit 1.1). As a result, the marketing manager has an urgent need for information—and that's where marketing research comes in. **Marketing research** is the organization's formal communication link with the environment. Through marketing research, the organization gathers and interprets data from the environment for use in developing, implementing, and monitoring the firm's marketing plans.

marketing research
The organization's formal communication link with the environment.

Solid marketing research is becoming increasingly important as the world moves to a global economy. For example, marketing research helped McDonald's adjust its positioning as attitudes toward the company changed in the United Kingdom. When the company first crossed the Atlantic in the mid-1970s, customers were attracted to its American origins and the novelty of fast food. Reflecting this appeal, McDonald's first

EXHIBIT 1.1

The Need for Information: Environments Affecting Marketing

U.K. ad slogan announced, "There's a difference at McDonald's you'll enjoy."

The fast-food giant used consumer research to keep tabs on opinions as the market matured. Fifteenyears after McDonald's began serving the U.K. market, consumers were describing McDonald's as inflexible and arrogant—and managers knew it was time to adjust. They softened their messaging strategy and began to depict McDonald's at the center of U.K. family life. The company has enjoyed double-digit sales growth in recent years and more than 2.5 million people in the United Kingdom visit McDonald's restaurants each day.[2]

WHO DOES MARKETING RESEARCH?

Although individuals and organizations have practiced marketing research for centuries—the need for information has always existed—the formal practice of marketing research can be traced to 1879 when advertising agency N. W. Ayer & Son collected data on expected grain production from state officials and publishers across the United States for a client who produced agricultural machinery. The agency constructed a crude market survey by states and counties; this was probably the first real instance of marketing research in the United States.[3]

Today three major categories of firms conduct marketing research: (1) producers of products and services, (2) advertising agencies, and (3) marketing research companies.

Producers of Products and Services

Marketing research really began to grow around the end of World War II when firms found they could no longer sell all they could produce but instead had to gauge market needs and produce accordingly. Marketing research was called on to estimate these needs. As consumers began to have more choices in the marketplace, marketing began to assume a more dominant role. The marketing concept emerged, and along with it came a reorganization of the marketing effort. Many marketing research departments were born in these reorganizations.

Most large firms (and many smaller ones, too) have one or more people assigned specifically to the marketing research activity. Organizations that produce products or deliver services for businesses or consumers often conduct research designed to develop and market their products and services. For

© BA LARUE/ALAMY

example, organizations as diverse as Kraft Foods, National Public Radio, Unilever, ESPN, and Southwest Airlines all have internal marketing research departments. Large retailers such as Target Corporation and Walmart also operate research departments to gather information about consumer preferences, store image, and so on.

Many companies use marketing research to track customer satisfaction and customer usage patterns. For example, researchers at Silver Dollar City, a popular theme park located near Branson, Missouri, found that visitors from over 301 miles away (outer market) took three times longer to plan their trips to Silver Dollar City than did guests who lived less than 100 miles away (core market). Based on these findings, the marketing department altered its promotions strategy and started advertising in outer markets several weeks before beginning those same ads in the core market. This resulted in more efficient advertising purchasing, and the message was presented to visitors at the time they were making plans to visit.

Advertising Agencies

As you might imagine, advertising agencies often conduct research designed to help create and measure the effectiveness of advertising campaigns. This may involve testing alternative approaches to the wording or graphics used in an ad or investigating the effectiveness of various celebrity spokespersons. However, many agencies also do marketing research for their clients to determine the market potential of a proposed new product or the client's market share.

Ad agencies sometimes do research to better understand consumers, their interests and behaviors in order to serve their corporate clients. For instance, media agency MEC conducted an extensive project to better understand women shoppers in 542 smaller Chinese cities, which agency executives saw as an important potential market for expansion in the Chinese market. The segmentation study uncovered five distinct segments characterized by the following labels: *The Pressure Cooker* (desire for personal success, family success, and a sense of identity as a woman); *The Traditional* (family comes first at all costs); *The Practical* (a pragmatic approach to life); *The Achiever* (desire to excel; open-minded and up to date); and *The Undecided* (not in touch with social and economic changes around her). Media usage trends differed across the segments. For example, the percentage that had accessed the Internet was relatively high for the Achievers (58%), the Practicals (48%), and the Undecideds (35%) but dropped significantly for the Pressure Cookers (20%) and the Traditionals (5%). The implications for reaching these women are important for MEC clients.[4]

Marketing Research Companies

Many companies specialize in conducting marketing research. The United States is home to 14 of the Top 25 largest market research firms in the world. Moreover, worldwide total revenues for these largest firms exceed $17.4 billion.[5] And don't forget that these numbers don't reflect the research done by organizations' own research departments or by advertising agencies or others.

© STEPHEN COBURN/SHUTTERSTOCK.COM

Although most specialized marketing research firms are small, a few are sizable enterprises. Exhibit 1.2 shows the names, home countries, and revenues of the 10 largest marketing research firms in the world. Some firms provide syndicated research; they collect certain information on a regular basis, which they then sell to interested clients. The syndicated services include organizations such as The Nielsen Company, which provides product-movement data for grocery stores and drugstores (not

EXHIBIT 1.2

The World's 10 Largest Marketing Research Firms

Rank/Organization	Parent Country	Worldwide Research Revenue (U.S. $, in millions)
1. The Nielsen Company	USA	$4,628.0
2. Kantar	UK	2,823.2
3. IMS Health Inc.	USA	2,198.7
4. GfK SE	Germany	1,622.8
5. Ipsos SA	France	1,315.0
6. Synovate	UK	816.4
7. SymphonyIRI Group	USA	706.3
8. Westat Inc.	USA	502.4
9. Arbitron Inc.	USA	385.0
10. INTAGE Inc.	Japan	368.6

Source: Developed from information in "2010 Honomichl Global Top 25," *Marketing News* (August 30, 2010), pp. 12–54. This report describes the services provided by the 25 largest global market research organizations.

to mention the popular TV ratings), and Arbitron, which measures U.S. radio audiences. Syndicated research is not custom designed for a particular client, but is designed and collected by the research company and sold to multiple clients.

Other firms, though, specialize in custom-designed research. Some of these provide only a field service; they collect data and return the data-collection instruments directly to the research sponsor. Some are limited-service firms, which not only collect the data but also analyze them for the client. And some are full-service research suppliers, which help the client in the design of the research as well as in collecting and analyzing data. For example, GfK SE provides full-service customized research services for numerous *Fortune* 500 clients. GfK can conduct large-scale qualitative or quantitative studies from start to finish, utilizing a range of data collection techniques.

Other organizations that provide or conduct marketing research include government agencies, trade associations, and universities. Government agencies provide much marketing information in the form of published statistics. In fact, the U.S. government is one of the world's largest producers of marketing facts through its various censuses and other publications. Trade associations often collect and share data gathered from members. Much university-sponsored research of interest to marketers is produced by the marketing faculty or by the bureaus of business research found in many schools of business. Faculty research is often reported in marketing journals; research bureaus often publish monographs on various topics of interest.

WHY STUDY MARKETING RESEARCH?

Almost all business schools offer courses in marketing research, and many require students who are completing majors in marketing to take a marketing research course. Why? (Maybe you're asking yourself this question right about now!)

We think there are three important reasons for learning about marketing research. First, some students will discover that marketing research can be rewarding and fun. For these students, learning how to be an "information detective" may lead to a career in marketing research. These students usually develop an early appreciation for taking data and converting them into information that can be used by marketing managers to make important decisions. So, for some people at least, the study of marketing research will be directly relevant to their careers.

Even if you don't go on to a career in marketing research, all of us are consumers of marketing and public opinion research, almost on a daily basis. The second reason for studying marketing research is to learn to be a *smarter* consumer of research results. Businesspeople are often exposed to research results, usually by someone trying to convince them to do something. Suppliers use research to promote the virtues of their particular products and services; advertising agencies use research to encourage a company to promote a product in particular media vehicles; product managers inside a firm use research to demonstrate the likely demand for the products they are developing to get further funding. Effective managers, however, know the right questions to ask to evaluate the research results they are shown.

A third key reason for studying marketing research is to gain an appreciation of the process, what it can and cannot do. As a manager, you will need to know what to expect marketing research to be able to deliver. The process of gathering data and generating information is full of opportunities for error to slip into the results. Thus, no research is perfect, and managers must take this into account when making decisions. Managers also need to understand what they are asking of researchers when requesting marketing research. The process is detailed, time consuming, and requires great amounts of thought and effort. As a result, marketing research is costly to an organization and should *not* be undertaken on trivial issues or to support decisions that have already been made.

THE MARKETING RESEARCH PROCESS

All marketing research efforts are unique, because the problems or opportunities they address are different. Even so, there is a general sequence of steps—the **research process** (see Exhibit 1.3)—that can be followed when designing and conducting research. This section provides a quick overview of the research process, and the remaining chapters in the book discuss the stages in more detail.

research process
A general sequence of steps that can be followed when designing and conducting research.

ONLY WHEN THE PROBLEM IS PRECISELY DEFINED CAN RESEARCH BE DESIGNED TO PROVIDE THE NEEDED INFORMATION.

EXHIBIT 1.3

Stages in the Research Process

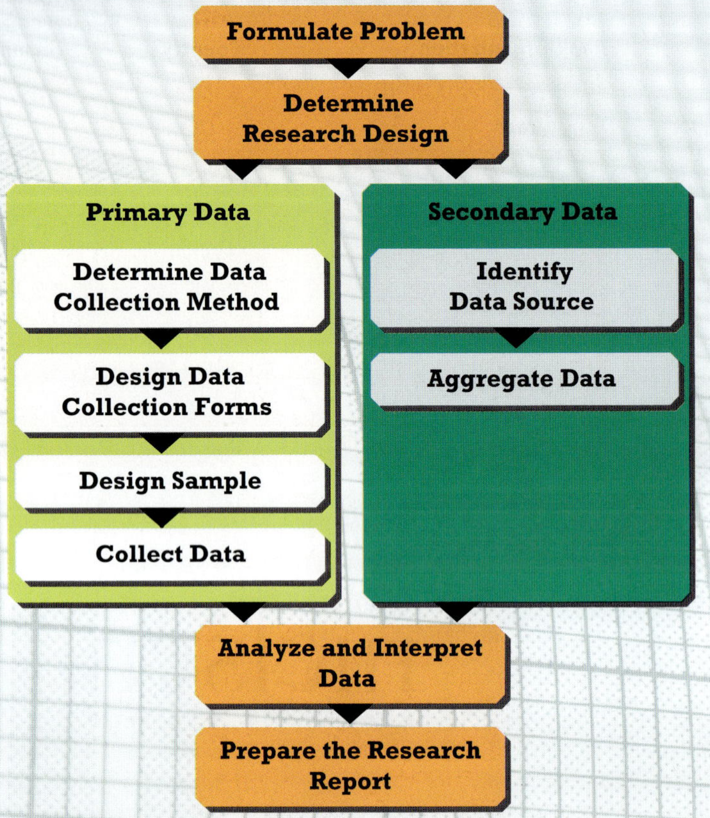

The first—and most important—step in the marketing research process is to define the marketing problem to be solved (*Chapter 2*). Only when the problem is precisely defined can research be designed to provide the needed information. The manager's decision problem and the research problem to be pursued by the researcher should be specified and agreed upon by researchers and managers in the form of a written research request agreement. The next step is to decide which research design (i.e., exploratory, descriptive, or causal) is appropriate (*Chapter 3*). The choice of research design depends on how much is known about the problem. If relatively little is known about the phenomenon to be investigated, *exploratory research* is needed. Some researchers apply the label "qualitative research" to this kind of research. If, instead of being broad or vague, a problem is well defined and clearly stated, *descriptive* or *causal research* is needed. Descriptive research focuses on describing a population, often emphasizing the frequency with which something occurs or the extent to which two variables are related to one another. The causal design often uses experiments to identify cause-and-effect relationships between variables. Sometimes descriptive or causal research is referred to as "quantitative research."

Sometimes the information that a firm needs to solve its problem already exists in the form of *secondary data*, or data that have already been collected for some purpose other than the question at hand (*Chapter 4*). Such data may exist in the firm's own internal information system as purchase or customer data, call reports from the sales force, or orders from wholesalers. If the firm itself doesn't have the necessary information, it may be available in the form of government statistics, trade association reports, or data from a commercial research supplier. Because such data are almost always less expensive and can be obtained and analyzed more quickly, researchers should look for existing sources of data first before launching a primary data collection effort. The Internet has greatly facilitated the discovery of secondary data.

© ASIA IMAGES GROUP/PHOTOLIBRARY

If good secondary data aren't available or don't fit the situation for some reason, the researcher will collect *primary data,* which are data collected specifically for the study (*Chapters 5 and 6*). There are lots of questions to be answered when collecting primary data, including: Should the data be collected by observation or questionnaire? How should these observations be made—personally or electronically? How should the questions be administered—in person, over the telephone, through the mail, or online? Once the researchers have settled on the method to be used for the study, they must design the data collection forms to be used on the project (*Chapters 7 and 8*).

Next comes the development of an appropriate sample (*Chapter 9*). Depending on the study, the *population* might be homemakers, preschoolers, sports car drivers, Pennsylvanians, tennis players, or so on. The particular subset of the population for whom data are available is known as a *sample.* There are two basic types of sampling plans, those that produce a *probability sample* (the preferred type) and those that lead to a *nonprobability sample.* The size of the sample depends upon how many members of the population it is necessary to use to get reliable answers without exceeding the time and money budgeted for the project. Once the sample design is in place, data collection can begin (*Chapter 10*).

Researchers may gather mountains of secondary or primary data, but data are useless unless they are analyzed and interpreted in light of the problem at hand (*Chapters 11–13*). Most data analysis is quite straightforward, involving frequency counts (usually, how many people answered a question a particular way) or simple descriptive statistics (for example, means and standard deviations). Sometimes the research calls for cross-tabulation, which allows a deeper look at the data by examining differences or relationships across groups, or some other type of multivariate analysis.

Finally, it's time to prepare the written research report (and oral presentation), including graphical representation of data, that summarizes the research results and conclusions (*Chapter 14*). This is a really important step, because this is the only part of the process that most other people will ever see. As a result, the research report must be clear and accurate, because no matter how well you've performed all the previous steps in the research, the project will be no more successful than the research report.

Before we move on, there's something important we need to point out about the research process shown in Exhibit 1.3. Although we've presented the stages in a particular order, some of the steps can be carried out at about the same time—and decisions about later steps will influence what should happen at earlier stages. It would get confusing, but Exhibit 1.3 probably should be drawn with a number of feedback loops representing the need to rethink, redraft, or revise the various elements in the process as it proceeds. For example, the problem may not be defined well enough to allow the development of the research design. If that happens, you'll need to return to stage one to define the research problem(s) more clearly. Or maybe the process goes smoothly all the way through the design of the data collection forms—and then the pretest of the survey identifies problems with the forms, methods used, research design, or even problem definition. The process isn't always as straightforward as it looks.

MARKETING RESEARCH ETHICS

Ethics are the moral principles and values that govern the way an individual or a group conducts its activities. Ethics apply to all situations in which there can be actual or potential harm of any kind (e.g., economic, physical, or mental) to an individual or a group. **Marketing research ethics** are the principles, values, and standards of conduct followed by marketing researchers.

THE GOAL OF ANY MARKETING RESEARCH PROJECT SHOULD BE TO UNCOVER THE TRUTH ABOUT THE TOPIC OF INTEREST.

marketing research ethics The principles, values, and standards of conduct followed by marketing researchers.

Unfortunately, there are lots of examples of organizations demonstrating questionable ethics. Several years ago the Coca-Cola Company wanted to increase sales through Burger King restaurants. Managers at Burger King were willing to sponsor a multimillion-dollar promotion for Frozen Coke if a two-week market test indicated that a Frozen Coke coupon would increase sales of value meals. When the results for the first week weren't so

good, Coke representatives rigged the market test by giving $9,000 in cash to kids' clubs and other nonprofits in the test market city to be used to buy hundreds of value meals. The resulting increase in sales was enough to convince Burger King to go forward with the national Frozen Coke promotion . . . which ultimately failed.[6]

Leading marketing and opinion research trade associations publish detailed codes of ethics for their members.

COURTESY OF THE MARKETING RESEARCH ASSOCIATION (MRA)

COURTESY OF CASRO

COURTESY OF ESOMAR

The goal of any marketing research project should be to uncover the truth about the topic of interest. In the previous example, the objective should have been to learn about the effectiveness of the Frozen Coke promotion, not to produce a result that somebody wanted to see. There's a name for research that is conducted to support a position rather than to find the truth about an issue: **advocacy research**. Researchers doing this type of research may word questions in such a way that they get the answers they want. They might select a sample of respondents known to support the position the researcher wants. They might do any number of other unethical things (like give kids money to buy value meals). These kinds of research practices are fraudulent and must be avoided if marketing research is to maintain its usefulness within the organization.

advocacy research
Research that is conducted to support a position rather than to find the truth about an issue.

It isn't just marketing researchers who could use research in unethical ways. For example, consider the use of **sugging**: contacting people under the guise of marketing research when the real goal is to sell products or services. Several years ago, one of us was contacted by a local automobile dealership and invited to a special "market test" at the dealership the following weekend. Inquiries with the dealership—and the promotions company they were working with—eventually revealed that the only "research" being conducted involved how many people they could get into the dealership to take a test drive . . . and buy a car. An employee of the promotions company admitted that they do this because it works.

sugging
Contacting people under the guise of marketing research when the real goal is to sell products or services.

Some researchers (and managers as well) often fail to think about whether it is morally acceptable to proceed in a particular way. Many think that if an action is legal, then it is ethical. It's not that simple, however. There can be differences between what is ethical and what is legal. Even among those who understand this, many don't seem to consider the ethical implications of their decisions. Some researchers probably just don't care; others may find it easier to ignore such considerations because doing the right thing isn't always easy.

Marketing researchers must recognize that their jobs depend on the goodwill of the public. "Bad" research that violates the trust of study participants will only make it more difficult and costly to recruit participants for data collection. Even researchers who don't care about whether their actions are right or wrong ought to be concerned about such issues from a business perspective. Good ethics is good business—and virtually all marketing and public opinion research associations have developed codes of ethics to guide the behaviors of their members.

2

The Research Question:

Formulation of the Problem

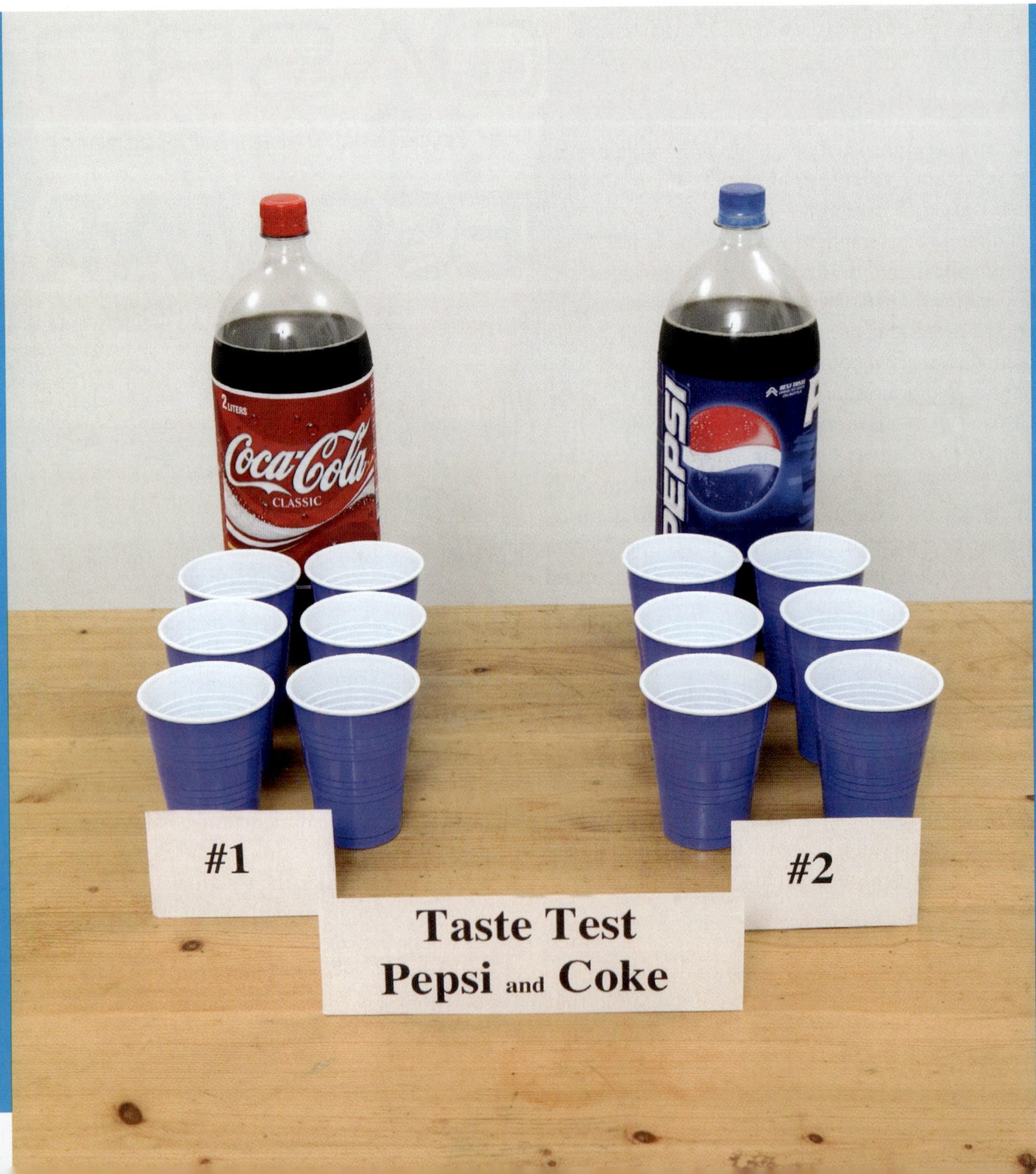

POLL QUESTION:

Using taste tests is a fool-proof method of conducting marketing research.

STRONGLY DISAGREE 1 ○ 2 ○ 3 ○ 4 ○ 5 ○ STRONGLY AGREE

Learning Objectives

1. Specify the key steps in problem formulation.
2. Distinguish between two types of decision problems.
3. Distinguish between a decision problem and a research problem.
4. Describe the research request agreement.
5. Outline the various elements of the research proposal.

INTRODUCTION

A business executive once remarked that he had spent his entire career climbing the ladder of success only to discover when he got to the top that the ladder was leaning on the wrong building. He wished that he had devoted more of his time to the things that really mattered. If we aren't careful, the same thing can happen with marketing research: We can take all the necessary steps and get perfectly valid answers—only to discover that we've been asking the wrong questions. It is unlikely that you will get the chance to "re-do" research if you find out that you missed something or that you went down the wrong path. As a result, it's critical that you properly design the research project up front so that you don't spend a lot of money on the wrong problem!

PROBLEM FORMULATION

The Coca-Cola Company's experience with New Coke in the 1980s is a classic example of how defining the problem incorrectly can lead to disastrous results.[1] Coca-Cola's market share had shrunk from 60 percent in the mid-1940s to less than 24 percent in 1983. Stung by Pepsi-Cola's "Pepsi Challenge" promotional campaign, which showed consumers consistently preferring the taste of Pepsi to Coke in blind taste tests, company researchers, managers, and executives became convinced that Coca-Cola had a "taste problem."[2]

Coca-Cola Company researchers proceeded to conduct extensive marketing research—including 190,000 blind taste tests with consumers, costing $4 million—to compare the taste of a new version of Coca-Cola with that of Pepsi and regular Coke. The new formulation was preferred by a majority of consumers. Further research demonstrated that the results held—in fact, were stronger—when consumers were allowed to glimpse the labels to see what they were tasting. Managers were confident that they had developed a product that would successfully solve the taste problem. On the basis of the research, the company introduced New Coke to the world in April 1984, replacing the original formula.

The decision to replace the original product with New Coke is recognized as one of the biggest marketing blunders in history.[3] The company reversed course less than three months later and reintroduced the original Coca-Cola product. What happened? The research was technically sound; people preferred the sweeter taste of New Coke. A far greater issue than taste for many consumers, however, was the idea that the original Coca-Cola—with a century's worth of history and imagery—was being discontinued. Although Coca-Cola managers recognized in advance that some consumers would probably not accept a change in the brand, they continued to focus on the "taste problem."

Fast-forward to the present day and Coca-Cola is again focusing on a "taste problem" but from a very different perspective. The Coca-Cola Freestyle is a fountain dispenser with over 100 flavor options.[4] Testing began in Orange County, California, and

Atlanta, Georgia, in mid-2009, with combinations of sodas, waters, juices, teas, or basically any combination a consumer could dream up.[5] If a consumer likes the taste of Classic Coke with a splash of Minute Maid Orange Juice, the Freestyle can deliver. The Freestyle is more of a taste opportunity than a taste problem.

© ANDREW HARRER/BLOOMBERG VIA GETTY IMAGES

TODAY'S OPPORTUNITY IS TOMORROW'S PROBLEM IF A COMPANY FAILS TO TAKE ADVANTAGE OF THE OPPORTUNITY.

Problems versus Opportunities

There isn't a perfect formula for defining marketing research problems, but in this chapter we'll describe a process that should help. When we talk about "defining the problem" or "problem formulation," we simply mean a process of trying to identify specific areas where additional information is needed about the marketing environment. A marketing manager might face a situation that has obvious negative ramifications for the organization (e.g., unexpected decreasing sales for an existing product). These situations are normally thought of as "problems."

On the other hand, the marketing manager might face a situation with potentially positive results for the organization (e.g., researchers have developed a new product with certain advantages over competing products). Marketers must decide how to exploit these "opportunities," if at all.

We prefer to think of problems and opportunities as two sides of the same coin. Regardless of perspective, both situations require good information about the marketing environment before managers make important decisions. Today's opportunity is tomorrow's problem if a company fails to take advantage of the opportunity . . . but its competitors do. And a company that successfully deals with a problem before its competitors do has created an opportunity to move ahead in the industry. So, we consider any situation in which a company needs information to be a marketing research problem.

© KILUKILU/SHUTTERSTOCK.COM

THE PROBLEM FORMULATION PROCESS

How can a company avoid the trap of researching the wrong problem? The best way is to delay research until the problem is properly defined. It takes time to fully understand what's going on in any given situation. Well-designed and executed research can't rescue a project (and the resulting business consequences) if a company fails to define the problem correctly.

Exhibit 2.1 presents the six key steps in problem formulation. Defining the problem is among the most difficult—and certainly most important—aspects of the entire marketing research process. Although we

EXHIBIT 2.1

Key Steps in Problem Formulation

- **Meet with client** to obtain (1) management statement of problem/opportunity, (2) background information, (3) management objectives for research, and (4) possible managerial actions to result from research.
- **Clarify the problem/opportunity** by questioning managerial assumptions and gathering additional information from managers and/or others as needed. Perform exploratory research as necessary.
- **State the manager's decision problem,** including source (planned change or unplanned change in environment) and type (discovery or strategy oriented).
- **Develop full range of possible research problems** that would address the manager's decision problem.
- **Select research problem(s)** that best address the manager's decision problem, based on an evaluation of likely costs and benefits of each possible research problem.
- **Prepare and submit research request agreement** to client. Revise in consultation with client.

provide some fairly specific directions, problem formulation involves both art and science. Approach it with care.

Step 1: Meet with Client

The first step toward defining the problem correctly is to meet with the manager(s) needing marketing research. This should be done at the earliest stages of the project for two important reasons. First, you must be able to communicate openly, and this won't happen until you begin to trust one another. It's important to keep everyone engaged and actively participating in the process, especially during problem formulation, but also at later stages.

The second reason to meet is straightforward. You must gather as much information as possible about the problem at hand. In particular, you must get a clear understanding of the problem from the client's viewpoint, along with all relevant background information. The broader context is critical, as many people will become very focused on a specific task (e.g., "I need a taste test") versus the broader issue (i.e., "We're losing market share"). Without the broader issue in mind, you can accidentally go down a very specific and possibly incorrect path!

Here are some questions that are appropriate at this point:

- What is the problem or opportunity you're facing right now? Can or should this be defined more broadly? Conversely, can it be defined more narrowly?
- What caused you to notice the problem? Is there any other evidence or information that you have?
- What factors do you think have created this situation? (Ask "Why?" five times to dive deeper into the possible causes.)
- What is likely to happen if nothing changes in the next 12 months?
- What do you hope to accomplish using market research?
- What actions will you take depending upon your answers?

Planned Change versus Unplanned Change In general, there are only two basic sources of marketing problems, planned and unplanned changes in the marketing environment. Understanding the basic source of the problem will provide clues about the nature of the problem and the type of research that is needed.

FAST FACT:

IN 2009, PACKAGED FOODS FORECASTED THAT **REFRIGERATED DOG FOOD** WOULD INCREASE AT A RATE OF 23% OVER THE NEXT THREE YEARS.

Some problems show up unexpectedly. How the firm responds to new technology or a new product introduced by a competitor or a change in demographics or lifestyles determines whether the unplanned change turns out to be a problem or an opportunity. Sometimes unplanned change involves serendipity, or chance ideas. An unexpected new idea might come from a customer in a complaint letter. Marie Moody, founder of Stella & Chewy's, a maker of premium pet foods, learned to listen carefully to customer complaints after finally agreeing to use opaque—rather than transparent—packaging on frozen pet foods in response to complaints. Consumers were choosing other brands because they could see ice crystals on the Stella & Chewy products. Customers responded favorably and sales began to soar.[6]

Other companies learn that customers are "misusing" products. Avon discovered that its Skin So Soft product was being used as a bug repellent, even though the company never marketed it that way. Managers seized the moment, however, and developed a brand extension, Skin So Soft Bug Guard Plus, that is available in various formats. In these cases, something unexpected happened, and managers needed information about how best to respond.

Not all change is unanticipated, though. Much of it is planned. Most firms want to increase their revenues, and they devise various marketing actions for doing so. These actions include the development and introduction of new products, improved distribution, more effective pricing, and promotion. Planned change is oriented more toward the future and is proactive; unplanned change tends to be oriented more toward the past and is often reactive. Planned change is change that the firm wishes to bring about—the basic issue is how. Often, the role of marketing research here is to identify alternatives to consider and to investigate the feasibility of any alternatives being considered. Your task at this stage is to get a sense of whether the issue needing information resulted from planned or unplanned change.

Step 2: Clarify the Problem/Opportunity

During the first step in problem formulation, the primary task of the researcher is to listen carefully as managers provide their perspective of the problem, its background and source (planned vs. unplanned change), and what they hope to learn through marketing research. Step Two involves helping managers get precisely to the heart of the problem. This may seem odd at first—after all, shouldn't managers have a better understanding of the problem than the researcher? However, it's best not to let a manager perform her own diagnosis and prescribe the treatment as well. Further, many people will get very focused on a specific solution or believe they already know the root issue when it may not be the real cause. Researchers must ultimately be consultants who are responsible for ensuring that root causes and clear paths of action are determined.

Many times preexisting assumptions must be challenged. At the very least they must be explicitly discussed. For example, in the case of a new service that hasn't lived up to revenue expectations, maybe there just isn't much need for the service. It may help to question clients about why the problem is important: "Why do you want to measure customer satisfaction? Have you seen signs that customers may not be satisfied? Are you concerned about a new competitor that has entered the market? Is there anything else that could explain why sales haven't met expectations?" The point isn't to put a manager on the spot; the point is to get to the true nature of the problem. As we discuss in the following chapter, exploratory research might be advisable to help pinpoint the problem.

One of the most important things a researcher can do for a manager is to provide a different perspective on the problem. Many managers, particularly those who have been with a company for a long time, are afflicted with **normal thinking**. That is, they have developed a routine way of looking at the business and responding to different situations. Usually, this is a good thing, but sometimes it can get in the way of understanding the true nature of a problem. It is your job as a researcher to provide a new perspective. Exhibit 2.2 offers an example of the perils of normal thinking.

normal thinking
A routine way of looking at a business situation. Researchers should offer a new perspective on the situation if possible.

Bringing a new perspective to a problem may sound like a good idea, but how is it actually done? How could The Coca-Cola Company have known to define its problem a bit more broadly than as simply one of taste? To be honest, it's tough. Because the researcher doesn't deal with the manager's issues on a daily basis, she is automatically less likely to fall victim to normal thinking. Until the problem is properly formulated, researchers must be asking key questions, listening carefully to the answers to those questions, asking more questions to clarify the situation further, and at all times carefully thinking about, or analyzing, the situation.

Step 3: State the Manager's Decision Problem

decision problem
The basic problem facing the manager, for which marketing research is intended to provide answers.

At this point, the researcher should be able to state the manager's **decision problem**, which is simply the basic problem facing the manager for which marketing research is intended to provide answers. A well-stated decision problem takes the manager's perspective, is as simple as possible, and takes the form of a question. For example, consider a new coffee shop that has been open for six months but has yet to make a profit. Costs have been held as low as possible; sales revenue simply hasn't materialized as quickly as expected. Although the owner no doubt has many questions about her business, its lack of success, and how to move forward successfully, her initial decision problem might best take the form, "Why are store revenues so low?" This situation was certainly unanticipated, so the problem has originated from unplanned change.

EXHIBIT 2.2

The Problem with Normal Thinking

There is an old story of a factory worker who left the factory each night, pushing a wheelbarrow piled high with scrap materials. At the factory gate, the security guard would tip his hat, say "Good evening," and wonder to himself why anybody would want to take that stuff home. But because the scraps held no value to the company, the guard let him pass each night. It was only later that the company discovered that the worker had been stealing wheelbarrows.

© INFOMAGES/SHUTTERSTOCK.COM

USING DISCOVERY-ORIENTED RESEARCH, THE RESEARCHER CAN OFFER FACTS AND FIGURES THAT HELP SHED LIGHT ON THE BASIC PROBLEM.

discovery-oriented decision problem
A decision problem that typically seeks to answer "What?" or "Why?" questions about a problem/opportunity. The focus is generally on generating useful information.

The decision problem facing the coffee shop owner is an example of a **discovery-oriented decision problem**. Discovery-oriented problems are common with unplanned changes in the marketing environment. In these situations, managers often simply need basic information—What is going on? Why is it going on?—and the researcher is asked primarily to provide facts that decision makers can use in formulating strategies to deal with the unexpected situation. For example, researchers could provide information about customer satisfaction (perhaps the shop doesn't consistently offer a quality product), or the overall awareness level among the target market (maybe most people don't know about the shop), or consumer perceptions of competing coffee shops (perhaps a nearby coffee shop is perceived as a better value for the money). In each case, the researcher can offer facts and figures that help shed light on the basic problem. Note, however, that discovery-oriented research rarely solves a problem in the sense of providing actionable results. This form of research simply aims to provide some of the insights and the building blocks necessary for managers to make better decisions.

strategy-oriented decision problem
A decision problem that typically seeks to answer "How?" questions about a problem/opportunity. The focus is generally on selecting alternative courses of action.

Discovery-oriented decision problems may also apply to situations of planned change, particularly in early stages of planning when the issue is to identify possible courses of action (as opposed to choosing a preferred course of action). In this situation, key questions are likely to include "What options are available?" or "Why might this option be effective?"

A second form of manager's decision problem, the **strategy-oriented decision problem**, aims more directly at making decisions. This type of decision problem is commonly used with planned change, with an emphasis on *how* the planned change should be implemented. It is also appropriate for problems originating from unplanned change, provided that enough is known about the situation (perhaps through discovery-oriented research) so that strategic decisions are possible. Suppose that initial research for the coffee shop indicated that only 38 percent of the customers in its target market were aware that the coffee shop existed. An appropriate strategy-oriented decision problem at this point might be "How do we best increase awareness?" and researchers might determine the effectiveness of two proposed advertising campaigns at generating awareness. Notice that the output from the research process in this situation will be a choice about which of two paths to choose. This is the key distinction between discovery-oriented and strategy-oriented decision problems.

If possible, researchers should attempt to conduct strategy-oriented research. Providing additional "facts" through discovery research doesn't necessarily get managers much closer to a good decision. And many companies place a preference on strategy-oriented research. At General Mills, for example, the emphasis is on research that evaluates alternatives. Thus, instead of asking the question, "What proportion of potato chips is eaten at meals?" General Mills would ask, "How can we advertise our potato chips for meal consumption?" or "Will a 'meal commercial' sell more chips than our present commercial?" (both strategy-oriented questions). Still, there are times when discovery-oriented research is absolutely essential, particularly when managers are confronted with unplanned changes in the environment.

© ISTOCKPHOTO.COM/RYASICK

Strategy-oriented decision problems produce a choice among alternative paths.

© ISTOCKPHOTO.COM/MING KAI CHIANG

Using discovery-oriented research, the researcher can offer facts and figures to provide insights and create building blocks managers can use to make decisions.

Step 4: Develop Possible Research Problems

The manager's decision problem describes the manager's view of the situation. A **research problem** is a restatement of the decision problem in research terms, from the researcher's perspective. A research problem states specifically what research can be done to provide answers to the decision problem.

research problem
A restatement of the decision problem in research terms.

Consider again the coffee shop owner facing the discovery-oriented decision problem "Why are store revenues so low?" As is true of most discovery-oriented problems, several avenues of research might provide insights into the problem, including these:

- Determine what sales levels are required for breakeven. (Researchers must first be good at overall business!)
- Assess store traffic and purchase patterns (i.e., whether low revenue is attributable to not enough customers, or low revenue per customer, or both).
- Investigate current customer satisfaction. Is the shop getting repeat business?
- Assess the target market's perceptions of the coffee shop and its competitors.
- Determine the target market's awareness of the shop.

Each of these possible research problems begins with an action word and describes information to be uncovered that might help solve the decision problem. At this stage, the researcher's primary task is to develop the full range of research problems for a given decision problem. Exhibit 2.3 provides examples of the relationship between decision problems and research problems.

EXHIBIT 2.3

The Relationship between Decision Problems and Research Problems

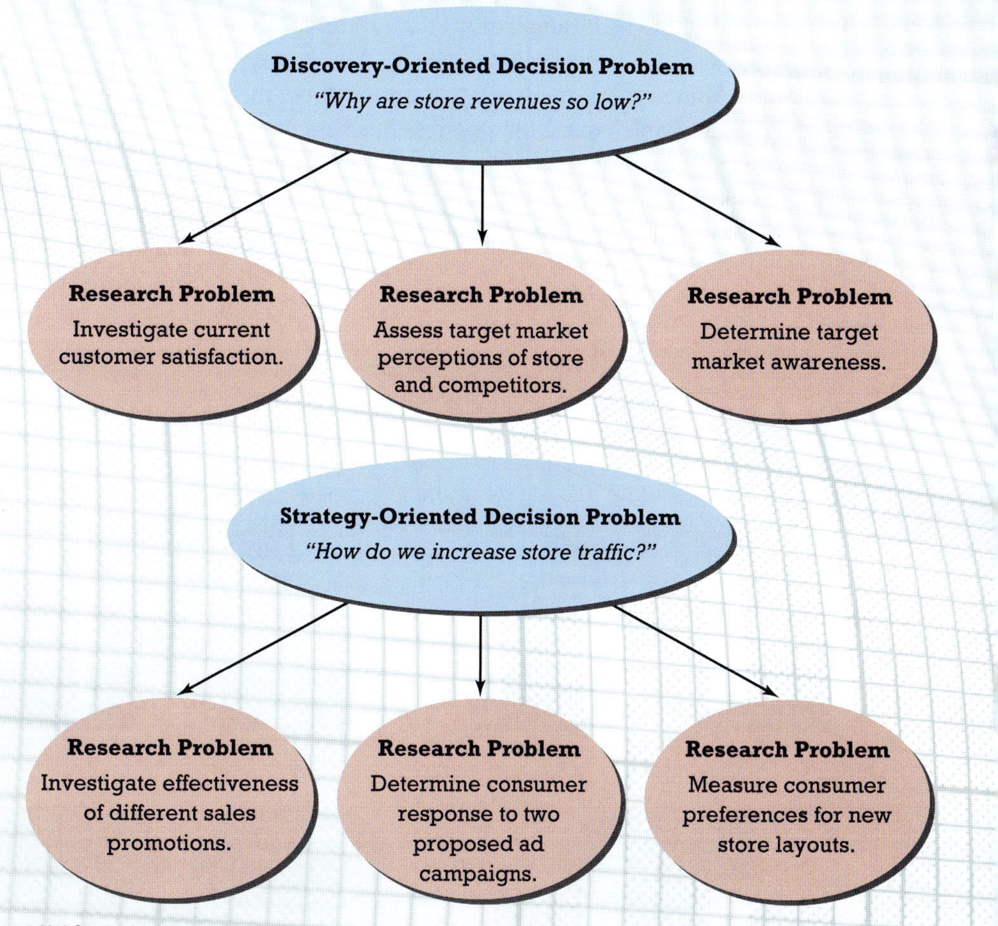

With strategy-oriented decision problems, there are typically fewer possible research problems because the focus has shifted onto making a choice among selected alternatives. At least, that's the way it's supposed to work. When the coffee shop owner shifted to the strategy-oriented decision problem "How do we increase store traffic?" there were still several strategic options available including increased levels of sales promotion, the introduction of an advertising campaign, rearranging the store layout, and so on. Possible research problems are again shown in Exhibit 2.3. Investigating any of these should result in a choice between strategic alternatives. The manager's experience, available budget, and/or discovery-oriented research might lead her to decide that advertising is the best area to consider for further research.

Where do ideas about possible research problems come from? Usually they come from the client during the process of clarifying the problem. Sometimes, however, new ideas will be uncovered through exploratory research, a determination of what information already exists, or as a result of a researcher's experience or insight. In any case, the key point at this stage of problem formulation is to specify the full range of potential research problems.

Many times you can develop a framework to identify the possible issues, the possible business outcomes needed, and ultimately the research approaches you may need to take to develop the right direction. Figure 2.1 provides a simple example:

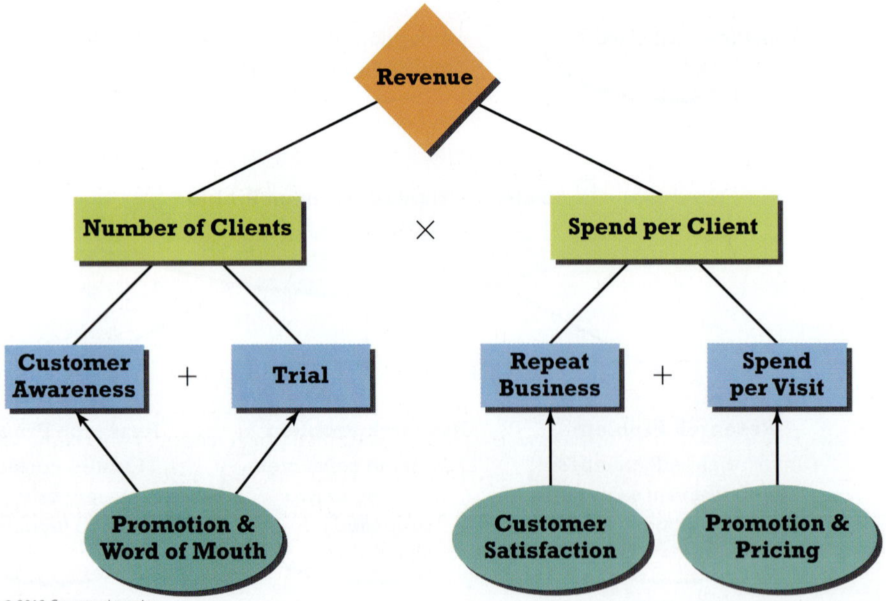

So, if revenue goals are not being met, the client might stop there in her assessment. However, if the researcher uses this framework, it could help to drill down into the core issue(s) at play. In other words, the driver of lower revenue could be the amount spent per client, which could be due to poor repeat business or smaller purchases per visit. Or it could be that the number of clients is too low, owing to low levels of awareness, which in turn could be driven by inadequate promotion or poor word-of-mouth. Research problems should be established with respect to repeat business, customer awareness, and/or spend per visit, not the revenue level alone.

Step 5: Select Research Problem(s) to Be Addressed

There are often many possible research problems that would provide useful information, especially with discovery-oriented decision problems. The trick is to figure out which research problem(s) to pursue given the normal resource constraints facing managers. You should carefully review each possible research problem in terms of the trade-off between the benefits of the information to be obtained, the importance of the subsequent decisions to be made, and the costs of obtaining that information. The costs may include money, time, and effort.

For example, we noted three of the possible research problems for the coffee shop owner facing the discovery-oriented decision problem, "Why are store revenues so low?" Investigating customer satisfaction will require gathering information from current customers. Assessing target market perceptions of the store and its competitors, as well as determining target market awareness require collecting data from the target market, many of whom are not current customers. To address all three research problems would be costly, and you would work closely with the coffee shop owner to determine the most profitable areas of research.

You should note that it is better to address one or two

REVIEW EACH POSSIBLE RESEARCH PROBLEM IN TERMS OF THE TRADE-OFF BETWEEN THE BENEFITS OF THE INFORMATION TO BE OBTAINED, THE IMPORTANCE OF THE DECISION(S) TO BE MADE, AND THE COSTS OF OBTAINING THAT INFORMATION.

research problems fully than to attempt too many and do a half-baked job on each. Our experience is that novice researchers, in their enthusiasm to do a good job, often try to do too much. Because of budget considerations, you usually cannot do all the things you'll want to do, which makes the choice of research problem so critical.

research request agreement A document prepared by the researcher after meeting with the decision maker that summarizes the problem and the information that is needed to address it.

Step 6: Prepare Research Request Agreement

One way to ensure that you and the client are in agreement with respect to problem definition is the written **research request agreement**. The research request agreement summarizes the problem formulation process and should include the following items:

1. **Background**—The events that led to the manager's decision problem. Although the events may not directly affect the research that is conducted, they provide a deeper understanding of the problem.

2. **Decision problem**—The underlying question confronting the manager. Include a brief discussion of the source of the problem (i.e., planned vs. unplanned change), along with a discussion of whether the problem is discovery oriented or strategy oriented.

3. **Research problem(s)**—The range of research problems that would provide input to the decision problem. Provide an overview of costs and benefits of each research problem. Indicate and justify the final choice of research problem.

4. **Use**—The way each piece of information will be used. For discovery-oriented decision problems, indicate key information to be obtained and how managers will use the information. For strategy-oriented decision problems, indicate the way the information will be used to help make the action decision. Supplying logical reasons for each piece of the research ensures that the research problem(s) makes sense in light of the decision problem.

5. **Population and subgroups**—The groups from whom the information must be gathered. Specify these groups so that an appropriate sample can be selected.

6. **Logistics**—Estimates of the time and money available to conduct the research. Both of these factors will affect the techniques finally chosen.

The research request agreement should be submitted to the decision maker for her approval. If possible, it is best to get that approval in writing, with a signature directly on the agreement. Exhibit 2.4 presents the research request agreement between a research group and a nonprofit organization seeking research on the topic of domestic violence.

FAST FACT:

34% OF YOUNG WOMEN (AGES 18–34) MAKE **FACEBOOK** THE FIRST THING THEY DO WHEN THEY WAKE UP.

EXHIBIT 2.4

Research Request Agreement presented to Stillwater Domestic Violence Services, Inc., by Research Partners, Ltd.

BACKGROUND

Stillwater Domestic Violence Services, Inc. (SDVS), was formed in 1979 as a nonprofit agency to offer services to individuals in the Stillwater, Oklahoma, area. Funded by the United Way, the Oklahoma Office of Attorney General, the Federal Office for Victims of Crime, the Elite Repeat Resale Shop, and by private donations from groups and individuals, the organization states its goal as follows:

> *Our goal is to provide comprehensive and confidential services to individuals and families experiencing domestic violence, sexual assault, stalking and child abuse or neglect. We also seek social change through community awareness and client advocacy.*

SDVS offers various services to the community, including sheltering for victims of domestic violence, a help line, counseling and consultation, a relief nursery, parenting education, community education on domestic violence, and a sexual assault response team. All services are offered to victims without consideration of individuals' ability to pay.

Despite the fact that university students make up about half of Stillwater's population, Dr. Ralph Lindsey, the SDVS director, has noted that the services offered by the organization are seriously underutilized by students at Oklahoma State University, which is located in Stillwater. This is unfortunate, because national statistics suggest that a significant number of college students are affected by domestic violence at some point during their college career. Dr. Lindsey is concerned that most students may not even know that SDVS exists and that its services are available to them when needed. In addition, SDVS relies upon volunteers in delivering many of its client support services. Perhaps more university students would volunteer their services if they knew of the existence of SDVS and the services it provides. SDVS has done no prior formal marketing research.

DECISION PROBLEM

"Why aren't more students utilizing the services of SDVS?" Dr. Lindsey desires to fulfill the organization's goals for all residents of Stillwater, including university students. This is a discovery-oriented decision problem that has arisen from an unplanned change in the marketing environment, an unexpectedly low number of university student clients.

RESEARCH PROBLEMS

There are several different research problems that might be addressed; each would offer insights into the general decision problem. This section discusses the most promising of these research problems and provides the rationale for selecting two of them for further attention.

Research Problem 1: Investigate student awareness of the services offered by SDVS. Dr. Lindsey has already noted that he believes that lack of awareness is the likely reason that so few university students utilize the services of SDVS. Awareness is relatively straightforward to measure, student respondents can be readily accessed, and costs would probably be low.

Research Problem 2: Determine the incidence level of domestic violence among university students in Stillwater.

Another possibility is that domestic violence is simply not very common in the Stillwater area among students. This seems unlikely to be true, but establishing that the problem exists might be a good first step. One difficulty is likely to be establishing a common understanding of what constitutes "domestic violence," but researchers should be able to offer a relatively clear definition of the concept before assessing the incidence level. A more difficult hurdle is the sensitivity of the issue to respondents who have experienced domestic violence or to those who will simply consider the questions to be "too personal."

Research Problem 3: Determine student satisfaction with the services provided by SDVS. If students have turned to SDVS for help in the past but have been disappointed in the services offered, they likely will not return—and they'll probably share their experiences with others. Given Dr. Lindsey's belief that few students have sought help and the difficulty of finding prior student clients because of confidentiality requirements, the costs of pursuing this research problem would likely be quite high.

Research Problem 4: Determine student awareness for any organization providing services to victims of domestic violence. It is conceivable that student need for assistance with domestic violence issues is being met by other organizations, either on campus, in the community, or in students' hometowns. If this is the case, Dr. Lindsey's fears that students don't know where to go for help may be unfounded. This research problem might be easily combined with Research Problem 1 or 2 because it would require the same general population of university students. As with these research problems, the costs would be relatively low.

Research Problem 5: Investigate student perceptions of the SDVS office location. Even if students are aware of the services offered by the organization, perhaps its location makes it less likely that students would go to SDVS for help. Although this could be an important issue, the research team believes that this is secondary to the basic awareness issue. In addition, unless the researchers can effectively describe the location to respondents, the sample would need to be drawn from among students who have actually visited the office. According to Dr. Lindsey, there just aren't many of these.

Research Problem 6: Determine which media outlets university students are most likely to utilize. If an awareness problem exists among students, SDVS may need to rethink its promotion strategy. Knowing which media vehicles (newspapers, radio stations, television stations, etc.) are routinely used by students could inform future decisions about advertising and other forms of promotion. Given the number of options available, collecting this information could take significant time with each student respondent, and the accuracy of the information would be questionable. It is difficult for individuals to communicate perceptual processes such as attention to all the different media they encounter in their daily lives. Plus, it is possible that awareness is not the issue at all, which would make the information obtained from pursuing this research problem less valuable.

Research Problems Selected After reviewing these research problems (and others), the research team has concluded that Research Problems 1 and 4 offer the greatest value in terms of providing information that is likely to address the decision problem. Each involves collecting information from the same population (see following); including both issues should not make the data collection forms too long.

USE

The key information to be obtained will include (1) unaided awareness and recognition of SDVS as an entity providing services for victims of domestic violence and (2) unaided awareness for any other organizations providing similar services. Dr. Lindsey plans to use the results to determine the degree to which a problem exists in terms of student awareness and to help in making decisions about increasing communications with students.

Population and Subgroups

Although the population will be formally defined in the Research Proposal, the researchers intend to collect data from Oklahoma State University students based in Stillwater. SDVS clients have primarily been women; most respondents should be women, but a small proportion of men (say, 20% of the sample) should be included. Because Research Partners, Ltd., is donating its services (see next), the sample size will be limited to 200–250 individuals.

Logistics

The project should be completed in approximately three months. As a nonprofit organization, SDVS has limited funds available that can be dedicated to marketing research. Research Partners, Ltd., has agreed to donate its services, although Dr. Lindsey has agreed to cover out-of-pocket expenses.

Source: The contributions of student researchers Jeff Blood, Trey Curtis, Kelsey Gillen, Amie Kreger, David Pittman, and Matt Smith are gratefully acknowledged.

THE RESEARCH PROPOSAL

Once the problem has been defined and research problem(s) agreed upon, it's time to think about the techniques that will be used to conduct the research. In the research request agreement, we paid little attention to research methods, other than a general specification of the population to be studied. That all changes with the preparation of the formal **research proposal**, which lays out the proposed method of conducting the research. The research proposal also gives you another opportunity to make sure the research will provide information needed to address the decision maker's problem.

research proposal
A written statement that describes the marketing problem, the purpose of the study, and a detailed outline of the research methodology.

Many research proposals are written in response to a **request for proposal (RFP)** issued by an organization that is seeking to choose a vendor to provide research services. A request for proposal is a document that describes the problem for which research is sought and asks providers to offer proposals, including cost estimates, about how they would perform the job. Generally, the RFP provides an idea of the degree of detail required in the research proposal. Some research proposals are very long and detailed; others are much shorter. Regardless of their length, however, proposals should contain most of the elements shown in the following sections (you'll learn about the necessary details in upcoming chapters).

request for proposal (RFP)
A document that describes the problem for which research is sought and that asks providers to offer proposals, including cost estimates, about how they would perform the job.

A. Problem Definition and Background

This section presents a short summary of the information contained in the research request agreement, including the background of the problem, the manager's decision problem, and the specific research problem(s) to be addressed by the project. It is often a good idea to include a few words justifying the particular research problem(s) under study.

B. Research Design and Data Sources

Type of research design (exploratory, descriptive, and/or causal) and type of data to be sought (primary, secondary), along with the proposed sources of those data, are discussed in this section. You'll need to include a brief explanation of how the necessary data will be gathered (e.g., surveys, experiments, library sources). "Sources" refer to where the data are located, for example, in government publications or company records, or as unpublished information held by people, and so forth. The nature of the problem will usually dictate the types of techniques to be employed, such as Web surveys, in-depth interviews, or focus groups.

C. Sampling Plan

The sampling plan starts with a detailed description of the population to be studied. You must specify the population, state the desired sample size (including the rationale for the proposed sample size), discuss sampling method, and identify the sampling frame. The reason for using the type of sample proposed must be justified.

D. Data Collection Forms

The forms to be used in gathering data are discussed in this section. For survey research, this usually involves a questionnaire. For other research, the forms could include inventory forms, guidebooks for focus groups, observation checklists, and so forth. You'll need to explain how these instruments have been or will be validated and provide any available evidence of their reliability and validity. The proposed data collection form itself will often be included in an appendix (see Section H).

E. Analysis

The primary information that appears in this section is the type of data analysis, including any specialized statistical techniques that are to be performed, to convert the collected data into usable information. If necessary, you may also include a discussion of editing and proofreading of questionnaires, coding instructions, and an explanation of how item nonresponse and missing data will be handled. Most importantly, you should include an outline of the tables and figures that will appear in the report (i.e., dummy tables). These tables and figures will likely be included in an appendix (see Section H).

F. Time Schedule

This is a detailed outline of the plan to complete the study. The study should be divided into workable pieces. Then, considering the persons involved in each phase, their qualifications and experience, and so forth, the time for the job is estimated. Some jobs may overlap. This plan will help in estimating the time required. Here is a simple example:

Timeline

1. Preliminary investigation	Jan. 10–Jan. 22
2. Final test of questionnaire	Jan. 24–Jan. 29
3. Sample selection	Jan. 31–Feb. 5
4. Mail questionnaires and field follow-up	Feb. 7–Apr. 2
5. Analysis and preparation of final report	Apr. 4–May 2

G. Personnel Requirements and Cost Estimate

This section provides a complete list of all personnel who will be required, indicating exact jobs, time duration, expected rate of pay, and each person's responsibility and authority. To estimate total personnel costs, personnel requirements are combined with time requirements for different phases. Estimates on travel, materials, supplies, drafting, computer charges, printing, and mailing costs must also be included. If an overhead charge is required, it should be calculated and added to the subtotal of the above items.

H. Appendices

This section will include data collection forms (including script for telephone interviewers and cover letter for written or electronic formats), any technical information or statistical information that would have interrupted the flow of the text, and dummy tables or figures included in the analysis plan.

THE NATIONAL ASSOCIATION OF HOME BUILDERS PREDICTS THAT **60%** OF CUSTOM HOMES WILL HAVE **DUAL MASTER BEDROOMS** BY 2015.

3 Exploratory, Descriptive, and Causal Research Designs

© ISTOCKPHOTO.COM/BART COENDERS

POLL QUESTION:

Focus groups are sufficient research tools for most decision problems.

STRONGLY DISAGREE 1 2 3 4 5 STRONGLY AGREE

Learning Objectives

1. Describe the major emphasis of each of the three basic types of research design.
2. Describe the key characteristics and basic uses of exploratory research.
3. Discuss the various types of exploratory research and describe each.
4. Discuss the difference between cross-sectional and longitudinal descriptive research designs.
5. Explain the difference between a continuous panel and a discontinuous panel.
6. Clarify the difference between laboratory experiments and field experiments.
7. Distinguish among a standard test market, a controlled test market, and a simulated test market.

INTRODUCTION

A research design is the framework or plan for a study used as a guide in collecting and analyzing data. There are three basic types of research design: exploratory, descriptive, and causal. In this chapter, we'll discuss these types of research design, give some examples, and note when each might be important.

TYPES OF RESEARCH DESIGN

The names of the three types of research design describe their purpose very well. The goal of **exploratory research** is to discover ideas and insights. **Descriptive research** is usually concerned with describing a population with respect to important variables. **Causal research** is used to establish cause-and-effect relationships between variables. Experiments are commonly used in causal research designs because they are best suited to determine cause and effect.

The popular crime investigation television shows (e.g., *CSI: Crime Scene Investigation*) provide a fairly good illustration of the three types of research design. These shows usually begin with a crime that must be investigated (an unplanned change has occurred in the marketplace). The first step is to search for clues that can help establish what has happened (exploratory research). The clues uncovered in the exploratory phase of the investigation often point toward a particular hypothesis or explanation of the events that occurred, and investigators begin to focus their efforts in this direction, conducting interviews with witnesses and suspects (descriptive research). Finally, a trial is held to determine whether the evidence is sufficient to convict a suspect of the crime (causal research).

Almost all marketing research projects include exploratory and descriptive research. How much of each is necessary depends mostly on how much managers already know about the issue to be studied. When a decision problem has arisen from unplanned changes in the environment, there is usually a need for exploratory

exploratory research
Design in which the major emphasis is on gaining ideas and insights.

descriptive research
Research design in which the major emphasis is on determining the frequency with which something occurs or the extent to which two variables covary.

causal research
Research design in which the major emphasis is on determining cause-and-effect relationships.

© JESSICA BURSTEIN/NBCU PHOTO BANK VIA AP IMAGES

research to better understand what is happening and why it is happening. Sometimes, however, managers know a lot about the situation—they understand the key issues and know what questions need to be asked—and the focus quickly shifts to descriptive research that is geared more toward providing answers than generating initial insights. Unlike crime investigations, however, in business situations managers are often perfectly happy with a "most likely" result produced by descriptive research. Only occasionally do they choose to establish cause-and-effect relationships through causal research. As you can probably tell, the three basic research designs can be viewed as stages in a continuous process. Exhibit 3.1 shows the interrelationships.

EXPLORATORY RESEARCH

Exploratory research is conducted to provide a better understanding of a situation. It isn't designed to come up with final answers or decisions. Through exploratory research, researchers hope to produce hypotheses about what is going on in a situation. A **hypothesis** is a statement that describes how two or more variables are related. For example, if sales for a particular line of vehicles dropped during the latest quarter, as a researcher you might use exploratory research to provide insights about what caused the decrease in revenue. Suppose that you conducted interviews with potential car buyers and noticed that they seemed to be more excited about the new styles of other car brands than they were about the brand in question. This might lead to the hypothesis that style preferences had changed, resulting in lower sales. You can't really confirm or reject the hypothesis with exploratory research, though. That job is left for descriptive

hypothesis
A statement that describes how two or more variables are related.

EXHIBIT 3.1

Relationships among Research Designs

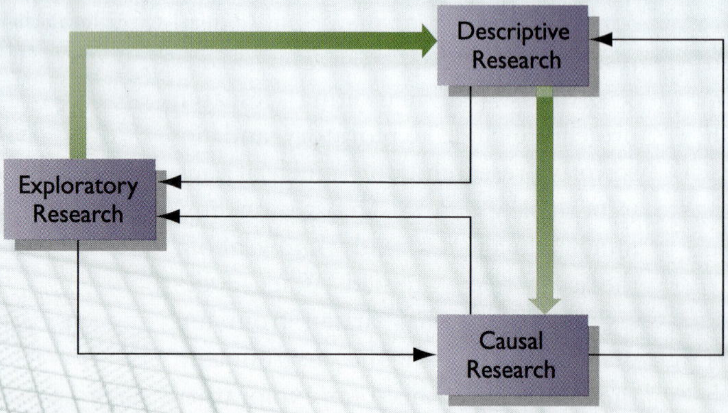

FAST FACT:

A RECENT GALLUP POLL REGARDING U.S. BUSINESS SECTORS SHOWED THAT THE **COMPUTER** INDUSTRY RATED MOST POSITIVELY AT **60%**, FOLLOWED BY THE **RESTAURANT** INDUSTRY AT **57%**.

and/or causal research (these are often called *quantitative research*).

This is an important point, so we'll stress it again: Exploratory research (sometimes referred to as *qualitative research*) shouldn't be expected to provide answers to the decision problem that you are attempting to solve for a client. It can provide very rich, meaningful information—or even definitive explanations—for particular individuals ("I hate the old-fashioned styling of that car; that's why I won't buy one"), but exploratory research doesn't provide definitive answers for the overall population. There are two reasons for this: (1) Exploratory research usually involves only a relatively small group of people, and (2) these people are almost never randomly selected to participate.

In addition to developing one or more hypotheses about actual (or potential) causes of changes in the marketing environment for an organization, exploratory research is also useful for other purposes. Sometimes it's necessary for helping define the problem, in particular, the research problems that might be addressed. There are often several possible hypotheses about a given marketing phenomenon, and exploratory research can help you identify which research problem(s) ought to be pursued. Exploratory research is also used to increase a researcher's familiarity with a problem, especially when the researcher doesn't know much about the organization and/or problem to be studied.

Regardless of the particular methods employed, exploratory studies should almost always be relatively small in size. You simply can't afford to devote the bulk of the research budget to exploratory research. And because we often don't know a lot at the beginning of a project, exploratory studies are very flexible with regard to the methods used for gaining insights and developing hypotheses. Basically, anything goes! Although there are a number of common types of exploratory research, be creative and follow your intuition.

Types of Exploratory Research

Some of the more popular methods of exploratory research include literature searches, depth interviews, focus groups, and case analyses (see Exhibit 3.2).

Literature Search

One of the quickest and least costly ways to discover hypotheses is to conduct a **literature search**. Almost all marketing research projects should start here. There is an incredible amount of information available in libraries, through online sources, in commercial data bases, and so on. The literature search may involve popular press (newspapers, magazines, etc.), trade literature, academic literature, or published statistics from research firms or governmental agencies such as the U.S. Census Bureau. Years ago, Miller Business Systems, Inc., used published industry sources to develop profiles of its competitors, which it then kept in its database. The company regularly scanned the database to monitor competitive actions. One day, they noticed that a competitor had hired nine furniture salespeople in a 10-day period, tipping them off that the competitor was about to make a push in the office-furniture market. They quickly scheduled extra sales calls and were able to hold on to their accounts.[1]

literature search
A search of popular press (newspapers, magazines, etc.), trade literature, academic literature, or published statistics from research firms or governmental agencies for data or insight into the problem at hand.

Depth Interviews

It's important to start with a good literature search, but at some point

EXHIBIT 3.2

Common Types of Exploratory Research

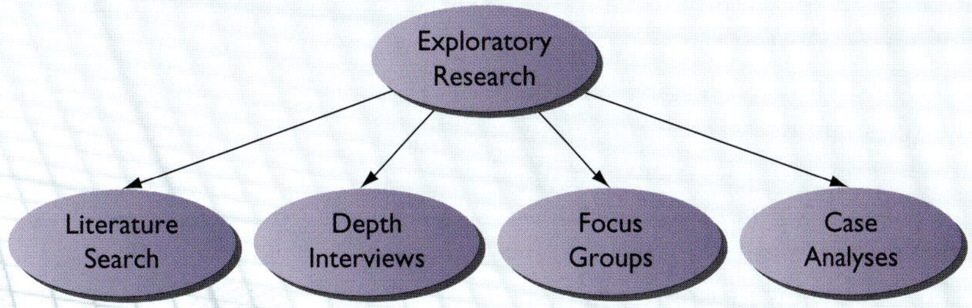

FAST FACT:

AN ANALYSIS OF CENSUS DATA BY **PEW RESEARCH CENTER** SHOWS THAT ABOUT 17% OF U.S. WOMEN WERE CHILDLESS AT AGE 40 COMPARED TO 22% IN ENGLAND.

depth interviews
Interviews with people knowledgeable about the general subject being investigated.

you'll probably want to talk to people and ask questions. **Depth interviews** are used to tap the knowledge and experience of those with information relevant to the problem or opportunity at hand. Anyone with relevant information is a potential candidate for a depth interview, including current customers, members of the target market, executives and managers of the client organization, sales representatives, wholesalers, retailers, and so on. For example, a children's book publisher gained valuable information about a sales decline by talking with librarians and schoolteachers who indicated that more and more people were using library facilities . . . and presumably buying fewer books for their children.

A series of depth interviews can be very expensive. Well-trained interviewers command high salaries; data are collected from one respondent at a time; and, if recorded, audio/video recordings must be transcribed, coded, and analyzed. This technique, however, can yield important insights and more often than not is well worth the effort.

focus group
An interview conducted among a small number of individuals simultaneously; the interview relies more on group discussion than on directed questions to generate data.

moderator
The individual who meets with focus group participants and guides the session.

Focus Groups Focus group interviews are among the most often used techniques in marketing research. Some would argue that they are among the most overused and *misused* techniques as well, a point we'll return to later. In a **focus group**, a small number of individuals (e.g., 8–12) are brought together to talk about some topic of interest to the focus group sponsor. The discussion is directed by a **moderator** who is in the room with the focus group participants; managers, ad agency representatives, and/or others often watch the session from outside the room via a two-way mirror or video link. The moderator attempts to follow a rough outline of issues while simultaneously having the comments made by each person considered in group discussion. Participants are thus exposed to the ideas of others and can respond to those ideas with their own.

Group interaction is the key aspect that distinguishes focus group interviews from depth interviews, which are conducted with one respondent at a time. It is also the primary advantage of the focus group over most other exploratory techniques. Because of their interactive nature, ideas sometimes drop "out of the blue" during a focus group discussion. In addition, there is a snowballing effect: A comment by one individual can trigger a chain of responses from others. As a result, responses are often more spontaneous and less conventional than they might be in a depth interview.

This is obvious, but focus group participants need to match the target market that the client is interested in learning more about. Aeropostale became one of the hottest performing clothing chains for teens in part by conducting focus groups with high school students.[2] Most firms using focus groups use screening interviews to determine who participates in a particular group. Clients normally have specific criteria for the kinds of people they want to participate. And that's a good idea: Usually, the more specific the criteria, the more useful the results will be. Recruiting people for focus groups is a critical task—and it isn't easy, especially as the criteria become more specific. For example, imagine recruiting people who enjoy eating Italian food. Now imagine trying to recruit people who enjoy cooking and eating a particular type of Italian food (say, veal parmigiana) at home. Which will be harder to find and convince to attend your focus group?

Given that the participants in any one group should be reasonably homogeneous, how can a firm

BECAUSE OF THEIR INTERACTIVE NATURE, IDEAS SOMETIMES DROP "OUT OF THE BLUE" DURING A FOCUS GROUP DISCUSSION.

be sure that the full range of opinions will be represented? The best way is to hold multiple groups. That way, the characteristics of the participants can vary across groups. How many groups should you hold? A typical number might be five or less, but sometimes companies choose to hold dozens of focus groups. For example, Visa used 58 focus groups during the process of developing a new brand logo.[3] Generally speaking, when focus groups begin to show diminishing returns in terms of new insights, it's time to move on to other forms of research.

Advancing technology has also created an explosion in the use of online, Internet-based focus groups. Such "groups," in which multiple respondents can "meet" electronically via chat rooms, instant messaging, Web cameras, and the like, offer tremendous speed and cost benefits, particularly when using an established online panel of respondents. There are other advantages of online focus groups, including the ability to form groups composed of people from far-flung locations, or to deal with sensitive topics.

In general, focus groups are less expensive to conduct than are individual depth interviews, mostly because multiple respondents are handled simultaneously. That's not to say that they are inexpensive, however. By the time the facility has been rented, an experienced moderator has been hired to conduct the session and write the report, and incentives paid to participants, a focus group has become costly. And that's just one focus group; add a series of focus groups and the costs can really rise.

The Role of the Moderator. The moderator in the focus group plays the single most important—and most difficult—role in the process. For one thing, the moderator typically translates the study objectives into a guidebook. The **moderator's guidebook** lists the general (and specific) issues to be addressed during the session, placing them in the general order in which the topics should arise. In general, a funnel approach is used, with broad general topics first and then increasing focus on the specific issues to be studied. As the moderator, you must understand the background of the problem and what the client needs to learn from the research process. Without this information, it's impossible to develop the guidebook and conduct a focus group effectively.

moderator's guidebook
An ordered list of the general (and specific) issues to be addressed during a focus group; the issues normally should move from general to specific.

The Dark Side of Focus Groups. Despite their benefits, focus groups have two major weaknesses. Actually, these weaknesses have little to do with focus groups as a technique. Instead, they arise from how they are often used. The first weakness has to do with how the results of a focus group session are sometimes interpreted. When managers—or researchers, for that matter—bring preconceived ideas about what they want or expect to see, it's no surprise when they find evidence in one or more of the group discussions that supports their position. The resulting biases may not be intentional, but they can still be harmful. As one observer put it, "The primary function of focus groups is often to validate the sellers' own beliefs about their product."[4]

Here is our second big concern about how focus groups are being used: Focus groups are only one type of exploratory research, yet for whatever reason they are just about the only kind of research—exploratory or otherwise—that some companies will use. Managers (and researchers too, unfortunately) tend to forget that the discussion—and consequently, the results—is greatly influenced by the moderator, the screening criteria, and the particular people who end up participating in the group. Like other forms of exploratory research, focus groups are better for generating ideas and insights than for systematically examining them. They are not designed to provide final answers, yet they are too often used for that purpose.

At Yoplait, yogurt moved from cups to tubes with the introduction of Go-gurt. In a follow-up move, the company developed carbonated yogurt in an attempt to make yogurt more palatable to "tweens." According to focus group results, the kids seemed to love it. In fact, the focus group results were so convincing that Yoplait's president skipped further marketing research for Fizzix and went straight to a national rollout for the product.[5] Not surprisingly, Fizzix fizzled on the market and the product is no longer available.

Why is focus group research so popular? Well, when used appropriately, it can be very effective, and this accounts in part for its popularity. And managers may be more comfortable supporting an activity in which they can participate. Plus, conducting focus groups has simply become the "norm" over the years. As one critic bluntly stated, "Focus groups are the crack cocaine of market research. You get hooked on them and you're afraid to make a move without them."[6]

Case Analyses

Often, researchers can learn a lot about a situation by studying carefully selected examples or cases of the phenomenon. This is the essence of **case analysis**, another form of

case analysis
Intensive study of selected examples of the phenomenon of interest.

exploratory research. As a researcher, you might examine existing records, observe the phenomenon as it occurs, conduct unstructured interviews, or use any one of a variety of other approaches to analyze what is happening in a given situation.

For example, when asked how Aeropostale selects the clothes it wants to carry in its stores, CEO Julian Geiger had this to say: "We don't look at what's on the selling floor of our competitors. We look at what's on the backs of our customers. Our design group goes all over. Sure, everybody goes to London and Paris and Barcelona. But we go to Great Adventure and concerts, spring break, train stations, and airports to see what the real kids are wearing."[7]

Case analyses can be performed in lots of different ways. Sometimes internal records are reviewed, sometimes individuals are interviewed, and sometimes situations or people are observed carefully. Several years ago, a company decided to improve the productivity of its sales force. A researcher carefully observed several of the company's best salespeople in the field and compared them to several of the worst. It turned out that the best salespeople were checking the stock of retailers and pointing out items on which they were low; the low performers were not taking the time to do this. Without being in the field with the sales force, this insight probably wouldn't have been uncovered.

benchmarking
Using organizations that excel at some function as sources of ideas for improvement.

Benchmarking. **Benchmarking** is a frequently used example of case analysis. It involves identifying one or more organizations that excel at carrying out some function and using their practices as a source of ideas for improvement. For example, L.L.Bean is noted for its excellent order fulfillment. Even during the busy Christmas season, the company typically fills over 99 percent of its orders correctly. As a result, other organizations have sought to improve their own order fulfillment by benchmarking L.L.Bean.

Organizations carry out benchmarking through activities such as reading about other organizations, visiting or calling them, and taking apart competing products to see how they are made. The process of benchmarking varies according to the information needs of the organization and the resources available. Xerox is widely credited with the first benchmarking project in the United States. In 1979, Xerox studied Japanese competitors to learn how they could sell mid-size copiers for less than what it cost Xerox to make them. Today, many companies commonly use benchmarking as a standard research tool.

Ethnography. An increasingly popular form of case analysis is **ethnography**. These procedures, which have been adapted from anthropology, often involve prolonged observation of consumers during the course of their ordinary daily lives. Unlike anthropologists, however, who might live in the group being studied for months or years, ethnographers use a combination of direct observations, interviews, and video and audio recordings to make their observations more quickly.

ethnography
The detailed observation of consumers during their ordinary daily lives using direct observations, interviews, and video and audio recordings.

Ethnography is useful as an exploratory research tool because it can allow insights based on real behavior, not just on what people say. Microsoft has used teams of researchers to observe and videotape computer users at home and at work. Not long ago, the researchers observed 50 families in seven countries as they used the next version of the company's operating system. Through this process, they found over 1,000 problems, about 800 of which hadn't been identified by company testers.[8]

We end this section on ethnography and other forms of case analysis with some words of caution about their (mis)use. Interpreting the rich, qualitative data produced by these techniques is very difficult to do. Remaining objective about the results (i.e., not allowing preconceived ideas and expectations to influence the interpretation) may be even harder to do.

And as with other exploratory methods, case analyses are not useful for discerning final answers and making decisions. We may learn the truth as it applies to a few individuals or situations, but we'll only have hypotheses about truth as applied to the larger group.

DESCRIPTIVE RESEARCH DESIGNS

Descriptive research is very common in business and other aspects of life. In fact, most of the marketing research you've heard about or participated in can be categorized as descriptive research. With a descriptive research design we are usually trying to describe some group of people or other entities. For example, Scion, a division of Toyota Motor Corporation, was designed from the start to be "cool" and "edgy" in an attempt to appeal to younger consumers. After the radical Scion xB had been in limited release in southern California for a while, researchers used descriptive research to confirm that the average Scion customer was 39 years old, the youngest in the automotive industry, compared with Toyota customers, who were 54 years old on average.[9]

Much of the information in the remainder of this book deals with how to collect this sort of descriptive data, but there are a few things we need to cover in this section. To begin, we use descriptive research for the following purposes:

1. **To describe the characteristics of certain groups.** For example, a research group gathered information from individuals who had eaten at a particular barbecue restaurant chain in a midwestern U.S. city to help managers develop a profile of the "average user" with respect to income, sex, age, and so on. The managers were surprised to learn that about half of their customers were women; they had started with the mistaken belief that a clear majority of their customers were men.
2. **To determine the proportion of people who behave in a certain way.** We might be interested, for example, in estimating the proportion of people within a specified radius of a proposed shopping complex who currently shop or intend to shop at the center. And most behavioral data are collected via descriptive research. For example, when a shopper makes a purchase at most retailers, the purchase behavior is recorded as part of scanner data.
3. **To make specific predictions.** We might want to predict the level of sales for each of the next five years so that we could plan for the hiring and training of new sales representatives.
4. **To determine relationships between variables.** It's very common to use descriptive research to examine differences between groups ("awareness levels for our product are higher for men than for women in the target market") or other relationships between variables ("as satisfaction increases, the intention to switch to another service provider decreases").

Descriptive research can be used to accomplish a wide variety of research objectives. However, descriptive data become useful for solving problems only when the process is guided by one or more specific research problems, much thought and effort, and quite often exploratory research to clarify the problem and develop hypotheses. A descriptive study design is very different from an exploratory study design. Exploratory studies are flexible in nature; descriptive studies are not.

FAST FACT:

ONLY **5%** OF U.S. ADULTS REPORT DOING A **VIGOROUS ACTIVITY** ON ANY GIVEN DAY COMPARED TO **80%** WHO REPORT **WATCHING TV** ON ANY GIVEN DAY.

They require a clear specification of the who, what, when, where, why, and how of the research.

Suppose a chain of electronics stores is planning to open a new store and wants you to investigate how customers choose particular stores for shopping. Here are a few of the questions—there are many more—that you'll need to answer before data collection for this descriptive study can begin.

- **Who** should be considered a customer? Anyone who enters the store? Someone who makes a purchase? Should we work at the individual or household level?
- **What** characteristics of customers should be measured? Are we interested in their age and sex, or in where they live and how they came to know about the store?
- **When** will we measure characteristics of the customers? While they are shopping or later? Should the study take place during the first weeks of operation of the store, or should it be delayed six months?
- **Where** will we measure the customers? Should it be in the store, immediately outside the store, or should we attempt to contact them at home?
- **Why** do we want to measure them in the first place? Are we going to use these measurements to plan promotional strategy? Are we going to use these measurements as a basis for deciding where to place other stores?
- **How** should we measure the customers? Do we use a questionnaire, or should we observe their purchasing behavior? If we use a questionnaire, what form will it take? How will it be administered?

Some of the answers to these questions will be fairly obvious from the hypotheses that guide the descriptive research. Others, however, may not be obvious at all. You might not have answers until after much thought or after a small exploratory study. In any case, the researcher should delay data collection until hypotheses are developed and clear answers about who, what, when, where, why, and how are available.

The Importance of Dummy Tables

dummy table
A table (or figure) with no entries used to show how the results of the analysis will be presented.

You shouldn't collect descriptive data until you know what you are going to do with them. To accomplish this, you should prepare a set of dummy tables before beginning the collection process. A **dummy table** is simply a table (or figure) used to show how the results of an analysis will be presented. It is a "dummy" table because there are no actual data in the table (they haven't been collected yet). Preparing a complete set of dummy tables forces you to think carefully about each piece of information to be collected. It also takes the guesswork out of the analysis phase of the project. Some will be simple tables or figures that show the results of individual items; others may show relationships between important variables. Exhibit 3.3 shows a dummy table that might be used by an athletic shoe retailer as it prepares to investigate store preference broken down by age.

Note that the table lists the age segments the company managers want to compare. It is crucial that the exact variables and categories to be investigated, as well as the necessary statistical tests, are specified before you begin to collect the data. Once data are

EXHIBIT 3.3

Dummy Table: Athletic Shoe Store Preference by Age

	Store Preference			
Age	**Finish Line**	**Foot Locker**	**The Athlete's Foot**	**Total**
Less than 18	XX%	XX%	XX%	100%
18–29	XX%	XX%	XX%	100%
30–39	XX%	XX%	XX%	100%
40 or over	XX%	XX%	XX%	100%

(Sample size = XX)

collected and analysis is underway, it's too late to say "Oops!" and start over. Dummy tables are particularly valuable in providing clues on how to phrase the individual questions and code the responses.

Two Types of Descriptive Studies

cross-sectional study
Investigation involving a sample of elements selected from the population of interest that are measured at a single point in time.

Exhibit 3.4 is an overview of various types of descriptive studies. The basic distinction is between cross-sectional designs, which traditionally have been the most common, and longitudinal designs. Typically, a **cross-sectional study** involves drawing a sample of elements from the population of interest. Characteristics of the elements, or sample members, are measured only once.

longitudinal study
Investigation involving a fixed sample of elements that is measured repeatedly through time.

A **longitudinal study**, on the other hand, involves a panel, which is a fixed sample of elements. The elements may be stores, dealers, individuals, or other entities. The panel, or sample, remains relatively constant through time, although members may be added to replace dropouts or to keep it representative. The sample members in a panel are measured repeatedly over time, in contrast with the one-time measurement in a cross-sectional study.

Longitudinal Analysis: Consumer Panels

There are two types of panels: continuous panels (sometimes called true panels) and discontinuous panels (sometimes called omnibus panels). In almost all cases, panel members are compensated in one way or another for their participation. **Continuous panels** rely on repeated measurements of the same variables. As a result, continuous panels allow for true time-series analysis. For example, Nielsen's Homescan product uses a panel consisting of more than 250,000 households across 27 countries to provide continuous tracking of consumer product purchases. The NPD Group maintains an online panel of 1.8 million consumers who regularly report purchases across a wide variety of product and service categories. In addition, many companies have set up their own continuous panels. If you use a shopping card at your favorite grocery store or other retailer, you're likely part of a continuous panel (and probably didn't know it). Tesco, one of the world's leading retailers, has done an amazing job setting up a frequent shopping program. Most of the purchases at its stores can be tied to particular shoppers using the Tesco Clubcard. The behavioral information obtained allows the company to better understand its customers and their needs.

continuous panel
A fixed sample of respondents who are measured repeatedly over time with respect to the same variables.

With a **discontinuous panel**, the information collected from panel members varies. Lands' End, for instance, has established a number of panels of 1,500 households each, to represent critical target segments. These households agreed to complete between six and eight online surveys a year in exchange for Lands' End gift cards. Panel members provide insights on creative concepts

discontinuous panel
A fixed sample of respondents who are measured repeatedly over time, but on variables that change from measurement to measurement.

EXHIBIT 3.4

Classification of Descriptive Studies

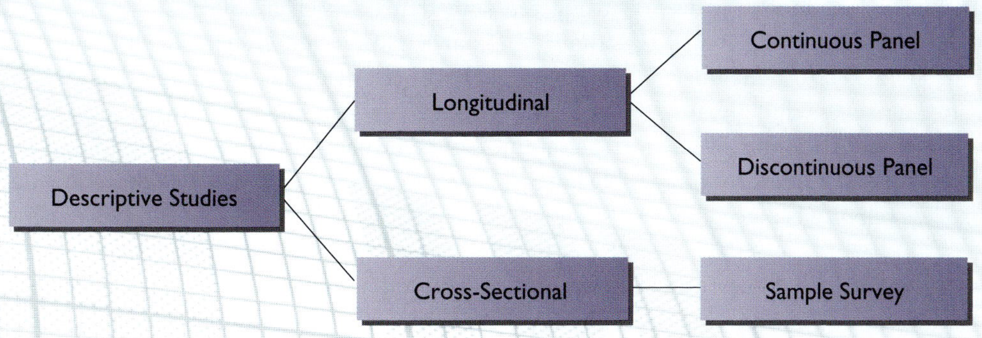

LANDS' END HAS ESTABLISHED PANELS OF 1,500 HOUSEHOLDS EACH TO REPRESENT CRITICAL TARGET SEGMENTS.

(e.g., catalogue covers) or product benefit statements. In other contexts, panel members might be asked for their attitudes about a new product at one point, and at another they might be asked to evaluate alternative advertising copy. With discontinuous panels, those chosen and the information sought vary from project to project. Several large marketing research companies operate discontinuous panels. For example, Synovate offers its Global Omnibus discontinuous panel, which has been in operation since 1986 and collects data in 55 countries via telephone survey.

If your research problem requires collection of things like purchasing behavior or watching and listening to media outlets, panel data are almost always more accurate than cross-sectional data. With cross-sectional designs, respondents are asked to remember and report their past behaviors, a process that always leads to mistakes because people tend to forget. With a panel, behavior often can be recorded as it occurs, electronically or manually, so less reliance is placed on memory.

The main disadvantage of panels is that they are almost always nonrepresentative and/or nonrandom. It is sometimes difficult to build a panel that represents the characteristics of the larger population. Even when the composition of the panel can be matched to the demographics of the target population, the results still can't be projected to the population because the participants were not randomly drawn from the population. Another big disadvantage is that most consumer panels have relatively low cooperation rates, even among households that agreed to participate in the panel.

Cross-Sectional Analysis: Sample Survey

As noted, a cross-sectional study involves drawing a sample of elements from the population of interest. Because a great deal of emphasis is placed on selecting sample members, preferably with a probability sampling plan, the technique is often called a **sample survey**.

sample survey
Cross-sectional study in which the sample is selected to be representative of the target population and in which the emphasis is on the generation of summary statistics such as averages and percentages.

A sample survey offers a couple of big advantages over panel designs. For one thing, you can target very specific populations. Targeted recruitment is possible with consumer panels, but only using the data that have been collected about the participating individuals or households. Here's a second big advantage of sample surveys: If you use a probability sampling plan, the results from the sample can be projected to the overall population. (Managers care more about populations than they do samples.) On the downside, survey research is expensive. It takes lots of time, energy, and money to successfully collect and analyze survey data. And unless you have the technical skills required for each aspect of the process, you'll have to hire others to help, adding to the overall cost of the project.

CAUSAL RESEARCH DESIGNS

Sometimes managers need stronger evidence that a particular action is likely to produce a particular outcome. For example, if you were considering a change in product packaging, you might want to test this hypothesis: "A redesign of the cereal package so that it is shorter and less likely to tip over will improve consumer attitudes toward the product." For really important decisions, sometimes we need stronger evidence than we can get with descriptive research. (Using descriptive research, we might have learned that there was a negative correlation between consumer ratings of likelihood of tipping over and attitude toward the product, but not a lot more.) Descriptive research is fine for testing hypotheses about relationships between variables, but we need causal designs for testing cause-and-effect relationships.

Concept of Causality

Everyone is familiar with the general notion of causality, the idea that one thing leads to the occurrence of another. The scientific notion of causality is quite complex, however; scientists tell us that it is impossible to prove that one thing causes another. Establishing that variable *X* causes variable *Y* requires meeting a number of conditions, one of which (the elimination of all other possible causes of *Y*) we can never know for certain no matter how carefully we have planned and conducted our research.

Does this mean that researchers shouldn't bother trying to establish causal relationships? Not at all! Although we can't prove with certainty that a change in one variable produces a change in another, we can conduct research that helps us narrow down the likely causal relationship between two variables by eliminating the other possible causes that we are aware of. Causal research designs work toward establishing possible causal relationships through the use of experiments.

Experiments as Causal Research

An **experiment** can provide more convincing evidence of causal relationships because of the control it gives investigators. In an experiment, a researcher manipulates, or sets the levels of, one or more causal variables (independent variables) to examine the effect on one or more outcome variables (dependent variables) while attempting to account for the effects of all other possible causal variables, usually by holding them constant.

experiment
Scientific investigation in which an investigator manipulates and controls one or more independent variables and observes the degree to which the dependent variables change.

laboratory experiments
Research investigation in which investigators create a situation with exact conditions in order to control some variables and manipulate others.

Sometimes we conduct experiments in "fake" or "sterile" environments so that we can carefully control exactly what research participants (called experimental subjects) see and experience. This allows us to observe the effect of the manipulated variables while the effect of other factors is minimized. **Laboratory experiments** allow us to be almost certain that the variables we manipulate produce the outcomes we observe because we can hold all other factors constant.

Here's an example: Researchers used a laboratory study to better understand "trip chaining," the practice of driving to more than one retail shop on the same shopping trip (as opposed to making separate trips to each retailer).[10] The researchers hypothesized that consumers prefer to drive short distances between retailers (i.e., the retailers are "clustered") rather than to drive longer distances between retailers ("nonclustered" retailers)—even when the total distance traveled from home, to the retailers, and back home again was the same. To test this hypothesis, the researchers

developed detailed maps and driving directions for both clustered and nonclustered trip chains and presented them to undergraduate students who agreed to serve as experimental subjects. Students saw both the clustered and the nonclustered manipulations of trip chains and then indicated which would be their preferred route. Confirming the researchers' hypothesis, 74 percent chose the clustered route.

In some ways, the task presented to subjects was similar to real life. When we shop for various items, we must choose which routes to take. In other respects, however, the study wasn't as realistic: these were not the real consumers living in the real geographic area represented on the maps. We can be pretty sure, though, that the outcome was due to differences in the maps and not to something else. This is the primary advantage of lab experiments. Marketing managers need to know whether or not changes in the experimental variable (degree of clustering) actually produced the observed changes in the outcome variable (consumer preference) so that they can formulate marketing strategy.

field experiment
Research study in a realistic situation in which one or more independent variables are manipulated by the experimenter under as carefully controlled conditions as the situation will permit.

A **field experiment** is a research study conducted in a realistic or natural situation. Just like lab experiments, one or more variables are manipulated to see their effect on an outcome variable. Because it's conducted in the field, you won't have the same degree of control as with a lab study, but you'll attempt to control as much as possible.

The researchers studying consumer preferences for clustered (versus nonclustered) trip chains also conducted a field experiment. In this case, the experiment was conducted with residents who actually lived in the area that had been mapped for subjects in the lab experiment. For the field study, however, researchers used a telephone survey and based the study on the subjects' home address and actual locations of retailers who were known to the subjects. They asked them to imagine that they needed to make trips to the two kinds of retailers and then presented them with two alternative routes (one that was clustered and one that was nonclustered). As in the laboratory experiment, subjects expressed a preference for the clustered trip chain compared with the nonclustered trip chain even though the overall travel distance was about the same.

Note how these two studies differed. In the field experiment, no attempt was made to set up special conditions—these were real consumers in their real environment. The laboratory experiment, on the other hand, was contrived. As we noted, the carefully controlled conditions of the laboratory let us make strong statements about how a manipulation led to a result. With field experiments, we can't make such strong statements, because there might be lots of things going on in a marketplace—things that we can't control—that affect the outcomes we observe. Field studies have a real advantage, though, when it comes to realism. The results of field studies can often be generalized, or extended, to other situations. In short, we may have less confidence that we understand exactly what produces a particular result, but the realistic conditions in the field allow us to be more confident that we can reproduce the result in other similar market conditions.

FAST FACT:

ACCORDING TO THE NPD GROUP, OVERALL **MAKE-UP USAGE IS DOWN FIVE PERCENTAGE POINTS** AMONG 18- TO 64-YEAR-OLD WOMEN FROM 2008 TO 2010.

MARKET TESTING

Market testing involves the use of a controlled experiment done in a limited but carefully selected section of the marketplace. Market testing is often used to predict the sales or profit outcomes of one or more proposed marketing actions. Very often, the action in question is the marketing of a new product or service. For example, in response to the rising popularity of specialty coffee drinks, McDonald's used test markets to determine that a market existed for McDonald's own higher-end coffee drink before beginning the commercialization process on a larger scale.[11]

market testing (test marketing)
A controlled experiment done in a limited but carefully selected sector of the marketplace.

Even if a company has performed previous tests of the product concept, the product package, the advertising copy, and so on, the test market is still the final gauge of consumer acceptance of the product. For example, a study on consumer packaged goods brands conducted by Information Resources reported that 80 percent of brands that are successful in live test markets go on to commercial success. Similarly, ACNielsen data indicate that roughly three out of four products that have been test-marketed succeed, but four out of five that have not been test-marketed fail.[12]

Test marketing is not restricted to testing the sales potential of new products; it has been used to examine the effectiveness of almost every element of the marketing mix. Market tests have been used to measure the effectiveness of new displays, the responsiveness of sales to shelf-space changes, the impact of changes in retail prices on market shares, the price elasticity of demand for products, the effect of different commercials on sales of products, and the differential effects of price and advertising on demand. General Motors even used it to test a proposed change in its distribution system. The Florida test involved keeping 1,200 new cars at a regional distribution center in Orlando for delivery to the state's 42 dealerships within 24 hours of an order. The approach was intended to whittle down the costly inventory that dealers have to maintain, improve manufacturing efficiency, and increase sales by allowing consumers to take quick possession of precisely the Cadillac model they wanted.[13]

Key Issues in Market Testing

The three key considerations of market testing are cost, time, and control.

Cost Cost is a big issue in test marketing. The cost includes the normal research costs associated with designing the data-collection instruments and the sample, the wages paid to the field staff who collect the data, and several other indirect expenses. In addition, with standard test markets (which we'll discuss a little later) you'll have to incur the usual costs of getting a new product in the channel of distribution (e.g., paying a sales force and—maybe—slotting fees). Ideally, the test market should reflect the marketing strategy to be used on the national scale, so the test can also include marketing costs for advertising, personal selling, displays, and so on. With new product introductions, there are also the costs associated with producing the merchandise. To produce the product on a small scale is typically inefficient. Yet to gear up immediately for large-scale production can be tremendously wasteful if the product proves a failure.

Time The time required for an adequate test market can also be substantial. In the 1960s, Procter & Gamble spent eight years testing Pampers disposable diapers before launching the product in the United States. In today's faster-paced globa environment, we simply don't have this luxury. This is unfortunate, because a test market's accuracy increases with time. Experiments conducted over short periods do not allow the cumulative impact of marketing actions. Consequently, a year is often recommended as a minimum before any kind of "go–no go" decision is made. Longer tests allow researchers to account for possible seasonal variations and to study repeat-purchasing behavior. For example, Altria tested a new cigarette called Marlboro Ultra Smooth—which was designed to be safer than regular cigarettes—for over three years in Atlanta, Tampa, and Salt Lake City, before deciding to discontinue the product; consumers didn't seem to care for it.[14] Such lengthy experiments are costly, however, and raise additional problems of control and competitive reaction.

Control The problems associated with control show up in several ways. First, there are the control problems in the experiment itself. What specific test markets will be used? How will product distribution be organized in those markets? Can the firm get wholesalers and retailers to cooperate? Can the test markets and control cities be matched sufficiently to rule out market characteristics as the primary reason for different sales results?

Chain retailers may have some advantage when it comes to control, because they can identify individual stores to serve as test sites and control the marketing mix elements inside the stores—including the products and services offered—in those specific geographic areas. For example, Chick-fil-A tested its new spicy chicken sandwich for two and a half years in Baltimore, Maryland, before rolling it out nationwide. McDonald's tested a variety of drinks such as Red Bull and Coca-Cola's vitaminwater in 150 of its stores, including 20 in the New York City area. Finally, Rite Aid Pharmacies introduced two Spanish-language stores in northern Philadelphia with bilingual staff, product selections, and in-store messages designed to appeal to the Hispanic market.[15]

One of the problems with market testing is the possibility that competitors can see a company's new product before it is fully commercialized. With many market tests, there are few secrets. When a Frito-Lay assistant brand manager would fly to a test-market city in Iowa to follow up with test sites selling the company's new Baked Lays product, the gate attendant at the small airport would routinely tell her which other snack foods companies had also had representatives in town to check the progress of the new product. In addition, competitors can, and do, sabotage marketing experiments by cutting the prices of their own products or by gobbling up quantities of the test marketer's product—thereby creating excitement and false confidence on the part of the test marketer.

Types of Test Markets

standard test market
A test market in which the company sells the product through its normal distribution channels.

There are three general categories of test markets: standard, controlled, and simulated. In a **standard test market**, such as those we've been describing, a company develops a product and then attempts to sell it through the normal distribution channels in a number of test-market cities. The potential success of the product can be gauged, and different elements of the marketing mix for the product can be experimentally varied with an eye toward developing the best marketing mix combination for the product. A key distinguishing feature of a standard test market is that the producer must sell the product to distributors, wholesalers, and/or retailers just as it would any other product.

What makes some cities better than others for standard test markets? Several factors are involved. The proposed test-market city needs to be demographically representative of the larger market in which the product will ultimately be sold. Most popular test-market cities are reasonably representative of the overall population, although some are more representative than others. If the product is geared more toward a specific segment of the population, however, then markets should be chosen with high representation of that segment. For example, for products targeted toward Hispanic consumers, test markets with higher proportions of Hispanic residents are obviously desirable.

Popular standard test-market cities also possess other features prized by researchers. The test market should be large enough that it has its own media outlets (e.g., newspapers and radio and television stations), which allow tests of advertising and promotion. It must also be large enough to have a sufficient number of the right kind of retail outlets. When Taco Bell was looking for a test market for its Grilled Stuft Burrito, for example, it was important to find a market with a good mix of company and franchise-owned restaurants, and Fresno, California, was selected.[16] It is also important that test markets be geographically isolated from other cities in order to avoid "spillover" effects from nearby markets where testing is not taking place. Such spillover effects might include advertising and other promotion or a significant percentage of consumers in the test market traveling outside the test market to shop.

controlled test market
An entire test program conducted by an outside service in a market in which it can guarantee distribution.

In a **controlled test market** (sometimes called a forced-distribution test market), the entire test program is conducted by an outside service. The service pays retailers for shelf space and can therefore guarantee distribution. For example, SymphonyIRI Group is a leading supplier of controlled test-market services. Its Behaviorscan service uses a number of smaller (populations of 75,000 to 215,000) demographically representative cities. Within each city several thousand panel households carry cards that are scanned when they purchase items from a variety of participating retail stores and use handheld scanners to record purchases from other stores. When marketers are planning to launch a new product, Behaviorscan gives them control over many important marketing and environmental variables. The company maintains its own warehouse and distribution system in each test city, and its employees routinely visit the stores each week to see that the distribution, shelf location, and point-of-sale promotions are executed as planned. The company also controls direct-to-consumer promotions and the targeting of specific advertising to subsets of the panel households.[17]

simulated test market (STM)
A study in which consumer ratings and other information are fed into a computer model that then makes projections about the likely level of sales for the product in the market.

A third type of market testing is the **simulated test market (STM)**. A simulated test market differs from standard and controlled test markets in that consumers do not purchase the product (or service) being tested from a retail store. In fact, in many cases, the product has not even been put into production. Instead, researchers will typically recruit consumers to participate in the simulated study. Consumers are shown the new product or product concept and asked to rate its features. They may be shown commercials for it and for competitors' products. All the information is fed into a computer model, which has equations for the repeat purchase and market share likely to be achieved by the test model. The key to successful simulation is the equations built into the computer model. Nielsen's BASES simulation approach, an industry leader, reports that in over 90 percent of cases,

COURTESY OF QUALTRICS LABS INC.

its STM models can come within 20 percent of actual results in the marketplace.[18]

Simulated test-market data are often collected via the Internet using consumer panels, although other data collection approaches are used where necessary. Members of an online panel may be recruited for participation in a particular study by letter and e-mail, which provide access to an online survey. Over the years, most simulated test markets have been conducted for consumer nondurable products. In recent years, however, more and more studies have focused on financial services, healthcare, consumer durables, pharmaceuticals, and other industries.[19]

Comparing the Three Types of Test Markets

Marketers who need to test-market a new product or to fine-tune an element of a marketing program must choose which type of test market to use. Each of the approaches has advantages and disadvantages.

One advantage of simulated test markets is the protection they provide from competitors. They are also good for assessing trial and repeat-purchasing behavior. They are faster than full-scale tests and are particularly good for spotting weak products, which allows firms to avoid full-scale testing of these products. Plus, of the three forms we've discussed, simulated test markets are the least expensive. The primary disadvantage of simulated test markets is that they do not provide any information about the firm's ability to secure trade support for the product or about what competitive reaction is likely to be. Thus, they are more suited for evaluating product extensions than for examining the likely success of radically different new products.

Controlled test markets are more expensive than simulated test markets, but less costly than standard test markets. One reason they cost less than standard test markets is that the research supplier provides distribution and handles all aspects of display, pricing, and so on. This perfect implementation of the marketing plan also represents one of the weaknesses of the controlled test market. Acceptance or rejection of the new product by the trade in the "real world" is typically critical to the success of any new product. A controlled test market guarantees acceptance by the trade for the duration of the test, but acceptance will not be guaranteed during the actual marketing of the product. When a new product fits in nicely with a company's existing line, for which it already has distribution, the controlled test market is a fairly good indicator. When the product is new or represents a radical departure for the manufacturer, the question of trade support is much more problematic, and the controlled test is much less useful under these circumstances.

The traditional, or standard, test market provides a more natural environment than either the simulated or the controlled test market and, as a result, offers the greatest degree of prediction accuracy. This advantage must be balanced against some important disadvantages, however. Standard test markets are the most expensive, take the most time, and are the most likely to tip off competitors compared with the other approaches. Even so, the standard test market may be a logical choice when (1) it is important for the firm to test its ability to actually sell to the trade and get distribution for the product; (2) the capital investment is significant and the firm needs a prolonged test market to accurately assess its capital needs or its technical ability to manufacture the product; and/or (3) the company is entering new territory and needs to build its experience base so that it can play for real, but wants to learn how to do so on a limited scale. The relative advantages and disadvantages of the three basic types of test markets are shown in Exhibit 3.5.

EXHIBIT 3.5

Relative Advantages and Disadvantages of Different Types of Test Markets

	Simulated	Controlled	Standard
Speed	1	2	3
Cost	1	2	3
Security	1	2	3
Experimental control	1	2	3
Realism	3	2	1
Prediction accuracy	3	2	1

1= most favorale; 3 = least favorable

4 Collecting Secondary Data from Inside and Outside the Organization

POLL QUESTION:

Internal secondary data, such as a firm's daily sales, are more important than external secondary data, such as a trade publication article.

STRONGLY DISAGREE 1 ○ 2 ○ 3 ○ 4 ○ 5 ○ STRONGLY AGREE

Learning Objectives

1. Explain the difference between primary and secondary data.
2. Cite two advantages offered by secondary data.
3. Explain the difference between internal and external secondary data.
4. Define what is meant by a decision support system (DSS).
5. List three common uses of the information supplied by standardized marketing information services.

INTRODUCTION

The fundamental purpose of marketing research is to help managers gather the information they need to make better decisions. Once you've defined the research problem and considered the type of research design to pursue, it's time to turn your attention to data collection. Regardless of research design, the natural temptation is to begin thinking about the questions you'd like to ask respondents.

Before you write questions for depth interviews, develop a moderator's guidebook, or craft a sample survey, however, you should look for existing information that might serve your purposes. **Secondary data** are information not gathered for the immediate study, but previously gathered for some other purpose. Secondary data often give good background information and fill in some gaps in the researcher's understanding. Data that you collect for the purpose of the investigation at hand are known as **primary data**. Primary data are very decision-focused and are tailored with a specific business issue in mind.

Here's an example of secondary data. Carol Tome, the chief financial officer at Home Depot, recently reported on changes in U.S. consumer spending habits. Because the company carefully tracks the size of purchase receipts, Home Depot analysts could report that the number of tickets of $50 or less had stayed about level during the economic downturn, but that tickets of $500 or more were down more than 10 percent.[1] Purchase receipts are an ongoing, everyday part of business—they certainly aren't produced for marketing research purposes—but they can serve as a useful source of secondary data. And note that the company could have chosen to survey their customers about their spending habits, which would have generated primary data.

secondary data
Information not gathered for the immediate study at hand but for some other purpose.

Successful projects should start with a careful search for existing secondary data. Most people usually have no idea just how much secondary data are available from sources inside and outside the organization. The U.S. Bureau of the Census (www.census.gov), for example, collects a wealth of information about people, households, and businesses, much of which is readily available for use by researchers. It is important to know what is available in secondary sources, not just in order to avoid "reinventing the wheel" but also because secondary data

primary data
Information collected specifically for the investigation at hand.

PURCHASE RECEIPTS ARE AN ONGOING, EVERYDAY PART OF BUSINESS . . . THEY CAN SERVE AS A USEFUL SOURCE OF SECONDARY DATA.

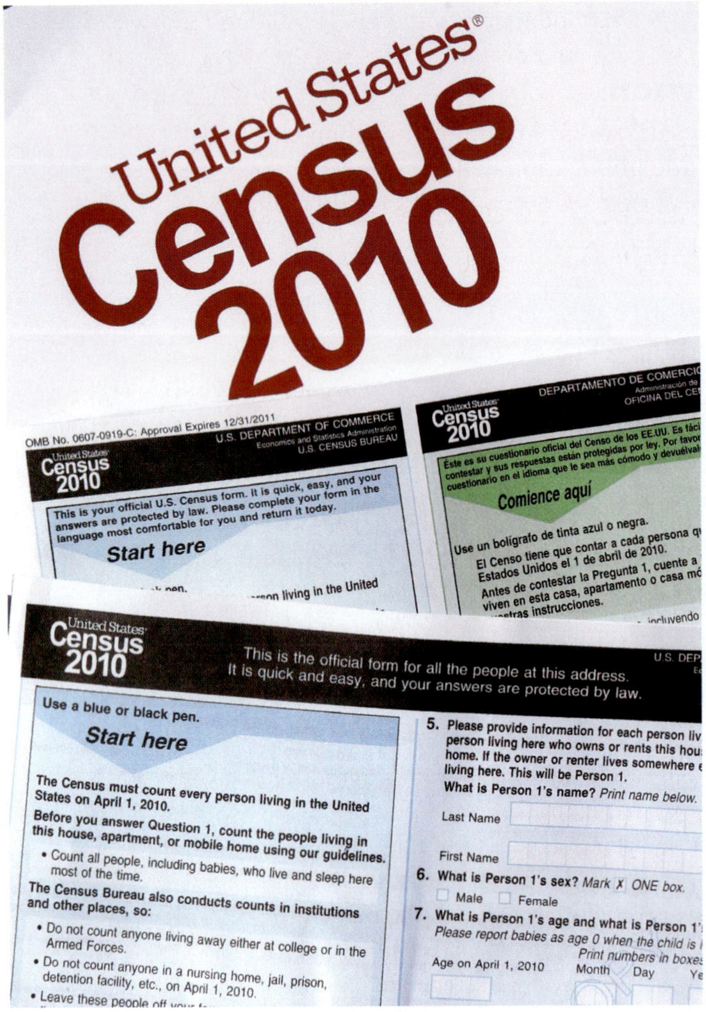

© AP IMAGES/ROSS D. FRANKLIN

possess some significant advantages over primary data. Some types of marketing research—in particular, market analysis—rely almost exclusively on secondary data.

ADVANTAGES AND DISADVANTAGES OF SECONDARY DATA

The most significant advantages of secondary data are the time and money they can save. If the information being sought is available as secondary data, you can simply go to the library or go online, locate the appropriate source(s), and gather the information desired. This shouldn't take much time or money. If you collected the same information using a survey, the process could take months and cost thousands of dollars. With secondary data, somebody else has already paid for data collection. Even if there is a charge for using the data (unlike statistics compiled by government or trade associations, commercial data are not free), the costs are generally less than they would be if you collected the information yourself.

FAST FACT:

COSTS FOR "THE TWELVE DAYS OF CHRISTMAS" ITEMS ROSE 9% IN 2010 TO $23,439. THE RISE WAS PRIMARILY BECAUSE THE COST OF "FIVE GOLD RINGS" **INCREASED 30%** DUE TO HIGH GOLD PRICES.

Given the substantial amount of time and money at stake, we offer this advice: Begin with secondary data and then proceed to primary data only if you still need more information. The secondary data might be sufficient, especially when all you need is a ballpark estimate. Realistically, though, secondary data don't often completely solve the problem under study, but they usually will (1) help you to better state the problem under investigation, (2) suggest improved methods or further data that should be collected, and/or (3) provide comparative data that can help interpret primary data if such data are eventually collected. So, secondary data are often a great place to gain exploratory insights.

The main disadvantages of secondary data are (1) they often don't fit the current problem very well and (2) they are sometimes not accurate. Because secondary data are collected for other purposes, it is rare when they perfectly fit the problem as defined. Sometimes this is due to the use of different units of measurement (e.g., secondary data reports retail store size in terms of profits, whereas you need it in terms of number of employees) or different class definitions (e.g., you needed a report of income broken down in $5,000 increments, but secondary data used categories with $7,500 increments). Sometimes they are just too general (e.g., you need data on organic free-range eggs, but natural dairy is the only available category.) An even bigger problem is that secondary data are often out of date. The time from data collection to data dissemination is often long, sometimes as much as two to three years, as, for example, with much government census data. Although census data have great value when they are current, the value decreases quickly with time. Most marketing decisions require current, rather than historical, information.

primary source The originating source of secondary data.

secondary source A source of secondary data that did not originate the data but rather secured them from another source.

The accuracy of much secondary data is also questionable. When you don't collect the data yourself, it's often difficult to assess just how accurate the data are. You can improve your confidence in the accuracy of the data by always going to the **primary source** of secondary data, the source that originated the data. A **secondary source** is a source that reproduces data taken from a primary source. Using the primary source allows you to have an idea of the quality of the original data collection effort because the primary source will typically be the only source that describes the process of collection and analysis. Plus, the primary source is usually more accurate and complete than a secondary source.

The owner of GrandKids Ltd. discovered the hard way why it is important to use primary sources of secondary data. After gathering secondary data on population from the local school district and a company that produces advertising brochures, she launched her store in an upscale suburb of New York, thinking it was an ideal location for a store catering to grandparents eager to spoil their grandchildren. Three years later, she was out of business. What happened? Based on the secondary data she used, she had grossly overestimated the size of her market. Had she checked census data, she would have discovered that the market contained less than half the number of households she thought there were—and that less than one-third of the residents were in her targeted age group of people 50 and older.[2]

There is one other thing we want you to consider when it comes to the accuracy of secondary data. It is important to consider the source, or sponsor, of a research project when evaluating the likely accuracy of the results. Unethical researchers will bend and twist the truth to suit their purposes. (In Chapter 1, we warned you about *advocacy research*, which is research conducted to support a position rather than to find the truth about a situation.) Be very cautious about relying upon secondary data for which you don't know the sponsor and/or important details about how the research was conducted (e.g., nature and size of sample, wording of questions).

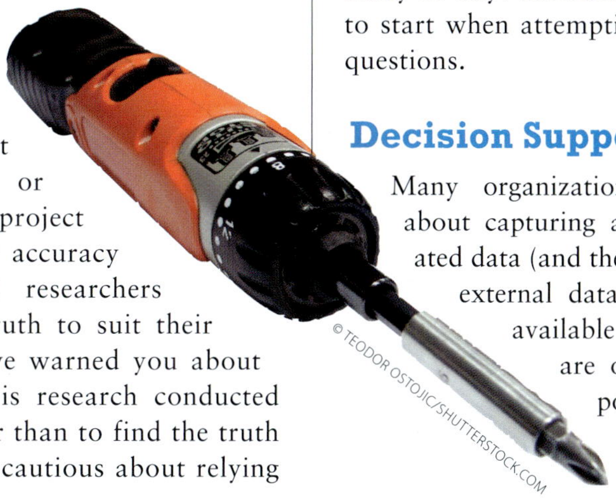
© TEODOR OSTOJIC/SHUTTERSTOCK.COM

INTERNAL SECONDARY DATA

Data that come from internal sources are known as internal secondary data. For example, the sales and cost data compiled in the normal accounting cycle represent promising internal secondary data for many research problems—such as evaluation of past marketing strategy or assessment of the firm's competitive position in the industry. Even something as simple as a product registration card can be used for marketing intelligence. Years ago, when the Skil Corporation was launching a cordless power screwdriver, management was surprised to find that a substantial proportion of the new screwdrivers were being sold to elderly people, based on information obtained from registration cards. Although marketing managers had positioned the product for the "do-it-yourself" market, the ease of use made the product attractive to older consumers. The company began advertising in publications targeting older Americans.[3]

Internal secondary data are often the least costly (assuming a database is already in place) and most readily available of any type of marketing research. Most studies should begin with a search for internal secondary data. For example, common questions that confront marketing managers are: How do we maximize sales (and profits) within our existing product lines? When consumers enter a store, what else might they also buy? What are they least likely to buy? Internal sales data are a great place to start when attempting to answer these types of questions.

Decision Support Systems

Many organizations are quite sophisticated about capturing and storing internally generated data (and they sometimes augment it with external data as well). Because the data available in a decision support system are often used for multiple purposes, they are considered an important source for internal secondary data.

decision support system (DSS)
A combination of database, analytical models, and dialog system that allows managers to develop and access customized information.

A **decision support system (DSS)** is a combination of database, analytical models, and dialog system that allows managers to develop and access customized information. Thus, besides storing information and producing standardized reports, the DSS allows managers to access the database and produce customized reports whenever they are needed. The DSS includes models for analyzing the data in the system—for example, creating tables or graphs of key data and seeing how a forecast changes if assumptions are changed. Exhibit 4.1 illustrates a basic DSS.

A good DSS has two key outputs: (1) standardized, up-to-the-minute reports needed for day-to-day operations and (2) custom reports that can easily be produced by managers when needed. In addition, they commonly include graphical interfaces and menu-driven procedures that make it easy to use for non-computer people.

Components of Decision Support Systems

Let's focus a bit more attention now on the various parts of a DSS. An organization-wide DSS has three primary components: the data system, model system, and dialog system. The data system includes the processes used to capture and store data coming from marketing, finance, and manufacturing, as well as information coming from any number of other internal (or external) sources. Essentially, this is a database. A typical data system has modules containing customer information, company operational data, general economic and demographic information, competitor information, and industry information, including market trends. Where do the data in a DSS come from? One survey of *Fortune* 500 companies indicated that 62 percent of the data come from internal accounting and data processing sources, with the remainder coming from marketing research and intelligence.[4]

© AP IMAGES/PRNEWSFOTO/SPRINT

EXHIBIT 4.1
Decision Support System

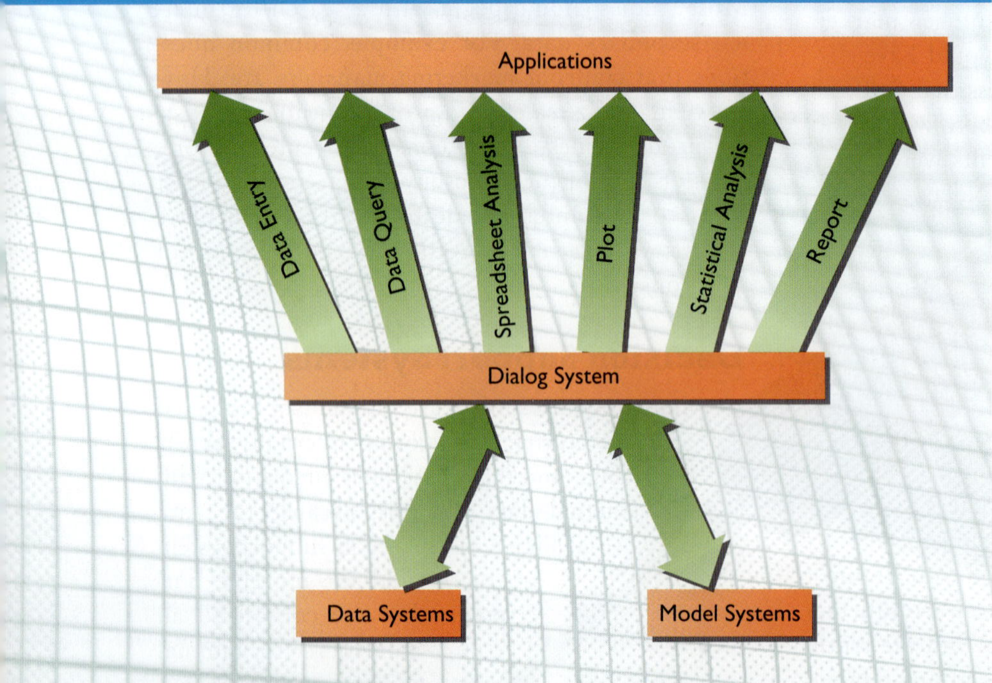

© 2012 Cengage Learning

The growth in computing power and sophisticated data-processing capabilities has led to the development of huge databases within companies. These *data warehouses* dwarf those available even a few years ago. For example, after Sprint and Nextel merged, one of the key challenges was data integration between the two firms. This included billing systems, data access, customer care, and retail store operations, among many others. Neither of the individual existing systems could handle the merger entirely, so the combined company sought a new solution. As an example of the challenge, whatever system used had to be able to quickly access 900 gigabytes of billing logs per day. Sprint's old system had a three-hour latency in retrieving this type of data. The new system—hosted on six database servers across four geographic locations—could execute data retrieval in 6 to 10 minutes. This allows Sprint/Nextel to handle customer care to retail store management in a timely manner.[5]

The model system in a DSS includes all the computerized routines that allow you to do the analyses you want to do. The most common procedures are the simple ones: counting the cases that fall into different groups, summing, averaging, computing ratios, building tables, and so on. Increasingly sophisticated models are being developed all the time, often for relatively specific purposes. For example, DSSs have been developed to enable brand managers to make better marketing mix decisions for their brands; help bankers make stronger credit management decisions; guide managers when they make new product development decisions; and assess alternative marketing plans for motion pictures before they are released.[6] In any case, the point is to use the model system to generate useful information for making decisions.

The explosion in recent years in the number of databases available and the size of some of them has triggered greater need for ways to analyze them efficiently. For example, store scanners provide massive amounts of data to marketing managers. The huge amounts of data require a great amount of time for even a well-trained analyst to come up with simple summaries that show the major trends. In response, a number of firms have developed **expert systems**—computer-based, artificial intelligence systems that attempt to model how experts in the area process information to solve the problem at hand.

expert system
A computer-based, artificial intelligence system that attempts to model how experts in the area process information to solve the problem at hand.

THE HUGE AMOUNTS OF DATA REQUIRE A GREAT AMOUNT OF TIME FOR EVEN A WELL-TRAINED ANALYST TO COME UP WITH SIMPLE SUMMARIES THAT SHOW THE MAJOR TRENDS.

Dialog systems allow users—including those with little technical or computer background—to explore the database and analyze data using the model system. Dialog systems are sometimes menu driven, requiring only a few clicks of a computer mouse or a few simple keystrokes to produce reports that satisfy the particular information needs of the user. This allows users to target the information they want and not be overwhelmed with irrelevant data. They can ask a question and, on the basis of the answer, ask a subsequent question, and then another, and another, and so on.

The dialog system puts data at your fingertips. Although that sounds simple enough, it's a difficult task because of the large amount of data available. Using the dialog system you can search for answers to particular questions or you can explore the data looking for important relationships among variables that help guide decisions. The technical term for the latter capability is **data mining**, the use of analytic techniques to explore the data held within a dataset to isolate useful information. Organizations typically use data mining to boost sales and profits by better understanding their customers. And there are other uses as well. Coaches and managers in Major League Baseball (MLB) have used data mining to sort through game statistics to determine their most productive combinations of players and measure the effectiveness of individual players.[7] Exhibit 4.2 discusses how data mining is being revolutionized by *Super Crunchers*.

data mining
The use of analytic techniques to explore the data held within a dataset in order to isolate useful information.

The sophistication in the design and uses of decision support systems opens up access to so much data that higher-level management of information becomes critical. An executive in charge of information can ensure that it is used in support of strategic thinking. In many organizations, this function is now the responsibility of a chief information officer, or CIO. The CIO's major role is to run the company's information and computer systems like a business. The CIO serves as the liaison between the firm's top management and its information systems department. He or she is responsible for planning, coordinating, and controlling the use of the firm's information resources. In many cases, the managers of the information system department report directly to the CIO.

EXHIBIT 4.2

Super Crunchers Are Thinking-by-Numbers

Can a credit card company examine a customer's charge history and determine whether he or she will get divorced? Can a hospital predict physician cleanliness based on infection rates? Ian Ayres, econometrician and attorney at Yale University, says the answer to both questions is yes in his book *Super Crunchers: Why Thinking-by-Numbers Is the New Way to Be Smart.*

Ayres details his own work, as well as recounting other studies, where large databases were analyzed to find relationships between seemingly unrelated things. For example, do race and gender have a role to play in such diverse areas as interest rates on car loans and the number of citations an academic article will receive? Well, yes again. Ayres and colleague Mark Cohen from Vanderbilt University found that African-American borrowers pay about $700 in markups compared to $300 in markups by Caucasians. Moreover, over half of Caucasian borrowers paid no markups, whereas African-American borrowers paid 19.9 percent of the markup profits.

Other data-driven discoveries from *Super Crunchers* include these: Netflix customers liking the movies the service recommends better than the ones they choose on their own, airlines predicting which customers are most vulnerable to being lured away by a competitor after a cancelled flight and giving them priority booking over the airline's own best customers, and baseball managers assessing prospects on quantifiable statistics instead of the seasoned observation of groups of scouts.

With the reams and reams of data that can be collected in a variety of industries, all it takes is a little mining to find business gold. So, with all this thinking-by-numbers success, are you ready to sign up with eHarmony.com? Its founder is a super cruncher, too.

Sources: Melissa Lafsky, "Attack of the Super *Crunchers:* Adventures in Data Mining," *New York Times,* August 23, 2007, accessed August 2, 2008, from http://freakonomics.blogs.nytimes.com/2007/08/23/attack-of-the-super-crunchers-ian-ayres-on-data-mining/; and Jerry Adler, "Era of the Super Cruncher," *Newsweek,* September 3, 2007, accessed August 8, 2008, from http://www.newsweek.com/id/40909.

© G FIUME/GETTY IMAGES

The process of data mining from game stats can enable professional sports managers and executives to tap into and use ideal player combinations.

EXTERNAL SECONDARY DATA

Although most people underestimate what is available, there is likely to be relevant external secondary data on many of the issues you'll confront. The problem usually isn't data availability; it's identifying and accessing what is out there. Some external secondary data are available from published sources and may be available for free from business periodicals or material published by trade associations. Other published sources might involve a fee or require you to purchase a directory. The other major sources of external secondary data are companies that sell standardized (or syndicated) marketing information. These companies collect primary data on various topics and then sell it to users. Regardless of whether you use published or syndicated sources, as we noted earlier, the cost is typically much less than collecting the needed primary data yourself.

EXHIBIT 4.3

Searching for Published Sources of External Secondary Data

1. Identify what you wish to know and what you already know about your topic.
2. Develop a list of key terms and names.
3. Search several of the general guides and directories, and Web sites for papers and/or reports.
4. Compile the literature you have found. Rework your list of key words and authors if necessary.
5. Consult the reference librarian.
6. Consult the various directory guides.
7. Identify authorities in the area and consult them.

Searching for Published External Secondary Data

The trick in locating published secondary data is to develop a systematic plan for finding relevant data. Exhibit 4.3 includes advice for getting started on a search of secondary data on a particular topic.[8]

As you can tell from the exhibit, one of the main issues is to identify a number of key words or phrases for searching. These terms will be used in your initial searches for information; you'll want to keep this list as long as possible during initial stages. Using your key terms, search the databases of popular press articles in newspapers and business periodicals that are typically available in libraries. Do a thorough search of online materials using a good search engine. And it really helps to secure the services of a good reference librarian in the process. Librarians are specialists who know the contents of many of the key information sources in a library and on the Web, as well as how to search those sources most effectively. (But remember that a reference librarian can't be of much help unless you provide specific details about what you want to know.)

If you have trouble finding what you need—and the reference librarian hasn't been able to help—use an authority. Identify some individual or organization that might know something about the topic. For example, the U.S. Census Bureau (http://www.census.gov/aboutus/subjects.html) allows you to contact specialists for information on any of the bureau's studies. These people are often quite knowledgeable about related studies in their areas of expertise. Faculty at universities, government officials, and business executives can also be useful sources of information.

Using Standardized Marketing Information Services

There are a number of standardized marketing information services that are available. These commercial services are more expensive than using published information. Suppliers of these data sell them to multiple companies, allowing the costs of collecting, editing, coding, and analyzing them to be shared. Because multiple companies must be able to use the data, however, the data to be collected—and how they are to be collected—must be standardized. As a result, such data may not always be a perfect fit for a company. This section describes some of the main types of external secondary data available from standardized marketing information service providers.

Profiling Customers

Market segmentation is common among organizations seeking to improve their marketing efforts. If firms can group their customers into relatively homogeneous groups, they can tailor marketing programs to the groups, making the programs more effective and the customers more satisfied. This only works, however, if the company can access information about its (potential) customers.

One of the commercial services that is especially popular among industrial goods and service suppliers is the Dun & Bradstreet International Business Locator, an index that provides basic data on over 28 million public and private companies worldwide in 200 countries. These records allow organizations to isolate potential new customers with particular characteristics, analyze and select the media to reach customer groups, assess market potential by territory, and accomplish lots of other things.

Firms selling consumer goods also need information about potential customer groups. Starting with the 1970 census, the U.S. Census Bureau has made available information that organizations have used for a multitude of purposes. Having the census data available in electronic form allows them to be analyzed by arbitrary geographic boundaries, and an entire industry has developed to take advantage of this capability. The **geodemographers**, as they are typically called, combine census data with their own survey data or data that they gather from administrative records such as motor vehicle registrations or credit transactions. Another important thing that geodemographers do is regularly updating the census data through statistical extrapolation to cover the 10 years between the censuses of population.

geodemography
The availability of demographic, consumer-behavior, and lifestyle data by arbitrary geographic boundaries that are typically quite small.

Mapping software, often called a geographic information system (GIS), combines various kinds of demographic data with geographic information on maps. The user can draw a map showing average income levels of a county and then zoom closer to look at particular towns in more detail. Most GIS programs on the market can show information as detailed as a single block; some programs can show individual buildings. Further, geodemographers use cluster analysis to produce "homogeneous groups" that describe the American population. Exhibit 4.4 shows the results of some of these data.

Measuring Product Sales and Market Share

Organizations need an accurate assessment of how they are doing if they are to succeed in an increasingly competitive environment. One way to accomplish this is to review internal records and determine how much they have sold into the channel of distribution (i.e., wholesalers, distributors, retailers, and the like). Knowing how much product has been shipped to wholesalers and retailers doesn't necessarily provide a good understanding of how the product is doing with consumers, however. In addition, simply totaling sales invoices provides no information at all about how a company's product is doing relative to products from other companies. Historically, there are several ways of measuring sales to final consumers, including the use of diary panels of households and the measurement of sales at the store level.

(Online) Diary Panels. As we discussed in the previous chapter, panels are sometimes used to track the products that households purchase. Whether recorded on paper or reported online, the key feature of a diary panel is that a representative group of individuals or households keeps track of purchases made or products consumed over a given period of time (a continuous panel). In this way, purchasing and/or consumption behavior can be projected to the larger population. Data are grouped by product category or household type, with a possible benefit being the discovery of competitive or even complementary products.

The NPD Group tracks a number of food-related trends in the United States. For example, the National Eating Trends (NET) service has operated a household diary panel since 1980. Participants keep a record of all food and drink consumed by all household members for a specified period of time. The company also tracks consumer purchasing using an online consumer panel. The panel offers access to more than 1.8 million individuals who have agreed to respond to surveys and to provide information on purchasing behavior. Ongoing tracking services are provided for a variety of product categories.

Scanners. Another way to assess product sales and market share is to work with retailers, rather than a panel of consumers, to get the data. In working with retailers, the usual approach is to use scanners that record purchases of products at the point-of-sale. Although old-fashioned store audits are still used in a few cases, the vast majority of consumer products in the United States are now tracked via scanner.

As you may be aware, there is a unique 12-digit Universal Product Code for each product sold in most stores. As the bar code is read by a fixed or handheld

FAST FACT:

SALES OF **OLD SPICE** BODY WASH HAVE **RISEN 11%** IN 12 MONTHS SINCE THE LAUNCH OF THE "SMELL LIKE A MAN, MAN" CAMPAIGN.

EXHIBIT 4.4

Sample Median Household Income Demographic Data

What does ESRI's Updated Demographics data show for your area?

Median Household Income ▾

This protracted recession/recovery has taken a toll on the earnings of every U.S. household. The median household income for the U.S. in 2010 is $54,442.

Zoom in and out using the slider bar on the left, or press SHIFT and drag the cursor to outline your area.

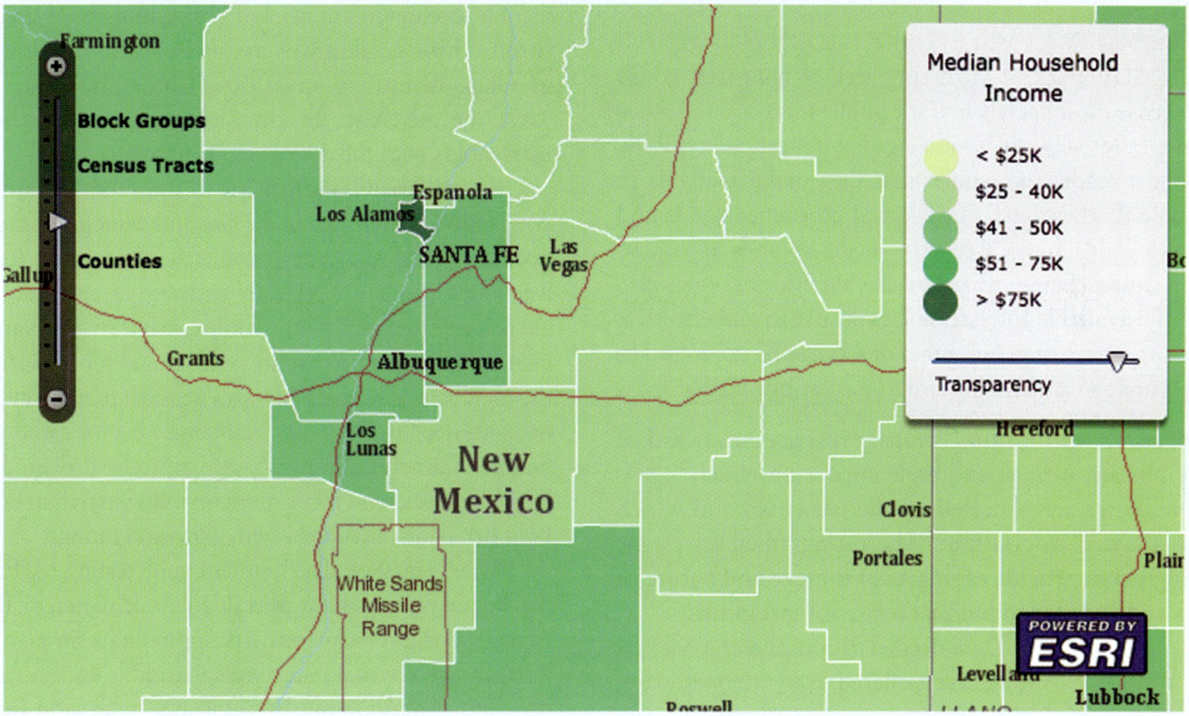

Source: http://www.esri.com/data/esri_data/demographic-map.html, downloaded March 29, 2011.

scanner
An electronic device that automatically reads the Universal Product Code imprinted on a product, looks up the price in an attached computer, and instantly prints the description and price of the item on the cash register receipt.

scanner, the scanner identifies the 12-digit number, looks up the price in the attached computer, and immediately prints the description and price of the item on the cash register receipt. At the same time, the computer can keep track of the movement of every item that is scanned. Where scanning is available, weekly sales (units sold at what price) are collected from a retailer's system. The research provider takes these data and matches the UPC to a description to make the information more useful.

In addition, other data sources can be combined with this information. For example, suppose that you or your research provider collected information about whether a product had been featured in a display or in advertising. You might also collect information about historical pricing for the product and compare it to the current pricing. In all of these cases, you would attempt to take the "causal" data and see whether it is related to changes in the sales of the product, thereby assessing the effectiveness of various marketing actions.

The effect of scanners on the collection of sales and market share data has been profound. Scanners can also be used to link purchase behavior with demographic information. As we noted in Chapter 3, it is possible to use scanners and consumer panels to link purchase behavior to particular households. Some systems take it a step further and measure or control media exposure in these households. Combining all of these data sources at the household level produces what has become known as **single-source data**.

single-source data
Data that allow researchers to link together purchase behavior, household characteristics, and advertising exposure at the household level.

Although single-source measurement offers the opportunity for new market insights, firms subscribing to these services need to prepare themselves for the incredible amounts of data they produce. Without proper planning, firms can literally drown in these data. That is why decision support systems for analyzing data (particularly expert systems) are becoming increasingly important in marketing research.

Measuring Advertising Exposure and Effectiveness

Most suppliers of industrial goods advertise most heavily in trade publications. To sell space more effectively, the various trade publications typically sponsor readership studies that they make available to potential advertisers. Suppliers of consumer goods and services also have access to media-sponsored readership studies. Standardized marketing information is also readily available for assessing exposure to and effectiveness of advertising. A number of services have evolved to measure consumer exposure to the various media.

Television and Radio. Almost everyone has heard of the Nielsen ratings and their impact on which television shows are canceled by the networks and which are allowed to continue. The ratings themselves are designed to provide estimates of the size and nature of the audience for individual television programs.

Data needed to compute the Nielsen ratings are gathered in a variety of ways. **People meters** attempt to measure not only the channel to which a set is tuned, but also who in the household is watching. Each member of the family has his or her own viewing number. Whoever turns on the set, sits down to watch, or changes the channel is supposed to enter his or her number into the people meter. All of this information is transmitted to a central computer for processing. In addition, Nielsen supplements people-meter data with information collected using simple electronic meters that record what channels are being watched (but nothing about who is watching), consumer diaries, and telephone interviews.

people meter
A device used to measure when a television is on, to what channel it is tuned, and who in the household is watching it.

Through the data provided by these basic records, Nielsen develops estimates of the number and percentage of all television households viewing a given television show. Nielsen also breaks down these aggregate ratings by numerous socioeconomic and demographic characteristics,

© THE NIELSEN COMPANY

including territory, education of head of house, household income, occupation of head of house, household size, and so on. These breakdowns assist the television networks in selling advertising on particular programs, while they assist the advertiser in choosing programs that reach households with the desired characteristics.

If your organization plans to use radio advertising, you'll also be interested in the size and demographic composition of the audiences various stations reach. Radio-listening statistics are typically gathered using diaries that are placed in a panel of households. Arbitron, for example, uses a random sample of households and sends diaries to the members of households who agree to participate. Participants keep track of their radio listening for a one-week period of time. Radio ratings are typically broken down by age and sex, and focus more on individual than household behavior, in contrast with television ratings.

After years of development and testing, Arbitron has begun rolling out a portable people meter, or PPM, in the 50 largest radio markets. Individuals simply carry a pager-sized device that senses inaudible codes embedded into programming by radio and television broadcasters (including cable TV) so that an accurate record can be made of actual exposure to media. This passive approach measures actual consumer behavior and should be much more accurate than the diary approach.

Print Media. There are several services that measure exposure to, and readership of, print media. For example, the Starch Ad Readership program, a service of the GfK Group, measures the effectiveness of magazine advertisements. Many thousands of advertisements in hundreds of individual issues are assessed each year. For each magazine issue, respondents are asked to indicate the degree to which they have read each ad. During the course of the interview, respondents also offer comments on the advertisements themselves as well as the brands featured in them.

Starch reports provide insights into readership for the ads; they also attempt to gauge reader interest and reactions to the editorial content and advertising in the magazine. An important feature of the reports is the ability to compare readership scores for a particular ad against (1) the other ads in the issue and (2) ads of similar size, color, and product category. These features of Starch scores help make them effective in assessing changes in theme, copy, layout, use of color, and so on.[9]

Internet. Advertisers also need information about consumers' online activities. It is relatively easy to count the number of times that a site or banner ad has been accessed, along with revenues from online transactions. As with other forms of media, however, it is a little more complicated to determine the demographics of those accessing a Web site—and this is important for decisions about which Web sites to choose for advertising purposes. Nielsen NetRatings offers a syndicated audience measurement service that assesses Internet usage at work and at home.

Regular reports detail a site's audience size and composition, time spent at the site, and so on. Exhibit 4.5 lists the top 10 Web brands based on the number of different Internet users who visited the brand's site(s) during a recent one-month period. For example, the top brand, Google, was visited by over 150 million people during the time period. Facebook came in second in terms of users, but they spent over six and a half hours on the site on average that month.

One additional area of Web-oriented measurement concerns mobile media (i.e., media consumption over cellular phones). Several companies have recognized the growing trends in mobile entertainment and advertising. For example, comScore tracks mobile web browsing to offer insights to its customers.

FAST FACT:

GOOGLE ACCOUNTED FOR **72%** OF ALL U.S. SEARCHES IN MAY 2010. **YAHOO!** WAS SECOND WITH **14%**.

Multimedia Services. Several companies offer syndicated research that measures media usage across categories. As an example, Experian Simmons uses a national probability sample of over 25,000 respondents. Its National Consumer Survey collects information on media exposure and product usage. Households agreeing to participate are sent a household survey booklet that collects information about household usage of an extensive list of products and services. In addition, each member of the household is sent a personal survey booklet that collects extensive media usage measures as well as personal information on demographics and lifestyle, product/service usage, shopping behavior, and so on. By taking into account both media habits and product usage, the Experian data allow companies to better segment, target, and communicate to the most promising groups.[10]

GfK MRI (formerly Mediamark Research and Intelligence) also makes available information on exposure to various media and household consumption of various products and services. Its annual survey of over 26,000 randomly selected respondents covers magazines, national and local newspapers, radio, television, and hundreds of product and service categories. Information is gathered from respondents in two stages. First, a lengthy personal interview is conducted to collect demographics and psychographics and data on media exposure. Second, at the conclusion of the personal interview, respondents are given a self-administered questionnaire that captures data on shopping behaviors and product usage. The questionnaire is typically picked up in person by the interviewer in about two weeks. Despite the length of both the personal interview and questionnaire, the company reports high response rates.[11]

EXHIBIT 4.5

Top 10 Web Brands for March 2011 (U.S., Home and Work)

Rank	Brand	Unique Audience (000)	Time Per Person (hh:mm:ss)
1	Google	152,333	1:21:51
2	Facebook	135,695	6:35:43
3	Yahoo!	131,319	2:16:10
4	MSN/WindowsLive/Bing	119,292	1:26:41
5	YouTube	105,203	1:17:52
6	Microsoft	88,114	0:42:31
7	AOL Media Network	75,206	2:26:30
8	Apple	63,017	1:12:36
9	Wikipedia	61,805	0:15:44
10	Ask Search Network	60,517	0:10:06

Source: The Nielsen Company. http://blog.nielsen.com/nielsenwire/online_mobile/march-2011-top-u-s-web-brands/ on May 9, 2011.

5 Collecting Primary Data by Observation

POLL QUESTION:

Recording license plate numbers in a mall parking lot is valuable observational research.

STRONGLY DISAGREE 1 2 3 4 5 STRONGLY AGREE

Learning Objectives

1. List the seven kinds of primary data about individuals that interest marketers.
2. Describe the two basic means of obtaining primary data.
3. State the specific advantages of each method of data collection.
4. List the important considerations in the use of observational methods of data collection.
5. Cite the main reason researchers may choose to disguise the presence of an observer in a study.
6. Explain the advantages and disadvantages of conducting an observational experiment in a laboratory setting.
7. Discuss four types of mechanical observational research.

INTRODUCTION

Although there are important advantages to using secondary data (see Chapter 4) where possible, we often find it necessary to collect primary data. In this chapter, we'll highlight the seven different types of primary data that might be collected from (or about) individuals and discuss key issues with collecting behavioral data (and maybe some types of demographic data) via observational research. In the following chapter, we'll turn our attention to collecting primary data using communication-based research.

The types of primary information about individuals that you will collect generally fall into one of seven categories: (1) demographic/socioeconomic characteristics, (2) personality/lifestyle characteristics, (3) attitudes, (4) awareness/knowledge, (5) intentions, (6) motivation, and (7) behavior. You need to understand each type of data and some of the issues involved in collecting it (see Exhibit 5.1).

EXHIBIT 5.1

Seven Types of Primary Data

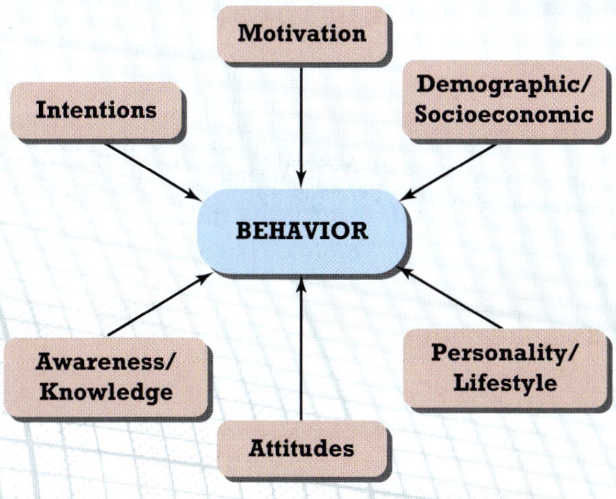

TYPES OF PRIMARY DATA

Demographic/Socioeconomic Characteristics

One type of primary data that marketers care about is the respondent's demographic and socioeconomic characteristics, such as age, education, occupation, marital status, gender, income, and social class. These variables are often used to break down a data set to help interpret the consumers' responses. Suppose we are interested in people's attitudes toward environmental sustainability. We might find that attitudes toward sustainability are related to the respondents' level of education or are different for men and women. Similarly, marketers often want to determine whether the consumption of particular products (e.g., digital music downloads, disposable diapers, vacation golf packages) is related to a person's age, education, income, and so on.

Demographic variables are often used as a basis for market segmentation. For example, gender has been used to segment categories as diverse as cigarettes (Marlboro vs. Virginia Slims), razors (Gillette Fusion vs. Venus), and athletic shoes (Foot Locker vs. Lady Foot Locker). Lots of other demographic and socioeconomic variables have been used as well.

Personality/Lifestyle Characteristics

personality
Normal patterns of behavior exhibited by an individual; the attributes, traits, and mannerisms that distinguish one individual from another.

Another type of primary data involves a respondent's personality and lifestyle characteristics in the form of personality traits, activities, interests, and values. **Personality** refers to the normal patterns of behavior exhibited by an individual—the attributes, traits, and mannerisms that distinguish one individual from another. We often characterize people by the personality traits—aggressiveness, dominance, friendliness, sociability—they display. Many marketers believe that personality can affect a consumer's choice of stores or products, or an individual's response to an advertisement or point-of-purchase display. Similarly, they believe that salespeople or front-line service workers who are extroverted or customer oriented are more likely to be successful. Although the empirical evidence regarding the ability of personality to predict consumption behavior is weak, we are beginning to see stronger evidence for the importance of recruiting and retaining employees who display higher levels of certain personality characteristics.[1]

Lifestyle analysis (sometimes called psychographic analysis) is based on the idea that a company can be more successful if it knows more about its customers in terms of how they live, what interests them, and what they like. For example, Frito-Lay conducted research that identified two broad categories of snackers, which it called "compromisers" and "indulgers." The compromisers are typically female and are more likely to exercise, read health and fitness magazines, be concerned about nutrition, and read product labels. Frito-Lay appeals to this group with its Baked Lay's potato chip, a reduced-fat snack.

FAST FACT:

ACCORDING TO GARTNER INC., **20% OF EMPLOYEES** WILL USE SOCIAL NETWORKS FOR BUSINESS COMMUNICATIONS BY 2014 DUE TO CHANGING DEMOGRAPHICS.

© TERRI MILLER/E-VISUAL COMMUNICATIONS, INC.

Frito-Lay's traditional potato chips are targeted to the other psychographic category, the indulgers, who are mostly male, in their late teens and early twenties, snack heavily, feel unconcerned about what they eat, and hesitate to sacrifice taste for a reduction in fat.[2]

Attitudes

attitude
An individual's overall evaluation of something.

An **attitude** refers to an individual's overall evaluation of something. Attitude is one of the more important notions for marketers. If you have a positive attitude toward a brand, aren't you more likely to buy it in the future? Marketers work hard to deliver products and services that customers will evaluate positively. As a result, it's very common in marketing research to measure people's attitudes toward product categories, brands, Web sites, retailers, and a whole host of other things. And the news isn't always good. For example, findings from recent studies suggest that teenagers' attitudes toward brand-name goods have declined, perhaps to a historic low. Energy/BBDO stated in its Gen World Report that two-thirds of the 3,322 teens surveyed worldwide are apathetic about brands, and only 37 percent like to wear the logos of their favorite brands.[3]

Attitudes and other psychological variables are so important for marketing researchers that we'll spend some time discussing how to measure them in Chapter 7.

Awareness/Knowledge

awareness/knowledge
Insight into, or understanding of facts about, some object or phenomenon.

Awareness/knowledge as used in marketing research refers to what respondents do and do not know or believe about some product, brand, company, advertisement, or so on. For instance, we're always interested in judging the effectiveness of ads in TV, radio, magazine, billboard, and Web banners. One measure of effectiveness is the product awareness generated by the ad, using one of the three traditional approaches described in Exhibit 5.2. All three tests of memory (unaided recall, aided recall, and recognition) are aimed at assessing the respondent's awareness of, and knowledge about, the ad. We assume that differences in awareness reflect differences in how deeply consumers have processed the ad (in detail or just superficially), the brand name, the featured attributes, and so on. Consumers have retained more knowledge from the ad when they can state the brand in an unaided recall test compared to a recall test where they have been given hints. Both measures of recall reflect more knowledge and retention than simple recognition.

EXHIBIT 5.2

Approaches Used to Measure Awareness

Unaided recall: Without being given any clues, consumers are asked to recall what advertising they have seen recently. An ad or a brand that can be remembered with no clues at all has made a deep impression. As a result, unaided recall represents the highest level of awareness.

Unaided Recall Cue

Aided recall: Consumers are prompted, typically with a category cue. That is, they are asked to remember all ads or brands that they have seen for products and services in a particular product category. Aided recall represents a relatively high level of awareness, but the presence of the cue makes the task easier than unaided recall.

Personal Computers

Aided Recall Cue

Recognition: Actual advertisements, brand names, or logos are shown or described to consumers, who are asked whether they remember seeing each one. Because the task is simply to recognize whether they have seen an ad, the recognition task is much easier for respondents but represents a lower level of awareness.

Recognition Cue

© STAFF/NEWSCOM

One way to measure the short-term success of an ad is "day-after recall," which involves a survey taken the day following the airing of a new ad (such as the day after the Super Bowl). Ad agencies can compare the day-after recall scores for an ad to their database of prior scores for other ads to project sales for the product being advertised.

Increasingly, psychologists and advertising researchers are exploring the idea that consumers do not have to explicitly remember an ad for that ad to have an impact on their behavior. For example, after airing an ad for Reebok, you could use "implicit"

IMAGE COURTESY OF THE ADVERTISING ARCHIVES

or indirect tests of memory. Rather than asking, "Do you remember any recent ads for athletic shoes or Reeboks?" you might instead ask consumers to list brand names of sporting shoes, shoes affiliated with athlete spokespersons, and so on, to assess the number of times the Reebok brand name appears. The assumption in these tests is that if Reebok appears more than it should (based on market shares), the ad was successful in bringing the Reebok brand name to mind.

In addition to ad testing, memory measures are used to assess awareness and knowledge of brands, products, companies, and the like. Marketers are often interested in understanding what different audiences know or believe about their brands and companies. This is the basis of countless brand image or company image studies. In general, awareness questions help the marketer assess consumers' knowledge of any element of the consumer experience—advertisements, products, retail stores, and so on.

Intentions

intentions
Anticipated or planned future behavior.

A person's **intentions** refer to her anticipated or planned future behavior. Most likely, you'll be interested in people's intentions with regard to purchase behavior. One of the better known studies regarding purchase intentions is that conducted by the Survey Research Center at the University of Michigan. The center regularly conducts surveys to determine the general financial condition of consumers and their outlook with respect to the state of the economy in the near future. The center phones a sample of 500 households monthly, asking 50 core questions about consumer confidence and buying intentions for durable goods such as appliances, automobiles, and homes during the next few months. The responses are then analyzed and used as one indicator of future economic activity.

Intentions are often gathered by asking respondents to indicate which of the following best describes their plans with respect to a new product or service:

- ☐ definitely would buy
- ☐ probably would buy
- ☐ undecided
- ☐ probably would not buy
- ☐ definitely would not buy

Intentions receive less attention in marketing than some other types of primary data, because there is often a big difference between what people say they are going to do and what they actually do. Estimating demand for products and services is very difficult—for example, in one study, consumers were asked to indicate how likely they were to buy a service when it became available. Less than half of the people who indicated that they *definitely would buy* the service actually did so within the first three months of its availability. And some of the respondents who indicated that they would not buy it actually did so.[4] Practicing marketing researchers have learned that they must discount people's stated intentions in most cases, based on the researchers' past experience in similar situations.

Although the prediction of behaviors by intentions is not perfect, sometimes behavioral data are too expensive, difficult, or even impossible to obtain. For example, if Apple were to create a new version of its popular iPod that was solar-powered and could receive satellite radio broadcasts, by definition no purchase data would exist because the product would not have been available yet for purchase. If the marketer had access to data on purchase levels of iPods, solar-powered

© X99/ZUMA PRESS/NEWSCOM

It is difficult to garner true and realistic purchase intentions when offering new, and untried, features for a product, such as the iPod.

radios, and satellite radio subscriptions among the target market, it might be possible to develop a rough sales forecast for the new product (this would require lots of assumptions, of course). Still, in many circumstances, consumer judgments of their purchase intentions are as close to actual behaviors as marketers can get.

The iPod example also demonstrates one of the reasons it's so hard to get accurate projections of future demand for new products and services. Until consumers can try out the new product or service, it's tough for them to know how they might behave with respect to the offering in the future. Artist renderings, written product concepts, and computer simulations simply can't replace product trial and use. Standard test markets are more accurate than simulated test markets. This is one reason why.

Motivation

A **motive** is a need, want, drive, urge, wish, desire, impulse, or any inner state that directs behavior toward goals. Marketers are in business to satisfy customer needs; it helps to know what these needs are! You'll often appeal to these motives in communications efforts. For example, the motive that underlies an ad for life insurance may be the desire to make certain that the family has adequate financial resources should something happen to a parent.

motive
A need, want, drive, urge, wish, desire, impulse, or any inner state that directs behavior toward goals.

A marketing researcher's interest in motives typically involves determining *why* people behave as they do. By understanding what drives a person's behavior, it is easier to understand the behavior itself. A desire for status may motivate one car buyer to purchase a Mercedes-Benz; a concern for safety may send another to the local Volvo showroom. If we understand the forces underlying consumer behavior, we are in better

© HANNU LIIVAAR/SHUTTERSTOCK.COM

FAST FACT:
MASSACHUSETTS RANKS FIRST IN THE U.S. WITH OVER 11% OF ITS HIGH SCHOOL STUDENTS IN **ADVANCED LEVELS OF MATH.** MINNESOTA IS SECOND WITH MORE THAN 10%.

position to design and offer products and services that can satisfy the motives driving that behavior.

Behavior

behavior
What individuals have done or are doing.

Behavior concerns what individuals have done or are doing. In marketing, this usually means purchase and use behavior. Behavior is a physical activity or action that takes place under specific circumstances, at a particular time, and involves one or more actors or participants. A marketing researcher investigating behavior would be interested in a description of the activity and its various components. One of the key issues in capturing behavioral data, however, is deciding exactly what behaviors to capture. You'll have to decide what behaviors to include or omit. The study of behavior, then, involves the development of a description of the purchase or use activity, either past or current, with respect to some or all of the following characteristics: what, how much, how, where, when, and who.

Behavioral data can be obtained by observing behaviors or by asking respondents to remember and report their behaviors. As we note elsewhere, however, asking people to report their behaviors can lead to more forms of bias because it depends on respondents' ability to accurately remember and report their prior behaviors. Even so, asking about specific behaviors performed during a specific time frame can yield solid information.

Behavioral data are becoming increasingly available through various technologies (e.g., scanners and the Web) and increasingly important to marketers, such as in building relationships with customers. Scanner data are probably the most common type of behavioral data. New technologies have given managers many innovative and effective ways of tracking consumer behavior. As a result, companies are increasingly placing a higher priority on tracking the behavior of target markets. Observational research could help you become more creative in identifying ways your organization might generate highly valuable behavioral data.

A different technology that yields similar behavioral data is the Web and all it entails, including the production of personal profile data, click-stream trails, and records of response to Web advertising. The process of tracking behavioral information via the Web is often referred to as *Web analytics*. A revolution is occurring regarding behavioral data access. The marketer talented at analyzing these data sets will derive great insights.

TWO METHODS OF OBTAINING PRIMARY DATA

communication
A method of data collection involving questioning of respondents to secure the desired information, using a data collection instrument called a questionnaire.

observation
A method of data collection in which the situation of interest is watched and the relevant facts, actions, or behaviors are recorded.

Once you've decided to collect primary data, there are still several choices to make about the method to use (see Exhibit 5.3). The primary decision is whether to use communication or observation. **Communication** involves questioning respondents to get the information you need using a questionnaire. The questions may be verbal or in writing, and the responses may also be given in either form. **Observation** does not involve questioning. Instead, you'll carefully watch what individuals do in a particular situation and record relevant details and behaviors. The observations can be recorded by a person or a mechanical device. For instance, supermarket scanners may be used to determine how many boxes of a particular brand of cereal are sold in a given region in a typical week. Alternatively, if you were interested in the brands of canned vegetables a family buys, you might arrange a pantry audit in which the family's shelves are checked to see which brands they have on hand. Some studies use both communication and observation to collect primary data.

EXHIBIT 5.3

Basic Approaches and Decisions for Collecting Primary Data

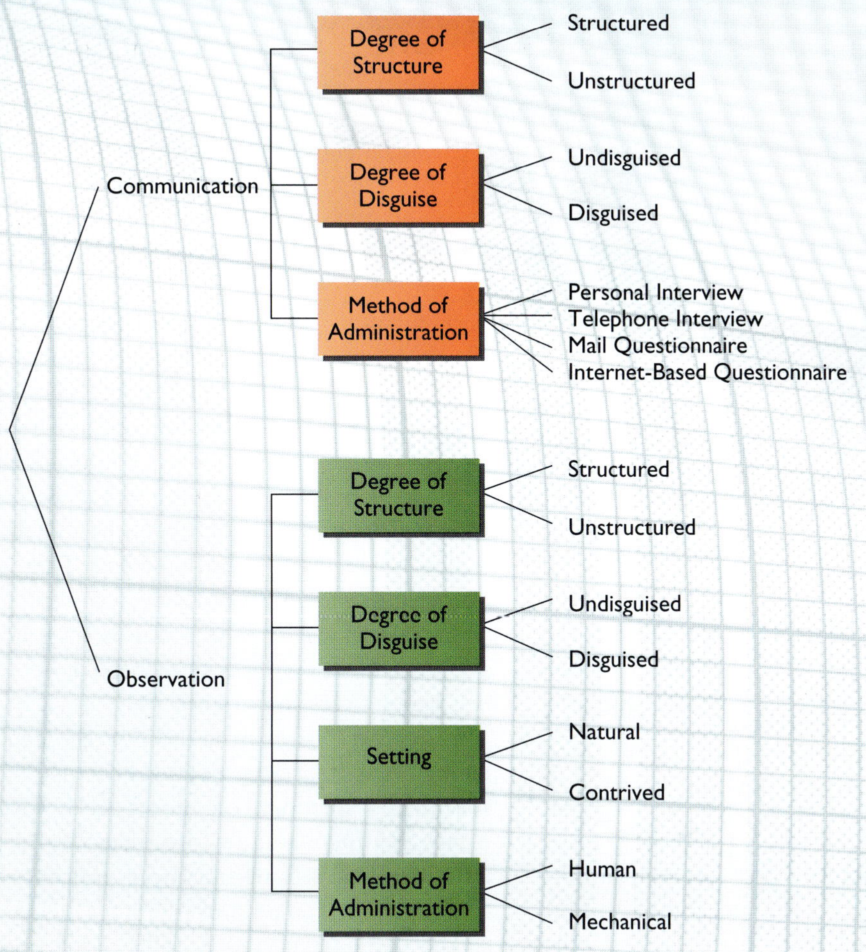

After choosing a primary method of data collection (communication vs. observation), you have more decisions to make. For example, should the questionnaires be administered by mail, over the telephone, in person, or on the Web? Should the purpose of the study be disguised or remain undisguised? Should the answers be open-ended, or should you ask respondents to choose from a limited set of alternatives? We'll return to these issues later in the chapter and in Chapter 6 as well.

Both the communication and observation methods have advantages and disadvantages. In general, the communication method of data collection has the general advantages of versatility, speed, and cost; observational data are typically more objective and accurate.

Versatility

Versatility refers to the ability to collect information on the different types of primary data that marketers care about. The communication approach can be used for collecting information about all seven categories of primary data from individuals. All we need to do is ask and get people to answer our questions . . . although the answers aren't necessarily correct.

Observation techniques, however, aren't nearly so versatile: they can provide us with information about behavior and certain demographic/socioeconomic characteristics (e.g., gender—most of the time—and age in very broad categories), but that's about it. And we can only assess current behavior; we can't observe a person's past behavior and we can't observe her intentions about future

Barcode scanners, such as shown in this photo, enable instantaneous recording of purchased items.

behavior. If we are interested in past behavior or intentions, we have to ask. The other basic types of primary data can't be measured effectively by observation. Questioning clearly allows us to gather more types of primary data.

Speed and Cost

The speed and cost advantages of the communication method are closely related. Communication is often a faster means of data collection than observation: you don't have to wait for behaviors to occur. In some cases, it is impossible to predict when an event will occur precisely enough to observe it. For other behaviors, the time interval between events can be substantial. If you've drawn a sample of households and want to know which brand of kitchen appliances is purchased most frequently, you might have to wait a long time to get enough observations to be useful.

In some cases, though, observation is faster and costs less than communication. A primary example involves the purchase of consumer nondurables. The use of scanners, for example, allows many more purchases to be recorded and at less cost than if purchasers were questioned about what they bought.

Objectivity and Accuracy

Although the observation method has some serious limitations in terms of scope, time, and cost, it has great advantages with regard to objectivity and accuracy. You can almost always gather behavioral data more accurately using observation because observation techniques usually don't depend upon the respondent's willingness and ability to provide the information needed. Here's what we mean: Respondents sometimes don't want to cooperate if their replies might make them look bad. They will sometimes shade their answers or even conveniently forget embarrassing events. In other cases, respondents don't even remember events or prior behaviors because they just weren't very important.

Because observation allows the recording of behavior as it occurs, it doesn't depend on the respondent's memory or mood in reporting what occurred and usually produces more objective data than do communication approaches. Sometimes people don't know they are being observed, so they aren't tempted to tell the interviewer what they think he wants to hear or to give socially acceptable responses that are not truthful. Because of the increased objectivity and accuracy of observation research, we generally recommend observation techniques when they can be used. In the remainder of this chapter, we'll discuss observation research in more detail.

FAST FACT:

IN 2010, ANGEL FLIGHT SOARS OF ATLANTA USED **87%** OF DONATED MONEY TO FUND ITS **CHARITY WORK,** MAKING IT ONE OF THE BEST AMONG U.S. CHARITIES.

OBSERVATION RESEARCH

Communication-based research relies on interviews and surveys and, as a result, there are lots of ways for error to enter into the analysis—things like people forgetting, trying to look better in the eyes of the interviewer, misunderstanding the question or the answer, and so on. Although observational research is not completely free from error, it is often the best method for generating valid data about what people *do*.

Observation is a fact of everyday life. We are constantly observing other people and events as a means of gaining information about the world around us. When researchers use this approach, however, the observations are systematically planned and carefully recorded. And they often lead to insights that might not be seen in any other way. For example, when researchers watched consumers buy dog food, they found that adults focused on buying dog *food* (which was usually stocked on lower shelves), but that senior citizens and children bought a bigger proportion of dog *treats* (which tended to be stocked on the top shelf). After the researchers' cameras "witnessed one elderly woman using a box of aluminum foil to knock down her brand of dog biscuits," the retailer moved the treats to where children and older people could reach them more easily—and sales soared.[5]

Observation research doesn't have to be sophisticated to be effective. It can be as basic as the retailer who used a different color of promotional flyer for each zip code to which he mailed. When customers came into the store with the flyers, he could identify which trading areas the store was serving. And consider these straightforward direct measures of behavior:

- A car dealer in Chicago checked the position of the radio dial of each car brought in for service. The dealer then used this information to decide on which stations to advertise.
- The number of different fingerprints on a page has been used to assess the readership of various ads in a magazine, and the age and condition of cars in a parking lot have been used to gauge the affluence of those patronizing a particular store.
- Scuff marks on museum floor tile have long been used as a means of measuring the popularity of a display.

Sometimes observational research is more sophisticated. Researchers have watched through two-way mirrors as consumers try to assemble a computer or use the computer to surf the Web. Many shopping malls determine their trading areas by hiring people to walk the parking lot and record every license number they find. These data can then be fed into computers that match the license plates to zip code areas or census tracts and prepare color-coded maps showing customer density from the various areas. And sometimes the degree of sophistication reaches levels that would make James Bond proud. A large sports/convention arena located in the eastern United States once built sensors into its outside walls that could determine which radio stations were tuned in on cars driven in its parking lot. This information would be useful for deciding which stations to use for advertising upcoming events at the arena.

Researchers can check what radio stations are preset in a vehicle to gauge on which stations to advertise.

Increasingly, marketing managers, consultants, and researchers have lobbied for observational research over communication research when it comes to assessing consumer behavior. It is often better to measure consumers' actual behavior and then work backward to determine what led to that behavior than it is to measure their attitudes and intentions and then hope that their future behavior matches their intentions. Plus, the best predictor of future behavior is usually past behavior. Doing it this way will almost certainly be more expensive, because the behaviors must be recorded and then connected back to their potential causes, which may mean developing a method of connecting each individual's attitudes, awareness, motivations, and the like, with his or her actual behaviors—but the information will almost always be far more useful. Tesco, the British grocery chain, is among the best companies in the world in understanding its customers and tracking their behavior. Tesco has taken the dominant position in U.K. grocery retailing based largely on its Clubcard program, which allows it to track the purchases of its members and connect them to demographic information about the cardholder. About one in three households in the United Kingdom has a Clubcard.

As indicated in Exhibit 5.3, you'll need to make several important decisions about the design of an observational study. We consider these decisions in the following sections.

structured observation
The problem has been defined precisely enough so that the behaviors that will be observed can be specified beforehand, as can the categories that will be used to record and analyze the situation.

unstructured observation
The problem has not been specifically defined, so a great deal of flexibility is allowed the observers in terms of what they note and record.

Structured versus Unstructured Observation

Structured observation applies when the research problem has been defined precisely enough so that you can specify the behaviors to be observed as well as the categories used to record and analyze the situation. **Unstructured observation** is used for studies in which the research problem has not been precisely defined and you have a great deal of flexibility in terms of what to note and record. Unstructured observation is much more likely to be used in exploratory research than in descriptive or causal research.

Imagine a study designed to investigate how consumers make decisions about purchasing soup. On the one hand, the observers could be told to stand at one end of a supermarket aisle and record whatever behavior they think is appropriate with respect to each sample customer's deliberation and search. This might produce the following record:

Purchaser first paused in front of the Campbell's brand. He glanced at the price on the shelf, picked up a can of Campbell's, glanced at its picture and list of ingredients, and set it back down. He then checked the label and price for Progresso. He set that back down and after a slight pause, picked up a different flavor can of Campbell's than he originally looked at, placed it in his cart, and moved down the aisle.

On the other hand, you might tell the observers to record a number of specific things, such as the first soup can examined, the total number of cans picked up by any customer, the brand of soup selected, and the time in seconds that the customer spent in front of the soup shelves—and to record these observations by checking the appropriate boxes on an observation form. This last situation represents a lot more structure than the first:

Record #: 83
❑ male ☑ female

First soup can picked up for examination:	☑ Campbell's ❑ Progresso ❑ Lipton ❑ Knorr ❑ other: ________
Total # cans picked up for examination, any brand: 3	
Brand selected: (leave blank if none selected)	☑ Campbell's ❑ Progresso ❑ Lipton ❑ Knorr ❑ other: ________
Time (in front of soup shelves):	12 seconds

To use the more structured approach, you must decide precisely which behaviors will be observed and which specific categories and units will be used to record the observations. To make these decisions, you'll need to have specific hypotheses in mind. As a result, the structured approach is more appropriate for descriptive and causal studies than for exploratory research.

Disguised versus Undisguised Observation

undisguised observation
The subjects are aware that they are being observed.

disguised observation
The subjects are not aware that they are being observed.

With **undisguised observation**, people know they are being observed; in **disguised observation**, they don't. In the soup purchase study described earlier, observers could stand next to the soup shelves in the grocery store in plain sight of customers, pencil and clipboard in hand, announcing their purpose to each customer. And they would probably get to watch consumers take much greater care than normal to read the labels for nutrition content, determine the best value, and all the other things that "smart" shoppers do, because the shoppers know they are being observed. On the other hand, the researchers might find a position where shoppers are less likely to notice them, or they could even observe the behavior using hidden cameras. The consumers' shopping behavior would be natural, but each consumer's right to be informed has been violated and debriefing would likely take place at the conclusion of the consumer's visit to the store. It is also possible that individuals could be told when they enter the store that their actions would be observed for research purposes and to please shop as they normally would. Most consumers will forget within minutes that they are being observed, that is, unless they see people walking around with white lab coats and clipboards!

Sometimes disguise is accomplished by having observers become part of the shopping scene. This is typically the case when it is a service worker or organization that you're observing, rather than a consumer. For example, some firms use paid observers disguised as shoppers, to evaluate important aspects of the shopping process. Krispy Kreme is one company that has hired mystery shoppers to visit their stores. The mystery shoppers use tiny cameras to record such things as the evenness of the jelly in doughnuts and the cleanliness of bathrooms. AT&T Wireless used mystery shoppers to visit its 2,700 locations. At a cost of about $50 per visit, the mystery shoppers visited each store monthly.[6] The Federal Trade Commission also employs mystery shoppers to ensure that children and teenagers cannot buy M-rated video games and R-rated DVDs.[7]

You'll need to consider a couple of issues about disguised observation, however. We've already noted the first: There are ethical concerns involved in observing people without their prior knowledge. Employees of an organization have reason to expect that their behaviors on the job will be observed; consumers do not. Thus, there are fewer ethical concerns with mystery shopping than with observing and recording consumer behavior. The second important issue with disguised observation is a practical one: How will you obtain other relevant background information, such as demographic and attitudinal information, if you don't identify yourself as a researcher? This highlights the primary difficulty with observational research in general: Many kinds of data simply cannot be observed. The use of disguise makes it even more difficult to tie data that might be obtained via communication to observational data.

FAST FACT:

ACCORDING TO SAVINGS.COM, ONLY **8%** OF ITS VISITORS **PURCHASED AFTER CLICKING** ON A COUPON.

Natural versus Contrived Setting for Observation

natural setting
Subjects are observed in the environment where the behavior normally takes place.

contrived setting
Subjects are observed in an environment that has been specially designed for recording their behavior.

Observations may be obtained in either **natural** or **contrived settings**. Sometimes we can alter the natural setting a little for experimental purposes. In the soup study mentioned earlier, researchers might choose to keep the setting completely natural and study only the activities that normally go into the purchase of soup in the normal setting. Alternatively, they might want to examine the effectiveness of point-of-purchase display materials and could include such materials in the stores where observations were taken. One measure of effectiveness might be the amount of time consumers spend reading the display materials or the time they spend looking at the brand being promoted.

FAST FACT:

ONLY **21%** OF AMERICANS SMOKED IN 2008 COMPARED TO **42%** IN 1965.

In a contrived setting, you might bring a group of people into a very controlled environment, such as a multiproduct display in a laboratory, and ask them to pretend that they are shopping. This controlled environment might contain, for example, a soup display that would allow researchers to study the degree of search and deliberation that participants go through as they decide what to buy. Taking it a step further, computer simulations and virtual reality can be used as well to assess customer reactions. These approaches allow marketers to display potential new products or product displays without going to the expense of physically building them.

The primary advantage of the laboratory environment is that researchers can control outside influences that might affect the observed behaviors. For example, a shopper in a natural setting might pause to chat with a friend while deciding what soup to buy. If you wanted to measure time spent in deliberation, this interruption could distort the accuracy of the measurement. Another advantage of the contrived setting is that you don't have to wait for events to occur but instead can ask the participants to engage in whatever behavior you want to study. Sometimes an entire study can be completed in a couple of days or a week, which can substantially reduce costs.

As you might guess, the great benefit of natural observation is that the recorded behaviors occur naturally, without prompting. In contrived observation, the prompting from researchers might be direct ("Pretend you are in a grocery store and show us how you would shop for soup") or through the creation of an artificial environment. Either way, the contrived setting may cause differences in behavior and thus raise real questions about the generalizability of the findings. This is much less of a problem with natural observation.

human observation
Individuals are trained to systematically observe a phenomenon and to record on the observational form the specific events that take place.

Human versus Mechanical Observation

With **human observation**, one or more people are trained to systematically watch consumers or whatever else is being studied and to record the events that take place. Researchers commonly use written field notes to record their impressions during observation in the field and later write-up summary thoughts back at the office. Although much field research still relies on human observation, **electrical or mechanical observation** has become increasingly important in marketing research. With electrical/mechanical observation, the behaviors of interest are recorded electronically or mechanically for analysis by researchers. (To simplify things, we'll just use the traditional term "mechanical observation" to refer to any type of technology used to record data.)

electrical or mechanical observation
An electrical or mechanical device observes a phenomenon and records the events that take place.

Although some technologies (such as tape recorders and video cameras) have been used for a long time, the development of new and less expensive technologies is expanding the role of mechanical observation. For example, ethnographic researchers increasingly rely on technology to assist them, particularly as various tools—such as audio and video recorders—get smaller in size, which means they are lighter in weight and less intrusive.

One of the most important methods of mechanical observation is the simple bar-code scanner. Bar codes are scanned billions of times a day; each item scanned is a potential data point for marketing researchers to analyze. Tesco's Clubcard program relies on scanner data for its success. And Cargill's meat-packing division was able to tailor its product mix, pricing, and product size to increase beef sales 10 to 12 percent in retail stores through the use of scanner data.[8]

Another well-known use of mechanical observation is Nielsen's use of people meters for tracking which family members are watching which television shows and when they are watching them. People meters are far more reliable at measuring viewing behavior compared with surveying viewers or even having them keep detailed diaries.

Mechanical observation can also be used to gauge the strength of respondents' feelings and/or uncertainty when they answer questions online or over the telephone. **Response latency** is the amount of time it takes a respondent to answer a question. Response time relates to the respondent's uncertainty in the answer and plays a role in assessing the individual's strength

response latency
The amount of time a respondent deliberates before answering a question.

of preference when choosing among alternatives. Measures of response latency can be programmed into a computerized survey.

Using Mechanical Observation in Advertising Tests

Other methods of mechanical observation have focused on testing advertising copy. The **galvanometer** is used to measure emotional arousal in response to seeing or hearing an ad. When a person experiences emotions, there are slight changes in the electrical resistance of the skin that aren't under the control of the individual. The galvanometer records these changes in electrical resistance. For example, a person could be fitted with small electrodes to monitor electrical resistance and then shown different advertising copy. The strength of the current induced would then be used to infer the subject's interest or attitude toward the copy.

galvanometer
A device used to measure changes in the electrical resistance of the skin which are associated with changes in emotion.

Voice-pitch analysis relies on the same basic premise as the galvanometer: Participants experience a number of involuntary physiological reactions, such as changes in blood pressure, rate of perspiration, or heart rate, when emotionally aroused by external or internal stimuli. Voice-pitch analysis examines changes in the relative vibration frequency of the human voice that accompany emotional arousal. Special audio-adapted computer equipment can measure abnormal frequencies in the voice caused by changes in the nervous system, changes that may not be discernible to the human ear. The more the voice pitch differs from the respondent's normal pitch, the greater the emotional intensity of the consumer's reaction. An **eye tracker camera** is used to study eye movements while a respondent reads advertising copy. Among other things, an eye tracker records where a subject's eye is focused (a fixation) and where it moves (a saccade): Where did the individual look first? Did she return to that place? How long did the person linger on any particular place? Did the consumer read the whole ad or just part of it? Exhibit 5.4 presents a "heatmap" that depicts aspects of an ad where subjects' eyes were focused while reading the ad. Following eye gaze paths has also been used to analyze package designs, package placements in the aisles of supermarkets, TV commercials, and billboards.

voice-pitch analysis
Analysis that examines changes in the relative frequency of the human voice that accompany emotional arousal.

eye tracker camera
A device used by researchers to study a subject's eye movements while he or she is reading advertising copy.

EXHIBIT 5.4
A "heatmap" produced using an eye camera

COURTESY OF TOBII TECHNOLOGY

6 Collecting Primary Data by Communication

© ISTOCKPHOTO.COM/WDSTOCK

POLL QUESTION:

A three percent response rate to an e-mail survey is a solid rate of response.

STRONGLY DISAGREE 1 ◯ 2 ◯ 3 ◯ 4 ◯ 5 ◯ STRONGLY AGREE

Learning Objectives

1. Explain the concept of *structure* as it relates to questionnaires.
2. Cite the drawbacks of using high degrees of structure.
3. Explain what is meant by *disguise* in a questionnaire context.
4. Differentiate among the main methods of administering questionnaires.
5. Discuss three important aspects used to compare the four different methods of administering questionnaires.

INTRODUCTION

Although observational research usually results in more accurate data about individual behavior, communication techniques must be used to capture most other kinds of data from individuals. In this chapter, we look closely at communication-based approaches. We'll discuss the three key decisions that you'll need to make when using communication: the degree of structure to use, whether to disguise the questionnaire, and which method to use. We end the chapter with a comparison of primary communication techniques across three levels of research control.

STRUCTURED VERSUS UNSTRUCTURED COMMUNICATION

The first decision is how much **structure**, or standardization, to use on the questionnaire. In a highly structured questionnaire, the questions and the response categories are completely standardized. That is, everyone receives the same questions, and everyone responds by choosing from among the same set of possible answers. These are known as **fixed-alternative questions**, or closed-ended questions, and they are very commonly used to collect primary data. Consider the following question regarding attitudes toward a company:

Considering all aspects, what is your overall evaluation of Microsoft Corporation?

- ☐ Extremely unfavorable
- ☐ Unfavorable
- ☐ Neither favorable nor unfavorable
- ☐ Favorable
- ☐ Extremely favorable

structure
The degree of standardization used with the data collection instrument.

Notice that the question itself is standardized, as are the response categories. Everyone asked to answer the question will get the identical question and respond with one of the five possible answers. These questions are like multiple-choice questions on an exam.

Now consider another way of asking a similar question, one involving much less structure:

Overall, how do you feel about Microsoft Corporation? Please write your answer in the space provided.

____
____
____
____
____

fixed-alternative question
A question in which the responses are limited to stated alternatives.

open-ended question
A question for which respondents are free to reply in their own words rather than being limited to choosing from among a set of alternatives.

This is an example of an **open-ended question**, a type of question for which respondents are free to reply using their own words and are not limited to a fixed set of possible answers. Most open-ended questions used for collecting primary data for descriptive research have a standardized question that everyone receives, but people get to answer in any way that they choose. These questions are similar to essay questions on an exam.

Highly structured questionnaires, like the first question above, are relatively simple to administer. No matter what method of administration you choose, once the questionnaire items are written, the questionnaire finalized, and data collected, the analysis is usually easy. There's no need to try to interpret open-ended responses, which saves a lot of time and money and avoids possible interpretation bias. Respondents respond, and that's about it.

Highly structured questions also help improve the consistency of responses across different people because standardized questions and responses provide respondents with an identical frame of reference. Consider the question, "How often do you watch television?" If you don't supply response categories, one respondent might say "every day," another might say "regularly," and still another might respond with the number of hours per day. Responses like that are far more difficult to interpret than those from a highly structured, fixed-alternative question that asks for responses with categories "every day," "at least three times a week," "at least once a week," or "less than once a week."

There are certain disadvantages associated with high degrees of structure, however. Although fixed-alternative questions tend to provide the most reliable responses, they may also encourage misleading answers. For example, fixed alternatives may force an answer to a question on which the respondent has no opinion. Suppose that an individual had never heard of Microsoft but encountered the first question shown above. Is this going to stop him from checking one of the boxes? Probably not. Some people will answer the question because they don't want to look dumb. And what if you don't include all of the possible answers to the question? Respondents will probably just choose the one closest to their true feelings, but using high structure in this situation means that you'll be missing out on what is true for some individuals.

High structure is most useful when the possible replies are well-known, limited in number, and clear-cut. They work well for obtaining factual information (age, education, home ownership, amount of rent, etc.) and for obtaining expressions of opinion about issues on which people hold clear opinions. They are not very good at getting primary data on motivations, but could certainly be used to collect data on attitudes, intentions, awareness, demographic/socioeconomic characteristics, and behavior.

FAST FACT:

79% OF U.S. WORKING ADULTS SAY THEY HAVE RECEIVED **WORK-RELATED E-MAILS** ON THANKSGIVING AND CHRISTMAS.

DISGUISED VERSUS UNDISGUISED COMMUNICATION

disguise
The amount of knowledge about the purpose or sponsor of a study communicated to the respondent.

The second consideration in the use of communication to gather primary data concerns **disguise**. A disguised questionnaire attempts to hide the purpose or the sponsor of the study. An undisguised questionnaire makes the purpose of the research obvious, either in the introduction, the instructions, or the questions themselves. For example, if Ford Motor Co. wanted to determine its customers' satisfaction with its cars and trucks, it could simply send out a survey with a cover letter printed on Ford letterhead stationery and the Ford logo appearing on the questionnaire itself. Doing so, however, means that respondents' answers are very likely biased toward Ford, because the survey's purpose and sponsor are clear. If Ford wants more objective data, it might go without the letterhead, go through an outside marketing research agency, or ask its drivers about Ford, GM, and Honda cars. In this scenario, the target of the research

FAST FACT:

THE NATIONAL HIGHWAY TRAFFIC SAFETY ADMINISTRATION REPORTS **84% SEAT-BELT USAGE** IN THE UNITED STATES.

is less clear, and we'd expect customers to answer more truthfully.

There are two general situations in which the use of disguise is often necessary. The Ford example illustrates the first: when knowledge of the sponsor or topic of the survey is likely to cause respondents to change their answers. Here's another example of this: Imagine asking people to "name the first three brands of cars that come to mind" or to "indicate their top two choices among the following brands of cars" when they can clearly see that the survey is sponsored by Ford. The researcher has "primed" a particular response, and the results will be of little value.

Disguise is also used to help create a more natural environment in which to collect data from individuals. Although this can apply to questionnaires, it more often applies to experimental research. Suppose that Ford wants to compare two television ads to see which could create greater awareness of a new Ford truck. Researchers run a lab study in which two groups of consumers are each shown one of the ads. The ads are imbedded in a 30-minute television show with other ads; consumers are told to watch the show as if they were watching TV at home. Later, they are asked to recall the brands advertised during the show.

What will happen if the sponsor and purpose of the study are fully disclosed? The subjects will be watching for anything in the show or ads related to Ford products and, as a result, recall for the test ads will be much higher than it would otherwise have been. In short, the results would be useless.

The Ethics of Disguise

It seems a little strange to suggest that deception can be used to get at the truth in a situation, doesn't it? The use of disguise makes some people and researchers

uncomfortable. Any way you look at it, the use of disguise amounts to a conscious effort to deceive the respondent, or at least to withhold information. Many people would argue that research participants have a right to know why they are being asked to provide answers, how those answers will be used, and/or who will use the information. On the other hand, as long as people understand the basic motivation for the study (i.e., in order to develop products and services that better meet their needs) and the reason for nondisclosure—so that the results will be more objective—they may not feel as deceived. If the emphasis is on the fact that you want their true response and that is more valuable than any perceived "right answer," they should feel okay with it. Researchers almost universally agree, that the benefits of true, usable information outweigh the costs of the deception to respondents, provided that they are given appropriate information following the task. This process is known as **debriefing**.

debriefing The process of providing appropriate information to respondents after data have been collected using disguise.

How much information should be shared in the debriefing process? If all you've done is withhold information from respondents, such as the sponsor or the specific purpose of the research, it's probably not a big deal. Respondents usually don't care, and sponsors normally prefer to remain anonymous. When disguise has involved an active deception, however, it is necessary to tell respondents that they have been misled, explain why the deception was needed, and provide a general overview of the purpose of the project. F or the most part, the use of disguise and the amount of debriefing necessary involve judgment calls on your part.

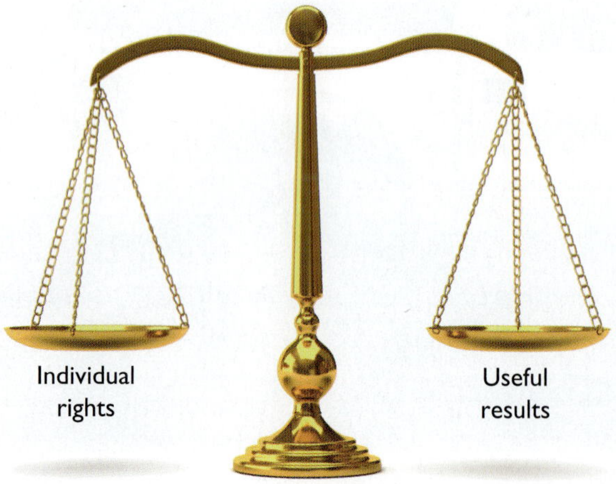

© VALDIS TORMS/SHUTTERSTOCK.COM

METHODS OF ADMINISTERING QUESTIONNAIRES

The third decision that you must make when collecting primary data via communication is which method(s) to use. The main methods include personal interviews, telephone interviews, mail questionnaires, and Internet-based questionnaires. Although there are others, most approaches can be categorized into one of these four types. Over time, there have been shifts in the frequency with which each method is used, as Exhibit 6.1 demonstrates.

For each general method, there are three key aspects to consider. *Sampling control* refers to the ability of a particular method to identify and obtain responses from a sample of respondents from the target population. Obtaining lists of population members and likely response rates are key issues in sampling control. *Information control* is concerned primarily with the number and types of questions that can be used and the degree to which researchers and/or respondents might introduce error into the answers or their interpretation. Finally, *administrative control* refers to resource issues such as the time and monetary costs of the different approaches.

Personal Interviews

A **personal interview** involves a direct face-to-face conversation between an interviewer and the respondent. Generally, the interviewer asks the questions and records the respondent's answers. Sometimes the interviewer may give all or part

personal interview Direct, face-to-face conversation between an interviewer and the respondent.

EXHIBIT 6.1

Percent of Marketing Research Revenues by Major Communication Methods

	2010
Personal Interviews	9%
Telephone Interviews	24%
Mail Questionnaires	3%
Internet-based Questionnaires	23%

Source: Marketing Research Association, 2010.

FAST FACT:

EXPEDIA IS THE MOST POPULAR U.S. TRAVEL WEB SITE, CONSISTENTLY EARNING OVER **14%** OF VISITS TO AN ONLINE TRAVEL AGENCY, MONTH AFTER MONTH.

of the questionnaire to the respondent and be available to answer questions while the respondent completes it. In still other cases, the researcher gets the respondent to agree to complete the survey, leaves the questionnaire, and returns to pick it up later (or has the respondent return it).

Personal interviews can take place just about anywhere. You can conduct them in a respondent's home or office, at the researcher's office, or at some other location. It depends on the needs of the research and the convenience of the respondents. We've even had a research group do interviews onboard rapid transit trains.

mall intercepts
A method of data collection in which interviewers in a shopping mall stop or interrupt a sample of those passing by to ask them if they would be willing to participate in a research study.

Mall intercepts are popular for conducting personal interviews among consumers. The technique involves exactly what the name suggests: Interviewers intercept, or stop, people in a shopping mall and ask them to participate in a research study. If you've spent much time in a larger shopping mall, you've probably seen interviewers in action. You may even have participated in an interview. Mall intercepts place the researcher in a location where people naturally gather together—consumers in their natural habitat. This approach is convenient for finding consumers to answer our questions. There's a cost to this convenience, however. For most purposes, the results cannot be projected to the overall population because the sample is not randomly drawn. Another significant cost is an interviewer who is not properly trained or compensated. It's not uncommon for an interviewer to fill in answers for the respondent in order to speed up the interview process, or to reword open-ended responses for the sake of time instead of accuracy. Still, for exploratory research and situations in which a nonrandom sample will work, mall intercepts can be quite useful.

Sampling Control

It's possible to draw some form of random sample when using personal interviews for data collection, but it tends to be a little more difficult than for most other methods. It's one thing to figure out whom to contact in a study; it is something else entirely to get that person to agree to participate. In this respect, the personal interview offers more sample control than other approaches. There are several reasons for this. The interviewer can verify the identity of the respondent; there is little opportunity for anyone else to reply. Response rates are also higher for personal interviews than most other methods, probably because the personal appeal makes it harder for respondents to say "no" compared with, say, simply tossing a mail questionnaire into the trash can.

© RICHARD LORD/PHOTOEDIT

Information Control

Personal interviews can be conducted using questionnaires with any degree of structure, from purely open-ended questions to purely fixed-alternative questions or any combination in between. One of the huge advantages of personal interviews is the ability to explain or rephrase questions and to have respondents explain their answers. In addition,

RESPONSE RATES ARE HIGHER FOR PERSONAL INTERVIEWS THAN MOST OTHER METHODS.

the personal nature of the interaction allows you to see the respondent interact with the product and show pictures, examples of advertisements, lists of words, scales, and so on, as needed. And there's no better approach for gaining a respondent's trust.

You can gather a lot of information in a personal interview, more than with any other approach under normal circumstances. Because of the personal interaction aspect, researchers can usually get respondents to spend more time in a face-to-face interview. Personal interviews also allow the sequence of questions to be changed by the researcher fairly easily in response to the answers provided by respondents. For example, if the answer to a question about home ownership is "no," you can skip questions about length of ownership, satisfaction with the current lender, recent remodels, and so on, and proceed to another point in the survey form, all without the respondent's knowledge.

On the downside, personal interviews are subject to several kinds of error that can bias the results away from the truth in a situation. For example, open-ended responses can be influenced by the biases of the researcher. In the classic form of a personal interview, the researcher is asking questions and then recording the respondent's answers. This process is full of opportunities for researcher bias to enter (e.g., mishearing the answer, writing it down incorrectly, truncating a written response to keep up with the spoken word, and misinterpreting later). And if the researcher changes the wording of questions or even the inflection in his or her voice—more possible error. Add to this the bias from the respondent's side of the equation—in particular the (un)conscious desires to appear knowledgeable, socially acceptable, and helpful to the researcher—and it should be clear that personal interviews must be undertaken with great care, including substantial interviewer training.

FAST FACT:
BRAZIL WAS THE TOP GLOBAL MARKET BY PERCENT REACH—**21%**—VIA TWITTER.

Administrative Control

In most cases, personal interviews cost more to conduct than any other communication method. It's easy to see why: Interviews take place one at a time; interviews tend to last longer; researchers must often travel from one interview to the next (unless all interviews are conducted in a central location, which leads to greater office overhead expense); interviewers must be well trained, which is expensive, and when they are trained, they command higher salaries; and coding and analysis can be much more involved, particularly if open-ended questions have been used. Further, as you might guess, using personal interviews generally takes a great deal of time.

Telephone Interviews

A **telephone interview** is similar in some ways to a personal interview, except that the conversation between researcher and respondent takes place over the telephone. It is still a social process involving direct interaction between individuals. Traditionally, response rates have usually been quite reasonable; costs are much lower than with personal interviews. As a result, telephone interviews have been a popular means of securing communication data for many years.

telephone interview
Telephone conversation between an interviewer and a respondent.

Sampling Control

Several companies generate and sell lists of consumer or business telephone numbers from which to draw a random sample. These lists can often be selected based on particular geographic or demographic variables, or even on variables representing consumer interests, occupations, lifestyles, hobbies, and so on. One or more telephone books might also serve as a list of potential sampling elements. Phone-book sampling frames are usually inadequate, however, because they do not include those without phones, those with unlisted numbers (including cell-phone users), or those who move into an area after the phone book is published. And some of the numbers that are in the phone book are disconnected because people have moved to another area.

The overall penetration rate of telephones in the United States is quite high—over 90 percent; however, there has been a dramatic shift in the types of service maintained. Landline (wireline) phones have given way, in large part, to wireless subscribers as cellular expenditures now exceed landline expenditures

EXHIBIT 6.2

Monthly Personal Consumption Expenditures for Telephone Service per Household

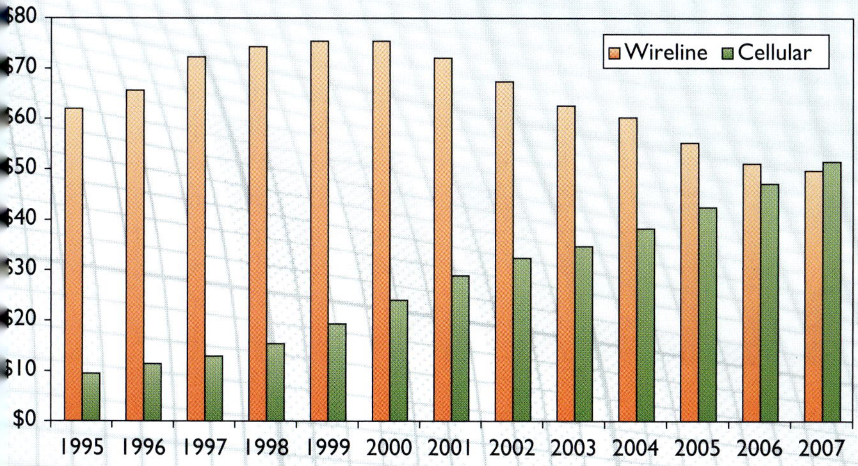

Source: United States Federal Communication Commission.

(see Exhibit 6.2). Normally, cell phone numbers are not available in telephone directories. This increases the challenge of sampling control.

random-digit dialing (RDD) A technique used in studies using telephone interviews in which the numbers to be called are randomly generated.

One way to overcome the error caused by unlisted numbers and the increasing presence of wireless phones is **random-digit dialing (RDD)**, which uses a computer to randomly generate numbers to be called. These systems usually automatically dial the calls as well. As a result, when a working number is reached, it makes no difference whether that number was listed in the telephone directory.

Finding a working number is only the first step, however, in getting feedback from a sample with the telephone interview method. The respondent must also be near the phone when it rings, answer the call, agree to participate, and then actually do so. Response rates that have traditionally been fairly good have begun to suffer in recent years, mostly as a result of caller ID and answering machines used for screening calls. Despite all this, telephone surveys are still productive; you just have to be persistent and make more calls to a given number.[1] As an example, Exhibit 6.3 illustrates the percentage of respondents who were contacted on the first, second, third, and so on, attempted contact for a study one of us conducted a few years ago. The overall response rate was very high (94%), but only because we didn't stop making callbacks after the first or second try.

Information Control

Most of the time, telephone studies use simple fixed-alternative questions that are easy to explain by the interviewer and easy to answer by the respondent. And it's easy to sequence questions based on the answers to earlier questions, especially with the use of **computer-assisted interviewing (CAI)** software. Using CAI, the computer screen displays each question exactly as it should be asked and will go on to the next question after an acceptable answer has been entered to the previous question. Question sequencing is handled seamlessly: Depending on the answer to the current question, the appropriate next question for the interviewer to ask the respondent is automatically shown on the screen.

computer-assisted interviewing (CAI) Using computers to manage the sequence of questions and to electronically record the answers.

Telephone interviews allow probing and follow-up on respondent answers when necessary. Questions

FAST FACT:

ACCORDING TO THE CENTER FOR DISEASE CONTROL, **34%** OF BREAST CANCER CASES ARE DIAGNOSED IN THE **LATTER STAGES.**

EXHIBIT 6.3

Percentage of Respondents Reached with Each Call in a Telephone Survey of University Seniors

Call	Number of Respondents	Percent*	Cumulative Percent*
1	35	20%	20%
2	31	18	38
3	34	20	58
4	14	8	66
5	40	23	89
6	17	10	99
7	1	1	100

*Percentages are based on total number of completed interviews. When refusals (4) and not-at-homes (2) are included, the overall response rate was 94%.

© ISTOCKPHOTO.COM/JUSTIN HORROCKS

and instructions can be repeated and answers verified. Because of the human contact, a degree of trust can be developed, particularly on longer surveys. Although there's still a chance that bias will enter because of the social interaction, it's less likely than with personal interviews.

One of the biggest disadvantages of telephone interviews is the limited amount of information that can be gathered from any given individual. Unless the topic is of great interest to respondents (or they are bored enough to talk to *anybody*, which actually happens), most are not going to be excited about staying on the telephone very long. How long should a telephone interview be? It depends on the likely interest level of the topic, but we recommend trying to keep the interview to 5 to 10 minutes.

If the telephone questionnaire is developed correctly, you can collect a lot of information in 5 to 10 minutes. It's usually smart to use common rating scales and response categories that people are familiar with and to keep them as consistent as possible throughout the interview. Remember that respondents are *listening* to the survey and cannot see it. Many respondents will have used 1–10 rating scales, formally and informally, for most of their lives. And they'll have little trouble understanding response categories anchored with words such as "not important–important," "unfavorable–favorable," "strongly disagree–strongly agree," and the like.

Administrative Control Although it is usually more costly to collect data using telephone interviews compared with mail or Web-based questionnaires, the solid response rates for this method have traditionally kept the cost-per-contact reasonable. Interviewers must be recruited and trained, and as with personal interviews, each interviewer can visit with only one respondent at a time. Quality control can be assured by having supervisors periodically listen in on interviews in progress. As a result, data from telephone interviews can be collected in a matter of days, rather than weeks or months.

Mail Questionnaires

The **mail questionnaire** approach involves surveys sent to designated respondents with an accompanying cover letter and reply envelope. Respondents complete the questionnaire and mail their replies back to the research organization. Variations to this classic form also exist. For example, a questionnaire might be dropped off at a residence (without direct contact between researcher and respondent), along with instructions to complete it and return it by mail to the researchers. Or you might simply attach questionnaires to products or put them in magazines and newspapers or even stuff them in shopping bags. Surveys can be e-mailed to respondents as well.

mail questionnaire
A questionnaire administered by mail to designated respondents with an accompanying cover letter.

Sampling Control If you want to be able to project the results of the survey to the overall population, you'll have to start with an accurate mailing list of the people in the population. This isn't a problem for companies doing customer surveys using customer records from an updated database. In other cases, companies can purchase mailing lists, often for very specific populations, although it isn't always clear how the information was obtained and how complete the list may be. Business-to-business marketing research

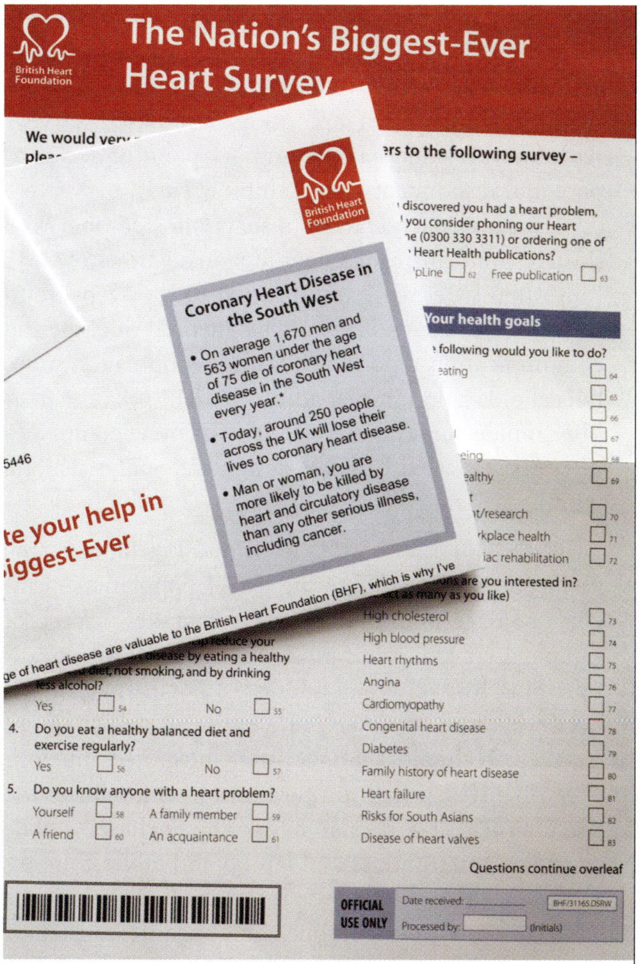

is usually easier in this regard—contact information for businesses is more stable than for consumers, and businesses are fewer in number.

When you purchase a mailing list from a list company, you normally get to use the list one time. How does the list provider know that you've used the list only once? It's easy: They normally include one or more "dummy" addresses that are delivered back to the list company or its employees. If a company tries to use the list more than once, the owner of the list will soon know about it.

On the downside, mail questionnaires provide little control in getting a response from the intended respondent. You can carefully identify desired respondents and offer them incentives, but you can't control whether the respondents actually complete and return the questionnaires. With no direct contact between researcher and respondent, there is less social pressure to agree to the researcher's request to complete the questionnaire. Although there are circumstances that produce big response rates, this isn't normally the case. On top of that, there's no way to know that the intended respondent really completed a returned questionnaire, or if someone else may have completed it. This is probably more of a problem with questionnaires sent to businesses than with consumer projects.

Information Control Mail questionnaires offer a couple of nice advantages when it comes to information control. For one thing, with written questions, there is no opportunity for interviewer bias from the wording of questions or the way that the questions are asked. It's also possible to include graphics, pictures, or other artwork if respondents need to see a stimulus in order to respond effectively. It may also be possible to collect a bit more information with mail surveys than with telephone interviews, but it is usually advisable to keep mail surveys under four pages long. Better yet, keep the survey to two pages (that is, one page, printed on both sides) if at all possible.

One of the biggest advantages of mail questionnaires is that they are the only method that can be truly anonymous. People are likely to be more candid in their responses. If your topic revolves around a sensitive issue (e.g., sexual behavior, participation in illegal or socially undesirable activities), the normal recommendation is to use mail questionnaires.

Despite these advantages, there are some shortcomings of mail questionnaires with respect to information control. Most importantly, mail questionnaires do not allow clarification of questions or response categories, and you can't ask follow-up questions or clarify answers. If open-ended questions are included, individuals must write out their answers, which is more difficult than answering a question orally. All else equal, more work for respondents translates into fewer questionnaires returned.

Here's another disadvantage: If they choose, respondents can review the entire questionnaire before answering the questions. This is a real problem if the researcher wants to assess awareness for certain brands and also ask specific questions about those brands in the same survey. If respondents see questions about Target in a survey, don't be surprised if "Target" is one of the most often mentioned answers to the item "list the first three department stores that come to mind." In addition, instructions for question sequencing ("If the answer to the previous question is "no," go to question 7") can quickly become complicated and should be avoided if possible with mail questionnaires.

Administrative Control Compared with hiring and training interviewers, it doesn't cost a lot to print

MAIL SURVEYS ARE FASTER THAN PERSONAL INTERVIEWS BUT TAKE LONGER THAN TELEPHONE SURVEYS.

surveys, buy a mailing list, and pay postage (outbound and inbound), so mail surveys have an advantage over personal interviews and telephone questionnaires when it comes to cost. These same cost advantages of mail surveys do not necessarily hold compared to the relative efficiency of electronic forms of communication (as noted below). Quality control is also an advantage for mail surveys. Supervisory responsibilities are limited to the management of the mailing process, both outgoing and incoming. This also serves to lower costs.

The only administrative disadvantage of mail questionnaires is that they take longer than telephone surveys (but they're often faster than personal interviews) because the surveys must go through the postal system going and coming, and respondents respond if and when they want to. As a result, you should budget at least two extra weeks in the timeline of a project using this approach. If you include follow-up mailings, you'll need to budget even more time.

Before we move on, we want to note that we consider e-mail surveys, in which a survey is embedded in (or attached to) an e-mail message, to be a special case of mail surveys. Respondents complete the survey and send them back via e-mail. We place e-mail surveys in this category because they share more similarities with mail surveys than they do Web-based studies, which we discuss next. The primary differences are that you'll have greater confidence that the correct person has responded with e-mail (which lowers anonymity and makes it more difficult to get personal information), and e-mail is faster and costs less. Although most people have a mailing address, however, keep in mind that not everyone can be reached by e-mail.

Internet-based questionnaires
A questionnaire that relies on the Internet for completion.

Internet-Based Questionnaires

In recent years we've witnessed an explosion in the use of **Internet-based questionnaires**. For instance, the cost of mail surveys coupled with the low response rates and increased reliance on electronic communications make online surveys increasingly attractive—so attractive, in fact, that more and more major research firms are using Web-based surveys with Internet panels as the primary point of access to potential respondents (see Exhibit 6.1).

This approach features a survey hosted on a Web site. Respondents can be recruited in a variety of ways (but often by e-mail) and directed to the Web site to complete the questionnaire. This method of gathering communication data is increasingly popular as more households gain Internet access. Dozens of companies offer online survey services; many of these companies offer assistance with survey design and analysis, along with basic data collection.

Sampling Control

As with all techniques, the ability to obtain an accurate list of population members' contact information is the first key aspect of sampling control. With most Web surveys, this means obtaining lists of e-mail addresses. For many populations, this isn't too much of a problem. For many of us, these technologies have been integrated into our everyday lives; a high proportion of people likely use the Internet on a regular basis. This includes mobile access on smartphones and laptop and tablet computers as well as in-home broadband users. This isn't the case, however, for everyone. Low-income consumers are not well represented online, but this is beginning to change.

Lists of e-mail addresses are available from numerous sources. Much like mailing lists, these lists can often be selected based on respondent demographics, interests, and so on. Several companies have developed panels of respondents that have agreed to answer survey questions. As an example, the online survey company Zoomerang boasts a panel of over 2.5 million consumers and businesspeople who have agreed to complete surveys. Exhibit 6.4 includes some of the variables available for fine-tuning sample selection if you are interested in drawing a U.S.-based sample with certain health and medical issues/interests. In addition, firms like Survey Sampling International provide strong panel management expertise to deliver high quality, representative samples. Given the current market landscape, it could be argued these firms, and firms like them, provide as good or better random sampling methods than personal intercept or random digit-dialing approaches discussed earlier.

You should note, however, that many e-mail samples are developed by encouraging individuals to

EXHIBIT 6.4

Zoomerang Sample Selection Variables, U.S. Health and Medical Categories

Diet and Exercise	Eating disorders
Body mass index	Female-associated ailments
Calories	Food absorption problems
Carbohydrates	Hair loss
Diet restrictions	Headaches
Diet type (vegan, vegetarian, meat eater)	Hearing loss
Eat ethnic food	Heartburn
Fat	Heart disease or angina
Frequency of exercise	Herpes
Health and exercise attitudes	High blood pressure
Height	High cholesterol
Meat	HIV/AIDS
Sodium	Impotence/erectile dysfunction
Sugar	Incontinence
Watch diet	Irritable bowel syndrome
Weight	Leukemia
Medical Ailments	Migraines
Allergies	Multiple sclerosis
Alzheimer's disease	Obesity
Anxiety	Obsessive-compulsive disorder
Arthritis	Organ transplant
Asthma	Osteoporosis
Athlete's foot	Physical handicap
Attention deficit disorder	Prescription anticoagulant
Baldness/hair loss	Restless leg syndrome
Bladder ailments	Seizures
Cancer (several types)	Sleep difficulty
Chemotherapy	Ulcers
Chronic back pain	Vision problems
Constipation/irregularity	**Prescription Fill Source**
Depression	Drugstore
Diabetes types 1 and 2	Grocery store
Dialysis	Mail

Source: Downloaded from the Zoomerang Web site, http://www.zoomerang.com/resources/Panel_Profile_Book.pdf, August 4, 2010.

join a panel in exchange for gifts and/or other incentives. This practice encourages "professional" panelists whose only interest may be in completing as many studies as possible to maximize rewards. Lying about interests, experiences, demographics, and so on, can often increase the number of surveys they can complete—and adds error to the results. In recent years, Zoomerang has begun to reject nearly 3 out of

COURTESY OF ZOOMERANG, A MARKETTOOLS COMPANY

10 of its online panelists because they are either not who they said they were; they completed multiple surveys (under different names); or they simply were not thinking about their answers (responding too quickly or selecting the same response for each item).[2]

As with any technique, though, we still must get people to respond to the questionnaire. Sometimes Web-based studies produce very respectable to excellent response rates. Studies using purchased e-mail lists or online panels, however, often have very low response rates just like other communication methods. The key is to do the necessary background work to distinguish the good panel that is managed properly from the one populated with "professional" panelists. Remember, in many respects, this type of behavior is not new. Research panels were in place before the Internet; however, the anonymity of the Internet makes this an issue of greater concern and a focal point of panel management relative to traditional mail panels, for instance. The good news is that established firms are well aware of these issues and take panel management quite seriously. The bad news is there is no perfect approach. That's why pros and cons of all communication methods are being discussed here.

A quick word of warning before we move on: Some companies who provide access to online panels are quick to tout the "completion rate" for a study (that is, the percentage of respondents who complete a survey once they've started it). Although this value can give an indication of the quality of the questionnaire, the completion rate is not the same thing as the overall response rate (the percentage of people who were given the opportunity to respond and completed the survey). The response rate is a much better indicator of the quality of the research effort and, in particular, of how concerned you should be about differences between those who responded and those who didn't.

Information Control Web-based questionnaires are very effective if you need to include pictures and/or other graphics with the questionnaire. Like mail surveys, you can collect a lot more information compared with telephone interviews. In addition, there is essentially no interviewer bias in the way questions are asked, and any type of question can be used. This approach also shares a disadvantage with mail surveys, though: There is no ability to probe, explain questions, or ask for respondents to explain their answers.

With Web surveys, question sequencing can be programmed into the survey, ensuring that the appropriate next question appears on the screen for the respondent. This feature offers greater flexibility with Web surveys than with e-mail or mail surveys. Another potential benefit is the reaction to open-ended questions. It is likely people will take more time and care responding to open-ended questions than is the case with nonelectronic formats. Many people are concerned about privacy when it comes to Web activity, though, believing that their answers could be traced back to them if someone wanted to do so. Still, the comfort level of respondents is likely higher with Web-based questionnaires than with any other approach except mail.

Administrative Control Web-based surveys offer two tremendous advantages in terms of administrative control: compared with other options, they are quite inexpensive and they provide very quick turnaround. In terms of cost, most companies already operate Internet servers, so the necessary hardware is probably already available if you want to host a Web-based questionnaire on your own, and the services of online survey providers are relatively inexpensive if you choose that route. Even better, because responses are normally automatically recorded in data files (and only valid responses are accepted), respondents effectively code their own responses when they reply to the questions on the survey. This eliminates one step where error can enter into the data set, not to mention a great deal of potential cost.

EXHIBIT 6.5

Primary Communication Methods of Data Collection: Relative Advantages (+) and Disadvantages (–)

	Personal Interviews	Telephone Interviews	Mail Questionnaires	Internet-Based Questionnaires
SAMPLING CONTROL				
Ability to secure list of population members		+	+	–
Ability to secure correct respondent	+	+	–	–
Response rate	+			
INFORMATION CONTROL				
Ability to probe for detailed answers	++	+	–	–
Ability to handle complex information	+	– –	–	+
Ability to clarify questions	++	+	–	–
Amount of information obtained	+	–		
Flexibility of question sequencing	+	+	–	+
Protection from interviewer bias	– –	–	+	+
Ability to obtain personal information	–	–	+	
Ability to show visual displays	+	–	+	+
Ability to offer anonymity	–	–	+	
ADMINISTRATIVE CONTROL				
Time requirements	– –	+	–	++
Cost requirements	–		+	++
Quality control/supervisory requirements	– –	–	+	+
Computer support		+	–	++

Comparing Methods of Administering Questionnaires

Each of these methods of communication possesses advantages and disadvantages. We've summarized our thoughts in Exhibit 6.5. If a modified form of administration is used (e.g., e-mail surveys), the general advantages and disadvantages may no longer hold. The advantages and disadvantages may also not apply when dealing with different countries with different cultures. We have provided a general overview.

The specific situation surrounding a project often dictates the actual approach chosen. For example, no matter how much you may want to use personal interviews, the budget may not support that option, and you'll have to do the best you can with the budget allocated, even if the final approach is suboptimal. Similarly, you'll need to endure the disadvantages of mail questionnaires if this is the only reasonable method of reaching the designated population.

Combining Administration Methods

Although none of the methods we have described for collecting communication data is superior in all situations, the research problem itself will often suggest one approach over the others. It is also possible that a combination of approaches may be productive. For example, a business manager could receive a letter, an e-mail, or a phone call asking for his or her help in a study, and after this notification the survey could be sent to his or her place of business. Web surveys can be initiated either by sending an e-mail to the sample of potential respondents that asks them to visit a certain Web address to complete the survey form, or by a cooperative relationship with another Internet vendor by placing a banner at its site. The respondent then just clicks through the survey. Self-administered questionnaires can be hand-delivered to respondents along with product samples, and telephone interviews can be used for follow-up.

7 Asking Good Questions

© DMITRIY SHIRONOSOV/SHUTTERSTOCK.COM

POLL QUESTION:

When comparing two products, it is better to rate them than it is to rank them.

STRONGLY DISAGREE 1 ○ 2 ○ 3 ○ 4 ○ 5 ○ STRONGLY AGREE

Learning Objectives

1. Define the term *measurement* as it is used in marketing research.
2. List the four scales (levels) of measurement.
3. Name some widely used attitude scaling techniques in marketing research.
4. List some other key decisions to be made when designing scales.
5. Explain the concept of validity as it relates to measuring instruments.

INTRODUCTION

Whether we ask questions or observe behaviors, marketing researchers are always attempting to measure things. Measurement is common to all aspects of life; most of us spend our days doing it, whether it's using a clock to measure time, bathroom scales to measure weight, scores to measure the outcomes of sporting events, stock prices to measure the value of investments, or so on.

Most things we measure are fairly concrete: pounds on a scale, teaspoons of coffee, the amount of gas in a tank. But how can we measure a person's attitude toward a company or the likelihood that a teenager will buy a ticket for a particular new movie? Marketers are interested in measuring many qualities that most people rarely think of in terms of numbers.

All of the questions on a survey or marks on an observation form are attempts at measuring important attributes or behaviors of some group or situation that is of interest to marketing managers. In this chapter, we discuss how marketing researchers go about measuring attributes and behaviors.

SCALES OF MEASUREMENT

Measurement consists of "rules for assigning numbers to objects in such a way as to represent quantities of attributes."[1] Note two things about this definition. First, we measure the attributes of objects and not the objects themselves. We don't measure a person, for example—but we can measure his or her income, education, height, weight, attitudes, and so forth. Second, the definition is broad; it doesn't specify how the numbers will be assigned. This is because different attributes have different qualities that dictate the rules for how numbers can be assigned. (As a quick example, the attribute *gender* can't be measured using a 1–5 rating scale—it doesn't make any sense and it can't support measurement at that level.)

So, the first step in measuring some attribute is to determine the properties of the attribute. Only then can we assign numbers that accurately reflect those properties. The numbering system is simply a tool that must be used correctly so that we don't mislead ourselves or our clients.

There are four types of scales used to measure attributes of objects: nominal, ordinal, interval, and ratio. Exhibit 7.1 summarizes some important features of these scales and provides some examples. These are often referred to as four "levels" of measurement because measures at higher levels of measurement (e.g., ratio scales) have more properties and can be used for more kinds of analyses than can measures at lower levels of measurement (e.g., nominal scales). That's why you should use the highest level of measurement possible when developing a measure for some attribute. Just remember, though, that the properties of the attribute itself determine which levels of measurement are possible.

measurement
Rules for assigning numbers to objects to represent quantities of attributes.

EXHIBIT 7.1

Scales of Measurement

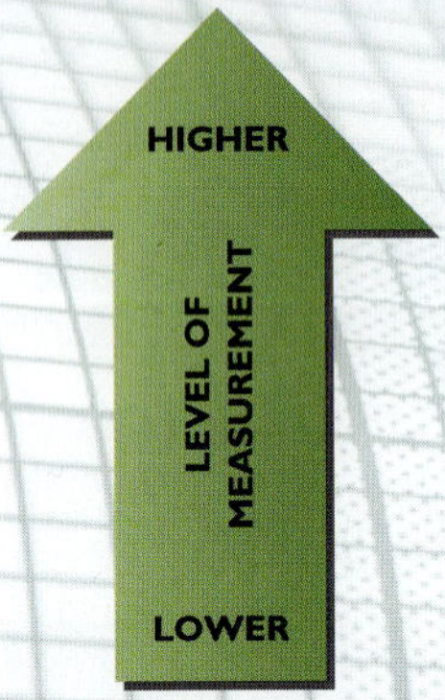

Scale	Basic Comparison[a]	Examples	Average[b]
RATIO	Comparison of absolute magnitudes	Units sold Income	Geometric mean Harmonic mean
INTERVAL	Comparison of intervals	Customer satisfaction Brand attitude	Mean
ORDINAL	Order	Brand preference Income (in categories)	Median
NOMINAL	Identity	Gender Brand purchase (yes/no)	Mode

[a]All the comparisons applicable to a given scale are permissible with all scales below it in the table. For example, the ratio scale allows the comparison of intervals and the investigation of order and identity, in addition to the comparison of absolute magnitudes.

[b]The measures of average applicable to a given scale are also appropriate for all scales below it in the table; for example, the mode is also a meaningful measure of the average when measurement is on an ordinal, interval, or ratio scale.

Nominal Scale

One of the most basic uses of numbers is to *identify* or categorize particular objects. A person's social security number is a **nominal scale**, as are the numbers on football jerseys, lockers, and so on. These numbers simply identify the individual or object that has been assigned the number. In these examples, the numbers are used to *uniquely* identify individuals, but nominal scales can also be used to categorize people or things into groups based on their attributes. For example, if we assign the number 1 to represent female respondents to a survey and the number 2 to represent male respondents, we've used a nominal scale that allows us to identify the gender of a particular respondent and to determine the relative proportions of each gender in our sample.

nominal scale
Measurement in which numbers are assigned to objects or classes of objects solely for the purpose of identification.

With nominal scales, the numbers don't mean anything other than simple individual or category identification. A basketball player wearing uniform number 15 isn't necessarily taller or a better shooter than a player wearing the number 14. Assigning the number 1 to represent women and 2 to represent men

© JOHN ANGELILLO/UPI/NEWSCOM

means nothing at all about men versus women on any attribute other than identification. As a result, the numbers we assign to represent the groups don't have any meaning beyond identification. We could actually use any numbers we want, because the numbers don't matter.

With a nominal scale, all you can do is count the number of people that fall into the various categories. As a result, the *mode* (the most frequently occurring category) is the only legitimate summary measure of central tendency or average. It doesn't make sense in a sample consisting of 60 women and 40 men to say that the average gender is 1.4, if females were coded 1 and males 2, even though the computer will calculate the mean *if you tell it to do so*. This is an incredibly important point: The numbers have been assigned by the researcher, and the researcher must be aware of what kinds of analyses are possible with different scales of measurement. In this example, all you can say is that there were more females in the sample than males, or that 60 percent of the sample was female. If you want to say more than that, you'll need to take additional measures.

Take a look at the first example in Exhibit 7.2; we'll use this exhibit as an ongoing example of the

FAST FACT:

SHARED E-MAIL MESSAGES CONTAINED **INFECTED ATTACHMENTS 6%** OF THE TIME IN THE THIRD QUARTER OF 2010 COMPARED TO 5% IN THE SECOND QUARTER OF THE SAME YEAR.

EXHIBIT 7.2

Assessing a Respondent's Preference for Soft Drinks with Nominal, Ordinal, Interval, and Ratio Scales

NOMINAL SCALE

Which of the soft drinks on the following list do you like? Check all that apply.

____ Coke
____ Dr. Pepper
____ Mountain Dew
____ Pepsi
____ 7 Up
____ Sprite

ORDINAL SCALE

Please rank the soft drinks on the following list according to your degree of liking for each, assigning your most preferred drink rank = 1 and your least preferred drink rank = 6.

____ Coke
____ Dr. Pepper
____ Mountain Dew
____ Pepsi
____ 7 Up
____ Sprite

INTERVAL SCALE

Please indicate your liking for each of the following soft drinks by circling the number that best reflects your opinion.

	Extremely Unfavorable						Extremely Favorable
Coke	1	2	3	4	5	6	7
Dr. Pepper	1	2	3	4	5	6	7
Mountain Dew	1	2	3	4	5	6	7
Pepsi	1	2	3	4	5	6	7
7 Up	1	2	3	4	5	6	7
Sprite	1	2	3	4	5	6	7

RATIO SCALE

In the past seven days, approximately how many 12 ounce servings of each of the following soft drinks have you consumed?

____ Coke
____ Dr. Pepper
____ Mountain Dew
____ Pepsi
____ 7 Up
____ Sprite

different types of scales. We might choose to score the individual responses as 1 if they check a particular soft drink on the list and as 0 if they don't. If a respondent puts a check mark next to Mountain Dew (a score of 1), what do we know? Only that she claims to like the brand. Taking all respondents, we can report the proportion that like Mountain Dew (and the proportion that don't). In terms of a summary response, we can report only the mode. Suppose that 68 percent of the people said they liked Mountain Dew; the modal response for this brand, based on the number of times marked, would be "like Mountain Dew" (because the majority said they liked the brand).

Ordinal Scale

With a nominal scale, the numbers assigned to individuals or categories are arbitrary. They can be changed or reversed—it doesn't matter as long as we know which number represents each category. This works because the numbers don't imply any order to the attributes you're trying to measure.

Many of the attributes that marketing researchers want to measure, however, are things that respondents can place in a certain order, and the numbers assigned can reflect this order. Consider the next example in Exhibit 7.2, which deals with preference for soft drinks. Can you put these soft drinks in order from least preferred to most preferred? Having a preference implies that you can order objects. As a result, with an **ordinal scale**, we could say that the number 2 is greater than the number 1, that 3 is greater than both 2 and 1, and that 4 is greater than all three of these numbers. The numbers 1, 2, 3, and 4 are ordered, and in this case the larger the number, the greater the property. You could also set up your ordinal scale so that lower numbers reflect more of the property; the important point is that there is a consistent order in whatever numbers you assign (the numbers are arbitrary except for order). If you assign the number 6 to identify the least preferred brand, 5 to identify the next-least-preferred brand, and so on, until 1 represents the most preferred brand, the numbers will reflect the *relative standing* of the different options for that particular individual. With an ordinal scale, the numbers have more meaning in that they represent this relative standing. But they don't go further than that; we know that one option has more of some attribute than some other option, but we don't know how much more.

ordinal scale
Measurement in which numbers are assigned to data on the basis of some order (e.g., more than, greater than) of the objects.

HAVING A PREFERENCE IMPLIES THAT YOU CAN ORDER OBJECTS.

Imagine that you've used the ranking task in Exhibit 7.2 with 1,000 college students because you're a brand manager for Mountain Dew and you want to see how your brand stacks up against the competition. Here's how it did: 172 people assigned Mountain Dew a ranking of 6 (dead last), 163 ranked it 5th, 301 ranked it 4th, 259 ranked it 3rd, 65 ranked it 2nd, and 40 ranked it 1st. So, the modal ranking for Mountain Dew was fourth out of six brands. Although that's interesting, we can go further: Because there is an order for the responses (i.e., first choice is better than second choice, and so on), we can also calculate an additional measure of central tendency, the *median*. Suppose you could line up the 1,000 student respondents according to their ranking of Mountain Dew. First might come the 172 who ranked it last, then would come the 163 who ranked it next to last, followed by the 301 who ranked it their fourth favorite brand, and so on. The median ranking for the soft drink would be the ranking provided by the person in the center of our line-up (with an even number of respondents, we would consider the scores of the two people in the center). In our example, the median ranking would thus be "fourth choice." If you wanted to see how the competing brands did, you could do the same analysis for each.

Whether we can use the ordinal scale to assign numbers to objects depends on the attribute in question. The attribute itself must possess the ordinal property to allow ordinal scaling that is meaningful. Note that it is impossible to say how much any individual respondent preferred one object to another; all we can say is that one is preferred over the other. In our soft drink example, one respondent might like all six brands, ranking them in the following order: first—Dr. Pepper; second—Coke; third—Pepsi; fourth—Sprite; fifth—Mountain Dew; and sixth—Seven-Up. Another respondent might really dislike all six brands, yet still rank them in the same order. Still another student may like Dr. Pepper, Coke, and Pepsi a lot, but dislike the others—and once again rank them in the same order. In each case, rank order is the same, but the underlying feelings about the brands are quite different. Representing those feelings requires a higher level of measurement.

Interval Scale

Some scales possess the following useful property: The *intervals* between the numbers tell us how far apart the objects are with respect to the attribute. This tells us that the differences can be compared. The difference between 1 and 2 is equal to the difference between 2 and 3.

Rating scales for measuring consumer attitudes are commonly used in marketing research and are great examples of **interval scales**. Consider the soft-drink example again and take a look at the third example in Exhibit 7.2. Here we're asking the respondents to rate their attitudes toward the brands, using 1–7 scales where 1 = "extremely unfavorable" and 7 = "extremely favorable." This interval scale will allow us to see the relative strength of a respondent's feelings toward each of the soft drinks. A respondent who really likes all six brands might assign each of them high scores, such as a 6 or 7. Someone who dislikes each brand might assign low scores to each. Respondents can indicate the full range of possible attitudes (extremely unfavorable to extremely favorable) toward each brand, a big step forward from simply knowing the order of preference.

interval scale
Measurement in which the assigned numbers legitimately allow the comparison of the size of the differences among and between members.

Thus, interval scales allow us to say that one brand is preferred over another by comparing scores and, even better, to say whether the brand is generally liked or disliked. Further, if we have measures on at least three brands, we can compare the intervals. That is, we can say that the difference in attitude between a brand with a score of 6 and a brand with a score of 4 is the same as the difference in attitude between brands with scores of 3 and 1. Or we could say that the difference between scores of 2 and 6 is twice as great as the difference between scores of 3 and 5.

What if one person rates Pepsi as a 6 on the 1–7 favorability scale, and another person rates Pepsi a 3; can we say that the first person's attitude is twice as favorable as the second? The answer is no. We can't compare the absolute magnitude of numbers when measurement is made on the basis of an interval scale. The reason is that on an interval scale, the zero point is established arbitrarily. Is there such a thing as having zero attitude toward some object? Attitudes may be negative or positive or neutral (or nonexistent for unknown objects), but there is no obvious point at which attitude is equal to zero.

With an interval scale, you can calculate *mean* scores or averages on measures in addition to median and modal scores. The mean is "meaningful" for interval scales because of the equal intervals between scale positions. So, if Mountain Dew achieves a mean score of 3.4 on the 1–7 favorability scale, compared with mean scores of 6.2 and 5.9 for Coke and Pepsi, respectively, we have much stronger information about the relative attitude toward Mountain Dew compared with what was available using only an ordinal measurement scale.

FAST FACT:

68% OF FACEBOOK USERS SAID THEY ARE **MORE LIKELY TO BUY** A PRODUCT OR VISIT A RETAILER BASED ON A POSITIVE FACEBOOK FRIEND REFERRAL.

Ratio Scale

A **ratio scale** differs from an interval scale in that it possesses a *natural,* or *absolute,* zero that reflects the complete absence of the attribute being assessed. Height and weight are examples. Because there is an absolute zero, comparison of the *absolute magnitude* of the numbers is legitimate. Thus, if a person were completing the final item in Exhibit 7.2 and reported consuming 20 servings of Mountain Dew and only five servings of Sprite, he has consumed four times as much Mountain Dew, an indication of a strong preference for Mountain Dew vs. Sprite.

ratio scale
Measurement that has a natural, or absolute, zero and therefore allows the comparison of absolute magnitudes of the numbers.

We've already noted that the more powerful scales include the properties possessed by the less powerful ones. Accordingly, with a ratio scale we can compare intervals, rank objects according to magnitude, or use the numbers to identify the objects (everything that interval, ordinal, and nominal scales can do). And the *geometric mean* (scores are multiplied and then the *n*th root is taken), as well as the more usual arithmetic mean, median, and mode, is a meaningful measure of average when attributes are measured on a ratio scale.

There are lots of attributes that can be measured using ratio scales, including age in years, income in dollars (or other monetary unit), units purchased or consumed, frequency of shopping behavior, and so on. Researchers should use ratio scales for measuring these sorts of attributes whenever possible, unless there is a compelling reason not to do so. (For instance, maybe some people are more likely to accurately provide their ages if you let them select age categories—an ordinal measure—rather than ask for age in years.) As we will see later when we discuss data analysis, using the ratio scale will allow us to compute a mean age across a sample of respondents; compute correlations between age and other variables such as product ratings, satisfaction scores, and the like; and perform other statistical techniques. Although there are analyses that can be performed with ordinal measures, they are less powerful.

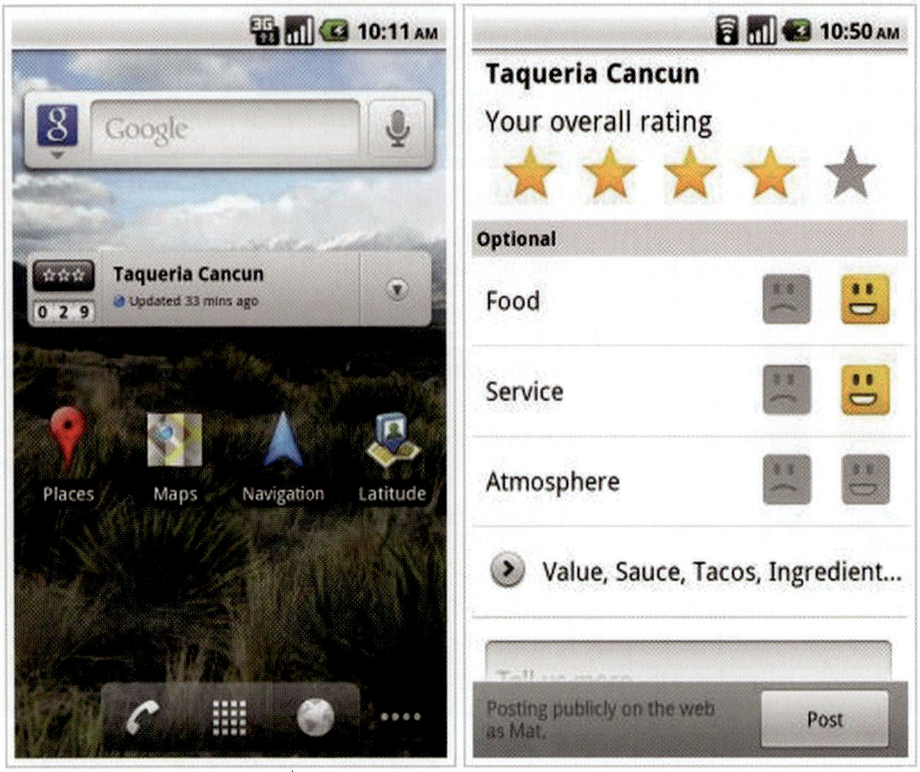

MEASURING ATTITUDES AND OTHER UNOBSERVABLE CONCEPTS

Some of the things we measure in marketing research are pretty straightforward. For instance, the fact that a company sold a certain number of units of a new product in a particular store in a test-market city can be confirmed relatively easily. The age, gender, ethnic background, zip code, and purchasing behavior for a particular consumer are real properties, although we often have to depend on the consumer to provide accurate responses to our measures.

Many of the qualities that we measure most often, however, can't be seen or touched. Have you ever seen someone's attitudes, motivations, or purchase intentions? You may have seen their expressions, heard their words, or observed the behaviors that might result from these qualities, but you haven't seen the characteristics themselves. And that's the dilemma that researchers face when it comes to measuring attitudes and other unobservable concepts. In this section, we'll show you some of the more popular ways of measuring people's attitudes. The ideas apply equally well to other types of unobservables.

By far, the most common approach to measuring attitudes is to obtain respondents' **self-reports**, in which people are asked directly for their beliefs or feelings about something. On BizRate.com, consumers can self-report ratings of their purchase experience with companies such as Zappos.com (current overall rating: 9.5 out of 10) and many, many more. This online business rating service uses graphic smiley/frowning face rating scales so that both online businesses and prospective customers can easily gauge customer attitudes toward stores across many product categories.

self-report
A method of assessing attitudes in which individuals are asked directly for their beliefs about or feelings toward an object or class of objects.

It won't surprise you that researchers have developed a number of different self-report methods to measure attitudes. Most approaches use itemized-ratings scales (a form of fixed-alternative response scale), but we'll describe a couple of other approaches as well.

© J.B NICHOLAS/SPLASH NEWS/NEWSCOM

Itemized-Ratings Scale

With **itemized-ratings scales**, the respondent selects from a limited number of response categories that typically reflect increasing amounts of the attribute (e.g., attitudes, satisfaction) being measured. So, if you wanted to measure an attitude toward a brand, you might develop a rating scale like that shown in Exhibit 7.2 to assess attitudes toward different brands of soft drinks: a 1–7 interval scale where 1 = "extremely unfavorable" and 7 = "extremely favorable." In general, five to nine categories work best; they permit fine distinctions but are easily understood by respondents.

itemized-ratings scale
A scale on which individuals must indicate their ratings of an attribute or object by selecting the response category that best describes their position on the attribute or object.

There are many different variations of itemized-ratings scales. Two of the most commonly used scales are summated-ratings scales and semantic-differential scales, which we'll describe next.

Summated-Ratings (Likert) Scale

The **summated-ratings scale**, also called a *Likert scale*, is one of the most widely used attitude-scaling techniques in marketing research.[2] With the summated-ratings scale, researchers write a number of statements that relate to the issue or object in question and then have respondents express how much they agree or disagree with each statement. Exhibit 7.3 is an example of a scale that you might use to compare the image of one bank with that of its competitors. The response categories represent varying degrees of agreement and are assigned scale values. Let's assume the values 1, 2, 3, 4, and 5 are assigned to the respective response categories shown in Exhibit 7.3. Then it's easy to calculate a total score for each respondent by adding (thus the name "summated-ratings") or averaging the scores across the items.

summated-ratings scale
A self-report technique for attitude measurement in which respondents indicate their degree of agreement or disagreement with each of a number of statements.

Suppose that one customer of the bank checked "agree" on items 1 and 4 and "strongly agree" on items 2 and 3. This customer's total attitude score toward the bank would thus be 18 if we add the scores, or 4.5 if we calculate the mean score.

Researchers often use variations of the scale we've shown in Exhibit 7.3, which is considered the classic version of a summated-ratings scale. For example, the version shown includes verbal descriptors, or *anchors,* for each scale position (i.e., "strongly disagree," "disagree," etc.). Some researchers will anchor only the endpoints of the scale. Another variation asks respondents to circle a number representing the level of agreement rather than check the appropriate category.

EXHIBIT 7.3

Example of Summated-Ratings Scale

	Strongly Disagree	Disagree	Neither Agree nor Disagree	Agree	Strongly Agree
1. The bank offers courteous service.	___	___	___	___	___
2. The bank has a convenient location.	___	___	___	___	___
3. The bank has convenient hours.	___	___	___	___	___
4. The bank offers low-interest-rate loans.	___	___	___	___	___

EXHIBIT 7.4

Example of Semantic-Differential Scaling Form

Service is discourteous. :___:___:___:___:___:___:___: Service is courteous.

Location is inconvenient. :___:___:___:___:___:___:___: Location is convenient.

Hours are inconvenient. :___:___:___:___:___:___:___: Hours are convenient.

Loan interest rates are high. :___:___:___:___:___:___:___: Loan interest rates are low.

And some researchers use more response categories than the traditional five categories. Regardless of how the particular scale is designed, the key features of the summated-ratings scale remain the same: a set of statements with which respondents indicate level of agreement.

semantic-differential scale
A self-report technique for attitude measurement in which respondents are asked to check which cell between a set of bipolar adjectives or phrases best describes their feelings toward the object.

Semantic-Differential Scale

Another very popular technique for measuring attitudes in marketing research is the **semantic-differential scale**. It is particularly useful in corporate, brand, and product-image studies. The scale grew out of research concerning the underlying structure of words but has since been adapted to make it suitable for measuring attitudes.[3]

Semantic-differential scales consist of pairs of bipolar words or phrases that can be used to describe the attitude object. Let's look again at measuring attitude toward a bank. Using the semantic-differential approach, the researcher would first generate a list of bipolar adjectives or phrases. Exhibit 7.4 is similar to Exhibit 7.3 in terms of the attributes used to describe the bank, but it is arranged in semantic-differential format. Respondents are instructed to read each set of phrases and to check the space that best represents their opinions. A respondent who believed that the hours were terribly inconvenient might check the space closest to the phrase "Hours are inconvenient"; someone who was about neutral on this issue would select the middle position on the scale.

Semantic-differential scales are popular in marketing for several reasons. They're flexible and easy to use for both researchers and respondents (although they don't work as well over the telephone). They are also good when it comes to presenting the results of a study. For example, suppose that respondents were asked to evaluate two or more banks, using the same scale. When several banks are rated, the different bank profiles can be compared. Exhibit 7.5 presents a

EXHIBIT 7.5

Snake Diagram Showing Contrasting Profiles of Banks A and B

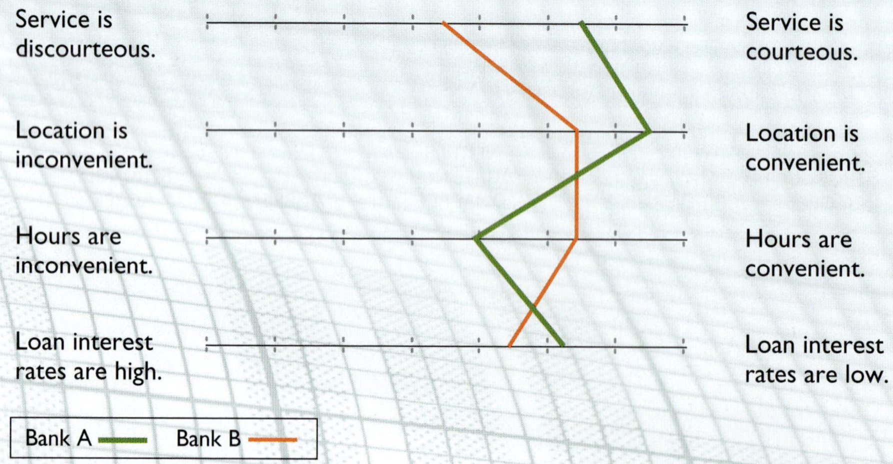

snake diagram (notice its shape), which illustrates that Bank A is perceived as having more courteous service and a more convenient location and as offering lower interest rates on loans, but as having less convenient hours than Bank B. The values on the chart represent the average score of all respondents on each item.

snake diagram
A diagram that connects the average responses to a series of semantic-differential statements, thereby depicting the profile of the object or objects being evaluated.

EXHIBIT 7.6

Graphic-Ratings Scale

Please evaluate each attribute, in terms of how important the attribute is to you personally, by placing an "X" at the position on the horizontal line that most reflects your feelings.

ATTRIBUTE	NOT IMPORTANT	VERY IMPORTANT
Courteous service	______________________	
Convenient location	______________________	
Convenient hours	______________________	
Low-interest-rate loans	______________________	

If you don't want to develop a profile, you can also total the scores on a semantic-differential scale in order to compare attitudes toward different objects. This score is computed by summing or averaging the scores for the individual scales. As was true for summated-ratings scales, variations in scale design are common. Numbers are sometimes substituted for blanks, and different numbers of scale positions can be used.

Other Itemized-Ratings Scales

There are endless possible varieties of itemized-ratings scales. The response categories for this type of scale are always limited in number, however, and they are almost always used to capture interval-level data. Beyond that, it's up to the creativity of the researcher and the demands of the situation. Thus, a set of faces, varying systematically in terms of whether they are frowning or smiling, used to capture a person's satisfaction or preference (appropriately called a *faces scale*) is an itemized-rating scale. Faces can also be useful when conducting marketing research with children.

Graphic-Ratings Scales

graphic-ratings scales
A scale in which individuals indicate their ratings of an attribute typically by placing a check at the appropriate point on a line that runs from one extreme of the attribute to the other.

Graphic-ratings scales are similar in most respects to itemized-ratings scales except for one very important difference: Instead of a limited set of response categories, there are a large number of possible response categories. For example, one common form of graphic-ratings scale asks people to indicate their ratings by placing a check at the appropriate point on a line that runs from one extreme of the attribute to the other (see Exhibit 7.6). Then, the attribute being assessed is scored by measuring the length of the line from one end to the marked position.

These scales offer respondents the greatest degree of freedom in providing answers. In theory, there are an infinite number of possible response positions along the continuous scale. Just how useful such fine differences in responses are is questionable, however, and the actual physical measurement of responses takes researcher time and attention. For these reasons, itemized-ratings scales have proven to be much more popular with researchers.

Comparative-Ratings Scale

In graphic and itemized scales, respondents are asked to consider attributes of an entity independently. For

EXHIBIT 7.7

Constant-Sum Comparative-Ratings Scale

Please divide 100 points between the following two attributes in terms of the relative importance of each attribute to you.

Courteous service	______
Convenient location	______

comparative-ratings scale
A scale requiring subjects to make their ratings as a series of relative judgments or comparisons rather than as independent assessments.

constant-sum method
A comparative-ratings scale in which an individual divides some given sum among two or more attributes on a basis such as importance or favorability.

example, you might ask respondents to indicate how important a convenient location is to them in choosing a bank. You might also ask how important having convenient hours are to them. With **comparative-ratings scales**, however, respondents are asked to judge each attribute with direct reference to the other attributes being evaluated. This is an important difference.

The constant-sum scaling method is a common example of a comparative-ratings scale. In the **constant-sum method**, the individual divides some given sum (often, 100 points) among two or more attributes on the basis of importance, favorability, purchase likelihood, or something else. (*Note:* Limiting the number of attributes to be assessed is important. The respondent should not need a calculator to divide the points.) Take a look at Exhibit 7.7, for example. If a respondent gave 50 points to courteous service and 50 points to convenient location, the attributes would be judged to be equally important. If she assigned 80 to courteous service and 20 to convenient location, courteous service would be considered to be four times as important. Note the difference in emphasis with this method. All judgments are made in comparison to some other alternative.

Comparative-ratings scales (such as the constant-sum scale) are good for eliminating the *halo effect* that is common in scaling. A halo effect occurs when there is carryover from one judgment to another. For example, suppose you were concerned about two key issues in a survey of department store customers: satisfaction with the service provided and satisfaction with store location. If you ask these questions back to back on the survey, a respondent with strong positive feelings about the service provided is likely to provide more positive assessments of store location than he might normally provide. Comparative-ratings scales help control this problem by requiring respondents to consider two or more attributes in combination.

Another problem that you might encounter when using graphic- or itemized-ratings scales to measure importance values is that respondents may be inclined to indicate that all, or nearly all, of the attributes are important. The comparative scaling methods allow more insight into the relative ranking, if not the absolute importance, of the attributes.

OTHER CONSIDERATIONS IN DESIGNING SCALES

There are a number of issues that must also be considered when designing scales for measuring concepts like attitudes. In this section, we'll deal with some of them.

Number of Items in a Scale

One consideration involves exactly how many items are needed to measure the concept you are trying to assess. Should attitude toward a company be assessed using a single item, 3 items, 10 items, or 35 items? The answer depends on the purpose of the measure. If an overall summary judgment of how consumers feel about the company is needed, then a single-item **global measure** of attitude on a "very unfavorable–very favorable" scale may be enough. The goal of a global measure is to provide an overall assessment of the attribute. Consider the following global measure of corporate reputation.

global measure
A measure designed to provide an overall assessment of an object or phenomenon, typically using one or two items.

What is your overall evaluation of Amazon.com? (Circle a number)

Very Unfavorable		Neither Favorable nor Unfavorable		Very Favorable
1	2	3	4	5

Sometimes, however, we need to develop a more comprehensive measure that will provide more information about how respondents view various aspects of the phenomenon being studied. These types of measures, often called **composite measures**, are more diagnostic in the sense that they provide more information for identifying strong or weak areas, particularly when aspects can be compared with one another or with measures for other entities. Suppose that marketing managers for a major retail chain are concerned about customer satisfaction. A global measure of satisfaction would provide an overall indication of how things are going, but a composite measure, consisting of measures of satisfaction with the location, product selection, prices, employees, and so on, would allow the managers to more easily diagnose any problem areas.

composite measures
A measure designed to provide a comprehensive assessment of an object or phenomenon, with items to assess all relevant aspects or dimensions.

How many items should be used with a composite measure? As many as it takes to fully capture the concept being measured. You'll have to use your best judgment to see that all important aspects of the concept are represented in the measure, but you don't want the survey to end up so long that nobody wants to complete it. Equally important, you don't want the survey to be so long that respondents get tired and start providing "garbage" data just to finish.

Number of Scale Positions

You also must decide how many response categories to include when designing measures. For most purposes, a minimum of five response categories should be included. What's the upper limit on number of response categories? With itemized-ratings scales, there's really no need to go beyond 9 or 10 scale positions. Scales with five to nine positions work quite well and are used routinely in marketing research.

There's a related decision that you also get to make: Should you include an even or an odd number of response categories? An odd number allows for a center position, usually interpreted as "neutral" by respondents. Sometimes it's easier for a respondent to choose the center position than to actually think about the right answer, so some researchers use an even number of scale positions (i.e., no middle position). On the other hand, there are plenty of issues on which a perfectly well-thought-out answer may be "neutral." As a result, some researchers routinely use an odd number of scale positions. Both even and odd numbers are used regularly in practice.

Including a "Don't Know" or "Not Applicable" Response Category

Sometimes researchers choose to include a "don't know" or "no opinion" option along with the regular scale positions for an item. The same is true with a "not applicable" option. This may be a good idea if a fairly sizable percentage of respondents are likely not to have encountered or thought about the object or issue being addressed in the study. Otherwise, any answers that they provide will probably have little meaning and as a result will simply add error to the study. Exploratory research and pilot studies can be used to shed light on the issue.

If you believe that most respondents should have an opinion, we advise against including a "don't know" category. If you include the "don't know" option, some respondents will choose it—including some who are simply looking for the easiest way to get through the survey. In fact, research has indicated that no opinion options are more frequently chosen (1) by individuals with lower levels of education, (2) by those answering anonymously, (3) for questions that appear later in a survey, and (4) by respondents who indicated that they had devoted less effort to the task of completing a survey.[4] As a result, including a "don't know" option could do more harm than good.

ESTABLISHING THE VALIDITY AND RELIABILITY OF MEASURES

Almost nothing in marketing research can be measured without error. Observation of behavior usually produces the most accurate measures—but most of the things we want to measure in marketing research simply can't be observed. How can we ever have much faith in our measures for things like attitudes, intentions, motivations, and so on?

Try this: Respond to the following question as if you saw it on a mail survey:

Taking everything you know about General Electric into consideration, how favorable are you toward the company? Please circle a number on the following scale:

Very Unfavorable	Unfavorable	Neither Favorable nor Unfavorable	Favorable	Very Favorable
1	2	3	4	5

Your observed response (i.e., the number you circled) is a combination of your true position on the issue plus any kinds of error that have influenced your response. We'll call these response errors. These errors fall into two general categories: systematic error and random error. Exhibit 7.8 provides an illustration of these ideas. Our goal, of course, is to minimize error. As systematic and random errors decrease, the validity of the measure increases.

systematic error
Error in measurement that is also known as constant error because it affects the measurement in a constant way.

Systematic error, which is also called constant error, is error that affects the measurement in a constant way. Some of these may have influenced how you responded to the question about General Electric. Sometimes personality traits or other stable characteristics of individuals add systematic error to the measurement process. For example, maybe you are more willing to express negative feelings than most other people; some people seem to be systematically negative in all their responses. On the other hand, maybe you tend toward more positive answers—which can introduce systematic error on the positive side. As another example, consumers sometimes have a hard time accurately reporting how frequently they perform behaviors. Those who perform behaviors frequently tend to underreport the level of behavior, and those who perform those behaviors less frequently tend to overreport the level of behavior.

EXHIBIT 7.8

Components of an Observed Response

Differences in how surveys are administered can also introduce systematic error into a project. Researchers at Silver Dollar City, a theme park located near Branson, Missouri, discovered that responses to the same satisfaction question were consistently higher when obtained via telephone compared with e-mail. Because there were no differences in answers for virtually all other questions, the researchers concluded that the telephone survey respondents were likely inflating satisfaction scores because of the social context: They were talking directly to someone else. With e-mail, there was less social pressure to say nice things.

The other general type of error, **random error**, is due to temporary aspects of the person or measurement situation; this can affect the measurement in irregular ways. Random error is present when we repeat a measurement on an individual and don't get the same scores as the first time we did the measurement, even though the characteristic being measured hasn't changed.

random error
Error in measurement due to temporary aspects of the person or measurement situation and which affects the measurement in irregular ways.

Your mood, state of health, fatigue, and so forth, might have affected your response to the question about General Electric, yet these factors are temporary. So, if you've had a hard day, your answer (assuming you chose to think about it at all) was probably more negative than if you'd read this section tomorrow. And it works the other way, too. Maybe you answered the question after finding out you did really well on a test; everything and everybody looks a little better than it did before, and your answer was a little higher than it might otherwise have been.

The situation surrounding the measurement also affects the score in random ways. Maybe the room temperature was too hot or too cold when you answered the question. Maybe you have a hundred other things to do and just didn't want to think about it very hard. And it's common for people to interpret questions—especially ambiguous ones—differently. Differences in the resulting scores may have more to do with interpretation than with true differences in the characteristic we wanted to measure. One of your main tasks is to write items or questions that mean the same thing

EXHIBIT 7.9

Illustration of Difference between Reliability and Validity

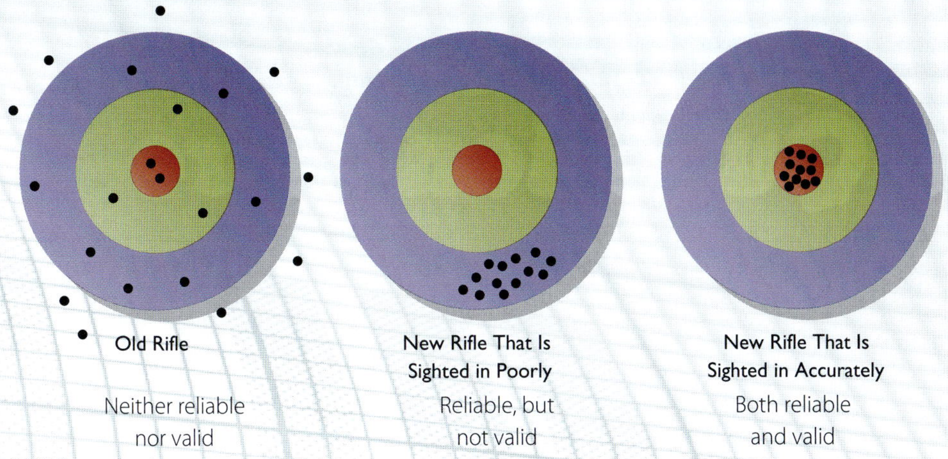

to all respondents. If you don't do this, you've added random error.

All of this matters, because the higher the levels of systematic and random error, the lower the **validity**, or correctness, of a measure. Any scale or other measure that accurately assesses what it was intended to assess is said to have validity. Although both types of error lower a measure's validity, in some ways systematic error is less troublesome than random error. If we know the source of the systematic error, sometimes we can adjust for it. For example, researchers know that consumers tend to overestimate their future purchase behaviors, so they can adjust for this as they analyze survey results. Random error, on the other hand, is just that—random—and we can't hold it constant or account for it statistically. The best we can hope is that random errors cancel themselves out across respondents.

validity
The extent to which differences in scores on a measuring instrument reflect true differences among individuals, groups, or situations in the characteristic that it seeks to measure, or true differences in the same individual, group, or situation from one occasion to another, rather than systematic or random errors.

reliability
Ability of a measure to obtain similar scores for the same object, trait, or construct across time, across different evaluators, or across the items forming the measure.

Reliability

Reliability refers to the ability of a measure to obtain consistent scores for the same variable or concept across time, across different evaluators, or across the items forming the measure. *Consistency* is the hallmark of reliability; as a result, improving reliability requires decreasing random error. A reliable measure isn't heavily influenced by transitory factors that cause random errors. However, a measure could be reliable, but not necessarily valid because of systematic error. A reliable measure is just consistent—it may not be measuring the right thing, but it returns consistent scores.

Suppose that a sportsman is comparing three different rifles—an old rifle and two new ones. He fires each of the rifles a number of times and each time he lines up the rifle's sights perfectly with the center of the target. Exhibit 7.9 illustrates the results for the three different rifles. The old rifle is unreliable; despite the fact that the sights are set on the center of the target, the shots go off in random directions. The first new rifle is relatively reliable—it hits about the same spot on the target each time—but its sights are set incorrectly in the center diagram. The error is systematic and not random, but the rifle still misses the mark. The right-hand diagram shows a new rifle with its sights set correctly. Only in the right-hand diagram could a user of any of the rifles be expected to hit the center of the target with regularity. This represents a measure that is both reliable *and* valid.

That's what asking good questions is all about. We need measures that display both reliability and validity.

8 Designing the Questionnaire

©LIGHTPOET/SHUTTERSTOCK.COM

POLL QUESTION:

Pretesting in a research context is similar to test marketing in a new product development context.

STRONGLY DISAGREE 1 2 3 4 5 STRONGLY AGREE

Learning Objectives

1. Cite some of the techniques researchers use to secure respondents' cooperation in answering sensitive questions.
2. List some of the primary rules researchers should keep in mind in trying to develop bias-free questions.
3. Explain what the funnel approach to question sequencing is.
4. Explain the difference between basic information and classification information, and tell which should be asked first in a questionnaire.
5. Explain the role of pretesting in the questionnaire development process.

INTRODUCTION

Most beginning researchers have no idea how difficult it is to develop an effective questionnaire. You may be saying to yourself, "How hard can it be to write a few questions?" It doesn't matter how perfectly data collection goes if the questions themselves are lousy and introduce error into the data set. As you read this chapter, we hope that you'll gain an appreciation for designing questionnaires carefully.

Exhibit 8.1 offers a method for developing an effective questionnaire.[1] Considering that many people think that 10 minutes is more than enough time to develop a questionnaire, a process with 10 steps may be surprising or seem a little extreme. As we describe these steps, however, we think you'll begin to understand why each is important.

Step 1: Specify What Information Will Be Sought

Both descriptive and causal research designs require that researchers have enough knowledge about the problem to frame some specific hypotheses to guide the research. The hypotheses also guide the questionnaire. They determine what information will be sought. If you've already developed a complete set of dummy tables, determining what information to collect is pretty easy. (Remember that a dummy table is a table that shows how the results of an analysis will be presented; at this early stage it has no numbers.)

EXHIBIT 8.1

Procedure for Developing a Questionnaire

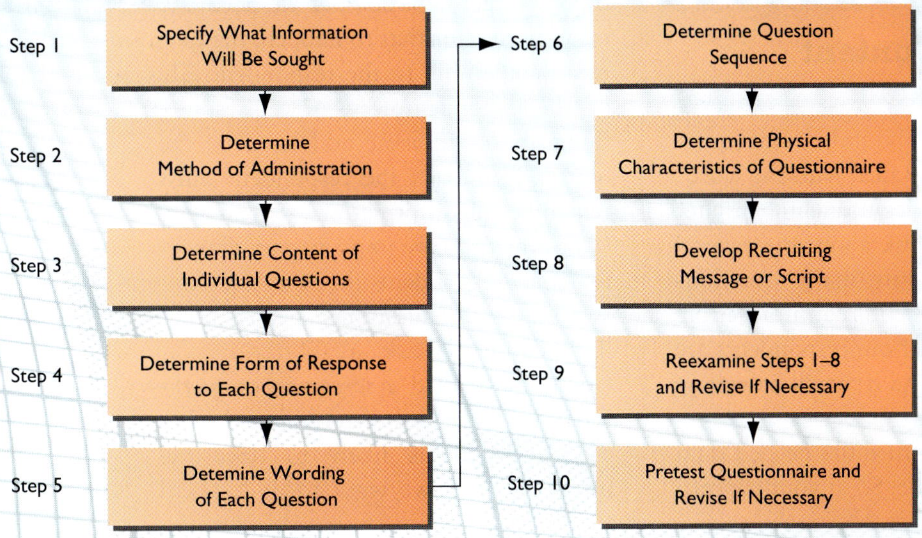

FAST FACT:

IT HAS BEEN ESTIMATED THAT **GOOGLE** INDEXES ONLY ABOUT **12%** OF THE URLs ON THE WEB.

Sometimes you'll think of other things you'd like to include as you design the questionnaire. Be careful here—if the information is truly important for the research problem you're studying, then go ahead and include the necessary questions. If it simply represents something that might be "nice to know," but isn't central to the purpose of the study, forget about it. Including extra questions makes the survey longer, which often causes response rates to go down.

Step 2: Determine Method of Administration

Once you know the basic information you need to collect, it's time to consider (again) the method of administration. As we noted in Chapter 6, there are four primary methods of collecting data via communication: personal interviews, telephone interviews, mail questionnaires, or Web-based questionnaires. You'll want to consider the specific circumstances of your project in light of the advantages and disadvantages of the different methods and verify that you've chosen the overall best method of administration. As we discussed earlier, the trick is to choose the method that best fits your information needs, time frame, budget, and the like. It's important to decide on a method as early as possible, because choice of method will influence the number and types of questions, wording of questions and response categories, question sequencing, and so forth.

Step 3: Determine Content of Individual Questions

Now it's time to begin thinking about the actual questions that should be asked. We'll deal with the words to use and the response categories to include in later stages—for now, we need to think about the general issues we're addressing and how many questions might be needed to deliver the required information. We also have to consider whether our respondents are likely to have the information and if they'll be willing to share it.

In general, we want to capture the needed data using as few questions as possible. So, if your concern is whether there are young children living in a household, it would be better to ask for the age of the youngest child living at home rather than to ask for the ages of all the residents in the household. Sure, it would be great to have the additional information, but if it isn't necessary, don't ask for it. On the flip side, lots of researchers try to get too much information using a single question, which often leads to confusion and unnecessary error in the results. Sometimes you'll need to ask several questions instead of just one.

Here's an example. Consider the question, "Why do you use Crest toothpaste?" One consumer might reply, "To reduce cavities"; another may say, "Because our dentist recommended it." The respondents are using two different frames of reference, the first replying in terms of why he is using it now and the second in terms of how she started using it. A better way is to break the question down into two separate questions, like this:

How did you first happen to use Crest?

____

What is your primary reason for using it?

____

If you wanted one or the other frame of reference, you could include response categories; these would indicate to the respondent the perspective you desire. Many times, you won't discover these sorts of subtle issues until you pretest the questionnaire with actual members of the population being studied. That's one reason that pretesting is so important—to make sure that a question won't be interpreted in different ways by different people.

Sometimes people don't know the answers to the questions we'd like to ask. Unfortunately, that probably won't stop them from answering! Most questions will get answers, but we need answers that are meaningful. For that to happen, the questions need to mean something to the respondent. This means that (1) the respondent needs to know something about the issue addressed by the question, and (2) the respondent must remember the information.

So how do we improve our chances that a respondent knows the answers to our questions? Many times it's helpful to ask a **filter question** (sometimes called a *screening* or *qualifying question*) to determine whether the individual is likely to have the information. If we want to understand

filter question
A question used to determine whether a respondent is likely to possess the knowledge being sought; also used to determine whether an individual qualifies as a member of the defined population.

FAST FACT:

FOUR OF THE FIVE MOST RECENT **U.S. PRESIDENTS** WERE **LEFT-HANDED**. THE EXCEPTION: GEORGE W. BUSH.

something about grocery store shopping behaviors and attitudes, a filter question like this might help: "Do you do the grocery shopping for your family?" Filter questions are regularly used at the start of interviews or questionnaires to determine whether the respondent is actually a member of the population being studied, particularly when names have been drawn from general lists (e.g., telephone directories).

Obtaining useful data from respondents also requires that they be able to remember the information we ask about. Very often we ask people about their purchase and/or use of products and services. No one goes through life trying to remember this sort of stuff, yet we have to depend on the respondent's ability to do so. (Note that observation data using scanner data and the like don't have this problem.) And as you might suspect, for a variety of reasons, an individual's memory for such things just isn't all that good. Returning to our toothpaste example, many people won't be able to recall the first brand they ever used, when they switched to their current brand, or why they switched. This is something we must keep in mind continually as we design questionnaires.

Even if respondents remember the information we want, there is always a question of whether they will share it. Unwillingness to respond to a question (or the whole questionnaire, for that matter) may be a function of the amount of work involved in producing an answer or the sensitivity of the issue. Although a purchasing agent might be able to determine to the penny how much the company spent on a particular brand of janitorial supplies last year, why would she want to take the time to look it up to answer a survey question? Would you? If you ask for something that requires a lot of effort, the respondent is likely to give an approximate answer, ignore the question, or refuse to complete the survey at all.

When an issue is embarrassing or otherwise threatening to respondents, they are naturally less likely to cooperate. Rule 1 about asking sensitive questions: Avoid them unless they are absolutely essential to your project. If you must ask one or more sensitive questions, do so with care. Respect the privacy of your respondents by maintaining the security of the information you collect and by fulfilling any promises of anonymity or confidentiality you have given. Exhibit 8.2 offers several techniques that can be used to more effectively handle sensitive issues.

Step 4: Determine Form of Response to Each Question

Once you've determined the general content of the individual questions, you must decide whether to use closed-ended (fixed alternative) or open-ended responses. Let's look at each in a little more detail.

Open-Ended Questions

Respondents are free to reply to open-ended questions in their own words rather than being limited to choosing from a set of alternatives. Here are some examples:

1. How old are you?__________ years
2. What is your opinion about laws requiring motorcycle riders to wear helmets?
____
____
____
3. Can you name three sponsors of the Monday night football games?
____
____
____
4. Do you intend to purchase an automobile this year?
____
5. Why did you purchase a Sony brand HDTV television?
____
____
____
6. In the past month, how many times have you purchased gasoline from a Shell service station?
__________ times

AVOID ASKING SENSITIVE QUESTIONS UNLESS THEY ARE ABSOLUTELY ESSENTIAL.

EXHIBIT 8.2

Handling Sensitive Questions

Here are some tips and techniques for obtaining sensitive information from respondents. We've already given you the most important tip: *Don't include sensitive questions unless you absolutely have to.* Here are some other ideas.

Tip: Guarantee respondents that their answers will be completely anonymous—but only if you will actually carry through on your promise. Anonymity is possible with any method of data collection, but with anything other than mail questionnaires, the respondent must rely on you to remove his or her name or other identifying information from the data record. If you cannot promise anonymity, at least promise that respondents' answers will be held in confidence and that information specific to them will not be given to anyone else. Then keep your word.

Tip: Put any sensitive questions near the end of the questionnaire. This will allow the researcher and the respondent a little time to develop trust and rapport, especially with personal interviews and telephone interviews. There's another practical advantage too: If the respondent decides to stop answering questions at that point, at least he or she has already completed most of the questionnaire.

Tip: Use a counter biasing statement that indicates that the behavior or attitude in question is not unusual. For example, a question about household financial difficulties might be preceded by the following statement: "Recent studies show that one of every four households has trouble meeting its monthly financial obligations." Doing it this way makes it easier for a respondent to admit the potentially embarrassing information.

Tip: Phrase the question in terms of other people and how they might feel or act; for example, "Do you think most people cheat on their income taxes? Why?" Respondents are more likely to reveal their attitudes and behaviors in sensitive areas when asked about other people than if you ask them directly about their own attitudes and behaviors.

Tip: Ask for general answers, rather than specific answers, when seeking sensitive information. One frequently used approach is to measure the response by having respondents check one of several categories instead of providing the precise answer. If you need to know a respondent's age, for example, rather than ask for his actual age in years, let him or her check one of the following boxes:

- Less than 20
- 20–29
- 30–39
- 40–49
- 50–59
- 60–69
- 70 or older

Although you won't be able to calculate the precise average age for the sample respondents, it usually isn't necessary to do so anyway.

Tip: Use the randomized-response model. With this technique, the respondent is typically given two questions, either of which can be answered "yes" or "no." One question deals with a simple, nonsensitive issue; the other specifically addresses the sensitive issue being studied. Using some random approach, such as flipping a coin, respondents are instructed to answer one or the other question, but the researcher never knows which question they actually answered. That's what makes the approach work: Respondents feel free to answer truthfully because they know that the interviewer will never know if "yes" is in reference to the sensitive or nonsensitive question. The rest is easy. Because we have chosen an innocent question for which we already know the probably of a "yes" answer (e.g., "Were you born in January?") and we know the probably that the respondent is answering the sensitive question (50% based on the coin flip), we can back our way into the proportion of the sample that answered "yes" to the sensitive question. Here's the only catch: Because we can never know specifically which respondents have admitted to the sensitive issue, there is no way for us to look at the relationship between their behavior and other variables such as demographic characteristics.

As these questions demonstrate, just about any kind of information can be gathered using open-ended questions. Open-ended questions are quite versatile.

Open-ended questions are often used to begin a questionnaire. An opening question such as, "When you think of flat-panel TVs, which brands come to mind?" gives some insight into the respondent's frame of reference and provides an easy way for the respondent to begin to focus on the topic at hand.

You may have noticed that some of the open-ended questions we presented seemed very straightforward; others were more subjective in nature. There are two general classes of open-ended questions. One type seeks factual information from a respondent. For example, look back at Questions 1, 3, 4, and 6. These questions seek direct answers from the respondent. There is a correct answer to each question, and the researcher assumes that the respondent can provide those answers (Questions 1, 4, and 6) or is testing to see whether the respondent is capable of providing the answers (Question 3).

The other type of open-ended question is more exploratory in nature (see Questions 2 and 5). Questions designed to uncover motivations and rich descriptions of feelings and attitudes (we sometimes refer to these as "touchy-feely" questions) are terrific for exploratory research. You can use them with descriptive research too, but they're difficult to code.

Closed-Ended Questions

With closed-ended questions, respondents choose their answers from a predetermined number of responses, using fixed alternative response scales. Many times, they respond using rating scales. In this section, we'll present several key issues with using closed-ended questions. Consider the examples below in which we've reframed some of the open-ended questions from the preceding list as fixed-alternative questions. Respondents would be instructed to check the box or boxes that apply.

© TERRI MILLER/E-VISUAL COMMUNICATIONS, INC.

Age

How old are you?

- ☐ Less than 20
- ☐ 20–29
- ☐ 30–39
- ☐ 40–49
- ☐ 50–59
- ☐ 60 or over

HDTV Television Purchase

Why did you purchase a Sony brand HDTV television (check all that apply)?

- ☐ Price was lower than other alternatives
- ☐ Feel it represents the highest quality
- ☐ Availability of local service
- ☐ Availability of a service contract
- ☐ Picture is better
- ☐ Warranty is better
- ☐ Other

Motorcycle Helmet Use Legislation

What is your opinion about laws requiring motorcycle riders to wear helmets?

- ☐ Definitely needed
- ☐ Probably needed
- ☐ Probably not needed
- ☐ Definitely not needed
- ☐ No opinion

Gasoline Purchase Frequency

In the past month, how many times have you purchased gasoline from a Shell station?

- ☐ 0
- ☐ 1–2
- ☐ 3 or more

These examples highlight some of the difficulties with closed-ended questions. None of the alternatives in the motorcycle helmet law question, for example, may capture the respondent's true beliefs on the issue. What if he believes that helmets should be required when riding on highways and streets, but not on private land or dirt tracks? The fixed-alternative question doesn't permit individuals to explain their true position.

The helmet law question also illustrates an issue we discussed in the previous chapter: Should respondents be provided with a "don't know" or "no opinion" option? The general rule is that if a sizable portion of respondents truly don't know an answer or hold an opinion on an issue, they ought to be allowed to say so. How do we define "sizable portion"? If exploratory research or questionnaire pretesting reveals that more than about 20 to 25 percent of respondents either don't know or don't hold an opinion, it's probably a good idea to include appropriate response categories to capture this. Another option is to use a filter question and avoid asking the question of these respondents altogether.

The HDTV television purchase question illustrates another problem with fixed-alternative questions. The list of reasons provided for purchasing a Sony brand HDTV television may not include all the reasons that could have been used by the respondent. Maybe a respondent purchased a Sony out of loyalty to a friend who owns the local electronics store or for some other reason not included on the list of possible reasons. *Response categories must be exhaustive;* that is, all reasonable possible responses must be included. The "other" response category attempts to solve this problem, but if many people are forced to check this response, the results for that question aren't worth much. How do you know that you've included all necessary responses? Through exploratory research and questionnaire pretesting.

Here's another thing to consider when determining the form of response for each question. If a respondent is supposed to select only one response category, then there must be only one response category that contains her answer. In addition to being exhaustive, *response categories must also be mutually exclusive.* Consider the age question above. What would happen if the response categories were "less than 20," "20–30," "30–40," and so on, and the respondent was 30 years old? Which category should she check? Unless it's a "check all that apply" question, researchers must be very careful that a respondent's answer will fall into only one category. Notice that the television purchase question includes the instruction to "check all that apply" because there might be several legitimate reasons for purchasing the Sony. On the other hand, if the instructions had said "check the most important reason," the categories would have been mutually exclusive because each represents a different reason.

Response categories are also susceptible to response order bias. **Response order bias** occurs when responses are likely to be affected by the order in which the alternatives are presented. The recommended procedure for dealing with order bias is known as the **split-ballot technique**. In this approach, multiple versions of the questionnaire are produced and distributed. Each version varies the order of the response categories so that each response category will appear in each position (e.g., first, in the middle positions, last) about equally across the sample. The idea is that any order biases will be averaged out across all respondents. This is very easily accomplished with Web-based surveys where response option randomization is available.

response order bias
An error that occurs when the response to a question is influenced by the order in which the alternatives are presented.

split-ballot technique
A technique used to combat response order bias, in which response options are reordered or randomized to create different versions of the survey.

Step 5: Determine Wording of Each Question

Step 5 in the questionnaire development process involves the phrasing—word by word—of each question. This is a critical task because a poorly worded question can cause respondents to refuse to answer it. This is known as *item nonresponse,* and it creates problems for data analysis. Even worse, poorly worded questions introduce error when people do respond, because people may misunderstand the question or interpret it in different ways.

Writing good questions is difficult. Here are some general rules of thumb that you can follow to avoid some of the more obvious problems. There is no substitute, however, for careful thought—and a good deal of pretesting to ensure that your respondents understand and can accurately respond to your questions.

Use Simple Words

Most researchers are more highly educated than the typical questionnaire respondent, and sometimes they use words that they are familiar with but that are not understood by many respondents. Your task is to use words that are precise enough to get the answers you need, but that will

© DEAN COPPOLA/MCT/NEWSCOM

be understood by virtually everyone in the designated population. Technical language on a survey is fine and may be even desired for its precision, with a technically oriented research topic and population. When seeking answers from the general public, however, it would be wise to remember that the average person in the United States has a high school, not a college, education. Even common words can cause difficulty on questionnaires as Exhibit 8.3 indicates. The best advice is to keep the words as simple as possible.

Avoid Ambiguous Words and Questions

Not only should the words and questions be simple, but they should also be unambiguous. Consider this question:

> **How often do you rent movies from a video rental store for viewing at home?**
>
> ☐ Never
> ☐ Occasionally
> ☐ Sometimes
> ☐ Often
> ☐ Regularly
> ☐ Always

For all practical purposes, the replies to this question would be worthless. The words *occasionally, sometimes, regularly,* and *often* are ambiguous. Even the words *never* and *always,* which are more concrete than the others on the list, can cause problems, as noted in Exhibit 8.3. So, although this question would get answers, it would generate little real understanding of the frequency of the behavior in question.

A much better strategy to use when asking about the frequency of some behavior is to ask how many times the behavior has been performed during a specific time period.

> **Over the past two weeks, how many movies have you rented from a video rental store for viewing at home?**
>
> ☐ 1
> ☐ 2
> ☐ 3
> ☐ 4
> ☐ 5
> ☐ More than 5

An even better approach might be to just let respondents provide the actual number:

> **Over the past two weeks, how many movies have you rented from a video rental store for viewing at home? Write a number on the following line:**
>
> ____________________

Avoid Leading Questions

Sometimes questions are written in such a way that they basically tell respondents what answer ought to be provided. A **leading question** might have been an accident by a careless researcher; more likely, it's an intentional attempt to manipulate the study's results. Remember that manipulating results produces advocacy research and is blatantly unethical. Under no circumstances should leading questions be used intentionally. Consider this question:

leading question
A question framed so as to give the respondent a clue as to how he or she should answer.

> **Do you feel that limiting taxes by law is an effective way to stop the government from picking your pocket every payday?**
>
> ☐ Yes
> ☐ No
> ☐ Undecided

This was one of three questions in a questionnaire sponsored by the National Tax Limitation Committee. The committee intended to make the results of the poll available to Congress and to state legislators. Given the name of the group, it's not surprising to see the leading

EXHIBIT 8.3

Some Problem Words and Possible Solutions

Word	Potential Problem	Possible Solutions
All	Potentially imprecise; for many respondents, "all" means "almost all"	(1) Avoid use; (2) carefully word question so that meaning is clear; (3) use clearly defined response categories (can help clarify meaning of question)
Always	Potentially imprecise; for many respondents, "always" means "almost always" or a goal they want to obtain—"I always do this"	(1) Avoid use, especially when trying to assess behaviors understood as socially desirable; (2) carefully word question so that meaning is clear; (3) use clearly defined response categories (can help clarify meaning of question); (4) allow respondents to provide open-ended count.
And	Possibly a double-barreled question	(1) Check carefully to see whether multiple thoughts are included in single question; (2) if so, divide the question into multiple items.
Dinner	Potentially ambiguous: for some, this is the midday meal, for others, it is the evening meal	(1) Avoid use and refer to the time of day of the meal (i.e., morning, midday, evening).
Feel	Potentially ambiguous; could mean mood or emotion or could mean attitude	(1) Avoid use and use more precise terminology (e.g., "emotions experienced," "evaluation"); (2) use clearly defined response categories (can help clarify meaning of question).
Government	"Loaded" term for many people; potentially ambiguous—does this mean "government in general" or a specific branch or agency of local, state, or federal government?	(1) Avoid use, referring instead to the specific entity.
If	Might signal a branching question; be careful that these are easy to understand for respondents	(1) Avoid branching questions if possible; (2) if necessary, carefully design them so that route through questionnaire is clear; (3) if possible, branch at end of questionnaire so that some respondents will complete the questionnaire at that point, whereas others will move to additional questions.
Never	Potentially imprecise; for many respondents, "never" likely means "almost never" or a goal they want to obtain—"I never do this"	(1) Avoid use, especially when trying to assess behaviors understood as socially desirable; (2) carefully word question so that meaning is clear; (3) use clearly defined response categories (can help clarify meaning of question); (4) allow respondents to provide open-ended count.
Occasionally	Imprecise	(1) Avoid use; (2) allow respondents to provide open-ended count.
Often	Imprecise	(1) Avoid use; (2) allow respondents to provide open-ended count.
Or	Possibly a double-barreled question	(1) Check carefully to see whether multiple thoughts are included in single question; (2) if so, divide the question into multiple items.
Rarely	Imprecise	(1) Avoid use; (2) allow respondents to provide open-ended count.
Regularly	Imprecise	(1) Avoid use; (2) allow respondents to provide open-ended count.
Sometimes	Imprecise	(1) Avoid use; (2) allow respondents to provide open-ended count.
Usually	Imprecise	(1) Avoid use; (2) allow respondents to provide open-ended count.
Where	Potentially ambiguous: "Where do you plan to work after graduation?" could refer to geography, industry, department within a company, etc.	(1) Avoid use; (2) carefully word question so that meaning is clear; (3) use clearly defined response categories (can help clarify meaning of question).
You	Potentially ambiguous: Does this refer to the specific person, his household, etc.?	(1) Avoid use; (2) carefully word question so that meaning is clear.

For additional information, see Norman Bradburn, Seymour Sudman, and Brian Wansink, *Asking Questions* (San Francisco, Calif.: Jossey-Bass, 2004), pp. 324–325, and Stanley L. Payne, *The Art of Asking Questions* (Princeton, N.J.: Princeton University Press, 1979), pp. 158–176.

words "picking your pocket" being used in this question, or the leading word "gouge" being used in another question. The problem is that it's unlikely that the questions themselves accompanied the report to Congress. Instead, it is more likely that the report suggested that some high percentage favored laws limiting taxes.

Leading questions like this have become commonplace. Here's a tip: When you see the results of surveys and public opinion polls presented in the news media, pay no attention whatsoever to any results that aren't accompanied by (1) the actual questions asked, (2) a description of how the study was conducted, and (3) what group was surveyed. Reputable media outlets will provide this information.

Avoid Unstated Alternatives

unstated alternative
An alternative answer that is not expressed in a question's options.

An alternative that is not expressed in the options is an **unstated alternative**. The results of one classic study from years ago demonstrate what can happen when unstated alternatives are made clear to respondents. Researchers wanted to know the attitudes of full-time homemakers toward the idea of having a job outside the home. They asked two random samples of homemakers the following two questions:[2]

> **Would you like to have a job, if this were possible?**
>
> ________
>
> **Would you prefer to have a job, or do you prefer to do just your housework?**
>
> ________

Although the two questions appear very similar, they produced dramatically different responses. In the first version, only 19 percent of the homemakers said "no." In the second version, 68 percent said they would prefer not to have a job—more than three and one-half times as many as in the first version. The difference in the two questions is that the second version makes explicit an important alternative: Doing housework is a job in itself. In many ways, this is consistent with our earlier advice that response categories must be exhaustive. Thorough exploratory research and questionnaire pretesting will help identify unstated alternatives.

FAST FACT:
83% OF TEEN GIRLS PLAY SPORTS.

Avoid Assumed Consequences

A question should be framed so that all respondents will consider all relevant information as they respond. Unfortunately, it's easy to ask questions that don't spell out what might happen as a consequence of certain actions. These questions leave **assumed consequences**. The question "Are you in favor of placing price controls on crude oil?" will generate different responses from individuals, depending on whether they think price controls will result in rationing, long lines at the pump, or lower prices. A better way of asking this question is to clearly state the possible consequence(s). For example, the question could be changed to ask, "Are you in favor of placing price controls on crude oil if it would produce gas rationing?" Another possibility is to place a statement that explicitly notes what the consequences might be before asking the question:

assumed consequences
A problem that occurs when a question is not framed so as to clearly state the consequences and thus generates different responses from individuals who assume different consequences.

> **Many experts believe that placing price controls on crude oil will result in lower gasoline prices, but may also mean lower gasoline production, gasoline rationing, and longer lines at the pump. Are you in favor of placing price controls on crude oil?**
>
> ☐ Yes
>
> ☐ No
>
> ☐ Undecided

Exhibit 8.4 shows that respondents can assume a wide range of possible alternatives if consequences are assumed instead of explicitly stated. The favorable or unfavorable nature of these consequences can also vary greatly. While some may view repairing aging bridges as justification of a state tax increase others may not feel as positively if the consequence is salary increases for state legislators. The key point is that it's important to ask questions that are precise and that don't require respondents to make assumptions.

Avoid Generalizations and Estimates

Questions should always be asked in specific, rather than general, terms. Imagine that you asked purchasing agents "How many salespeople did you see last year?" To answer the question, the agent would probably estimate how many salespeople call in a typical week and would multiply this estimate by 52. Don't place this sort of burden on your respondents. Instead,

EXHIBIT 8.4

Illustration of What Can Happen If an Assumed Consequence is Made Explicit

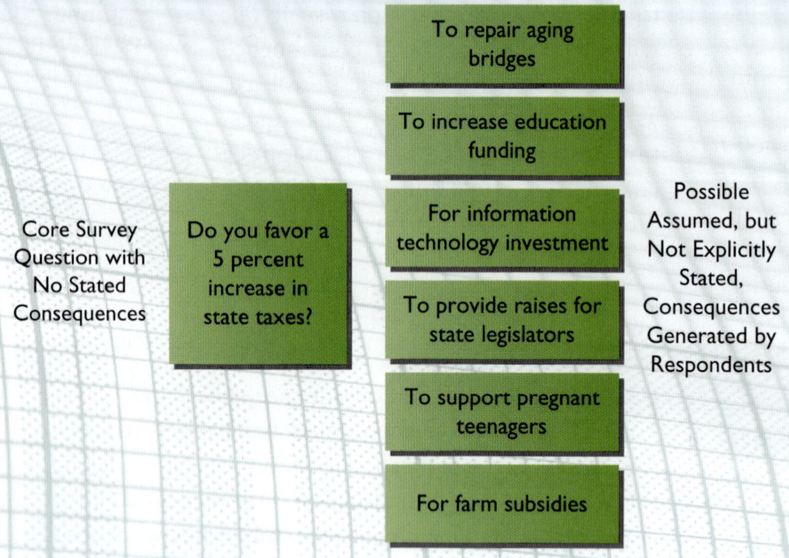

ask about a shorter time frame that won't force a respondent to provide an estimate. For this question, it would be better to ask "How many representatives have you seen in the last two weeks?" If you need an estimate for the year, you can multiply the answer by 26. The important point is to choose the appropriate time frame—and this will differ depending upon what you want to know.

Avoid Double-Barreled Questions

Try to answer the following question:

> **Think back to the last meal you purchased at a fast-food restaurant. How satisfied were you with the price and the quality of service that you received?**
>
> ☐ Very Dissatisfied
> ☐ Dissatisfied
> ☐ Neutral
> ☐ Satisfied
> ☐ Very Satisfied

Was it difficult to answer the question? Maybe not, if both the price and service quality were consistently satisfactory or unsatisfactory. But what if the service was great but the price was too high? Now how should you answer the question? With **double-barreled questions**, two questions are rolled into one, leading to confusion for respondents.

> **double-barreled question** A question that calls for two responses and creates confusion for the respondent.

Most of the time double-barreled questions are fairly easy to spot. Just look over your questionnaire closely, circling the words *and* and *or*. Finding one of these words doesn't necessarily mean you've written a double-barreled question, but it often does. Usually, a double-barreled question (or a *triple-barreled question,* for that matter) can easily be fixed by splitting the question into two or more separate questions.

Step 6: Determine Question Sequence

Once you have the questions and responses developed, you're ready to begin putting them together into a questionnaire. The order in which the questions are presented can be crucial to the success of the research effort. There are no hard-and-fast principles, but only rules of thumb to use as guides.

Use Simple and Interesting Opening Questions

The first questions asked are really important. If respondents can't answer them easily—or if they find them uninteresting or threatening in any way—they may refuse to cooperate at all. As a result, it's essential that the first few questions be simple, interesting, and nonthreatening. Questions that ask respondents for their opinions on some issue are often good openers if they help get the respondent engaged.

Use the Funnel Approach

One approach to question sequencing is the **funnel approach**, which gets its name from its shape: Start with broad questions and progressively narrow down the scope. For example, if you wanted to measure customer satisfaction, it's best to start with the overall satisfaction questions first before getting down to satisfaction with

> **funnel approach** An approach to question sequencing that gets its name from its shape, starting with broad questions and progressively narrowing down the scope.

individual attributes of the products and services provided. If you start with some of the particular attributes, the later overall satisfaction question may be strongly influenced by answers to one or more of the particular attributes selected provided. This is an example of **question order bias**, the tendency for earlier questions to affect respondents' answers to later questions. In general, the funnel approach helps prevent problems with question order bias.

question order bias
The tendency for earlier questions on a questionnaire to influence respondents' answers to later questions.

When measuring awareness, the sequence of the questions is a very important concern. Recall questions ("Which three financial institutions located in Taylorville come to mind first?") must always be asked before recognition questions ("Tell me whether or not each of the following financial institutions is located in Taylorville") if the results of the recall question are to be meaningful.

There should also be some logical order to the questions. This means that sudden changes in topics and jumping around from topic to topic should be avoided. When it's time to change the topic, most researchers simply insert a brief explanation as a way of moving to the new topic.

Design Branching Questions with Care

A direction as to where to go next in the questionnaire based on the answer to a preceding question is called a **branching question**. For example, the initial question might be, "Have you bought a car within the last six months?" If the respondent answers "yes," she is instructed to go to another place in the questionnaire, where questions are asked about specific details of the purchase. Someone replying "no" to the same question would be directed to skip the questions relating to the details of the purchase. The advantage to branching questions is that those for whom a question is irrelevant are simply directed around it.

branching question
A technique used to direct respondents to different places in a questionnaire, based on their response to the question at hand.

Through the use of computer technology, branching questions and directions are much easier to develop for telephone interviews, personal interviews, and Web-based questionnaires than they are for mail surveys. With mail questionnaires, the number of branching questions must be kept to an absolute minimum so that respondents don't become confused—or refuse to cooperate because the task becomes too difficult. If possible, it's best to place branching questions near the end of the survey so that those who need to continue do so, but those who don't are simply done with the questionnaire.

Ask for Classification Information Last

The typical questionnaire contains two types of information: basic information and classification information. *Basic information* refers to the subject of the study, for example, intentions or attitudes of respondents. *Classification information* refers to the other data we collect to classify respondents, typically for demographic breakdowns. For instance, we might be interested in determining whether a respondent's attitudes toward a new product or service are affected by the person's income. In this case, income would be a classification variable. Demographic/socioeconomic characteristics of respondents are often used as classification variables for understanding the results.

Except under rare circumstances, *basic information should be obtained first,* followed by classification information. There is a logical reason for this. The basic information is most critical. Without it, there is no study. The researcher shouldn't risk alienating the respondent by asking a number of personal questions before getting to the heart of the study. Respondents who readily offer their opinions about television programming may balk when asked about their income.

Place Difficult or Sensitive Questions Late in the Questionnaire

The basic information itself can also present some sequence problems. Some of the questions may be sensitive. Early questions should not be sensitive, for the reasons we mentioned earlier. If respondents feel threatened, they may refuse to participate in the study. Thus, sensitive questions should be placed near the end of the questionnaire. Once respondents have become involved in the study, they are less likely to react negatively or refuse to answer when delicate questions are posed.

FAST FACT:

LESS THAN 1% OF U.S. CITIZENS OVER THE AGE OF 25 HAVE A DOCTORAL DEGREE.

Step 7: Determine Physical Characteristics of Questionnaire

The physical appearance of the questionnaire can influence respondents' cooperation. This is particularly true with mail questionnaires, but it applies as well to any method in which respondents will be able to see the survey form. If the questionnaire looks sloppy, respondents are likely to feel the study is unimportant or unprofessional and refuse to cooperate no matter how important the researcher says it is. If the study is important (and why would you be conducting it if it isn't?), make the questionnaire reflect that importance. Exhibit 8.5 offers some specific suggestions that can improve the initial "look" and likely acceptance of a questionnaire. All of these apply to mail questionnaires; many apply to other methods as well.

There's one other thing to consider. Don't bother with long, drawn-out sets of instructions unless you are doing something new and different and they are absolutely necessary. Most people have completed enough surveys to know how to respond to them, so a sentence or two ought to be enough. Keep instructions simple and short.

Step 8: Develop Recruiting Message or Script

The introduction to the research can also affect acceptance of the questionnaire. With personal interviews and telephone interviews, the opening script used to recruit potential respondents is probably your only chance to secure their participation, so put some thought into what you'll say. In fact, your "script" needs to be carefully developed and pretested to ensure that it is effective in getting people to agree to participate. Then you must make certain that the people making the contacts actually follow the script. Note that it is important that the recruiters practice the script until it sounds as natural as possible; nobody likes to hear someone reading or reciting a "canned" presentation to them.

EXHIBIT 8.5

Improving the Appearance of a Questionnaire

- Use good-quality paper and a good photocopier. If you will be distributing enough questionnaires to make it cost effective, have the surveys printed rather than photocopied.
- The questionnaire must not appear to be cluttered. Don't be afraid to leave margins and other empty space on the form, because this will make the questionnaire seem less intimidating to respondents.
- Keep the questionnaire to a single page, printed on front and back, if it is possible to do so. Shorter surveys almost always achieve higher response rates than longer surveys. Even if you have to use a smaller font to keep the survey to a single page, we recommend that you do so. Use common sense, however. If your respondents are elderly and therefore more likely to have poor eyesight, don't try to use a very small font just to keep the survey on a single page. Plenty of three- to five-page surveys have been used effectively when necessary. When more than a single page is needed, make the questionnaire into a booklet rather than staple or paper-clip the pages together. It just looks better and more professional to the respondent.
- If you must use branching questions, make certain that the instructions are clear. It might even be possible to include arrows pointing from each answer on a branching question to the next question the respondent should read. Some researchers have effectively used color-coding to connect answers on a branching question to the next section to be completed.
- Use the graphics available in word processing software to improve the appearance of the survey form. Put boxes, lines, circles, shadows, shading, and so on, to good use.
- If your questionnaire will contain more than about 8 to 10 questions, try numbering the questions within sections. That is, if you had a 30-question survey, instead of numbering the questions 1 through 30, put the questions into sections and restart numbers within each section. So, the first four questions might be numbered 1-1, 1-2, 1-3, 1-4, and the next three questions numbered 2-1, 2-2, 2-3, and so on.
- Include the name of the sponsoring organization and the name of the project on the first page. Both of these lend credibility to the study. However, because awareness of the sponsoring firm may bias respondents' answers, many firms use fictitious names for the sponsoring organization.

With mail and Web-based projects, the questionnaire is typically introduced with a written message, either a cover letter or an e-mail message. Because there's no direct social connection between you and the potential respondent, the task of introducing the survey and gaining cooperation is even more difficult.

Good cover letters and scripts are rarely written in a hurry. Like the questionnaire itself, they usually require a series of painstaking rewrites to get the wording just right. The most important things to communicate are (1) who you are, (2) why you are contacting them, (3) your request for their help in providing information, (4) how long it will take, (5) that their responses will be anonymous and/or confidential (if this is true), and (6) any incentives they will receive for participating. Regardless of method of administration, the recruiting message needs to convince respondents about the importance of the research and the importance of their participation.

Step 9: Reexamine Steps 1–8 and Revise If Necessary

Never expect the first draft of the questionnaire to be the one that is ultimately used. Questionnaire development is an iterative process, even for professional researchers. Each question should be reviewed to ensure that the question is easy to answer and not confusing, ambiguous, or potentially offensive to the respondent. Questions must not be leading or likely to bias respondents' answers. How can you tell? An extremely critical attitude and good common sense should help. You need to examine each word in each question. When a potential problem is discovered, the question should be revised. After examining each question, and each word in each question, for its potential meanings and implications, test the questionnaire by having different members of the research team answer the questions, using the method of administration to be used in the actual study. Call them on the telephone, send them an e-mail, walk up and ask for their participation, or let them find the questionnaire with their mail. This sort of role playing should reveal some of the most serious shortcomings and should lead to further revision of the questionnaire.

DATA COLLECTION SHOULD NEVER BEGIN UNTIL YOU HAVE PRETESTED—AND PROBABLY REVISED AGAIN—THE QUESTIONNAIRE.

Step 10: Pretest Questionnaire and Revise If Necessary

The real test of a questionnaire is how it performs under actual conditions of data collection. For this assessment, the questionnaire **pretest** is vital. The questionnaire pretest serves the same role in questionnaire design that test marketing serves in new product development. Although the product concept, different advertising appeals, alternative packages, and so on, may all have been tested previously in the product development process, test marketing is the first place where they all come together. Similarly, the pretest provides the real test of the questionnaire and the mode of administration.

pretest
Use of a questionnaire (or observation form) on a trial basis in a small pilot study to determine how well the questionnaire (or observation form) works.

Data collection should never begin until you have pretested—and probably revised again—the questionnaire. Better yet, use two pretests. Do the first as a personal interview, no matter how you actually plan to administer the actual survey. Watch your respondents to see whether they actually remember the data requested of them or whether some questions seem confusing or produce resistance or hesitancy for whatever reason. The pretest interviews should be conducted among respondents similar to those who will be used in the actual study, by the firm's most experienced interviewers. Then make any necessary changes and do a second pretest, using the chosen method of administration for the project.

There are no strict guidelines for how many respondents to include in a pretest. We recommend using at least five people with the face-to-face pretest and probably 5 to 10 more with the actual pretest. If changes are still necessary, it will be important to make the changes and then roll in more pretest participants.

If you fail to pretest your data collection forms, you are asking for trouble. The pretest is the most inexpensive insurance you can buy to ensure the success of the questionnaire and the research project. A careful pretest along with proper attention to the dos and don'ts presented in this chapter and summarized in Exhibit 8.6 should make the questionnaire development process successful.

EXHIBIT 8.6

Questionnaire Preparation Checklist

STEP 1: SPECIFY WHAT INFORMATION WILL BE SOUGHT

- Make sure that you have a clear understanding of the issue and what it is that you want to know. Frame your research questions, but don't write the actual questions just yet.
- Write the research problem(s) you're addressing on a card and keep it in front of you. Review it often as you are working on the questionnaire.
- Use the dummy tables that were set up to guide the data analysis to suggest questions for the questionnaire.
- Conduct a search for existing questions on the issue and revise to meet your current purposes.

STEP 2: DETERMINE METHOD OF ADMINISTRATION

- Use the type of data to be collected as a basis for deciding on the type of questionnaire.
- Use the desired degree of structure and disguise to guide selection of method of administration.
- Compare your situation against the advantages and disadvantages of the different approaches.

STEP 3: DETERMINE CONTENT OF INDIVIDUAL QUESTIONS

- For each possible question, ask yourself, "Why do I want to know this?" Answer it in terms of how it will help your research. "It would be interesting to know" is not an acceptable answer.
- Make sure each question is specific and addresses only one important issue.
- Ask yourself whether the question applies to all people who receive the questionnaire; if it doesn't, either the population must be redefined, or you need a filter question and/or a branching question.
- Split questions that can be answered from different frames of reference into multiple questions, one corresponding to each frame of reference. If you don't need each frame of reference, carefully rephrase the question to provide only the perspective you need.
- Ask yourself whether respondents will be informed about, and can remember, the issue that the question is dealing with.
- Make sure the time period of the question is appropriate for the topic.
- Avoid questions that require excessive effort or that deal with sensitive (embarrassing or threatening) issues.
- If sensitive questions must be asked,
  - (a) guarantee respondent anonymity or confidentiality.
  - (b) use a counter-biasing statement.
  - (c) phrase the question in terms of others and how they might feel or act.
  - (d) put sensitive questions near the end.
  - (e) use categories or ranges rather than specific numbers.
  - (f) use the randomized-response model.

STEP 4: DETERMINE FORM OF RESPONSE TO EACH QUESTION

- Determine which type of question—open-ended or closed-ended—provides data that fit the information needs of the project.
- Use structured questions whenever possible.
- Consider using open-ended questions that require short answers to begin a questionnaire.
- Try to convert open-ended questions to fixed-response questions to reduce respondent work load and coding effort for descriptive and causal studies.
- If open-ended questions are necessary, make the questions fairly specific to give respondents a frame of reference when answering.
- Provide for "don't know" and "no opinion" responses, if these are likely to apply to a significant proportion of the population.
- When using fixed-alternative questions, be sure the choices are exhaustive and mutually exclusive.
- If multiple responses are possible, use "check all that apply" in the instructions.
- Watch out for response order bias when using closed-ended questions. Consider the use of a split-ballot procedure to reduce order bias.

- Use the highest level of measurement possible for each question unless there is a solid reason to do otherwise.

STEP 5: DETERMINE WORDING OF EACH QUESTION

- Use simple words.
- Avoid ambiguous words and questions.
- Avoid leading questions.
- Avoid unstated alternatives.
- Avoid assumed consequences.
- Avoid generalizations and estimates.
- Avoid double-barreled questions.
- Make sure each question is as specific as possible.

STEP 6: DETERMINE QUESTION SEQUENCE

- Use simple, interesting questions for openers.
- Use the funnel approach, first asking broad questions and then narrowing them down.
- Design branching questions with care.
- Ask for classification information last so that if respondent refuses, the other data are still usable.
- Ask difficult or sensitive questions late in the questionnaire, when rapport is better.
- Watch out for question order bias; use a split-ballot procedure if necessary.

STEP 7: DETERMINE PHYSICAL CHARACTERISTICS OF QUESTIONNAIRE

- Make sure the questionnaire looks professional and is relatively easy to answer.
- Use quality paper and printing.
- Attempt to make the questionnaire as short as possible while avoiding a crowded appearance; aim for a single page, printed on the back if necessary.
- Use a booklet format for ease of analysis and to prevent lost pages, if multiple pages are necessary.
- List the name of the organization conducting the survey on the first page; a fictitious name may be necessary if disguise is used.
- Number the questions to ease data processing; if there are more than about 8 to 10 questions, number within sections.
- Use concise, clear instructions, especially with branching questions.
- Use appropriate graphics to improve the appearance of the questionnaire.

STEP 8: DEVELOP RECRUITING MESSAGE OR SCRIPT

- Keep the message as brief as possible, especially with personal and telephone interview scripts, but include the following information at a minimum:
  (a) Who you are
  (b) Why you are contacting the respondent
  (c) Your request for his or her help in providing information
  (d) Approximately how long it will take to participate
  (e) That responses will be anonymous or confidential (if this is true)
  (f) Any incentives the respondent will be given
- Practice the script until it sounds natural, rather than "canned" or memorized.

STEP 9: REEXAMINE STEPS 1–8 AND REVISE IF NECESSARY

- Examine each word of every question to ensure that the question is not confusing, ambiguous, offensive, or leading.
- Have members of the research team complete the surveys using the method of administration selected.

STEP 10: PRETEST QUESTIONNAIRE AND REVISE IF NECESSARY

- Pretest the questionnaire first by personal interviews among respondents similar to those to be used in the actual study.
- Obtain comments from the interviewers and respondents to discover any problems with the questionnaire, and revise it if necessary.
- Pretest the questionnaire using the method chosen for the study.

9

Developing the Sampling Plan

POLL QUESTION:

Telephone books are a good source of potential respondents for telephone surveys.

STRONGLY DISAGREE 1 2 3 4 5 STRONGLY AGREE

Learning Objectives

1. Explain the difference between a parameter and a statistic.
2. Explain the difference between a probability sample and a nonprobability sample.
3. List the primary types of nonprobability samples.
4. List the primary types of probability samples.
5. Discuss the concept of total sampling elements (TSE).
6. Cite three factors that influence the necessary sample size.
7. Explain the relationship between population size and sample size.

INTRODUCTION

Once you've specified the problem, developed an appropriate research design, and carefully crafted your data collection instrument, it's time to think about the people (or other units) from which you'll collect data. If you collect information from or about each member of the relevant population, you are conducting a **census**. When the overall population is limited in size, it is usually smart to attempt a census, even if you can't get information from everyone.

Most of the time, however, we develop a sampling plan, the process of selecting the people or objects (i.e., companies, products, etc.) to be surveyed, interviewed, or observed. With a sampling plan, we collect information from a **sample**, or subset, of elements from the larger group, with the goal of making projections about what would be true for the population. As we'll see, the ability to make inferences about the overall population from a sample of population members depends on how we select the sample. Exhibit 9.1 lays out a six-step process for drawing a sample and collecting data.

census
A type of sampling plan in which data are collected from or about each member of a population.

sample
Selection of a subset of elements from a larger group of objects.

EXHIBIT 9.1

Six-Step Procedure for Drawing a Sample

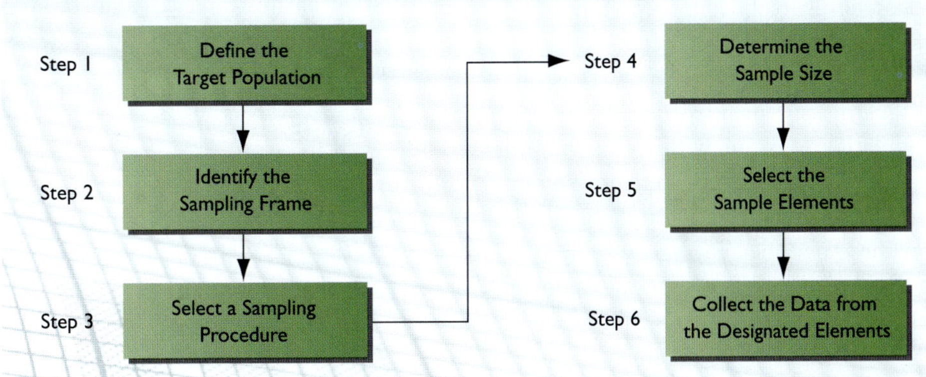

DEFINING THE TARGET POPULATION

The first step in the process outlined in Exhibit 9.1 is to define the target population. By **population**, we mean all the individuals or objects that meet certain requirements for membership in the overall group. We often refer to those who qualify as *population elements*. You must be very clear and precise in defining the population. For example, does the population consist of individuals, households, business firms, other institutions, credit card transactions, light bulbs on an assembly line, or something else? When the elements are individuals the relevant target population might be defined as all those over 18 years of age, or females only, or those with a high school education only, or those who have visited a certain restaurant within the last 30 days. The point is that you must be painfully explicit about who or what qualifies to be a member of the population.

population
All cases that meet designated specifications for membership in the group.

In general, the simpler the definition of the target population, the easier (and less costly) it will be to find the sample. Alternatively, as the number of criteria for population membership increases, so do the cost and time necessary to find them. But ease and cost don't outweigh the importance of defining the population that is relevant to your study, even if it means adding criteria. If you need the opinions of left-handed women between the ages of 65 and 75 located in Southern California, then you'll just have to find a way to locate them.

Parameters versus Statistics

Before we go on, let's revisit why we are drawing a sample in the first place. Our goal with a sample is to determine what is likely to be true for a population based on data obtained from only a subset of that population. We typically work with a sample, rather than a census, because a sample is often easier and less costly to obtain than is a census.

Any population has certain characteristics; these characteristics are called **parameters**, and we assume that if we could take measurements of these characteristics from all population elements without any kind of error getting into our data that we would know what is true about the population on these parameters. For example, suppose the population for a study consists of all adults living in Phoenix, Arizona. We could describe this population on a

parameter
A characteristic or measure of a population.

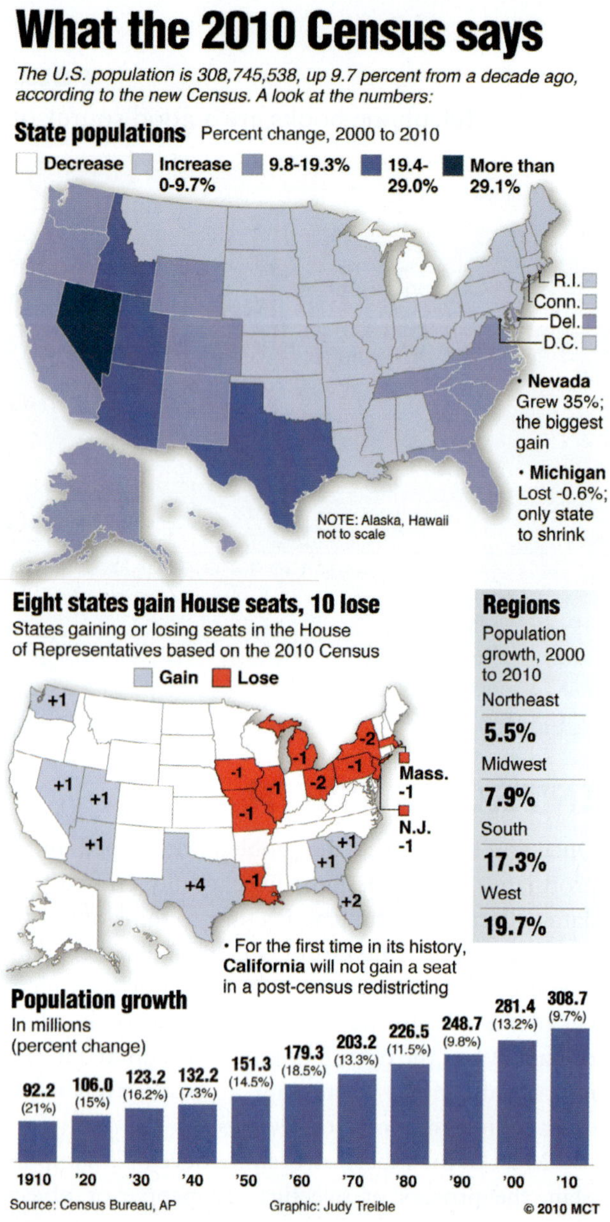

number of parameters, including average age, proportion with a college degree, range of incomes, attitude toward a new service offering, awareness of a new retail store that has just opened, and so on. Note that within

FAST FACT:

17% OF U.S. ADULTS HAVE **BUMPED INTO AN OBJECT** OR OTHER PERSON WHILE **TALKING OR TEXTING** ON A MOBILE TELEPHONE.

the population, there is a real quantity or value for each of these parameters, even though we'll never know for sure what these true values are (because as a practical matter, we can never measure something without error).

When we work with a sample drawn from a population, we are attempting to describe the population parameters based on the measures we take from the sample members. That is, we calculate the average age, range of income, or awareness level for the sample as a means of gaining insights into what likely would be true for the population. In short, we work with **statistics**, which are characteristics or measures of a sample, to draw inferences about the larger population's parameters. When we work with a sample instead of a census, it is likely that our results will be at least a little different than they would have been had we gathered information from every member of the population. This difference is known as **sampling error**.

statistic
A characteristic or measure of a sample.

sampling error
The difference between results obtained from a sample and results that would have been obtained had information been gathered from or about every member of the population.

How big a problem is sampling error? Well, it's something that you'll want to take into account, but unless you're working with a really small sample, it's probably not as much a problem as are other kinds of errors. Fortunately, you can estimate sampling error fairly easily—provided that you've drawn the right kind of sample. We'll get to this shortly.

sampling frame
The list of population elements from which a sample will be drawn; the list could consist of geographic areas, institutions, individuals, or other units.

IDENTIFYING THE SAMPLING FRAME

Once you've carefully defined the population, the next step is to find an adequate **sampling frame**, a listing of population elements from which you'll draw the

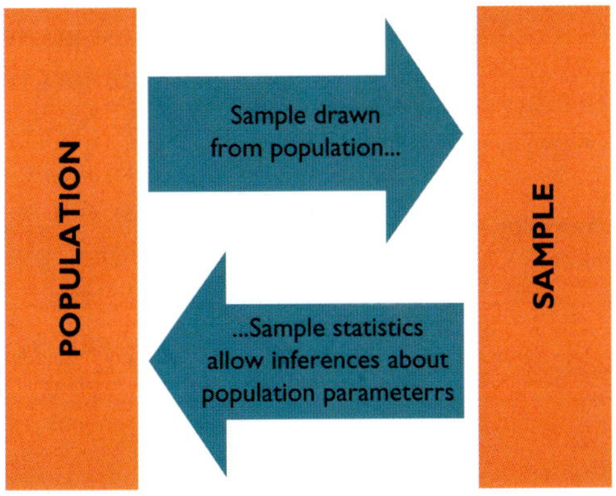

sample. Suppose that the target population for a telephone survey is all the households in the metropolitan Dallas area. Your first thought will probably be to use the Dallas phone book as your sampling frame. When you examine it a little more closely, however, you'll realize that there are problems with this approach: those with unlisted numbers or who only use cell phones or who have recently moved into the area won't be included; there are some people with multiple numbers listed; and there are some people who are included on the list, but no longer live in the area. One way around this problem is the use of random-digit dialing, as we discussed in an earlier chapter. Still, there will be situations in which the telephone directory is the best available choice.

Unfortunately, perfect sampling frames usually don't exist except in unusual circumstances. That makes developing an acceptable sampling frame one of your most important and creative tasks. For instance, trying to survey individuals who have visited a specific fast food restaurant in the last 60 days is very challenging. No directory exists of this group. Thus, the sampling frame is used like a fisherman uses a large net. Not every fish caught will be kept but casting a wide net is necessary to find qualified individuals.

Sometimes you'll work with sampling frames that have been developed by companies that specialize in

infoUSA CALLS EACH BUSINESS IN ITS DATABASE TO VERIFY THE ACCURACY OF INFORMATION.

compiling databases and then selling the names, addresses, phone numbers, and/or e-mail addresses. For example, infoUSA, a database company located in Omaha, Nebraska, employs over 600 data compilers who gather information from a broad range of sources. Its list of millions of businesses is updated regularly based on telephone directory listings, annual reports, government data, the business press, and other sources. The company calls each business in its database to verify the accuracy of the information. As a result, you can easily develop a sampling frame for a fairly specific population of businesses based on the variables coded in the company's database.

SELECTING A SAMPLING PROCEDURE

Unless you've decided to attempt a census (which, again, is probably a good idea if your population is relatively small), your next task is to choose a particular sampling procedure. Because your client will be interested in what would likely be true for the whole population, rather than just the sample, it's important to draw the right kind of sample. Sampling techniques can be divided into two broad categories: probability and nonprobability samples. Exhibit 9.2 shows the basic types of samples.

nonprobability sample
A sample that relies on personal judgment in the element selection process.

Nonprobability Samples

Nonprobability samples involve personal judgment somewhere in the selection process. Not all elements have an opportunity to be included so we can't estimate the probability that any particular element will be included in the sample. As a result, it's impossible to assess the degree of sampling error. And that means that we can't say anything at all about what would have been true for the overall population—we're stuck with sample statistics and don't know whether they apply to the population as a whole. Managers may still choose to use the results from nonprobability samples, but they are taking risks when they do so. Foremost among these risks is attempting to apply the outcomes of the research to the population in total. This is not advisable as we can only talk about the sample, not the population.

WITH NONPROBABILITY SAMPLES, WE'RE STUCK WITH SAMPLE STATISTICS AND DON'T KNOW WHETHER THEY APPLY TO THE POPULATION AS A WHOLE.

Three common types of nonprobability samples are convenience samples, judgment samples, and quota samples.

Convenience Samples With **convenience samples**, the name says it all: Being included in the sample is a matter of convenience. People or objects are selected for the sample because they happen to be in the right place at the right time to be included. Convenience samples are easy—just go out and find a location where lots of people who are likely to be members of the population are located and do interviews or pass out surveys. Lots of organizations put surveys on Web sites so that people who visit the sites can respond electronically—but what about

convenience sample
A nonprobability sample in which population elements are included in the sample because they were readily available.

EXHIBIT 9.2
Classification of Sampling Techniques

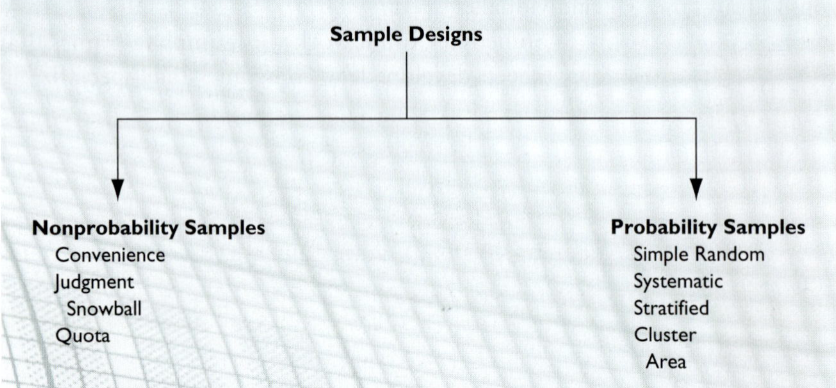

people who don't visit the Web site? Still, sometimes convenience samples are just fine. For instance, convenience samples are commonly used with exploratory research, where the goal is to generate insights or to develop hypotheses.

Problems arise, however, when people begin to draw important conclusions based on data from convenience samples. The main problem is that we have no way of knowing if those included in a convenience sample are representative of the larger target population. As a simple example, passing out surveys to passersby at the corner of Manvel Avenue and Tenth Street in a certain city during business hours on a Tuesday means that anyone who happened *not* to be at that corner during that time period had no chance of participating. It's very likely that important points of view may have been missed.

Judgment Samples

With **judgment samples**, the sample elements are handpicked by the researcher because she believes that they can serve the research purpose. Procter & Gamble (P&G) used this method once when it advertised for interns ages 13 to 17 from the area around its Cincinnati headquarters. The company selected a group of teenagers to serve as a kind of consumer panel. Working 10 hours a week in exchange for $1,000 and a trip to a concert, they reviewed television commercials, visited the mall with P&G managers to study retail displays, tested new products, and discussed their purchasing behavior. By selecting the panel members through a hiring process rather than randomly, the company could focus on traits it considered helpful—for example, the teenagers' ability to articulate their views clearly—at the risk that their views might not be representative of their age group.[1]

judgment sample
A nonprobability sample in which the sample elements are handpicked because they are expected to serve the research purpose.

snowball sample
A judgment sample that relies on the researcher's ability to locate an initial set of respondents with the desired characteristics.

A **snowball sample** is a judgment sample that is sometimes used to sample special populations, in particular populations that are difficult to find and identify. This type of judgment sample relies on the researcher's ability to locate an initial set of respondents with the desired characteristics. These individuals are then asked to help identify others with the desired characteristics.

As long as the researcher is at the early stages of research when ideas or insights are being sought—and when the researcher realizes its limitations—the judgment sample is perfectly appropriate. In some cases, it may be about the only way to develop a sample of people who meet specific criteria that don't occur frequently and/or cannot easily be observed. A judgment sample becomes dangerous, however, when it is used in descriptive or causal studies and its weaknesses are ignored.

FAST FACT:
25% OF TEENAGERS HAVE USED **EMOTICONS** IN THEIR SCHOOL WORK.

Quota Samples

Researchers sometimes use a **quota sample** that mirrors the population on one or more important aspects. For example, if you are asked to draw a quota sample of 1,000 undergraduate students, you'll make sure that your sample contains the right proportions of freshmen, sophomores, juniors, and seniors. You might also want to ensure that you have the right proportions of men and women in the sample, or maybe you'd want to have the right proportions of students from the various colleges or majors across campus. The goal would be to build a sample that looks like the larger population of students. And once you've identified the kinds of students that you need—that is, you've developed a quota for different types of people to be included—you're ready to go.

quota sample
A nonprobability sample chosen so that the proportion of sample elements with certain characteristics is about the same as the proportion of the elements with the characteristics in the target population.

Many online panels in use today are essentially large quota samples. The better panels are constructed by asking a potential panel member to opt in, and then comparing his data against U.S. Census demographic characteristics. These panels are widely used in both consumer and business research and often contain millions of panel members.

Note, however, that the specific sample elements to be used in a quota sample are left to the discretion of the researcher. That's what makes a quota sample a nonprobability sampling plan. And even though the resulting sample *looks* like the overall population on key aspects, it may not accurately reflect other aspects of the population.

Probability Samples

probability sample
A sample in which each target population element has a known, nonzero chance of being included in the sample.

In a **probability sample**, each member of the target population has a *known, nonzero* chance of being included in the sample. The chances of each member of the target population being included in the sample may not be equal, but everyone has some chance of being included. Plus, there is a random component in how population elements are selected for the sample to ensure that they are selected objectively and not according to the whims of the researcher or fieldworker. Because of this objectivity, we can make inferences to the larger population based on the results from the sample and estimate the likely amount of sampling error.

Probability samples depend on the sampling distribution of the particular statistic being considered for the ability to draw inferences about the larger population. That is, we'll be able to project the range within which the population parameter is likely to fall in the population based on the sample statistic. (This range is known as the *confidence interval;* we'll discuss the calculation of confidence intervals later on in the book.) In this section, we'll introduce several different types of probability samples.

Simple Random Samples

simple random sample
A probability sampling plan in which each unit included in the population has a known and equal chance of being selected for the sample.

Most people have had experience with **simple random samples** either in beginning statistics courses or in reading about results from such samples in newspapers or magazines. In a simple random sample, each unit included in the sample has a known and equal chance of being selected for study, and every combination of population elements is a sample possibility. For example, if we wanted a simple random sample of all students enrolled in a particular college, we might have a computer pick a sample randomly from a list of students in that college.

FAST FACT:

7% OF THE WORLD'S POPULATION HAS A **COLLEGE DEGREE.**

Drawing a simple random sample depends mainly on having a good sampling frame. For some populations, this isn't a problem—a list of population members is readily available. For many target populations, however, a list of population elements simply doesn't exist, and you'll need to resort to other sampling methods. If the population is moderate to large in size, you'll normally use a computer to randomly select the sample from the sampling frame, so having a digital version of the sampling frame is a real advantage.

Systematic Samples

Suppose you were asked to conduct telephone interviews with 250 college students at a particular school and that the university published a directory that contained the names and telephone numbers of all 5,000 of its students. If you had access to a computer file containing the information, it would be a relatively easy matter to draw a simple random sample from the list. If you don't have such a computer file, however, drawing a simple random sample isn't so simple. It is difficult to randomly select each sample member.

systematic sample
A probability sampling plan in which every *k*th element in the population is selected for the sample pool after a random start.

A **systematic sample** offers an easy, but very effective, solution in situations like this. With a systematic sample, you'll randomly select the first population element to be included in the sample and then select every *k*th element following it in the sampling frame. In our example, let's assume for a moment that we'll be able to interview all 250 college students who are selected for the sample. We'll end up interviewing one out of every 20 students on campus (5,000/250 = 20). So, you would randomly select one of the first 20 names in the student directory, then count down 20 names on the list and select that name, count down 20 more names and select that name, and so on, until you have gone through the entire directory. (It may not sound like it, but this is *much* easier than trying to randomly select each member of the sample by hand.)

So what makes this a probabilistic sampling plan? It's because the first element is randomly selected, and every other element selected for the sample is a function of the first element, which makes them all randomly selected, in effect.

sampling interval
The number of population elements to count (*K*) when selecting the sample members in a systematic sample.

Calculating the **sampling interval** (i.e., *k*, the number of names to count when selecting the sample members) is easy—sort of. In general, we simply divide the number of population elements in the sampling frame by the number of elements that we need to draw to obtain the sample size we want. In the example above, $k = 5{,}000/250$, so our sampling interval was 20. Here's where it gets a little tricky, though. Remember how we assumed that we could conduct telephone interviews with all 250 students selected for the sample? For lots of reasons, it almost never works out that way.

If we selected only 250 students for our sample, it is almost a certainty that we'll end up with fewer than 250 respondents—maybe a whole lot fewer. Why? Some people won't be home to answer their telephones, even if we try multiple times to reach them. Others will have changed telephone numbers since the directory was published. A few people will refuse to answer our questions because they are too busy or just don't care to help. As a result, in almost all cases we need to start with a larger number of population elements in our initial sample pool in order to end up with the desired sample size. We refer to the total number of elements to be selected for inclusion in the initial sample pool as **total sampling elements (TSE)**.

total sampling elements (TSE)
The number of population elements that must be drawn from the population and included in the initial sample pool in order to end up with the desired sample size.

The notion of TSE is general and applies to any type of sample, not just systematic samples. Anytime it is necessary to select a larger initial sample in order to reach the necessary sample size, the calculation of TSE becomes important. Calculating TSE typically requires making predictions about the proportion of sample elements that (1) have incorrect contact information (telephone number, e-mail address, or mailing address); (2) are ineligible because they don't meet criteria for inclusion in the sample; (3) refuse to participate; and (4) cannot be contacted, even after multiple tries.

THE NOTION OF TSE IS GENERAL AND APPLIES TO ANY TYPE OF SAMPLE, NOT JUST SYSTEMATIC SAMPLES. ANYTIME IT IS NECESSARY TO SELECT A LARGER INITIAL SAMPLE IN ORDER TO REACH THE NECESSARY SAMPLE SIZE, THE CALCULATION OF TSE BECOMES IMPORTANT.

The formula for TSE looks like this:

$$\text{total sampling elements } (TSE) = \frac{\text{sample size}}{(1 - BCI)(1 - I)(1 - R)(1 - NC)}$$

where BCI = estimated proportion of bad contact information (wrong telephone numbers, mailing or e-mail addresses), I = estimated proportion of ineligible elements in the sampling frame (i.e., people or entities that don't meet the criteria to be population members but were included in the sampling frame anyway), R = estimated proportion of refusals, and NC = estimated proportion of elements that cannot be contacted after repeated attempts.

Returning to the current problem, we need a sample of 250 respondents from the 5,000 students in the directory. Even if the directory is updated annually, we should assume that some of the telephone numbers won't be working, because some people may have left school and others will have changed telephone numbers. Let's assume that percentage is 15 percent; thus, $BCI = 0.15$ Because some of the people who left school (and are no longer eligible to be included in the population) might still have working telephone numbers, we also need to include an ineligibility proportion. That proportion is likely to be low, however, so we'll set it at 2 percent ($I = 0.02$). Refusal rates aren't typically all that high, but we want to be conservative to ensure that we end up with at least 250 respondents, so we'll set the refusal rate at 20 percent ($R = 0.20$). Finally, and this is often the biggest issue of all—we'll assume that we won't be able to reach 30 percent of the people selected for the sample; thus, $NC = 0.30$. Putting it all together, we need to draw a total of 536 students from the population in order to obtain a sample size of 250:

$$\text{total sampling elements } (TSE) = \frac{250}{(1 - 0.15)(1 - 0.02)(1 - 0.20)(1 - 0.30)} = 536$$

FAST FACT:
THAILAND HAS THE HIGHEST PERCENTAGE OF FEMALE ENTREPRENEURS, AT **45%.** THE **U.S.** RANKED 16TH, WITH **11%.**

Once we know how many elements we need to draw from the population, it's a simple matter to determine the sampling interval:

$$\text{sampling interval} = \frac{\text{number of elements in the sampling frame}}{\text{total sampling elements}} = \frac{5{,}000}{536} = 9.3$$

To draw the sample, you would randomly select one of the first 9 names in the directory, maybe using a random-number generator on a computer or even something as simple as pulling a number out of a hat. Once that name is selected, you'll draw every ninth name following the first one. Because drawing every ninth name will result in a list of 556 students instead of the 536 that you want, you might choose to count down 9 names to get the second sample element and another 9 names to get the third sample element—and then count down 10 names to get the fourth. It doesn't matter, provided that you follow the same pattern throughout the whole sampling frame (i.e., down 9, down 9, down 10, down 9, down 9, down 10, and so on); each name after the first is still a function of the position of the randomly selected first sample element.

Stratified Samples

Our goal in drawing a probabilistic sample from a population is to describe the population's characteristics, or parameters, based on statistics calculated from the sample. Stratified samples sometimes allow researchers to do this more efficiently. A **stratified sample** is a probability sample in which (1) the population is divided into mutually exclusive and exhaustive subgroups (i.e., each population element fits into one—and only one—subgroup) and (2) samples are chosen from each of the subgroups.

stratified sample
A probability sample in which (1) the population is divided into mutually exclusive and exhaustive subsets, and (2) a simple random sample of elements is chosen independently from each group or subset.

Stratified samples take advantage of the fact that, all else equal, smaller samples are required to estimate a population parameter if there is little variation on the characteristic in the group being sampled. (If everyone's opinion is exactly the same about some issue, we only need to ask one person to be able to project to the population.) So, if we can find a way to group together population elements that are similar on some characteristic we're trying to study, we can be more efficient by drawing a smaller sample within that subgroup. We can use the extra efficiency in a couple of ways, either by increasing sample size in subgroups that have greater variation on the characteristic to get greater precision or confidence (we'll discuss these notions later) or by saving money thanks to the overall lower sample size.

To make this work, you'll have to be able to group population elements that are likely to be similar to one another on the parameter of interest into subgroups. That is, the subgroups should be *homogenous within* the groups. Once the subgroups have been formed, samples are taken from each of them so that all subgroups are represented in the final sample.

There is one other reason that stratified samples might be used, and this has more to do with effectiveness than efficiency. Sometimes it is necessary to work with stratified samples as a means of ensuring that particular categories of respondents are included in the final sample. Suppose, for example, that a manufacturer of diamond rings wants to conduct a study of sales of the product by social class. Unless special precautions are taken, it is possible that the upper class—which represents only about 3 percent of the total population—will not be represented at all, or will be represented by too few cases. Yet this may be an extremely important segment to the ring manufacturer. Stratified sampling is one way of ensuring adequate representation from each subgroup of interest.

Cluster Samples

Sometimes researchers use **cluster samples**, another type of probability sampling. Cluster sampling is similar to stratified sampling in that the population is divided into mutually exclusive and exhaustive subgroups, but the similarities stop there. With cluster sampling, you'll randomly select one or more subgroups, and then either select all the elements included in those subgroups for the sample *(one-stage cluster sampling)* or a

cluster sample
A probability sampling plan in which (1) the parent population is divided into mutually exclusive and exhaustive subsets, and (2) a random sample of one or more subsets (clusters) is selected.

probabilistic sample of elements from the randomly selected subgroups for the sample *(two-stage cluster sampling)*.

Notice the difference here. With stratified sampling, a sample of elements is selected from each subgroup, but with cluster sampling a sample is selected only from the randomly selected subgroups. Because of this, it is important that each cluster reflect the diversity of the whole population. The goal with cluster sampling is thus to have clusters that are as heterogeneous as possible on the key issues. That way, no matter which cluster(s) are randomly selected, the full range is represented. (Recall that we wanted the subgroups to be as homogeneous within each subgroup as possible with stratified sampling.)

area sample
A form of cluster sampling in which areas (e.g., census tracts, blocks) serve as the primary sampling units. Using maps, the population is divided into mutually exclusive and exhaustive areas, and a random sample of areas is selected.

An **area sample** is a special form of cluster sample in which geographic areas (city blocks, neighborhoods, housing additions, etc.) serve as the clusters. With area samples, you'll randomly select one or more geographic clusters and then take population elements from these clusters for the sample. This approach is particularly useful when no good sampling frame is available. Suppose, for example, that you needed to draw a sample of households in Chicago, Illinois. One approach would be to identify the residential areas throughout the city and then draw a sample of these areas. The next step would be to contact a probabilistic sample (two-stage sampling) or all (one-stage sampling) of the households in the selected areas, maybe by knocking on doors, gathering addresses for mail surveys, or some other method. The difficulty with area samples is that the people who live in the same area often share many characteristics. As a result, the area clusters often don't represent the full variability on important parameters that we'd like to see. Still, unless the degree of homogeneity is very high within areas, we can often reduce (but not eliminate) the problem by drawing from a larger number of clusters.

DETERMINING HOW BIG A SAMPLE YOU NEED

The next step of the process is to determine the necessary sample size for your study. You might be tempted to assume that the sample should be as large as the client can afford, but there's more to it than that—and in many cases the advantages of a larger sample (i.e., lowered sampling error) don't outweigh the costs of gathering it.

Computer programs are routinely used to calculate the needed sample size in a given situation, so we'll avoid specific formulas in this section. It's important, however, that you understand the simple factors that influence the size of sample needed.

Basic Considerations in Determining Sample Size

Three basic factors affect the size of sample needed when working with a probabilistic sample. The first of these, the amount of diversity or variation of the parameter in question within the population, is beyond your control. As we noted earlier, when there is very little variation across elements on some characteristic, it doesn't take a very large sample to estimate the value of that characteristic. As variation increases, larger samples are required, all else equal.

A second consideration is how precise the estimate must be—this depends on the importance of the issue. For example, suppose that you were asked to develop a profile of the "average" diner in a particular restaurant. One thing the client will probably want to know is the mean income of the restaurant's diners. Should your estimate be within $100, high or low, of the true population value? Or can you get by with a less precise estimate—say, within $500 or $1,000 of the true value? The closer we need the estimate to be to the true value in the population (i.e., the more **precision** we need), the larger the sample that will be required, all else equal.

precision
The degree of error in an estimate of a population parameter.

The other factor that affects sample size is the degree of confidence you'd like to have in the estimate. By **confidence**, we mean the degree of certainty that the true value of the parameter that we are estimating falls within the precision range that we have established. For example, suppose that you have decided that in describing the average diner in the restaurant, an acceptable precision range for mean income is ±$500 and that the mean income in the sample is $45,300. Does mean income *necessarily* fall between $44,800 and $45,800 in the population? No, it doesn't. Because we are working with the sampling distribution of sample means, however, we can have a certain level of confidence that the population parameter does fall within the precision range that we have established. How much confidence? With a given precision range, the amount of confidence is directly related to the size of the sample. The bigger the sample, the more certain we can be that the true value in the population falls within the precision range, which is calculated based on the sample estimate.

confidence
The degree to which one can feel confident that an estimate approximates the true value.

At any given sample size, there is a trade-off between degree of confidence and degree of precision. Higher precision means lower confidence unless we can increase the sample size. As a result, the desire for precision and confidence must be balanced.

In sum, in order to determine the necessary sample size you need three basic pieces of information: (1) how homogeneous or similar the population is on the characteristic to be estimated, (2) how much precision is needed in the estimate, and (3) how confident you need to be that the true value falls within the precision range you've established. Increases in desired precision, confidence, or the variation of the characteristic in the population lead to increases in the necessary sample size. Armed with this information, it is relatively easy to calculate a precise sample size, using a computer program.

Multiple Estimates in a Single Project

You might have noticed that our discussion of precision, confidence, and variation referred to determining sample size for a single parameter. Most projects, however, ask questions about lots of characteristics, not just a single one. A natural question, then, is "How do I calculate sample size if I'm asking more than one question on a survey?"

Because sample size is calculated based on individual items, you will usually end up with different sample size requirements for many of the items when you are measuring multiple characteristics in a study. Somehow you'll have to come up with an overall sample size for the project. The best approach is to focus on the variables that are most critical and select a sample that is big enough to estimate them with the required precision and confidence.

Population Size and Sample Size

You may not have noticed it before, but so far we haven't talked at all about the size of the population as we've discussed determining the necessary sample size. It may seem odd, but the size of the population has no direct effect on the size of the sample (with one exception that we'll discuss shortly).

As we've noted before, if all population elements have exactly the same value of the characteristic, then a sample of 1 is all that is needed to represent the population. And this is true whether there are 1,000, 10,000, or 100,000 elements in the population. As a result, it is desired precision, confidence, and variation of the characteristic in the population that drive sample size, not the size of the population itself. Many managers have a hard time accepting this, because it isn't intuitive.

The exception to this rule occurs when the calculated sample size is more than about 5 to 10 percent of the population. In this case, the calculated sample size can safely be reduced using the finite population correction factor. If, for example, the population contained 100 elements and you needed a sample of 20 elements, fewer than 20 observations would, in fact, be taken if the finite population correction factor were used. The good news is that computer programs can also handle this calculation in practice.

Other Approaches to Determining Sample Size

So far, we've taken a statistical approach to calculating sample size. Researchers and companies often use other approaches to determine sample size. We'll discuss a few of these in this section.

Marketing research can be an expensive proposition. For the most part, data collection is a variable cost; the bigger the sample size, the greater the cost. Because it takes about the same amount of money to design a data collection form for a project with 100 respondents as it does for a project with 10,000 respondents, when the research budget is limited, sample size is often a function of the amount of money "left over" after taking other research costs into consideration. So, one common method of determining sample size, unfortunately, is to take the remaining budget and divide by the expected cost per contact of the method of administration.

Another consideration is the type of analysis to be conducted on the data. One very common type of analysis (cross-tab analysis) requires that a minimum number of respondents (say, 10–20) fall into each of the different categories based on the variables used in the analysis (this will make more sense once you've read the analysis chapters). As a result, the sample size must be big enough to ensure that the minimum requirements are met for the particular type of analysis to be conducted.

One final method used by some researchers to determine the size of the sample is to use the size that others have used for similar studies in the past. Although this may be different from the ideal size in a given problem, the fact that the sample size is in line with that used for similar studies is psychologically comforting, particularly to inexperienced researchers. One of us once had a client who had just taken a marketing research position with an organization. When asked about the sample size that she had selected on a particular project, the client responded with a particular number of mail surveys that were going to be sent. When asked how she had arrived at that number, she said "because we always send out that many." Many companies operate in a similar fashion.

Using history as a guide might not be a bad strategy. At some point in time, someone may have determined that a certain number of mail surveys sent will deliver enough confidence and precision for the types of assessment needed by the client company. Until things change—more confidence or precision is needed, response rates decrease significantly, or a parameter with much wider variation in the population is estimated—the necessary sample size probably won't change much.

10 Data Collection:

Enhancing Response Rates while Limiting Errors

POLL QUESTION:

A well-written survey can enhance response rates.

STRONGLY DISAGREE 1 2 3 4 5 STRONGLY AGREE

Learning Objectives

1. Describe the five types of error that can enter a study.
2. Give the general definition for response rate.
3. Discuss several ways in which response rates might be improved.

INTRODUCTION

Once you've developed data collection forms and a sampling plan, it's time to collect the data. In this chapter, we focus on the different kinds of error that can enter a project at this point. We'll also show you how to calculate the response rate for a study, an important consideration for assessing the overall quality of the data collection effort. Finally, we offer several suggestions for improving response rates.

EXHIBIT 10.1

Five Types of Error

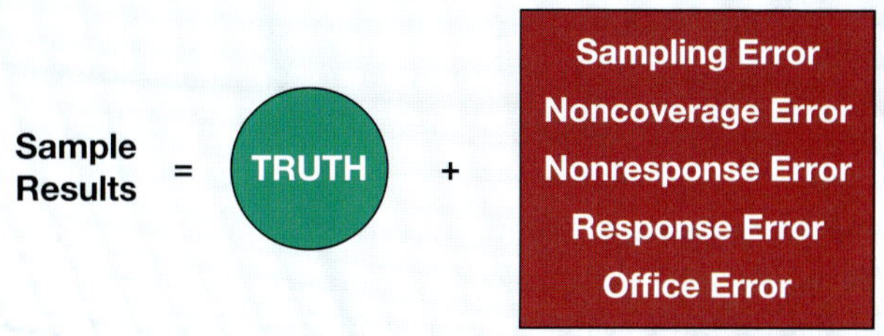

TYPES OF ERROR

Exhibit 10.1 presents the different types of error that can enter a project and illustrates how they can bias results away from the truth about a population. You'll notice that this illustration is similar to one we showed you earlier in which an individual's response to a survey item is a combination of truth, systematic error, and random error. Exhibit 10.1, however, shows that the results of a study based on a sample are a combination of truth, sampling error, noncoverage error, nonresponse error, response error, and office error.

Sampling Error

We've already mentioned one kind of error—sampling error—that affects projects that rely on samples drawn from a population. Recall that sampling error is the difference between results obtained for a sample and the results we would have obtained had we gathered information from the whole population. Sampling error often is less troubling than the other sorts of errors that can find their way into your study—there are easy ways to reduce it (increase the sample size) or account for it statistically (calculate the margin of sampling error). If you don't use a probability sampling technique, it is impossible to estimate the degree of sampling error.

As an example of the impact of sampling error versus other kinds of errors, consider how a random sample of consumers might respond to the following question on a survey: "On average, how many times per week do you brush your teeth?" Suppose that the mean response was 21 brushings per week. Further, we could be 95 percent confident that had we talked with all consumers in the population, the answer would fall between 19 and 23. In our analysis, we have fully accounted for possible sampling error. That doesn't really buy us all that much, however, because many of our respondents probably overstated their brushing behavior in order to be seen as socially acceptable. Estimating sampling error can't correct for errors caused by the questions themselves, the manner in which they were asked, or a host of other factors.

So, if sampling error isn't really that big of a deal, what kinds of errors should you be watching for? We'll talk about those next. Unfortunately, the other kinds of errors aren't as manageable as sampling errors. They don't necessarily decrease with increases in sample size and may, in fact, increase. And in many cases, it's difficult to even estimate the size and effects of these errors.

Noncoverage Error

Noncoverage error arises when we fail to include qualified elements of our defined population in the sampling frame. That is, one or more consumers, households, and so on, which met the criteria for membership in the population, weren't included in the list of population members—and thus they had no chance of being included in the sample. Noncoverage error, then, is essentially a sampling frame problem.

noncoverage error
Error due to the failure to include some elements of the defined target population in the sampling frame.

It is common to conduct projects with populations for which no lists of members exist. In these cases, one of your key tasks is to develop a reasonable sampling frame so that the project can proceed ... and most of the time it's going to be nearly impossible to get it completely right. Even if a list of population members is available, it is often dated and inaccurate (take the telephone directory as a sampling frame for households in an area, for instance). As a result, noncoverage error enters the project.

Noncoverage error isn't a problem in every survey. For some studies, clear, convenient, and complete sampling frames exist. For example, a furniture store that wants to survey its past customers should have little trouble with noncoverage error, assuming that it kept accurate records. Still, accurate sampling frames seem to be the exception.

FAST FACT:

31% OF 9TH–12TH GRADE STUDENTS REPORTED HAVING BEEN IN A **PHYSICAL FIGHT** AT LEAST ONCE IN THE LAST 12 MONTHS.

Given that noncoverage bias is likely, how can you reduce its effect? The most obvious step is to improve the quality of the sampling frame. This may mean taking the time to bring available city maps up to date (for area samples), or taking a sample to check the quality and representativeness of a mailing list with respect to a target population. Telephone surveys can take advantage of computerized dialing approaches to handle unlisted numbers, but this won't help with households that don't have phones.

Nonresponse Error

Nonresponse error can occur when you fail to obtain information from elements of the population that were selected for the sample. Suppose that five years from now a university were to conduct a survey among this year's senior class to determine how "successful" the school's graduates were based on their current salary. Who would be most likely to respond to the survey? Probably those who were pleased with their salaries. Who would be least likely? Probably those who were not happy with their salaries. As a result, those who responded to the survey would likely be systematically different from those who didn't respond, and the results would be biased upward. This upward bias reflects nonresponse error.

nonresponse error
Error from failing to obtain information from some elements of the population that were selected and designated for the sample.

Nonresponse error is a potential problem in any project for which data are not collected from all respondents selected for the sample. It is a *potential* problem, because it only occurs when those who respond are systematically different in some important way from those who do not respond. The degree of nonresponse error, however, is difficult to assess because we obviously don't have answers from those who didn't respond.

The two main sources of nonresponse bias are refusals, which apply to projects using all forms of data collection, and not-at-homes, which apply mainly to telephone surveys and some types of personal interviews. In almost every study, some respondents will refuse to participate. The rate of **refusals** depends on many factors. Different methods typically produce different response rates. All else equal, personal interviews seem to be most effective, and mail and Web-based questionnaires least effective, in generating responses. Telephone survey response rates usually fall somewhere in between. The most obvious reason for the superiority of personal interviews and telephone surveys over other methods is the social nature of the contact: A respondent doesn't run the risk of hurting someone's feelings by deleting an e-mail message or throwing a mail survey in a trash can.

refusals
Nonresponse error resulting because some designated respondents refuse to participate in the study.

In general, there is a tendency for females, nonwhites, those who are less well educated, those who have lower incomes, and those who are older to be more likely to refuse to participate in a study.[1] Cultural factors can also make a difference; for example, in some cultures like Saudi Arabia, it is difficult to interview women. Some additional reasons for refusing to participate in a survey include lack of time, contacting respondents at an inappropriate time, and lack of interest in the subject matter. Interviewers themselves can have a significant impact on the number of refusals they obtain. Their approach, manner, and even their own demographic characteristics can affect a respondent's willingness to participate.

Not-at-homes present a different sort of problem. Sometimes we simply can't reach some of the designated sampling units at home during the data collection time frame. The probability of finding someone home traditionally has been greater for low-income families, rural families, and families with younger children. Seasonal variations, particularly during the holidays, occur, as do weekday-to-weekend variations. And technological advancements have made the not-at-home problem even worse, especially with telephone surveys. As answering machines have become more prevalent in households, more and more people are using them to screen their calls. A substantial portion of households—not to mention individuals with cell phones—use caller ID, a technique for identifying the source of an incoming telephone call, to screen calls. Many people ignore calls coming from sources they do not recognize. As the movement from land-phone to cell-phone-only homes continues to grow, this challenge will only intensify.

not-at-homes
Nonresponse error that arises when respondents are not at home when the interviewer calls.

Because the not-at-home problem is serious, you'll definitely want to use *callbacks*, in which you'll attempt to reach people selected for the sample by calling them back on different days and times. The nonresponse problem due to not-at-homes is so important to the accuracy of most surveys that experts have been suggesting for many years that small samples with multiple callbacks are better than large

FAST FACT:

ACCORDING TO A REPORT BY THE U.S. CENSUS BUREAU, A COLLEGE MASTER'S DEGREE IS WORTH **$1.3 MILLION** MORE IN LIFETIME EARNINGS THAN A HIGH SCHOOL DIPLOMA.

samples without callbacks, unless the percentage of initial response can be increased considerably above normal levels.[2]

This is an important general point, so we'll repeat it: It is usually better to work hard at generating responses from a smaller sampling pool (i.e., lower TSE) and perhaps end up with a smaller sample than to start with a (much) larger sampling pool and obtain a larger sample without concern for obtaining feedback from nonrespondents. Beware of any data collection tool that offers thousands of respondents but must send surveys to millions of people to accomplish it. Unless the 98 percent who do not respond are the same as the 2 percent who do respond on the key issues, the risk of nonresponse error is too high.

Response Error

Response error occurs when an individual provides a response to an item, but the response is inaccurate for some reason. There are many factors that can cause response error, ranging from poorly written items that respondents misinterpret, to characteristics of the respondent that subconsciously influence his or her responses, to a variety of other things. The responsibility for response errors can lie with the researcher, the respondent, or both.

response error
Error that occurs when an individual provides an inaccurate response, consciously or subconsciously, to a survey item.

The following questions are useful for considering the different ways response errors can affect individuals' responses.[3] These questions might also be used to anticipate possible problems when developing questionnaire items in the first place.

Does the respondent understand the question?

As we mentioned in Chapter 8, survey items must be written using simple, direct language, especially when a general audience is being surveyed. If respondents don't understand a question, one of two things is likely to happen: They will either skip the question, leading to potential nonresponse error, or they will answer the question based on their interpretation, which may not match your intentions. Neither of these outcomes is good. Pretesting the questionnaire with members of the relevant population can usually eliminate this source of error.

FAST FACT:

19% OF U.S. ADULTS HAVE **TRIED VIDEO CALLING** ONLINE OR ON MOBILE TELEPHONES.

Several years ago, we conducted a satisfaction study among patients of a number of healthcare providers. The questionnaire included items assessing patient expectations and perceptions of service-provider performance across a range of relevant dimensions. One respondent appeared to have read the directions and (we presume) accurately responded to the first of the items on the rating scale, then proceeded to provide open-ended responses to most of the other items. The respondent, a 92-year-old woman, was doing her best to answer our questions. It was clear that she understood the questions, for the most part, but she didn't understand how we wanted her to respond. Was this her fault? Not really; it was our job to make sure that the instructions were clear.

Does the respondent know the answer to the question?

Just because a respondent understands a question doesn't mean that he actually knows the answer to the question. The problem is that many people will answer the question anyway. This is especially common with closed-ended questions for which respondents simply choose a response category. Dealing with this issue is a bit trickier. Providing a "don't know" response category is one option, but this strategy will often create difficulties in data analysis (i.e., lots of missing cases). People will sometimes select the "don't know" option as a way of not having to think about a particular item, even when they do know the answer to the question. A preferred strategy is to perform sufficient exploratory research and questionnaire pretesting to understand what population members are likely—and not likely—to know.

Is the respondent willing to provide the true answer to the question?

Respondents who understand a question don't always provide a truthful answer. There are lots of reasons for this. Respondents may consciously lie because they want to make themselves look better or to avoid appearing "dumb" when they don't know the answer to a question. Sometimes respondents are angry or in a bad mood and they knowingly provide inaccurate answers. Some respondents just don't care, even though they could understand the questions and provide accurate responses if they wanted to. Others simply don't want to say something negative about a product, store, or service provider.

To study people who buy and fly airplanes, the Advanced General Aviation Transport Experiment

FAST FACT:

SMALL ACCOUNTS (I.E., LESS THAN $100,000 IN ASSETS) COMPRISE **52%** OF NORTH AMERICAN BROKERAGE FIRM ACCOUNTS.

(AGATE) conducted online surveys. The developers of the AGATE questionnaire noted that when surveys ask how much people are willing to pay for some item, respondents typically give an answer near the bottom of the true acceptable range. When they asked a yes/no question like "Are you willing to pay $200?" however, the responses were much more accurate.[4]

Here's another kind of response error: Respondents' current attitudes and emotions sometimes influence their responses. We once conducted a study with dental patients that included a question about patient moods prior to treatment. One elderly respondent was less than thrilled with our questionnaire, writing on the form that he was "crotchety enough without seeing questionnaires like this!" His attitude toward the questionnaire also seemed to influence his response to the mood item: he checked the category nearest "good" (on a "bad" to "good" semantic differential scale) and added, "I always experience absolute euphoria at the prospect of going to the endodontist. I sing the 'Ode to Joy' at the top of my lungs all the way."

What can you do about these sorts of response errors? Once again, the key is thorough exploratory research and questionnaire pretesting. Questions that might cause respondents to be even slightly defensive—especially sensitive questions—must be carefully designed and tested. When the data collection forms are designed, careful attention must be given to the questions (and the order in which they are asked) so as to hold the respondent's attention.

Is the wording of the question or the situation in which it is asked likely to bias the response? As noted, the wording of a question and its response categories has a strong influence on individuals' responses. Leading questions must be avoided, and researchers must be careful not to accidentally use "loaded" words if they are to uncover the truth about an issue. Watch out for unstated alternatives, assumed consequences, and double-barreled questions—and don't ask respondents for estimates (see Chapter 8).

Personal interviews and telephone surveys create an opportunity for interviewers to influence, or bias, the results of the study. Interviewers must be trained not to let the tone of their voice or inflections in their speech vary from one interview to the next. You'll probably guess that interviewer bias is worse with open-ended questions because interviewers both ask the questions and record the answers, creating lots of opportunities for error. Closed-ended questions aren't immune from the problem, though, because interviewers sometimes emphasize one of the response categories, and changes in emphasis or tone can change the meaning of the question entirely. As a result, interviewer training—and clear instructions—are very important.

There are two other sources of response error that the interviewer might cause. One of the interviewer's main tasks is to keep the respondent interested and motivated. At the same time, the interviewer must try to record what the respondent says by carefully writing down the person's answers to open-ended questions or checking the appropriate box with closed-ended questions. That's a tough job and sometimes interviewers make mistakes. Recording errors can be forgiven; interviewer cheating is another matter. Cheating can range from the fabrication of a whole interview to making up one or two answers to make the response complete. Because of interviewer cheating, most commercial research firms validate 10 to 20 percent of the completed interviews through follow-up telephone calls or by sending postcards to a sample of respondents to verify that they have, in fact, been contacted.

Office Errors

Unfortunately, error can enter a project even after the data are collected. **Office error** can show up during the process of editing, coding, and analyzing the data. In many ways, office error is the most frustrating kind of error. Suppose that a survey question has been carefully designed, a respondent understands it and provides the true response—and then someone makes a simple keystroke error that transforms the true response into something else. The efforts of all involved have been wasted, at least for that question and that respondent. For the most part, office errors can be reduced, if not eliminated, by exercising proper controls in data processing. We address some of these issues in the following chapter.

office error
Error due to data editing, coding, or analysis errors.

FAST FACT:

40% TO 50% OF AMERICANS **RECYCLE** COMMON MATERIALS "ALL OF THE TIME."

Total Error Is the Key

It is important to understand that total error, rather than any single type of error, is the key in a research project. We believe that far too many researchers focus too much on decreasing sampling error when they should be focusing more closely on other potential sources of error. Managers, students (especially those with a course in statistics behind them), and some researchers often argue for the "largest possible sample," reasoning that a large sample is much more likely to produce a "valid" result than a small sample is. Increasing the sample size does, in fact, decrease sampling error, but it also can increase other types of errors. If you want to be an effective researcher, try to manage total error, not just one particular kind of error.

Exhibit 10.2 attempts to summarize the sources of errors and how they can be reduced and controlled. You could use this table as a sort of checklist for evaluating the quality of research prior to making important decisions based on the research results.

CALCULATING RESPONSE RATES

Once the data have been collected, the researcher must calculate the **response rate** for the project. The response rate—the number of completed interviews with responding units divided by the number of eligible responding units in the sample—serves two important functions. First, it allows an assessment of the potential influence of nonresponse error on the study's results. Although this assessment is qualitative in nature (because even if you were to obtain responses from 90 percent of those chosen for the sample, the other 10 percent could have been very different on the issue in question), higher response rates generally suggest fewer problems with nonresponse bias. Second, the response rate serves as an indicator of the overall quality of a data collection effort. Very low response rates may indicate poor questionnaire design, lack of interest among respondents, failure to gain the intended respondents' attention, and so on. Unless the client is willing to collect more data, however, it is too late to do anything about these problems. To avoid this outcome, use enough exploratory research and questionnaire pretesting in advance to be comfortable about what will happen when you collect your data.

response rate
The number of completed interviews with responding units divided by the number of eligible responding units in the sample.

The following general formula is used to calculate a project's response rate:

$$\text{response rate} = \frac{\text{number of completed interviews with responding units}}{\text{number of eligible responding units in the sample}}$$

How this formula is applied depends upon the data collection method used. "Completed interviews" includes completed survey forms for methods that don't include an actual interview. We address the most common approaches in the following sections.

Web-Based and Mail Surveys

With these forms of data collection, response rate calculation is usually straightforward. The first step is to determine the number of usable questionnaires completed. Not every completed questionnaire is usable, as we'll see in the following chapter, and you'll need to exclude the bad ones. Common reasons for excluding a questionnaire include evidence that a respondent wasn't really paying attention to the questions, or a large percentage of items weren't answered by the respondent.

Once the number of usable questionnaires is known, the number of eligible response units must be determined. With these types of data collection, it is usually assumed that all elements or people in the sampling frame meet the criteria for membership in the population and sample, which makes calculating the number of eligible response units quite simple. All you have to do is take the number of sample elements that you attempted to contact and subtract the number of e-mail (or mail) addresses that turned out to be invalid. With both approaches, you'll normally know very soon which addresses weren't valid because the surveys will be returned to you in the mail or in your e-mail system. Thus, for these methods of data collection, response rate (RR) is calculated as:

$$RR = \frac{\text{number of usable questionnaires}}{\text{number of contacts attempted} - \text{number of wrong addresses}}$$

EXHIBIT 10.2

Types of Errors and Methods for Handling Them

Type	Definition	Methods for Handling
Sampling	Difference between results for the sample and what would be true for the population.	1. Increase sample size.
Noncoverage	Failure to include some units or entire sections of the defined target population in the sampling frame.	1. Improve sampling frame using other sources. 2. Adjust the results by appropriately weighting subsample results (assuming weighting scheme is known).
Nonresponse	Failure to obtain information from some elements of the population that were selected for the sample. *Not-at-homes:* Designated respondent is not home when the interviewer calls. *Refusals*: Respondent refuses to cooperate in the survey.	1. Have interviewers make advance appointments. 2. Call back at another time, preferably at a different time of day. 3. Attempt to contact the designated respondent using another approach. 1. Attempt to convince the respondent of the importance of his or her participation. 2. Frame the study to enhance respondent interest. 3. Keep the survey as short as possible. 4. Guarantee confidentiality or anonymity. 5. Train interviewers well and match their characteristics to those of the subject pool. 6. Personalize the recruiting message/script where possible. 7. Use an incentive. 8. Send follow-up surveys.
Response	Although the individual participates in the study, he or she provides an inaccurate response, consciously or sub-consciously, to a survey item.	1. Match the background characteristics of interviewer and respondent as closely as possible. 2. Make sure interviewer instructions are clear and written down. 3. Conduct practice training sessions with interviewers. 4. Examine the interviewers' understanding of the study's purposes and procedures 5. Have interviewers complete the questionnaire and examine their replies to see whether there is any relationship between the answers they secure and their own answers. 6. Verify a sample of each interviewer's interviews. 7. Avoid using ambiguous words and questions. 8. Avoid the use of leading questions. 9. Avoid unstated alternatives; include all reasonable response options. 10. Avoid assumed consequences; write clear questions. 11. Don't ask respondents for generalizations or estimates. 12. Don't include double-barreled questions.
Office[a]	Errors that arise when coding, tabulating, or analyzing the data.	1. Use a field edit to detect the most glaring omissions and inaccuracies in the data. 2. Use a second edit in the office to decide how data collection instruments containing incomplete answers, obviously wrong answers, and answers that reflect a lack of interest are to be handled. 3. Use closed-ended questions to simplify the coding process, if possible, but when open-ended questions need to be used, specify the appropriate codes that will be allowed before collecting the data. 4. When open-ended questions are being coded and multiple coders are being used, divide the task by questions and not by data collection forms. 5. Have each coder code a sample of the other's work to ensure that a consistent set of coding criteria is being used. 6. Follow established conventions; for example, use numeric codes and not letters of the alphabet, when coding the data for computer analysis. 7. Prepare a codebook that lists the codes for each variable and the categories included in each code. 8. Use appropriate methods to analyze the data.

[a]Steps to reduce the incidence of office errors are discussed in more detail in the analysis chapters.

Suppose that an online retailer decided to conduct an online survey among its past customers. A sample of 1,000 customers is randomly selected to receive an e-mail survey. A total of 202 customers respond to the survey; 58 of the e-mail addresses are no longer valid. Here's how to calculate the response rate:

$$RR = \frac{202}{1{,}000 - 58} = 21\%$$

Telephone Surveys (No Eligibility Requirement)

Things get a little more complicated with telephone surveys—but not much. In cases where there is no eligibility requirement (i.e., everyone in the sample pool meets the criteria for being included in the sample, which isn't always the case depending upon the source and quality of the sampling frame), we can categorize the attempted contacts into three groups: completed interviews, refusals, and not-at-homes (which includes when no one answers as well as when someone who isn't the correct respondent answers the telephone). The response rate formula looks like this:

$$RR = \frac{\text{number of completed interviews}}{\text{number of completed interviews} + \text{number of refusals} + \text{number of not-at-homes}}$$

Notice that wrong numbers or nonworking numbers are automatically excluded from the formula and thus don't lower the calculated response rate. You'll want to keep track of the number of bad telephone numbers (along with completed interviews, refusals, and not-at-homes), however, as an indication of the quality of the sampling frame.

Consider the following scenario: A researcher has designed a project using a telephone survey as the method of data collection. The respondents are current members of a health club. Using the membership roster as a sampling frame, the researcher has randomly selected 200 members. At the conclusion of the data collection phase, 112 interviews have successfully been conducted, 27 people refused to participate in the study, 57 people could not be reached after at least three tries, and 4 telephone numbers were no longer in service. What is the response rate for this project?

$$RR = \frac{112}{112 + 27 + 57} = 57\%$$

In addition, the quality of the sampling frame appears to be very good, with only 4 nonworking numbers, or 4/200 = 2 percent.

Before moving on, there's an important issue we need to address, and it applies to all methods of administration. What exactly counts as a "completed" interview? Once in a while respondents hang up the phone before they have completed the telephone survey (or they will only answer some of the questions on a mail or Web-based survey). In these cases, you need to use good judgment. Usually, a response that is nearly complete should be included in the data set and counted as a completed interview. At the other extreme, a respondent who answers only one or two questions should probably not be included. The troubling cases are those lying between these extremes. Our general recommendation is to count any interview (or survey) as completed if the respondent provides answers for most of the survey items.

Telephone Surveys (with Eligibility Requirement)

Sometimes researchers are forced to work with sampling frames that include response units that are not members of the population being studied. Suppose, for example, that a department store wants to know shoppers' opinions of a new store layout. Unfortunately, the store can't keep records on who has shopped at the store and who hasn't (because not all shoppers actually buy something and get into its database). Store managers believe that at least half of the households in a test market city contain at least one adult who has visited the store since the new layout was introduced. To conduct a telephone survey, researchers working with the company might choose the local telephone directory as a sampling frame. The trouble is that some of the households won't include anyone who has shopped at the store during the relevant time frame and is ineligible to complete the telephone survey. To identify these households, a screening question will be included ("Has any adult in this household visited Smart's Department Store in the previous three months?"); interviews with those that haven't visited the store will end at that point.

Because some households are ineligible, how would you calculate the response rate? The first step is to count the number of completed interviews, refusals, not-at-homes—*and* the number of ineligible response units. If you're wondering why you must keep track of the number of ineligibles, we need them to help adjust for the likelihood that many of the people who refused to take the survey or who weren't at home wouldn't have qualified anyway. We need to adjust the response rate to account for this; otherwise, the response rate will be lower than it really was. The *eligibility percentage (E%)* is computed as follows:

$$E\% = \frac{\text{number of completed interviews}}{\text{number of completed interviews} + \text{number of ineligibles}}$$

The eligibility percentage is then used to adjust the number of refusals and not-at-homes to reflect the fact that many of them would not have qualified to participate in the survey even if we had successfully contacted them and gotten them to agree to participate. Response rate is calculated as follows:

$$RR = \frac{\text{number of completed interviews}}{\text{number of completed interviews} + E\% \,(\text{number of refusals} + \text{number of not-at-homes})}$$

Imagine that researchers working with the department store had randomly selected 1,000 telephone numbers from the local telephone directory and had attempted to contact each household. Here are the final results of the calls, along with the correct response rate calculation:

Completed interviews	338
Refusals	89
Not-at-homes	169
Ineligibles	292
Nonworking numbers	112
	1,000 telephone numbers

$$E\% = \frac{338}{338 + 292} = 54\%$$

$$RR = \frac{338}{338 + (0.54)(89 + 169)} = 71\%$$

Without adjusting for ineligibles, the calculated response rate would have been only 57 percent, so it is important to keep track of the number of response units that don't qualify for the survey.

Other Methods of Data Collection

So far, we've talked about calculating response rates for most of the major types of data collection. What about other types, such as personal interviews or the residential "drop-off" surveys common with area samples? Regardless of the type of data collection, the same logic is applied: The response rate equals the number of completed interviews with responding units divided by the number of eligible responding units in the sample. If the method used allows a distinction between refusals and not-at-homes, one of the formulas shown above for telephone surveys can likely be utilized or adapted. If not, then a variation of the formula for mail surveys is likely to apply. If there is an eligibility requirement, start with the formula for telephone surveys with an eligibility requirement. Regardless of the circumstances, the researcher can usually use common sense and the basic formulas we've discussed to arrive at the appropriate response rate.

IMPROVING RESPONSE RATES

As noted, the lower the response rate, the more likely it is that nonresponse error will affect research results. Because of this potential problem, researchers have suggested numerous techniques over the years for improving response rates. In this section, we briefly discuss a few of the most promising techniques for increasing response rates.

There's one factor, however, that probably has more effect than any other on response rates: how interested the sample pool is in the topic. Unfortunately, this factor isn't really under the control of the researcher. Some topics are inherently more interesting than other topics to particular respondents. Although you can't change the topic of a research project, you might consider different approaches for introducing and framing the issue under study. Use exploratory research for gauging respondent interest in the topic and to give trial runs to different introductory scripts.

FAST FACT:

24% OF NORTH AMERICANS ACTIVELY **BUY ORGANIC** PRODUCTS.

Survey Length

Although there are exceptions, respondents typically do not appreciate or respond well to long surveys. As surveys get longer, respondents get tired, lose focus, become inattentive and start speeding through the survey just to finish. None of these are good things, especially in terms of response quality. Survey Sampling International (SSI) conducted a study in 2004 and repeated it in 2009, comparing a 20-minute survey to a shortened version. Pete Cape, SSI's global knowledge director concluded, "In both 2004 and 2009, the long survey proved itself too long." The challenges of the long survey included respondent fatigue and satisficing behavior; the benefits of the shortened version included more motivated and responsive respondents.[5] Thus, all else equal, short surveys are more likely to be completed than are long surveys. This is one reason for researchers to include only questions that are truly important and that will be used in the analysis.

Guarantee of Confidentiality or Anonymity

It is routine practice to promise respondents that their answers will be held in confidence by the researcher. This is especially important when the topic or specific questions are likely to be sensitive to the respondent. With mail surveys, you can also guarantee that responses will be anonymous, providing an even greater sense of security to the respondent. By the way, if you promise confidentiality or anonymity, you are ethically bound to keep the promise. Sometimes managers will want access to respondent names, addresses, or telephone numbers—particularly those who have expressed interest in a proposed product or service. Even if you made no promises at all, you shouldn't share this information with managers because it blurs the line between research and sales.

RESPONDENTS TYPICALLY DO NOT APPRECIATE OR RESPOND WELL TO LONG SURVEYS.

Interviewer Characteristics and Training

An interviewer is likely to get better cooperation and more information from a respondent when the two share similar backgrounds. This is especially true for characteristics like race, age, and gender. Sufficient training is also important so that interviewers can learn to quickly convince potential respondents of the value of the research and the importance of their participation. So, you'll want to develop an effective recruiting script and train your interviewers to follow the script. To the extent possible, the script should also communicate information about the content and purpose of the study so that respondents may develop greater involvement and interest in the topic.

Personalization

Anything you can do to make the data collection process seem more personalized will improve response rates. For example, hand-addressed envelopes, handwritten signatures on cover letters, and the use of actual stamps should increase the odds that a respondent opens a mail survey (and they need to open it before they can respond to it!). And a personalized e-mail message ("Hello Amjad") is always better than a generic greeting ("Hello").

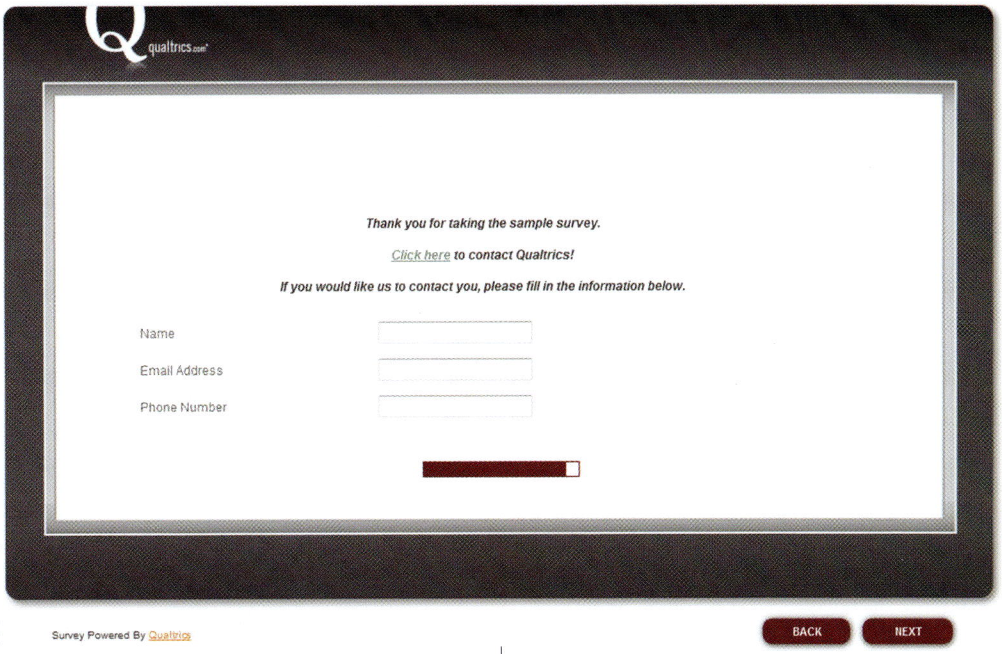

COURTESY OF QUALTRICS LABS INC.

Response Incentives

Considerable research has shown that offering an incentive to respondents usually increases response rates on a project. Response incentives can take several forms ranging from money to lotteries to donations for charity. Monetary incentives often have the greatest influence on response rates. Including a reasonable amount of money as a token of appreciation is often a good idea—but it obviously raises the cost of data collection.

Many researchers have effectively used lotteries as a means of generating response. By participating in the survey, the respondent is typically entered into a drawing for a prize. The difficulty, if there is one, lies in the amount of trust that the respondent must place in the researcher. From the respondents' perspective, there may or may not be an actual lottery; they may or may not actually be entered in such a lottery; and their responses may not be confidential or anonymous if name, address, and telephone number are to be kept for contact purposes (in order to notify the winner). Be careful here; remind respondents that the information will be held in confidence and don't do anything to violate that trust.

Follow-Up Surveys

In some cases, the circumstances surrounding a contact are responsible for a respondent's refusal to participate. Because these circumstances may be temporary or changeable, follow-up reminder contacts are sometimes useful for generating a response. With mail surveys, it's not uncommon at all to receive additional responses with second and third mailings; the same applies to Web-based studies. Of course, sending a follow-up survey might require identification of those who didn't respond earlier, which removes the possibility of anonymity. The alternative—resending the survey to everyone in the sample pool—is irritating for those who have already responded, and costly in the case of mail surveys.

11 Data Preparation for Analysis

POLL QUESTION:

If a respondent skips a question (i.e., fails to answer), all of his/her responses should be discarded due to incompleteness.

STRONGLY DISAGREE 1 2 3 4 5 STRONGLY AGREE

Learning Objectives

1. Explain the purpose of the editing process.
2. Define what coding is.
3. Describe the kinds of information contained in a codebook.
4. Describe common methods for cleaning the data file.
5. Discuss options for dealing with missing data in analyses.

INTRODUCTION

In a marketing research project, several things have to happen before the data can be analyzed. This chapter presents and explains a number of these preliminary steps.

EDITING

The basic purpose of editing is to make certain that the raw data meet minimum quality standards. **Editing** involves the inspection and, if necessary, correction of the data received from each element of the sample (or census).

Here's an example of the kinds of things you're watching for in the editing process: Suppose that you have used an open-ended question to ask a company's customers how many years they have been shopping at the store. What if someone wrote in "8 months"? You'll have to convert this answer to one that can be used in the analysis (in this case, probably "1 year"); the units must be consistent.

FAST FACT:

37% OF CONSUMERS SURVEYED OWNED OR WERE PLANNING TO OWN AN **iPAD** AS THEIR FIRST APPLE, INC., PRODUCT PURCHASE.

During the editing process, you also must decide what to do about cases with incomplete answers, obviously wrong answers (especially invalid or inaccurate responses), and answers that reflect a lack of interest. It is not uncommon for respondents to leave one or more questions blank. In such situations, the researcher must decide how to treat the missing data.

editing
The inspection and correction of the data received from each element of the sample (or census).

Unless you are using an online survey that forces respondents to complete each item before they can move on in the survey (and we don't necessarily recommend that strategy), it's very likely that many respondents won't complete all of the items on your survey. Some surveys will have complete sections omitted. In the case of forced response in an online context, the respondent could break off her participation mid-way through the survey. It's not a formal rule, but if half or more of the responses are missing on a survey, we usually recommend dropping that case entirely. Questionnaires containing only isolated instances of item nonresponse should be kept.

Sometimes the answers that people provide are simply incorrect. For example, a researcher at a consumer panel research company once reviewed data that indicated that 45 percent of the households in the panel had purchased dog food, but only 40 percent of the households reported that they owned a dog.[1] Although we can't be certain, it looks as though some

IF HALF OR MORE OF THE RESPONSES ARE MISSING ON A SURVEY, WE USUALLY RECOMMEND DROPPING THAT CASE ENTIRELY.

of the questionnaires contained incorrect answers. In a case like this, it might be possible to determine which of the two answers (i.e., 45% purchasing dog food vs. 40% owning a dog) is correct from other information in the questionnaire.

You also must be on the alert to spot "completed" questionnaires that don't really have true responses. Consider, for example, a respondent who checked the "5" position on a five-point scale for each of 20 items in an attitude questionnaire, even though some items were expressed negatively and some positively. This sort of *response set bias* occurs fairly frequently and is fairly easy to detect with a hard-copy survey—but it's not as obvious with an online survey. Great care should be taken regardless of communication context. We've also seen returned surveys on which respondents created patterns out of their responses, for example, circling the numbers 1, 2, 3, 4, 5, 6, 7, 6, 5, 4, 3, 2, 1, and so on, for successive items. When it's obvious that a respondent hasn't taken the study seriously, his or her answers should not be recorded, at least for that section of the survey.

Any additional codes that need to be placed on the data collection forms should be added during the editing process. For example, a unique identifying number of some type should be added unless one already exists on the form. This number will be coded in the data file along with the answers provided by the respondent and will be used to look up the data record or original questionnaire if necessary. Exhibit 11.1 provides a list of the primary tasks involved in the editing process.

coding
The process of transforming raw data into symbols (usually numbers); it involves specifying the alternative categories or classes into which the responses are to be placed and assigning code numbers to the classes.

CODING

Coding is the process of transforming raw data into symbols. Most often, the symbols are numerals, because they can be handled easily by computers. The task

EXHIBIT 11.1

Primary Tasks in the Editing Process

1. ***Convert all responses to consistent units.*** For example, if income is to be measured in thousands of dollars, convert the response "46,350" to 46.
2. ***Assess degree of nonresponse.*** If limited, keep the survey; if excessive, eliminate the survey.
3. ***Where possible, check for consistency across responses.*** For example, if the respondent indicates in one part of a survey that he has never been seen by a particular healthcare provider but later reports that he was "very satisfied" with the service provided by that healthcare provider, the editor must decide whether to correct one or the other answer or to treat both responses as if they were missing.
4. ***Look for evidence that respondent wasn't really thinking about his or her answers.*** This typically takes the form of response set bias in which the respondent provides the same answer to a series of rating scale items. Responses that are clearly due to response set should be treated as missing. If this creates an excessive degree of nonresponse, eliminate the survey.
5. ***Verify that branching questions were followed correctly.*** From time to time, sections are only to be answered based upon answers to earlier questions. For instance, survey instruction might say, "if yes, continue to Question 3; if no, skip to Question 12." It is important to verify that respondents followed directions properly. Respondents answering "yes" in this example should have answered Questions 3–11, whereas "no" responses should not. If those answering "no" did answer Questions 3–11, this data should be omitted.
6. ***Add any needed codes.*** For example, each completed survey must have an identification number.

FAST FACT:
16% OF 2009 TRAFFIC FATALITIES WERE LINKED TO **DISTRACTED DRIVING** ACTIVITIES, INCLUDING TEXTING, GROOMING, AND WATCHING VIDEO CONTENT.

© POULSONS PHOTOGRAPHY/SHUTTERSTOCK.COM

is to transform respondents' answers (or other information to be coded) into numbers representing the answers. Sometimes the transformation is almost automatic (e.g., when respondents have circled numbers on rating scales); sometimes, however, the coding process involves considerable effort on the part of the coder (e.g., when respondents answer certain types of open-ended questions).

Coding Closed-Ended Items

In descriptive research, most of the items included in a questionnaire are likely to be closed-ended. That is, most questions will provide a limited number of response categories and will ask the respondent to choose the best response or, sometimes, all responses that apply. These types of items are generally quite simple to code. When there is a single possible answer to a question (e.g., male or female), the researcher uses one variable for the question and simply assigns a character (almost always a number) to each possible response (e.g., 1 = female, 2 = male). The appropriate code number is then recorded in the data file. The coding process is made simpler by using numerical rating scales, but it really isn't necessary. If you ask respondents to check boxes or to provide some other form of response, it's usually easy to assign a number to represent each particular response. For example, the following semantic differential item to measure attitude toward a service provider can easily be coded with the numbers 1–7, where 1 represents the box nearest "unfavorable" and 7 represents the box nearest "favorable:"

unfavorable ☐ ☐ ☐ ☐ ☐ ☐ ☐ favorable

For purposes of analysis, there will be a single variable representing this item, with possible codes 1 through 7 representing increasing levels of favorability.

The coding process for closed-ended items becomes a bit more complex when respondents can indicate more than one answer for a given question, as with "check all that apply" types of items. For example, consider the following question:

How did you learn about Brown Furniture Company? (check all that apply)

☐ newspaper advertising
☐ radio advertising
☐ billboard advertising
☐ recommended by others
☐ drove by the store
☐ other

In this situation, using a single variable coded 1–6, representing the different options, won't work very well; how would you code responses for someone who checked both "newspaper advertising" and "billboard advertising"? A simple solution is to create six variables to represent the six possible answers and to indicate for each whether the option was selected. An easy coding scheme is to record a "1" if a respondent selected a response and to record a "0" if she didn't. For the respondent who checked "newspaper advertising" and "billboard advertising," the variables representing these two responses would be coded "1" and each remaining variable would be coded "0."

Coding Open-Ended Items

Recall that open-ended items don't provide response categories for respondents; respondents answer them using their own words. Coding open-ended responses is typically much more difficult than coding closed-ended responses.

Coding Factual Open-Ended Items

There are two general classes of open-ended questions. One type seeks factual information from a respondent. For example, consider the following open-ended questions:

In what year were you born? __________

How many times have you eaten at Streeter's Grill in the last month? __________

Each of these questions seeks a factual answer from the respondent. There is a correct answer to each question, and the researcher assumes that the respondent can provide that answer. This type of open-ended question is easy to code by simply coding the actual response (or, if the actual responses aren't numeric, converting the responses to numbers). Numerical data should be recorded as they were reported on the data collection form, rather than be collapsed into smaller categories. For example, don't code age as 1 = under 20 years, 2 = 20 − 29, 3 = 30 − 39, and so on, if actual ages of the people were provided. Instead, record age in years so that information isn't sacrificed. If you need the information in categories, it's easy to do the conversion later. (Remember our earlier advice: Always use the highest level of measurement possible. In this case, recording the actual age results in ratio-level measurement; recording age in categories would result in ordinal-level measurement.)

Coding Exploratory Open-Ended Items

The other type of open-ended question is often more exploratory in nature and, as a result, usually much more difficult and expensive to code. For many open-ended questions, there are multiple legitimate responses, some of which you might not anticipate in advance. Suppose that you wanted to determine the causes of so-called "brain drain," the migration of college graduates from one state to another after graduation. In response to the question, **"In your own words, give us two or three reasons why you prefer to leave the state after graduation,"** students provided answers such as "my family lives in another state," "want to try something different," "going to graduate school in another state," and so on. Some people provided a single reason to leave, while others provided multiple reasons to leave. The process of coding the answers to this sort of question involves a number of steps.

Step 1: *The first step is to go through each questionnaire and highlight each separate response given by each individual. Some respondents can provide multiple answers in only a few words, but others can write whole paragraphs and communicate only one answer, so be careful at this stage. Normally, at least two coders should review all of the responses separately and then compare results to ensure that all responses are considered.*

Step 2: *The next step in coding is specifying the categories or classes into which the responses are to be placed. The goal is to reduce the great number of individual responses into a much smaller set of general categories so that insights may be drawn from the results. The categories must be mutually exclusive and exhaustive, so that every open-ended response logically falls into one and only one category. Usually, a researcher can anticipate some or most of the categories in advance—but don't become "locked in" on those categories alone. Respondents' actual answers will often reveal categories that were initially overlooked or anticipated categories that turn out to have very few responses. For example, the brain drain researcher may not have anticipated that some graduates want to leave just to try something new. To make the categories exhaustive, it is often necessary to include an "other" category for responses that simply don't fit anywhere else. However, if the number of responses in the "other" category rises to more than 5 to 10 percent of the total number of responses, the researcher should consider whether additional categories are needed.*

Step 3: *After an appropriate set of categories is identified, the actual coding of responses into the categories begins. Each response identified during the first step must be given the code number for one and only one of the categories developed in the second step. Unless the questions (and responses) are very straightforward (rarely the case for this type of open-ended question), at least two coders who have been trained to understand the types of responses that should be placed in each category should code the responses. Multiple coders help reduce bias in the interpretation of the different responses, a form of office error. Each coder will individually decide which category is appropriate for a response and then assign the numerical code for that category to the response.*

Step 4: *When each coder has coded all responses, the coders meet to compare results, discuss differences in the codes assigned to particular responses, and assign a final code for each response. The coders must keep careful records of the number of codings for which initial disagreement existed so that a summary measure of percentage agreement (or other measure of reliability) can be computed. The lower the overall level of agreement, the greater the possibility that either the categories aren't mutually exclusive or that one or more coders didn't do a thorough job.*

Building the Data File

To use a computer to analyze the data, the codes representing respondents' answers must be placed in

a data file that the computer can read. With online data collection tools, this process is automatic; data are normally stored in spreadsheet format and can be downloaded for further analysis. This is also the case for other computer-assisted forms of data collection (e.g., telephone surveys or personal interviews with direct computer entry). In some cases, however, you'll need to manually enter the data yourself.

There are numerous methods of entering data, including creating text data files in word processing software, using spreadsheet software, using database software, entering data directly into statistical software packages such as SPSS, or using optical scanning. Regardless of how the data input process will be handled, it helps to visualize the input in terms of a multiple-column record where columns represent different variables (based on items from the questionnaire) and rows represent different respondents.

The Codebook Consider the brief questionnaire presented in Exhibit 11.2. Suppose that researchers used this questionnaire with randomly selected members of a fitness center to determine member demographics and usage characteristics, among other things. After receiving surveys back, researchers carefully tracked the fees paid by the respondents over the next 12 months; total revenues per respondents were added later to the data file. The survey was administered via mail survey, but it could just as easily have used some other method.

FAST FACT:

11% OF HEISMAN TROPHY WINNERS HAVE BEEN INDUCTED INTO THE NFL HALL OF FAME.

During the editing and coding process, the researcher added a respondent identification number, code numbers for the open-ended responses, and as noted, revenues received over the next year from the respondent (based on internal records). The **codebook**, presented in Exhibit 11.3, contains explicit directions about how raw data from the questionnaires are coded in the data file. At a minimum, the codebook must provide (1) the variable name to be used in statistical analyses for each variable included in the data file; (2) a description of how each variable is coded; and (3) an explanation of how missing data are treated in the data file. In a very real sense, the codebook is a map to help the researcher navigate from completed questionnaires to the data file.

codebook
A document that contains explicit directions about how data from data collection forms are coded in the data file.

Although there are numerous ways to code and enter data into the data file, we suggest the following standards:

- Assign specific column locations for particular variables. That way, the same variable is recorded in the same columns for each respondent. This is handled automatically with online and computer-assisted methods.
- When a question allows multiple responses, assign separate variables for each response option. Look at Question 1 on the Avery Fitness Center survey (Exhibit 11.2). Because this question allows multiple answers ("please check all that apply"), the researchers have assigned separate variables for each option in the data file. Similarly, if Question 7 had asked for two reasons that members began using the fitness center, the coder would have provided separate columns for each of the answers.
- Use only numeric codes, not letters of the alphabet or special characters, like @. Follow this suggestion

EXHIBIT 11.2

Avery Fitness Center Questionnaire

AVERY FITNESS CENTER SURVEY

Thank you for taking time to provide important feedback about ***Avery Fitness Center*** (AFC). Please answer the following questions. Your candid responses will help us provide better services in the future. No one at AFC will see your specific responses, so please be honest.

(1) Which of the following AFC services have you utilized at least once in the last 30 days? (Please check all that apply)

- ☐ Weight Training
- ☐ Exercise Circuit
- ☐ Therapy Pool
- ☐ Classes
- ☐ Circulation Station

(2) Within the past 30 days, approximately how many times have you visited AFC to exercise?

______Times in the last 30 days

(3) During what part of the day have you normally visited AFC? (Please check only one)

- ☐ morning
- ☐ afternoon
- ☐ evening

(4) How did you learn about AFC? (Please check all that apply)

- ☐ Recommendation from Doctor
- ☐ Recommendation from Friend or Acquaintance
- ☐ Advertising (including Yellow Pages)
- ☐ Heard AFC director speak
- ☐ Drove by location
- ☐ Article in Paper
- ☐ Other

(5) How important to you personally is each of the following reasons for participating in AFC programs? (Circle a number on each scale)

	not at all important				very important
General Health and Fitness	1	2	3	4	5
Social Aspects	1	2	3	4	5
Physical Enjoyment	1	2	3	4	5
Specific Medical Concerns	1	2	3	4	5

(6) How likely is it that you would recommend AFC to a friend or colleague?

not at all likely					neutral					extremely likely
0	1	2	3	4	5	6	7	8	9	10

(7) What was the original event that caused you to begin using services from AFC?

____

(8) Current Age________

(9) Gender ☐ Male ☐ Female

(10) Highest Level of Education Achieved:

- ☐ Less than High School
- ☐ High School Degree
- ☐ Some College
- ☐ Associates Degree
- ☐ Four-year College Degree
- ☐ Advanced Degree

(11) What is your approximate annual household income from all sources, before taxes? (Please check the appropriate category & employment status)

- ☐ $0–15,000
- ☐ $15,001–30,000
- ☐ $30,001–45,000
- ☐ $45,001–60,000
- ☐ $60,001–75,000
- ☐ $75,001–90,000
- ☐ $90,001–105,000
- ☐ $105,001–120,000
- ☐ more than $120,000

- ☐ Employed
- ☐ Retired

THANK YOU!

EXHIBIT 11.3

Codebook for Avery Fitness Center Questionnaire

Variable Name	Description	Response Options
ID	Questionnaire identification number	
WEIGHT	Utilized weight training in previous 30 days?	0 = no 1 = yes
CLASSES	Utilized classes in previous 30 days?	0 = no 1 = yes
CIRCUIT	Utilized exercise circuit in previous 30 days?	0 = no 1 = yes
STATION	Utilized circulation station in previous 30 days?	0 = no 1 = yes
POOL	Utilized therapy pool in previous 30 days?	0 = no 1 = yes
VISITS	Number of visits to AFC in previous 30 days?	(record number)
DAYPART	Normal time to visit AFC?	1 = morning 2 = afternoon 3 = evening
DOCTOR	How learned about AFC? Doctor Rec.	0 = no 1 = yes
WOM	How learned about AFC? Friend Rec.	0 = no 1 = yes
ADVERT	How learned about AFC? Advertising	0 = no 1 = yes
SPEAKER	How learned about AFC? Heard director speak	0 = no 1 = yes
LOCATION	How learned about AFC? Drove by location	0 = no 1 = yes
ARTICLE	How learned about AFC? Article in newspaper	0 = no 1 = yes
OTHER	How learned about AFC? Other	0 = no 1 = yes
FITNESS	Importance for participation: General Health and Fitness	(1–5, "not at all important – very important")
SOCIAL	Social Aspects	SAME
ENJOY	Physical Enjoyment	SAME
MEDICAL	Specific Medical Concerns	SAME
RECOM	How likely to recommend?	(1–10, "not at all likely–extremely likely")
EVENT	What original event caused you to begin AFC? (open ended)	1 = general health / exercise 2 = pool / facilities 3 = rehab / specific medical needs 4 = social considerations 5 = transfer from another center 6 = other
AGE	Current Age	(record number)
GENDER	Gender	1 = male 2 = female
EDUCAT	Highest level of education achieved?	1 = less than high school 2 = high school degree 3 = some college 4 = associates degree 5 = four-year college degree 6 = advanced degree
INCOME	Annual household income before taxes	1 = $0 – 15,000 2 = $15,001 – 30,000 3 = $30,001 – 45,000 4 = $45,001 – 60,000 5 = $60,001 – 75,000 6 = $75,001 – 90,000 7 = $90,001 – 105,000 8 = $105,001 – 120,000 9 = more than $120,000
STATUS	Work Status	1 = employed 2 = retired
REVENUE	One–year Revenue from Respondent	($$$ from secondary records)

MISSING = BLANK

© JGI/TOM GRILL/BLEND IMAGES/GETTY IMAGES

for open-ended responses if possible. For instance, note that Question 7 is open-ended. The EVENT variable associated with this question in the codebook (see Exhibit 11.3) shows five common, general responses provided as answers to this question, "1 = general health/exercise, 2 = pool/facilities," and so on, plus a "6 = other" category.

- Use standard codes for "no information." Thus, all "don't know" responses might be coded as 8, "no answers" as 9, and "does not apply" as 0. It is best if the same code is used throughout the study for each of these types of "no information." If "don't know" and "does not apply" are not response options (and thus there is no distinction between different types of "no information"), it is often best to just leave the column(s) blank.
- Code a respondent identification number on each record (with online surveys this is often done automatically). This number normally won't identify the respondent by name. Instead, the number simply ties the questionnaire to the coded data. This is often useful information in data cleaning.

CLEANING THE DATA

blunder
An error that arises during editing, coding, or data entry.

Blunders are office errors that occur during editing, coding, or, especially, data entry when done by hand. Of all possible sources of error in a marketing research project, blunders are among the most frustrating because they are usually caused by simple carelessness. In this section, we will talk about how to identify blunders and discuss several data entry options that might limit this source of error. One of the advantages of online data collection is that when respondents answer questions, they automatically enter their responses into the data file, reducing the number of potential blunders.

Sometimes blunders are relatively easy to find. For example, suppose that you were coding a 1–5 Likert scale and accidentally entered a 7 instead of the 4 that the respondent circled on the questionnaire. The blunder can be seen by performing a simple univariate analysis known as a frequency count (which we will introduce in the next chapter). A frequency count tells us all of the different responses coded for a variable along with how many cases responded in each way. In our example, the miscoded 7 will turn up as a response in the frequency analysis, and we will immediately know that a mistake has been made (remember that only the numbers 1 through 5 are valid responses to the question). At this point, it's only a matter of identifying which questionnaire was coded 7 for that variable, pulling the actual questionnaire to find the correct response (i.e., 4), and correcting the mistake in the data file. On most projects, frequencies should initially be run on all variables to help identify blunders.

Other blunders are more difficult to detect. In the previous example, suppose that you accidentally entered a 1 instead of the 4 circled by the respondent. Because a 1 is one of the possible valid responses to this item (i.e., a 1–5 scale), a frequency analysis will not uncover this blunder; more involved types of examination are required. One possibility, which is similar to quality control in manufacturing processes, is to select a sample of questionnaires that have been coded and entered and compare the data file against the original questionnaires to find discrepancies. If no blunders are found, there is less concern about data entry error. If several blunders are identified, it may be necessary to check additional records or even examine all records.

A better option, known as **double-entry** of data, requires that the data be entered by two separate people in two separate data files and then the data files be compared for discrepancies. The differences are resolved by referring to the original questionnaires. Because it's unlikely that two different people would make the same blunders during data entry, this approach is likely to produce the "cleanest" data file possible with manual data entry. Using modern word processing software packages, the file comparison process is quite straightforward. Note, however, that this technique requires greater resources (i.e., time, effort, money).

double-entry
Data entry procedure in which data are entered separately by two people in two data files, and the data files are compared for discrepancies.

Finally, **optical scanning** of data collection forms takes information directly from the data collection form

optical scanning
The use of scanner technology to "read" responses on paper surveys and to store these responses in a data file.

FAST FACT:

MORE HISPANICS USE **TWITTER** (18%) THAN DO ALL ONLINE ADULTS (8%).

and reads it into a data file. The Gallup Organization routinely uses optical scanning for mail or other self-administered questionnaires. The company claims an extremely high accuracy rate; any responses that the scanner can't read with 100 percent confidence are sent for verification to company employees.[2]

HANDLING MISSING DATA

item nonresponse
A source of nonsampling error that arises when a respondent agrees to an interview but refuses, or is unable, to answer specific questions.

As we noted earlier, **item nonresponse** is often a significant problem. Unless you "force" respondents to complete each item before moving on in an online survey, it's almost a sure thing that some respondents will skip questions or even whole sections. Although forcing answers is convenient for the researcher (i.e., it eliminates missing data), it will likely lead to (1) response error when respondents simply choose a response so that they can get on with the survey, or (2) nonresponse error when individuals become frustrated and simply terminate the process. Researchers planning to use this approach must ensure that all or most potential respondents know the answers to the questions and that all potential responses are represented (i.e., the response categories are exhaustive). As always, we advise careful exploratory research and pretesting in order to avoid problems.

The degree of item nonresponse often serves as a useful indicator of the quality of the research. When there are lots of missing items, you should question the whole research effort and critically review your objectives and procedures. Even when there's not a lot of missing information, you still must decide what to do about it before you analyze the data. Here are several possible strategies:

- **Eliminate the case with the missing item(s) from all further analyses.** This extreme strategy results in a "pure" data set with no missing information at all. The sample size will thus be equal for all analyses. This strategy, however, excludes data that may be perfectly useful for some analyses. In the extreme, you might throw out a questionnaire from which only a single piece of information was missing. Given that data are so valuable and sometimes difficult to collect, we would rarely recommend this strategy. Any case with a significant amount of missing information should have been eliminated during the editing process.
- **Eliminate the case with the missing item in analyses using the variable.** When using this approach, you'll need to continually report the number of cases on which an analysis is based, because the sample size won't be constant across analyses. The obvious advantage to this strategy is that all available data are used for each analysis.
- **Substitute values for the missing items.** Sometimes you can estimate a value for the missing item based on responses to other related items on the respondent's questionnaire, perhaps using a statistical technique known as regression analysis, which measures the relationship between two or more variables. Or you can use the values from other respondents' questionnaires to determine the mean, median, or mode for the variable and substitute that value for the missing item. The substitution of values makes maximum use of the data, because all the reasonably good cases are used. At the same time, it requires more work from the analyst, and it contains some potential for bias, because the analyst has "created" values where none previously existed.
- **Contact the respondent again.** If the missing information is critical to the study and responses were not anonymous, it is sometimes possible to contact the respondent again to obtain the information. This approach is especially applicable if it appears that the respondent simply missed the item altogether or if the respondent tried to answer the question but didn't follow the instructions.

There is no "right" or simple answer as to how missing items should be handled. It all depends on the purposes of the study, the incidence of missing items, and the methods that will be used to analyze the data.

12 Analysis & Interpretation:
Individual Variables Independently

POLL QUESTION:

A researcher should always report percentages to help readers interpret results.

STRONGLY DISAGREE 1 ○ 2 ○ 3 ○ 4 ○ 5 ○ STRONGLY AGREE

Learning Objectives

1. Distinguish between univariate and multivariate analyses.
2. Describe frequency analysis.
3. Describe descriptive statistics.
4. Discuss confidence intervals for proportions and means.
5. Overview the basic purpose of hypothesis testing.

INTRODUCTION

There are some aspects of marketing research that are fairly difficult. Fortunately, data analysis usually isn't one of them, despite what you may have heard. Data analysis hinges on two considerations about the variable(s) to be analyzed. First, will the variable be analyzed in isolation (univariate analysis) or in relationship to one or more other variables (multivariate analysis)? Second, what level of measurement (nominal, ordinal, interval, ratio) was used to measure the variable? If you can answer those questions, data analysis usually isn't that difficult—especially because a computer can do the analysis for you!

In this chapter, we present some common types of univariate data analysis techniques and introduce the concept of hypothesis testing. Many analyses in applied marketing research involve simple univariate analyses. For example, the publisher of a magazine might want to know the proportion of the magazine's readers who are male; a restaurant might like to know the average income of its typical diner; a service provider might need to know her customers' average level of satisfaction with the services provided. In each of these cases, a single variable is analyzed in isolation—gender, income, satisfaction.

THE AVERY FITNESS CENTER (AFC) PROJECT

Recall the Avery Fitness Center (AFC) project that we introduced in the previous chapter. Located in a mid-size city in the southeastern United States, the company offers a variety of exercise programs to its members under the supervision of personal trainers. The company was founded 10 years ago and operates from a single location in an old shopping center near a large university. AFC primarily targets "prime-timers"—men and women ages 55 years and older, some of whom are struggling with health issues. Many customers are attracted to the large indoor therapy pool that allows exercise using water resistance, which is much easier on bones and joints than traditional exercise options. Individuals become members of the fitness center by paying a monthly fee; they pay additional fees for special classes, use of personal trainers, etc. Although business has been steady, AFC managers believe that the company could grow substantially without adding additional facilities. As a result, AFC managers are interested in better understanding the kinds of individuals that are attracted to AFC and how best to recruit more of these kinds of people. More specifically, the AFC researchers are addressing two research problems: (1) Determine member demographics and usage patterns, and (2) investigate how members learn about AFC.

FAST FACT:

ONLINE BLACK FRIDAY 2010 SALES WERE UP **16%,** WITH AVERAGE ONLINE ORDERS RISING FROM $170.19 TO $190.80.

To address these research problems, researchers decided to conduct a mail survey of AFC's customer base (see the questionnaire in Exhibit 11.2 in the previous chapter). "Customer" was defined as any individual in the company's member database who had visited AFC at least once in the previous 12 months. Surveys were sent to 400 members drawn using a simple random sample; respondents completed and returned 231 usable surveys for a response rate of 58 percent. Survey respondents were then matched with total fees paid over the next 12 months. After editing, coding, and cleaning the data, the researchers were ready to begin data analysis (see the codebook in Exhibit 11.3).

BASIC UNIVARIATE STATISTICS: CATEGORICAL MEASURES

Because both nominal and ordinal measures are easily used to group respondents or objects into groups or categories, researchers often refer to these types of measures as **categorical measures**. For example, the AFC survey included measures of (1) the gender and (2) the highest level of education achieved of the population of AFC members. The first of these measures is clearly at the nominal level of measurement: Each responding individual belongs to either the "male" or the "female" category.

categorical measures
A commonly used expression for nominal and ordinal measures.

The second measure was assessed at the ordinal level of measurement. Respondents indicated the highest level of education they had achieved by choosing one of six categories ordered from low ("less than high school") to high ("advanced degree"). Sample statistics for both items are easily obtained via frequency analysis.

Frequency Analysis

A **frequency analysis** consists of counting the number of cases that fall into the various response categories. This is a very simple analytic tool, yet it is incredibly important and commonly used to report the overall results of marketing research studies. You can produce frequencies for any of the variables in a study; any packaged statistical program such as SPSS and even spreadsheet programs such as Excel can perform frequency analysis.

frequency analysis
A count of the number of cases that fall into each category when the categories are based on one variable.

EXHIBIT 12.1

Avery Fitness Center: Gender

Gender	Number	Percent	Valid Percent	Cumulative Valid Percent
Male	45	19%	20%	20%
Female	177	77	80	100
Total	222	96	100%	
Missing	9	4		
Overall total	231	100%		

Some programs will calculate summary statistics and plot a histogram of the values (discussed later) in addition to reporting the number of cases in each category. Additionally, many of the current Web-based survey tools will provide summary statistics in the form of frequency analyses.

Exhibit 12.1 presents the frequency analysis for the gender of the AFC study respondents (SPSS Menu Sequence: Analyze > Descriptive Statistics > Frequencies). As indicated, 177 of the 222 individuals who responded to the gender item (9 respondents did not answer the question) were women. The second column in Exhibit 12.1 includes percentages calculated using all respondents, including those who didn't answer the question. The third column presents "valid" percentages (the missing cases are excluded). Although the number of missing cases in a frequency analysis should be indicated, valid percentages are normally reported along with the count. The final column in Exhibit 12.1 reports the cumulative valid percent associated with each level of the variable. This is the percentage of observations with a value less than or equal to the level indicated.

Exhibit 12.2 presents frequency results for the highest level of education reported by the AFC

EXHIBIT 12.2

Avery Fitness Center: Level of Education

Level of Education Achieved	Number	Valid Percent	Cumulative Percent
Less than high school	4	2%	2%
High school degree	34	15	17
Some college	46	20	37
Associates degree	7	3	40
Four-year college degree	52	23	64
Advanced degree	82	36	100%
Total	225	100%	

(number of missing cases = 6)

members. As you can see, 15 percent of respondents reported a high school degree as the highest level of education achieved. Working with the cumulative percentages, however, it is probably more informative to report that 81 percent of respondents indicated having taken courses beyond the high school level. The results in Exhibit 12.2 indicate that AFC members tend to be well educated (60% have at least a four-year college degree).

About Percentages

Before going further, let's think about using percentages for reporting results. First, you'll almost always want to include percentages along with the raw count for frequency analyses—percentages help readers interpret results. (Which do you think is more informative—that "80 percent of respondents were women" or that "177 of 222 respondents were women"?) Second, percentages should be rounded off to whole numbers (i.e., no decimals) because whole numbers are easier to read and because decimals might make the results look more accurate or "scientific" than they really are, especially in a small sample. In some cases, it might be reasonable to report percentages to one decimal place (rarely two decimal places), but the general rule is to use whole numbers.[1]

Other Uses for Frequencies

In addition to communicating the results of a study, frequency analysis is useful for several other purposes. For example, frequencies can help determine the degree of item nonresponse for a variable as well as help locate blunders, as we discussed in the previous chapter. You really ought to run frequencies for all the variables in a study before you do anything else.

Another use of frequency analysis is to locate **outliers**, valid observations that are so different from the rest of the observations that they ought to be treated as special cases. This may mean eliminating the observation from the analysis or trying to determine why this case is so different from the others. For instance, consider the histogram of AFC respondents' ages presented in Exhibit 12.3. A **histogram**

outliers
An observation so different in magnitude from the rest of the observations that the analyst chooses to treat it as a special case.

histogram
A form of bar chart on which the values of the variable are placed along the *x*-axis and the absolute or relative frequency of the values is shown on the *y*-axis.

EXHIBIT 12.3

Avery Fitness Center: Histogram of Respondent Age (SPSS Output)

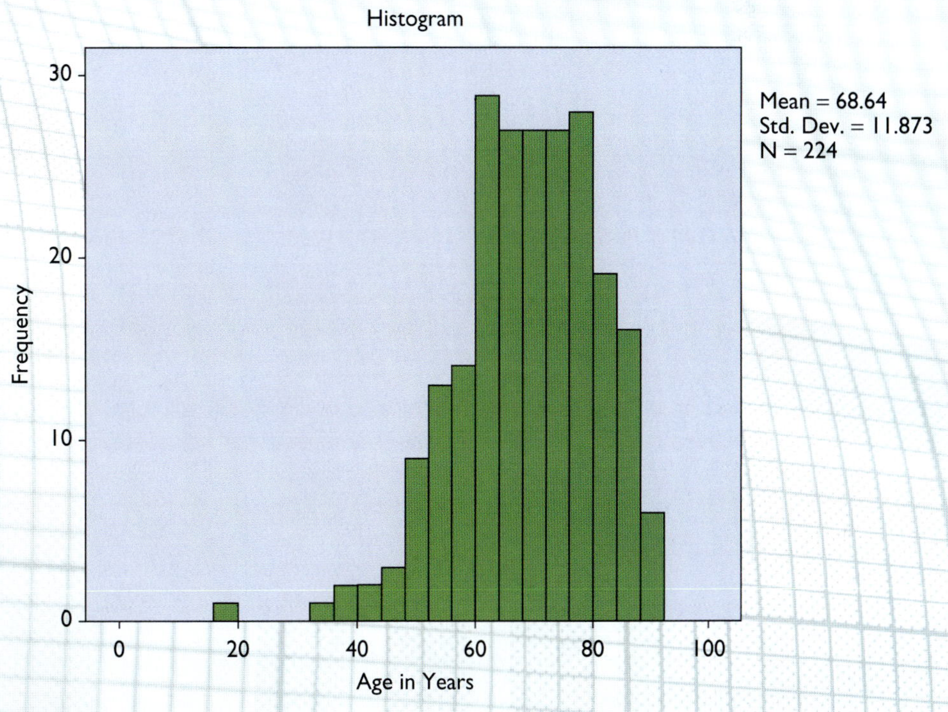

is a form of bar chart that is based on information from a frequency count. The values of a variable—age, in this example—are placed along the x-axis, and the raw count or proportion of cases that occur at each level is plotted on the y-axis.

A quick look at the histogram shows that one respondent reported an age that is considerably younger than all the other cases. The SPSS frequency analysis output (see Exhibit 12.4) shows that this particular customer is 18 years old; the next youngest customer among the respondents was 35 years old. This case is clearly out of line with the rest of the sample—it should be considered an outlier. What you choose to do with this observation depends on the objectives of the study. In this case, it's reasonable for a respondent to be 18 years old (although unusual), so we'll keep it in the data file for now.

EXHIBIT 12.4

Avery Fitness Center: Age (SPSS Output)

Age in Years

		Frequency	Percent	Valid Percent	Cumulative Percent
Valid	18	1	.4	.4	.4
	35	1	.4	.4	.9
	36	1	.4	.4	1.3
	38	1	.4	.4	1.8
	40	1	.4	.4	2.2
	43	1	.4	.4	2.7
	45	1	.4	.4	3.1
	46	1	.4	.4	3.6
	47	1	.4	.4	4.0
	48	2	.9	.9	4.9
	49	2	.9	.9	5.8
	50	3	1.3	1.3	7.1
	51	2	.9	.9	8.0
	52	1	.4	.4	8.5
	53	4	1.7	1.8	10.3
	54	4	1.7	1.8	12.1
	55	4	1.7	1.8	13.8
	56	1	.4	.4	14.3
	57	3	1.3	1.3	15.6
	58	3	1.3	1.3	17.0
	59	7	3.0	3.1	20.1
	60	6	2.6	2.7	22.8
	61	7	3.0	3.1	25.9
	62	3	1.3	1.3	27.2
	63	13	5.6	5.8	33.0
	64	6	2.6	2.7	35.7
	65	5	2.2	2.2	37.9
	66	8	3.5	3.6	41.5

Age in Years

	Frequency	Percent	Valid Percent	Cumulative Percent
67	8	3.5	3.6	45.1
68	4	1.7	1.8	46.9
69	6	2.6	2.7	49.6
70	6	2.6	2.7	52.2
71	11	4.8	4.9	57.1
72	4	1.7	1.8	58.9
73	6	2.6	2.7	61.6
74	9	3.9	4.0	65.6
75	8	3.5	3.6	69.2
76	6	2.6	2.7	71.9
77	7	3.0	3.1	75.0
78	7	3.0	3.1	78.1
79	8	3.5	3.6	81.7
80	5	2.2	2.2	83.9
81	2	.9	.9	84.8
82	11	4.8	4.9	89.7
83	1	.4	.4	90.2
84	3	1.3	1.3	91.5
85	4	1.7	1.8	93.3
86	4	1.7	1.8	95.1
87	5	2.2	2.2	97.3
88	2	.9	.9	98.2
89	3	1.3	1.3	99.6
90	1	.4	.4	100.0
Total	224	97.0	100.0	
Missing System	7	3.0		
Total	231	100.0		

The frequency count for age presented in Exhibit 12.4 also allows us to point out one final use of frequency analysis. With ordinal-, interval-, or ratio-level measures, it is often useful to identify the median point as a measure of "average" for the distribution. It is a simple matter to locate the value of age at which the 50th percentile (the observation in the middle of the distribution when ordered from low to high) lands; in this case, the median age is 70. (And, if it matters, the first quartile falls at age 61 and the third quartile at age 77.)

So, what have we learned so far about AFC members from frequency analysis? They are mostly female, well educated, and older. Additional analyses on customer demographics (try these on your own using the data file located at www.cengagebrain.com) reveal that most are retired (77%) and have household incomes above $45,000 (70%). In addition, Exhibit 12.5 presents information about AFC service usage behavior—all of these results were obtained using simple frequency analysis.

Confidence Intervals for Proportions

We learned from the results presented in Exhibit 12.1 that 80 percent of the respondents in the sample were women. Although this sample statistic is interesting, AFC managers care more about the entire population of AFC customers than they do about a particular sample. Recall that we draw a sample to represent the population. In this case, our best guess is that 80 percent of the members in the population are female, but because of sampling error (not to mention the other types of error, but let's not worry about those right now), we can't be confident that this estimate is precisely true for the population.

EXHIBIT 12.5

Avery Fitness Center: Services Utilized within Past 30 Days

Service	Number	Percent Respondents Utilizing
Weight training	73	32%
Classes	61	26
Exercise circuit	51	22
Circulation station	28	12
Therapy pool	104	45

(n = 231; no missing cases)

confidence interval
A projection of the range within which a population parameter will lie at a given level of confidence, based on a statistic obtained from a probabilistic sample.

Fortunately, because the researchers drew a sample using a probabilistic sampling plan, we can account for sampling error and make inferences about the population as a whole based on the results from the sample. A **confidence interval** is a projection of the range within which a population parameter will lie at a given level of confidence based on a statistic obtained from an appropriately drawn sample.[2] To produce a confidence interval, all we need to do is calculate the degree of sampling error for the particular statistic. To calculate sampling error for a proportion, we need three pieces of information: (1) z, the z score representing the desired degree of confidence (usually 95% confidence, where $z = 1.96$); (2) n, the number of valid cases overall for the proportion; and (3) p, the relevant proportion obtained from the sample. The sample size and the proportion are easily obtained from the frequency analysis output. These pieces of information are entered into the following formula for sampling error for a proportion:

$$\text{sampling error for proportion} = z\sqrt{\frac{p(1-p)}{n}}$$

The resulting value is also frequently called the *margin of sampling error*. Using the information in Exhibit 12.1, the margin of sampling error for the proportion of women in the AFC customer population is calculated as follows:

$$\text{sampling error} = 1.96\sqrt{\frac{0.80(1-0.80)}{222}} = 0.05$$

You calculate the confidence interval itself like this:

$$(p - \text{sampling error} \le \pi \le p + \text{sampling error})$$
$$(0.80 - 0.05 \le \pi \le 0.80 + 0.05)$$
$$\text{or } (0.75, 0.85)$$

Here's how to interpret the confidence interval: We can be 95 percent confident that the actual proportion of women in the population (π) lies between 0.75 and 0.85, inclusive. This is a strong statement that highlights the beauty of probabilistic sampling. Even though the AFC researchers had responses from only 222 individuals, they have a strong notion of what the answer would have been had they taken measures from all the customers in the population. If they want a narrower confidence interval (i.e., greater precision), they can decrease the degree of confidence desired (e.g., at 90% confidence, $z = 1.65$) or increase sample size.

A Word of Caution Before we start letting the numbers do the thinking for us, recognize that the confidence interval only takes sampling error into account. To the extent that other types of error have entered the study—and you can be sure that they have to some degree—the confidence interval is less likely to have "captured" the population parameter within its bounds. Unfortunately, there is no quantitative way of adjusting the confidence interval to reflect these types of errors.

BASIC UNIVARIATE STATISTICS: CONTINUOUS MEASURES

Because interval- and ratio-level measures are similar when it comes to analysis (the mean is the most commonly calculated statistic for both types), many researchers refer to both types as **continuous measures**, even though the label is not technically correct, especially for interval measures such as rating scales.

continuous measures
A commonly used expression for interval and ratio measures.

Descriptive Statistics

For continuous measures, numerous types of descriptive statistics can be calculated. **Descriptive statistics** describe the distribution of responses on a variable, including measures of central tendency (mean, median, and mode), measures of the spread, or variation, in the distribution (range, variance, standard deviation), and various measures of the shape of the distribution (e.g., skewness, kurtosis). In this section, we discuss the calculation and interpretation of two commonly used descriptive statistics, the mean and standard deviation. These descriptive statistics are easily obtained from any statistical software package (SPSS Menu Sequence: Analyze > Descriptive Statistics > Descriptives).

descriptive statistics
Statistics that describe the distribution of responses on a variable. The most commonly used descriptive statistics are the mean and standard deviation.

The **sample mean** ($\overline{x}$) is simply the arithmetic mean value across all responses for a variable and is found using the following formula:

sample mean
The arithmetic average value of the responses on a variable.

$$\overline{x} = \frac{\sum_{i=1}^{n} x_i}{n}$$

where x_i is the value of the variable for the ith respondent and n is the total number of responses. In the AFC customer study, mean age is found by summing the age values across respondents and dividing by 224, the total number of valid cases. In this example, the computed mean age turns out to be 68.6 years.

Although means are easy to calculate or obtain from computer output, there are several issues to keep in mind. First, although mean values can be calculated for any variable in a data set, they are only meaningful for continuous (i.e., interval, ratio) measures. Thus, knowing that the mean level of education is 4.4 is of little value at best—and misleading at worst—because this variable is at the ordinal level of measurement (i.e., "1 = less than high school, 2 = high school degree," etc.; not years of education or some other continuous measure). The mean is only useful with equal-interval scales, one of the common characteristics of interval and ratio measures.

A second issue with respect to interpreting mean values concerns spurious precision. Just as we warned you about the use of decimals with percentages, you'll need to be careful about just how precise a mean value can be. Consider the original values of respondent age shown in Exhibit 12.4. Each respondent provided his or her age in years, as a whole number. Knowing this, would it be reasonable to report that mean age for the sample was 68.6437261 years? No. Round the result off to a whole number (69 years) or use a single decimal (68.6 years) at the most. Anything more suggests a level of precision that simply isn't justified or necessary.

The third issue about mean values concerns their use with variables with one or more extreme cases, or outliers. As noted earlier, one AFC customer reported being only 18 years old, while most members were 60 years or older. In this case, leaving the respondent in the data set has only a slight effect on the mean age

FAST FACT:
CURTIS INSTITUTE OF MUSIC HAD THE LOWEST ACCEPTANCE RATE OF U.S.-BASED COLLEGES: **5%** ACCEPTANCE IN FALL 2009.

© ROBERT KNESCHKE/SHUTTERSTOCK.COM

calculated for the sample, so it really isn't much of an issue. There are situations, however, where outliers can have a very strong influence on the sample mean. In general, it is better to report the median value when there are outliers in a distribution because it more accurately represents the vast majority of cases. Another option is to temporarily ignore the extreme cases and calculate the mean across the remaining cases.[3]

sample standard deviation
A measure of the variation of responses on a variable. The standard deviation is the square root of the calculated variance on a variable.

The **sample standard deviation**(s) provides a measure of the variation in responses for continuous measures. If everyone were basically the same on some characteristic or felt the same way about some topic or object, then the standard deviation would be very small. If, on the other hand, responses were different—some high, some low—then the standard deviation for the variable would be larger.

If you don't take the variation of responses into account, you'll sometimes end up making bad decisions. Consider the classic case of a new sauce product:

> *On the average, consumers wanted it neither really hot nor really mild. The mean rating of the test participants was quite close to the middle of the scale, which had "very mild" and "very hot" as its bipolar adjectives. This happened to fit the client's preconceived notion. However, examination of the distribution of the ratings revealed the existence of a large proportion of consumers who wanted the sauce to be mild and an equally large proportion who wanted it to be hot. Relatively few wanted the in-between product, which would have been suggested by looking at the mean rating alone.*[4]

The following formula is used to calculate the sample standard deviation:

$$s = \sqrt{\frac{\sum_{i=1}^{n} (x_i - \bar{x})^2}{n - 1}}$$

© MEL SVENSON/WHITE/PHOTOLIBRARY

where x_i is the value of the variable for the *i*th respondent; $\bar{x}$ is the mean value of the variable; and n is the total number of responses. Again, statistical software packages easily calculate descriptive statistics, including the standard deviation. For the age of the AFC members, the sample standard deviation turns out to be 11.9 years, providing evidence of considerable spread in ages around the sample mean. As demonstrated by the hot sauce example above, this could have important implications for AFC managers if different marketing mix elements are found to be more or less effective among different age groups, for example.

In almost all cases, it's important to report standard deviations along with mean values. A word of caution, however: Issues related to spurious precision and the presence of outlier cases apply to standard deviations as well as to means. And remember, the standard deviation is meaningful only for interval- and ratio-level measures.

Converting Continuous Measures to Categorical Measures

Sometimes it is helpful to convert interval- or ratio-level measures to categorical measures. Because higher levels of measurement have all the properties of lower levels of measurement, this conversion is perfectly acceptable—and in many cases it's really useful for interpreting the results. Exhibit 12.3 was created by converting open-ended responses to the age question (ratio-level measure) into a number of age categories (ordinal-level measure) and plotting the results on the graph. Was this conversion necessary for describing the sample with respect to age? No. The researchers could simply have reported descriptive statistics for the original measure ($\bar{x}$ = 68.6 years, s = 11.9 years, median = 70 years). On the other hand, Exhibit 12.3 allows a condensed picture of the distribution that should be easy for managers or other readers to grasp, particularly when presented in combination with the descriptive statistics.

There aren't a lot of rules for the actual conversion process. Sometimes, you'll just use your best judgment to determine relevant categories. Occasionally, a client will have a predetermined structure for categories. In other cases, the data themselves determine category divisions. For example, if you want to convert a continuous measure into two approximately equal-sized groups, you'll probably create the categories based on a **median split**. That is, the cumulative percent column of the frequency analysis output will identify a value at the 50th percentile, and values up to and including this value will form one group (typically the "low" group for ratio measures) and values above the median value will form the second group (the "high" group).

The median split is actually just one case of the **cumulative percentage breakdown**, a technique in which groups are created using cumulative percentages. For example, look again at the age data in Exhibit 12.4. If we wanted to convert these data into three approximately equal-sized groups, which categories would be combined? Based on the cumulative percent breakdown, the three groups would be as follows:

Less than 64 years

64 to 74 years

More than 74 years

When using statistical software for analyses—which is almost always—we strongly recommend that you create a new variable whose values are initially identical to the original continuous variable. Then you can recode the new variable into the desired categories, using data manipulation commands. This way, both the original variable and the new categorical variable are available for analyses (SPSS Menu Sequence: Transform > Recode into Different Variables).

Here's another example: Analysts often report the results of rating scale questions by presenting the percentage of respondents who checked one of the top two positions on a rating scale. This is known as the **two-box technique**. As an example, look at the response frequencies (and percentages) presented in Exhibit 12.6. The AFC researchers wanted to understand the importance of various reasons for participating in AFC programs. The researchers could correctly report that the mean rating score for the importance of physical enjoyment was 3.9 on a 5-point importance scale. To make this result easier to grasp, they might also report that 70 percent of

median split
A technique for converting a continuous measure into a categorical measure with two approximately equal-sized groups. The groups are formed by "splitting" the continuous measure at its median value.

cumulative percentage breakdown
A technique for converting a continuous measure into a categorical measure. The categories are formed based on the cumulative percentages obtained in a frequency analysis.

two-box technique
A technique for converting an interval-level rating scale into a categorical measure, usually used for presentation purposes. The percentage of respondents choosing one of the top two positions on a rating scale is reported.

EXHIBIT 12.6

Avery Fitness Center: Reasons for Participation

"How important to you personally is each of the following reasons for participating in AFC programs?" Number (Percentage) of Respondents Selecting Each Response Category

	Not at All Important				Very Important
General health and fitness	5 (2)	26 (11)	4 (2)	26 (11)	192 (84)
Social aspects	27 (13)	35 (17)	59 (29)	48 (24)	35 (17)
Physical enjoyment	8 (4)	10 (5)	43 (21)	67 (33)	74 (37)
Specific medical concerns	17 (8)	8 (4)	22 (11)	62 (30)	100 (48)

respondents selected one of the top two levels of importance on the 5-point scale. Responses for the other reasons for participation are interpreted in the same way. The next table, Exhibit 12.7, presents two-box results and descriptive statistics as they might appear in the research report.

You need to understand that converting from continuous to categorical measures results in the loss of information about a variable. Most of the time, conclusions drawn using categorical approaches will roughly parallel those drawn using the full information from the continuous measure, but this isn't always the case. To be safe, always perform data analysis using the continuous version of a variable. Then, if it will help managers interpret the results, use the categorical version to present the results. A simple solution for many univariate analyses is to provide both types of results (see Exhibit 12.7).

EXHIBIT 12.7

Avery Fitness Center: Two-Box Results, with Descriptive Statistics

	Two-Box	Mean	(s.d.)	*n*
General health and fitness	95%	4.7	(1.3)	203
Social aspects	41	3.2	(0.7)	229
Physical enjoyment	70	3.9	(1.1)	202
Specific medical concerns	78	4.1	(1.2)	209

Confidence Intervals for Means

The sample mean ($\bar{x}$) is an important piece of information about a variable, but as we noted earlier, managers care more about the population than they do any particular sample. Our job, as a result, is to make projections about where the population mean (μ) is likely to fall, rather than to be satisfied with the sample mean. One important piece of information that the fitness center researchers gathered with respect to usage was the number of times that the respondents had visited AFC over the previous 30 days. Note that the number of visits is a ratio-level measure, with the mean number of visits equal to 10.0, and standard deviation of 7.3, based on the responses of the 198 AFC members who answered the question on the survey. So, 10 visits per month on average per individual is our best point estimate about the mean value of the population parameter (μ), but we have so little confidence that this point estimate is correct that we need to construct an interval that will allow us greater confidence that we have actually "captured" the parameter within its bounds. As with proportions, to establish the confidence interval, we must estimate the degree of sampling error for the sample mean. The following formula is used:

$$\text{sampling error} = z\frac{s}{\sqrt{n}}$$

where z = z score associated with confidence level (for 95% confidence, z = 1.96), s = sample standard deviation, and n = total number of cases (standard deviation and number of cases are part of the standard output for descriptives analysis). Thus, at the 95 percent confidence level,

$$\text{sampling error} = 1.96\frac{7.3}{\sqrt{198}} = 1.0$$

Thus, the margin of sampling error for this estimate is approximately 1.0.

© ROBERT KNESCHKE/SHUTTERSTOCK.COM

Substituting this value and the sample mean ($\bar{x}$ = 10.0) into the following formula

$$(\bar{x} - \text{sampling error} \leq \mu \leq \bar{x} + \text{sampling error})$$
$$(10.0 - 1.0 \leq \mu \leq 10.0 + 1.0)$$
$$\text{or } (9.0, 11.0)$$

results in a 95 percent confidence interval ranging from 9 to 11. We can therefore be 95 percent confident that the mean number of visits to the fitness center in the past 30 days in the population lies somewhere between 9 and 11, inclusive.

Think about what we've accomplished. On the basis of only 198 observations, we can say with 95 percent confidence that had we taken measures on number of visits to AFC from every individual in the population, the mean number of visits would fall in the range 9 to 11. We note again, however, that the confidence interval takes only sampling error into account. To the degree that other types of error are present, our estimates may be off target.

HYPOTHESIS TESTING

The fact that marketing researchers are almost always working with a sample rather than full information from all population members creates something of a dilemma for managers who must make decisions based on research results. *How can we tell whether a particular result obtained from a sample would be true for the population as a whole and not just for the particular sample?* In truth, we can never know for sure that a sample result is true for the population. Through hypothesis testing, however, we can establish standards for making decisions about whether to accept sample results as valid for the overall population. We introduce hypothesis testing at this point because it applies to both univariate analyses (the remainder of this chapter) and multivariate analyses (the next chapter).

When marketers prepare to launch a research study, they generally begin with a hypothesis. "I'll bet," the advertising manager might say to the marketing director, "that if we hired an attractive actress to promote our shampoo, sales would increase." Using inferential statistics, we are often able to determine whether there is empirical evidence from a sample to confirm that a **hypothesis** like this may be true for the population.

hypothesis
Unproven propositions about some phenomenon of interest.

Null and Alternative Hypotheses

Marketing research studies can't "prove" results. At best, we can indicate which of two mutually exclusive hypotheses is more likely to be true, based on the results of the study. The general forms of these two hypotheses and the symbols attached to them are as follows:

- H_0, the hypothesis that a proposed result is not true for the population.
- H_a, the alternate hypothesis that a proposed result is true for the population.

The first of these hypotheses, H_0, is known as the **null hypothesis**. The typical goal is to reject the null hypothesis in favor of the **alternative hypothesis**. (Note, however, that we can't prove that the alternative hypothesis is true even if we can reject the null. A hypothesis can be rejected, but it can never be accepted completely because further evidence may prove it wrong.) You should frame the null hypothesis so that its rejection

null hypothesis
The hypothesis that a proposed result is not true for the population. Researchers typically attempt to reject the null hypothesis in favor of some alternative hypothesis.

alternative hypothesis
The hypothesis that a proposed result is true for the population.

leads to the tentative acceptance of the alternative hypothesis. As a quick example, suppose your company wanted to introduce a new product if more than 20 percent of the population could be expected to prefer it to the competing products. Here's the way to frame this sort of hypothesis.

$$H_0 : \pi \leq 0.20$$
$$H_a : \pi > 0.20$$

If the results of the study lead you to reject H_0, you would tentatively accept the alternative hypothesis and the product would be introduced, because such a result would have been unlikely to occur if the null were really true. If H_0 could not be rejected, however, the product wouldn't be introduced.

Hypothesis Testing in Practice

In a technical sense, hypothesis testing involves a number of steps, ranging from specifying hypotheses, to calculating the appropriate inferential statistics, to specifying the significance level for the test. In practice, researchers learn very quickly to let the computer run the basic analyses as well as handle the more technical aspects of hypothesis testing.

With any type of hypothesis testing, you'll need to select an appropriate level of error related to the probability of rejecting the null hypothesis (H_0) when it is actually true for the population. This is usually referred to as the **significance level** or alpha level of the test and is symbolized by alpha (α). We prefer, not surprisingly, that the probability of this type of error be as small as possible. By convention, most social scientists have decided that an α level of 0.05 is an acceptable level, which means that we'll end up rejecting a true null hypothesis 5 percent of the time. If the consequences of an error are particularly bad, it's appropriate to lower the α level, maybe to 0.01 or 0.001.

significance level (α)
The acceptable level of error selected by the researcher, usually set at 0.05. The level of error refers to the probability of rejecting the null hypothesis when it is actually true for the population.

FAST FACT:
26% OF VIDEO GAMES SOLD IN THE U.S. ARE **RATED "M"** FOR MATURE CONTENT.

As noted, when you conduct an analysis, statistical software is usually used to calculate the appropriate inferential statistic that allows you to decide whether a sample result can reasonably be projected to the overall population. Actually, the software also takes it a step further by calculating the **p-value** associated with the test statistic. (Some statistical software packages place p-values in a column labeled "significance.") The p-value represents the likelihood of obtaining the particular value of a test statistic if the null hypothesis were true. Once you have the p-value, it's a simple matter to compare it with the significance level of the test to determine whether the result can be considered "statistically significant" (that is, the sample results can be projected to the population). If the p-value is less than the significance level established, you can reject the null hypothesis and tentatively accept the alternative hypothesis.

p-value
The probability of obtaining a given result if in fact the null hypothesis were true in the population. A result is regarded as statistically significant if the p-value is less than the chosen significance level of the test.

Think about the logic of this for a second and it will make sense. A statistically significant result simply means that the probability that you could have obtained a particular result if the null hypothesis were really true (the p-value) is less than the level of error that you're willing to tolerate (the significance level). So, researchers virtually always want to obtain low p-values, and as long as the p-value is lower than the significance level (typically $\alpha = .05$), the results can be applied to the population. If the p-value isn't lower than the established significance level, then there's just too much risk that the results were a fluke produced by chance.[5]

TESTING HYPOTHESES ABOUT INDIVIDUAL VARIABLES

There are numerous occasions when you'll want to compare univariate sample statistics against preconceived standards. Maybe, for instance, you'll need to compare the mean customer satisfaction score for a particular department store against the overall mean satisfaction score for all department stores in the chain, or to determine whether the characteristics of sample respondents match those of the overall

© BEN WELSH/AGE FOTOSTOCK/PHOTOLIBRARY

population from which the sample was drawn. Each of these examples calls for a researcher to test a hypothesis about a univariate measure.

Testing Statistical Significance with Categorical Variables

Suppose that AFC managers wanted to know whether their current customers were different from the overall population of people who lived in their trading area. Although you could make this comparison on several different classification variables, the managers are especially interested in whether their customers have higher or lower levels of education than the population in general. To determine whether this is the case, you need to compare the results from the sample (see Exhibit 12.2) with those for the overall population in the trade area. In this case, we'll compare the sample results with the results of a larger general opinion survey conducted at about the same time that included a similar measure of respondent education.

Exhibit 12.8 presents data from the general opinion survey alongside the data from the AFC study. You'll notice quickly that a bigger proportion of AFC customers fall in the highest education category (and lower proportions fall in the lower categories). But is this enough evidence to reject the null hypothesis that the education levels are the same? This is the type of problem for which the **chi-square goodness-of-fit test** is ideally suited. Using SPSS (SPSS menu sequence: Analyze > Nonparametric Tests > Legacy Dialogs > Chi-square) we obtained $X^2 = 118.38$, on 5 degrees of freedom,[6] and the associated p-value, $p < .001$. Because the p-value is much lower than the significance level we established for the test ($\alpha = .05$), we have evidence to suggest that AFC customers are different in terms of education level from the general population in the city. In particular, they appear to be considerably more highly educated.

chi-square goodness-of-fit test
A statistical test to determine whether some observed pattern of frequencies corresponds to an expected pattern.

EXHIBIT 12.8

AFC Customer Education Level versus Education Level in Trade Area

Level of Education Achieved	AFC Number	AFC Valid Percent	Trade Area Number	Trade Area Valid Percent
Less than high school	4	2%	147	10%
High school degree	34	15	294	20
Some college	46	20	412	28
Associates degree	7	3	59	4
Four-year college degree	52	23	368	25
Advanced degree	82	36	191	13
Total	225	100	1,471	100

The chi-square test can also be applied when there are only two levels for a variable, for example, gender. An alternative approach is the binomial test (SPSS Menu Sequence: Analyze > Nonparametric Tests > Legacy Dialogs > Binomial).

Testing Statistical Significance with Continuous Variables

When the variable to be compared against a standard is a continuous measure, the approach is a little different and allows us to take advantage of increased statistical power. As an example, AFC managers learned from a trade association that, nationwide, members of fitness centers visit a center eight times per month on average. For years, AFC trainers had been encouraging clients to come to the center more frequently, even if they stayed less time per visit. The results of the current study suggest that clients do visit the center more frequently per month compared with fitness center clients overall (recall that mean visits per month for the sample was 10), but can we say with any certainty that the population of AFC members does, in fact, visit the center more frequently than the national average? In this situation, we'll use SPSS (or another software package) to compare the sample mean against an external standard. The analysis (SPSS menu sequence: Analyze > Compare Means > One-Sample T Test) returns the following results—t-value = 3.82, on 197 degrees of freedom, $p < .001$. So, the probability that we could have obtained a difference this large (a mean of 10 visits vs. 8 visits) if there truly were no difference between the mean visits for AFC members and the standard is less than 1 in 1,000. The p-value is lower than the conventional standard for significance level ($\alpha = .05$), and we would conclude that AFC members visit the center more frequently per month than the national average.

WORLDWIDE NUMBER OF MOBILE APPLICATION DOWNLOADS EXPECTED TO **RISE 117%** TO 17.7 BILLION IN 2011.

13 Analysis & Interpretation:
Multiple Variables Simultaneously

POLL QUESTION:

A significant correlation between two variables means one variable causes the other variable.

STRONGLY DISAGREE 1 2 3 4 5 STRONGLY AGREE

Learning Objectives

1. Discuss why a researcher might conduct a multivariate analysis.
2. Explain the purpose and importance of cross tabulation.
3. Describe a technique for comparing groups on a continuous dependent variable.
4. Explain the difference between an independent sample *t*-test for means and a paired sample *t*-test for means.
5. Discuss the Pearson product-moment correlation coefficient.
6. Discuss a technique for examining the influence of one or more predictor variables on an outcome variable.

INTRODUCTION

Sometimes univariate analyses are enough for providing answers for a research problem. Lots of times, however, you'll need to use multivariate analyses to get the information you need—in many cases, adding one or more additional variables to an analysis can provide a much deeper understanding of the situation.

Here's an example: In an awareness test for an ice cream shop, 58 percent of survey respondents could name the shop in a recall task. Closer analysis revealed several insights, however. Only 45 percent of male respondents could name the shop, compared with 71 percent of female respondents. And age also seemed to be related to awareness: 69 percent of respondents 20 years old and younger could name the shop, but only 54 percent of those who were 21 to 40 years old, and 39 percent of those over 40 years old could do so. If you stopped with the univariate analysis result (i.e., 58% correct in recall task), you would miss important managerial insights about gender and age. Exhibit 13.1 presents the information graphically; note how conclusions change when we consider the additional variables.

In this chapter, we present some commonly used multivariate analysis techniques. Although we'll barely scratch the surface of the full range

EXHIBIT 13.1

Univariate versus Multivariate Analysis

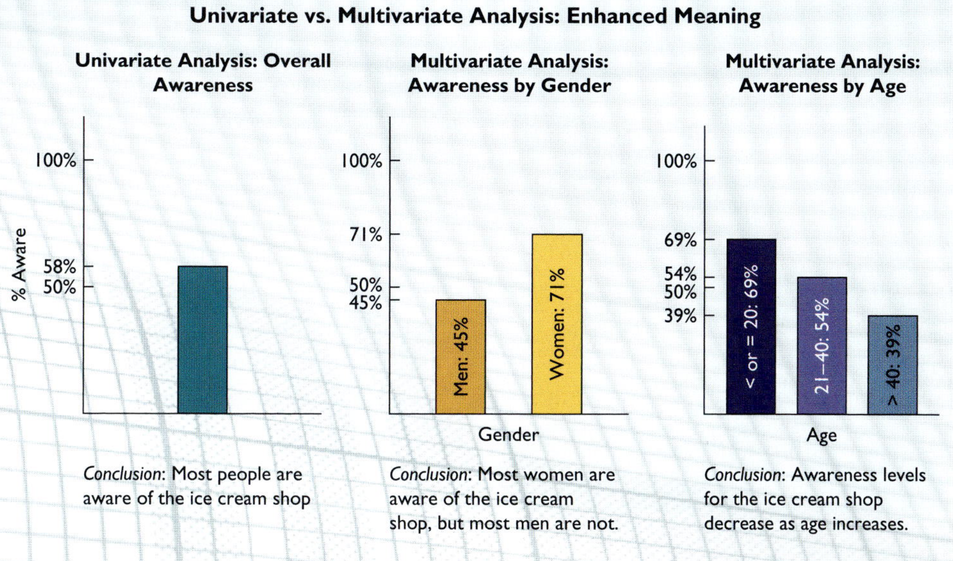

of techniques that are available and used in industry, we'll provide enough detail to get you started on the most common analyses. As with the univariate analyses presented in the previous chapter, the computer does most of the work—including providing tests of statistical significance—but you'll need to know when to use each of the approaches and how to interpret the results. Interpretation is the key!

CROSS TABULATION

cross tabulation
A multivariate technique used for studying the relationship between two or more categorical variables. The technique considers the joint distribution of sample elements across variables.

Cross tabulation is an important tool for studying the relationships between two (or more) categorical variables. It is the most used multivariate data analysis technique in applied marketing research. Many marketing research studies go no further than simple cross tabulations between two variables at a time. Because they are so commonly used, you'll want to take the time to fully understand how cross-tabs are developed and interpreted.

In most multivariate analyses, you'll be trying to see whether one variable (the independent or predictor variable) has an influence on another variable (the dependent or outcome variable). With cross-tabs, the respondents are divided into groups based on the independent variable in order to see how the dependent variable varies from group to group. For example, consider again the Avery Fitness Center project discussed in previous chapters. AFC researchers wanted to know whether being referred by a doctor to the fitness center led to greater usage of the therapy pool. A quick look back at Exhibit 12.5 reveals that the therapy pool was the service used by the highest percentage (45%) of respondents in the 30 days prior to the survey. Does this percentage differ for people who were recommended by a doctor compared with people who were not? This is an ideal problem for a cross-tab analysis, because both pool usage ("yes" or "no") and learning about AFC from a doctor ("yes" or "no") are measured on categorical scales.

CROSS TABULATION IS THE MOST USED MULTIVARIATE DATA ANALYSIS TECHNIQUE IN APPLIED MARKETING RESEARCH.

Exhibit 13.2 presents SPSS output for the two-way classification of the sample respondents by pool usage and whether they learned about AFC from a doctor (SPSS Menu Sequence: Analyze > Descriptive Statistics > Cross-tabs). There's a lot going on in this table, so take some time to look it over carefully. First, note the *marginal totals* for each variable: 104 (45%) respondents had used the therapy pool (127, or 55%, had not), and 54 (23%) respondents had learned about AFC from a doctor (177, or 77%, did not). The marginal totals represent the frequency counts for each of the variables independently.

With a cross-tab analysis, however, you can also examine the joint distribution of the two variables. This will allow us to see whether the outcome (% of people using the pool) is different for those who learned about AFC from a doctor versus those who did not. Because there are two levels for each of the variables being considered, there are four possible combinations when both variables are considered together ($2 \times 2 = 4$). These combinations are represented by four *cells* in the cross tabulation. For example, of the 54 respondents who had learned about AFC from a doctor, 34 of them had used the therapy pool in the past 30 days and 20 of them had not. Of 177 who did not learn about AFC from a doctor, 70 had used the pool and

© FRANCESCO RUGGERI/PHOTOGRAPHER'S CHOICE/GETTY IMAGES

EXHIBIT 13.2

Avery Fitness Center: Therapy Pool Usage by Doctor's Recommendation (SPSS Output)

Doctor recommendation? * Utilized therapy pool? Cross Tabulation

			Utilized therapy pool?		
			No	**Yes**	**Total**
Doctor recommendation?	No	Count	107	70	177
		% within doctor recommendation	60.5%	39.5%	100.0%
		% within utilized therapy pool	84.3%	67.3%	76.6%
	Yes	Count	20	34	54
		% within doctor recommendation	37.0%	63.0%	100.0%
		% within utilized therapy pool	15.7%	32.7%	23.4%
	Total	Count	127	104	231
		% within doctor recommendation	55.0%	45.0%	100.0%
		% within utilized therapy pool	100.0%	100.0%	100.0%

107 had not. But what does this mean for AFC managers? Does it appear that there is some connection between doctors' recommendations and therapy pool usage?

We've noted before that percentages are incredibly useful for interpreting results. Each of the cells in Exhibit 13.2 contains two different percentages (because we asked for them as part of the analysis in SPSS) that differ depending upon what number is used as the denominator in the calculation of the percentage. The first percentage in each cell, sometimes called the "row percentage," is calculated using the row total as the denominator. For example, consider the cell representing respondents who neither used the pool nor learned about AFC from a doctor. The row percentage is 61 percent (i.e., 107/177 = 0.605). The next percentage in each cell is the "column percentage" and is calculated using the column total as the denominator. Thus, for those who neither used the pool nor learned about AFC from a doctor, the column percentage is 84 percent (i.e., 107/127 = 0.843).

Which of these percentages should you use? To answer this question, think about which of the variables being studied is likely to be the independent variable (cause) and which is likely to be the dependent variable (effect). *Percentages are always calculated in the direction of the causal variable.* That is, the marginal totals for the causal variable are always used as the denominator when calculating percentages in cross tabulations. We've already theorized that a doctor's recommendation might have caused respondents to utilize the therapy pool; because the different levels of the causal variable are represented by the rows in the cross tabulation (see Exhibit 13.2), the row percentages should be used.

Now back to the original question: Does it appear that people who are recommended by doctors are more or less likely to use the therapy pool? Looking only at the row percentages, can you detect a different pattern of responses for the two groups (i.e., those who learned about AFC from doctors and those who did not)? From the sample results, it looks as though people who learn about AFC from doctors are more likely to use the therapy pool than people who don't learn about it from a doctor (63% vs. 40%, respectively). Thus, from a manager's perspective, it appears that if the proportion of AFC customers who come because of a doctor's recommendation increases (perhaps through increased promotion to doctors), utilization of the therapy pool may go up significantly. The trick is to determine whether this is likely to be true for the population and not just for the sample.

The **Pearson chi-square (X^2) test of independence** assesses the degree

Pearson chi-square (X^2) test of independence A commonly used statistic for testing the null hypothesis that categorical variables are independent of one another.

FAST FACT:

4% OF ADULTS USE **LOCATION-SHARING SERVICES** LIKE FOURSQUARE OR GOWALLA.

to which the variables in a cross-tabulation analysis are independent of one another. The value can range from zero to some upper value limited by sample size and the distribution of cases across the cells. The chi-square value, degrees of freedom for the chi-square test, and the *p*-value are provided in the output for standard statistical analysis software packages.

For the analysis presented in Exhibit 13.2, the Pearson chi-square value is 9.17, on 1 degree of freedom (df), and the associated *p*-value is 0.002; we obtained this value by selecting the appropriate statistics option in the cross-tabs analysis in SPSS. Thus, if these variables are truly independent of one another in the population, the probability that we could have obtained a chi-square value this large is less than 1 percent, and we can reject the null hypothesis that the variables are independent. (Recall that for most purposes *p*-values have to be under 0.05 for a result to be "statistically significant;" this is the case for the analysis in Exhibit 13.2.)

Although the chi-square test indicates whether two variables are independent, it doesn't measure the strength of association when they are dependent. One popular approach for measuring the strength of the relationship between two categorical variables is **Cramer's *V***, which is scaled to range between 0 and 1, with higher values representing a stronger relationship between the variables. For our analysis, Cramer's *V* is equal to 0.195, an indication of a modest degree of association between the variables.

Cramer's *V*
A statistic used to measure the strength of relationship between categorical variables.

INDEPENDENT SAMPLES *T*-TEST FOR MEANS

Researchers commonly encounter situations in which a continuous outcome measure must be compared across groups. For instance, imagine that a brand manager wanted to know whether men and women held different attitudes toward her brand. Or maybe a manager for a small hospital chain wanted to compare patient perceptions of service quality across two different hospitals in the chain. In these and many other cases, the task is to test for differences across groups (i.e., men vs. women; hospital A patients vs. hospital B patients) on some important variable assessed using a continuous measure (i.e., attitude toward the brand; perceptions of service quality). In situations like this, the **independent samples *t*-test for means** is the correct method of analysis.

independent samples *t*-test
A technique commonly used to determine whether two groups differ on some characteristic assessed on a continuous measure.

The AFC managers had begun to wonder if the space within the facility might be better utilized. They were especially concerned that a great deal of floor space—not to mention equipment—was currently dedicated to circuit training, a form of exercise in which participants move fairly rapidly from one exercise to another. The goal of the exercise circuit is to provide a workout for all muscle groups in the body. It wasn't clear, however, whether they could continue

FAST FACT:
ALMOST **25%** OF ALL FORD AND GM **HYBRID VEHICLES** WERE SOLD TO THE FEDERAL GOVERNMENT IN 2009 AND 2010.

© ZHANG JUN/XINHUA /LANDOV

to justify the amount of space dedicated to circuit training.

The managers knew that about 22 percent of AFC members had used circuit training in the past month (see Exhibit 12.5 in the previous chapter), but that alone wasn't enough to justify the space requirements. If there were evidence, however, that participants who used circuit training were more involved in the center, as evidenced by visiting AFC more frequently than those who don't use the circuit, they decided that they would leave the status quo. Otherwise, they intended to use the space for things that might be more appealing. Because of the importance of the decision, they decided to consider only the responses of AFC members who had actually visited the center during the previous 30 days. (In the SPSS analysis, this is easily accomplished using the following SPSS menu sequence: Data > Select Cases.)

Do the data obtained from AFC members verify that those who used circuit training visited the fitness center more regularly than those who didn't? Given that the outcome variable is continuous (number of visits; see Question 2 on the survey presented in Exhibit 11.2) and the independent variable is categorical (use of circuit training; see Question 1), this is an ideal situation to use the independent samples *t*-test to determine whether the two groups (i.e., those who used circuit training vs. those who did not) truly differ with respect to how frequently they visit the fitness center.

Just about any statistical software package can be used to easily perform the analysis. Exhibit 13.3 presents the output from an SPSS analysis. (SPSS Menu Sequence: Analyze > Compare Means > Independent-Samples T Test) First, notice that the mean number of visits over the 30-day period does appear to be different for members who used circuit training (mean = 14.2 visits) compared with those who did not (mean = 11.8 visits). Can we conclude, however, that this is the case? Not yet.

As usual, we must test to determine how likely it is that we could have obtained these *sample* results (a difference of 2.4 visits per month) if there really were no difference in the overall *population* from which the samples were drawn. The test statistic, t, is found in the SPSS output in Exhibit 13.3. In this case, the calculated t-value is -2.31 with 156 degrees of freedom. The associated p-value is less than 0.05. Thus, if there really were no difference in number of visits for those who used circuit training versus those who didn't, the probability that we could have obtained the results we did in our sample is less than the conventional standard for achieving statistical significance ($p < 0.05$). As a result, we can conclude that members who use the exercise circuit do, in fact, visit the fitness center more frequently than those who don't. The managers decided to keep the exercise circuit.

EXHIBIT 13.3

Avery Fitness Center: Number of Visits (Past 30 Days) by Exercise Circuit Usage (SPSS Output)

Group Statistics

	Utilized exercise circuit?	N	Mean	Std. Deviation	Std. Error Mean
Number of visits	no	114	11.83	5.782	0.542
	yes	44	14.20	5.773	0.870

Independent Samples Test

		Levene's Test for Equality of Variances		t-test for Eqality of Means					95% Confidence Interval of the Difference	
		F	Sig.	t	df	Sig. (2-tailed)	Mean Difference	Std. Error Difference	Lower	Upper
Number of Visits	Equal variances assumed	0.196	0.658	−2.312	156	0.022	−2.371	1.026	−4.397	−.345
	Equal variances not assumed			−2.313	78.276	0.023	−2.371	1.025	−4.412	−.331

PAIRED SAMPLE *T*-TEST FOR MEANS

paired sample *t*-test

A technique for comparing two means when scores for both variables are provided by the same sample.

The independent samples *t*-test for means always compares mean scores for the same variable measured in two groups (for example, people who have used circuit training versus those who haven't). What happens when you need to compare two means when both measures are provided by the same people? In that case, you'll use the **paired sample *t*-test** for means.

As with the independent samples *t*-test, the paired sample *t*-test is common in marketing research. For example, take a quick look back at Question 5 on the Avery Fitness Center survey presented in Exhibit 11.2. The researchers wanted to understand what motivates people to participate in AFC programs. If the results indicated that the social benefits of meeting with other people were especially important, managers planned to develop additional social activities for members and were even considering rearranging the layout of the center to encourage greater interaction among members while they exercise.

Exhibit 13.4 presents the mean importance scores for four possible reasons for participating in AFC programs in graphic format. The results indicate that social aspects are the least important of all the possible reasons for participating in AFC programs. Managers wanted to be sure, however, before giving up their plans. Is there evidence in the sample data to support the conclusion that social aspects are least important to population members?

Exhibit 13.5 presents SPSS output for three different paired sample *t*-tests, one each for comparing the importance of social aspects with the importance of the other three possible reasons for participating in AFC programs. (SPSS Menu Sequence: Analyze > Compare Means > Paired-Samples T Test) As an example, the paired sample *t*-value comparing the importance of social aspects with the importance of general health and fitness is $t = -18.05$, on 189 degrees of freedom, and the associated p-value is well under 0.05, so we can conclude that AFC members place greater importance on general health and fitness than social considerations when it comes to program participation. Now, take a close look at Exhibit 13.5 and see whether there is evidence that the members think that the other reasons are also more important.

EXHIBIT 13.4

Avery Fitness Center: Importance of Various Reasons for Participating

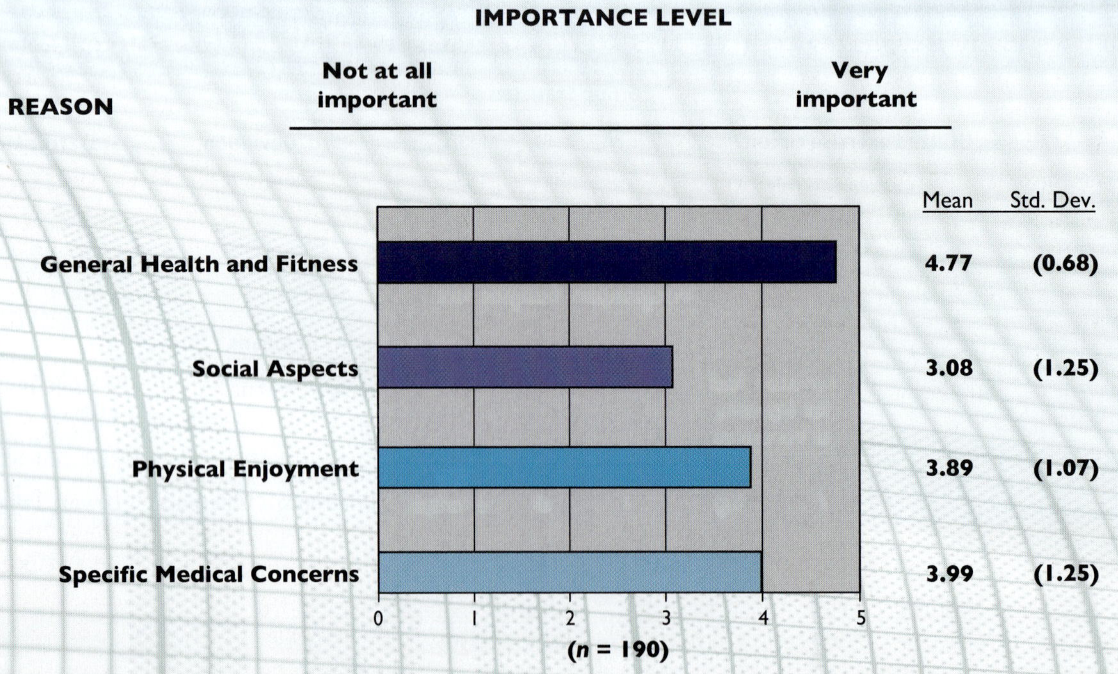

(n = 190)

EXHIBIT 13.5

Avery Fitness Center: Paired Sample *t*-Tests (SPSS Output)

Paired Samples Test

	Paired Differences							
				95% Confidence Interval of the Difference				
	Mean	Std. Deviation	Std. Error Mean	Lower	Upper	*t*	df	Sig. (2-tailed)
Pair 1 Importance: Social Aspects – Importance: General Health and Fitness	−1.689	1.290	.094	−1.874	−1.505	−18.048	189	.000
Pair 2 Importance: Social Aspects – Importance: Physical Enjoyment	−.811	1.111	.081	−.969	−.652	−10.058	189	.000
Pair 3 Importance: Social Aspects – Importance: Specific Medical Concerns	−.911	1.552	.113	−1.133	−.688	−8.085	189	.000

PEARSON PRODUCT-MOMENT CORRELATION COEFFICIENT

So far, we've looked at relationships in which the causal, or independent, variable was a categorical measure. What happens when both the independent variable(s) and the dependent variable are measured on continuous scales? One option is to calculate the degree of correlation between two continuous variables.

The correlation coefficient is a fundamental building block of data analysis. You probably have a basic understanding of what it means when someone says that two things are "correlated." You might not know the technical details, but you have an intuitive understanding that the two concepts, events, or ideas somehow "go together," that there is some sort of association or even relationship between them. As one thing changes, so does the other.

Pearson product-moment correlation coefficient
A statistic that indicates the degree of linear association between two continuous variables. The correlation coefficient can range from −1 to +1.

The **Pearson product-moment correlation coefficient** provides a means of quantifying the degree of association between two continuous variables. Essentially, the Pearson product-moment correlation coefficient assesses the degree to which two continuous variables change consistently across cases. That is, are higher or lower scores on one variable associated with higher or lower scores on the second variable as we go across cases? The correlation coefficient can range from −1 (representing perfect negative linear correlation) to +1 (representing perfect positive linear correlation). In practice, correlations rarely approach −1 or +1.

Is there a relationship between an AFC member's age and the total fees that he or she pays the center? Managers thought that there might be—and if so, they planned to pay a little closer attention to their older customers. To find out, they used SPSS (SPSS Menu Sequence: Analyze > Correlate > Bivariate) to obtain the Pearson product-moment correlation coefficient. Exhibit 13.6 presents the output for the correlation between age and revenues over a one-year period. Notice that the output provides the correlation coefficient, the corresponding *p*-value (Sig.), and the number of cases in the analysis (*N*). In this case, the correlation coefficient equals 0.25, which is evidence of a modest relationship between the two variables in the sample data. As always, though, the bigger question is whether there is an association between the variables in the population of all AFC members, not just within the sample. The *p*-value for the analysis is below the usual significance level (i.e., 0.05), and we can conclude that there is a statistically significant relationship between age and revenue.

© PIXSOOZ/SHUTTERSTOCK.COM

Caution in the Interpretation of Correlations

Before going further, we need to offer a quick caution about interpreting correlation coefficients (and this also applies to other multivariate analyses as well). Sometimes you'll be tempted to assume a causal relationship between two variables when you obtain a statistically significant correlation coefficient. Just because two variables are correlated doesn't mean that one variable necessarily caused the other one. There is nothing in correlation analysis, or any other mathematical procedure, that can be used to establish causality. All these procedures can do is measure the nature and degree of association between variables. Statements of causality must come from underlying knowledge and theories about the phenomena under investigation. They do not come from the mathematics. Here's an example to drive home this point:

> ***News Flash: Ice cream purchases are correlated with murder rates!***

From what you know about ice cream, or what you could theorize about murder rates, how would this information help you to know why a relationship might exist between these two variables? Would you ever be tempted to say purchasing ice cream causes someone to take another person's life? What we know is people purchase more ice cream when the weather is warmer and the days are longer. What we could theorize is murder rates are higher when more people are outside. So, what do these two activities have in common? If you said they both happen during the summer, you are correct! Ice cream sales and murder rates are higher during summer months, so the relationship between the two is due to a third variable (i.e., time of year, which itself reflects temperature). Yes, ice cream purchases and murder rates are correlated, but this in no way provides evidence that one causes the other.

So, in the AFC case, managers can theorize that growing older causes members to spend more money with AFC, but the correlational data alone cannot prove this to be true. The available evidence is consistent with this theory, but not sufficient to establish causality.

EXHIBIT 13.6

Avery Fitness Center: Correlation between Age and Revenues (SPSS Output)

Correlations

		Age in Years	One-Year Revenue ($)
Age in Years	Pearson Correlation	1	.246**
	Sig. (2-tailed)		.000
	N	224	224
One-Year Revenue ($)	Pearson Correlation	.246**	1
	Sig. (2-tailed)	.000	
	N	224	231

**Correlation is significant at the 0.01 level (2-tailed).

REGRESSION ANALYSIS

regression analysis
A statistical technique used to derive an equation representing the influence of a single (simple regression) or multiple (multiple regression) independent variables on a continuous dependent, or outcome, variable.

Regression analysis provides a means for getting at the nature of the relationship between one or more predictor variables and an outcome variable. If there is a single predictor variable, the technique is referred to as *simple regression*; with multiple predictors, it's called *multiple regression*. Usually, you'll have reason to believe that the predictor variable(s) somehow influence the dependent variable (keeping in mind that the mathematics alone cannot prove causation), although this doesn't have to be the case.

We've already established that there is a correlational relationship between age and revenues for AFC members. Managers also wanted to see whether they could pinpoint any basic motivations that were associated with spending more money at the fitness center. Recall that respondents provided importance ratings for four different reasons for participating in AFC programs (see Question 5 in Exhibit 11.2). Is it possible that the importance of visiting the center for (1) general health and fitness, (2) social aspects, (3) physical enjoyment, and/or (4) specific medical concerns leads to spending more money with AFC? If so, managers might try to attract new members by appealing to those needs in their promotional efforts.

In regression analysis, the dependent variable (revenues) is "regressed" on the set of predictor, or independent, variables (SPSS Menu Sequence: Analyze > Regression > Linear). Mathematically, an equation is produced that represents the best fit between the predictors and the outcome. As shown in Exhibit 13.7, the analysis produces regression coefficients for each

EXHIBIT 13.7

Avery Fitness Center: Regression of Revenues on Several Predictors (SPSS Output)

Model Summary

Model	R	R Square	Adjusted R Square	Std. Error of the Estimate
1	.408[a]	.166	.143	156.24062

[a] Predictors: (Constant), Importance: Specific Medical Concerns, Age in Years, Importance: Physical Enjoyment, Importance: General Health and Fitness, Importance: Social Aspects

ANOVA[b]

Model		Sum of Squares	df	Mean Square	*F*	Sig.
1	Regression	861276.227	5	172255.245	7.056	.000[a]
	Residual	4320770.289	177	24411.132		
	Total	5182046.516	182			

[a] Predictors: (Constant), Importance: Specific Medical Concerns, Age in Years, Importance: Physical Enjoyment, Importance: General Health and Fitness, Importance: Social Aspects
[b] Dependent Variable: One-Year Revenue ($)

Coefficients[a]

		Unstandardized Coefficients		Standardized Coefficients		
Model		B	Std. Error	Beta	*t*	Sig.
1	(Constant)	−88.819	108.633		−.818	.415
	Age in Years	4.334	.996	.304	4.351	.000
	Importance: General Health and Fitness	14.850	18.769	.060	.791	.430
	Importance: Social Aspects	36.637	11.224	.273	3.264	.001
	Importance: Physical Enjoyment	−29.639	13.609	−.188	−2.178	.031
	Importance: Specific Medical Concerns	2.486	9.828	.018	.253	.801

[a] Dependent Variable: One-Year Revenue ($)

of the predictor variables. These coefficients represent the average change in the outcome variable per unit change in the associated predictor variable, holding all other predictor variables constant. For example, the sample results indicate that for each additional year in age we can expect an average increase in yearly revenues of a little more than $4. Similarly, increasing the importance of social aspects one position on the rating scale (say, from 3 to 4) is associated with an increase of nearly $37 in annual revenue. But we're getting ahead of ourselves.

Before we try to interpret the individual regression coefficients, it's important to check a couple of things first. Start by looking to see whether there is an overall statistically significant relationship between the set of predictors and the outcome variable; if there isn't, there's no point in looking at any of the individual predictors. In Exhibit 13.7 you'll see a section of SPSS output labeled "ANOVA" (which stands for "analysis of variance"). The overall model is tested on the basis of the amount of variance in the dependent variable that can be explained by the regression relative to the variation in the dependent variable that cannot be explained. In this case, the *F*-statistic equals 7.06, and the corresponding *p*-value is less than 0.001, so there is a statistically significant relationship between the amount of fees members pay and the predictor variables (age plus the four importance ratings).

We also need to verify that our set of predictors can explain (or predict) a meaningful portion of the variation in the outcome variable. (If you work with a large enough sample, almost any relationship at all between variables will become statistically significant, even if the effects are trivial from a managerial standpoint.) If some or all of our predictor variables are causing changes in the outcome variable, then there has to be some degree of association between changes in the predictors and changes in the outcome variable. The **coefficient of multiple determination** calculates the closeness of the relationship between the predictor variables and the outcome variable in a multiple regression analysis and is symbolized by R^2. (In simple regression, this is called the *coefficient of determination.*) The AFC researchers found this value in the "Model Summary"

coefficient of multiple determination (R^2)

A measure representing the relative proportion of the total variation in the dependent variable that can be explained or accounted for by the fitted regression equation. When there is only one predictor variable, this value is referred to as the *coefficient of determination.*

FAST FACT:

COMPARING Q1 2009 TO Q1 2010, **LAPTOP SALES INCREASED 43%,** FOR THE BEST QUARTERLY MOBILE COMPUTER SALES IN EIGHT YEARS.

section (see Exhibit 11.7); R^2 was equal to 0.17. This means that the predictors have a small to modest association with the outcome variable; together they can account for 17 percent of the variation in revenues for the one-year period. We'd like the coefficient of multiple determination to be higher, but considering all of the many other things that might influence how much a member spends with the center, this result was meaningful to AFC managers.

Now we'll shift our attention back to the individual predictors. Looking at the *t*-values associated with the five predictors (see Exhibit 13.7), we see that age ($t = 4.35$), the importance of social aspects ($t = 3.26$), and the importance of physical enjoyment ($t - 2.18$) are statistically significant predictors of revenues, but that importance of attending the center for general health and fitness and the importance of attending because of specific medical concerns do not seem to influence the amount of money people spent over the year at AFC. (For the latter two predictor variables, the *p*-value, the probability that we could have seen an effect of this magnitude if there truly were no relationship between the predictor and revenues, is greater than 0.05.)

So what do these results mean? First, it appears that older people spend more money each year at the center compared with younger people. Managers might want to adjust their promotional efforts to appeal to older customers. And more importantly, maybe they could spend more time determining what this important market really needs with respect to fitness and how to satisfy these needs.

Second, people who place greater importance on social aspects as a reason for going to AFC seem to spend more money than those who place less importance on social aspects. Interestingly, we saw earlier that this is the least important reason for attending the center on average across all respondents, which suggests that there is an opportunity for growth in this area. Specifically, managers might want to promote the importance of social interaction as an ingredient in maintaining health and fitness as people grow older.

Finally, look closely at the coefficient that represents the influence of the perceived importance of physical enjoyment as a reason for visiting AFC on one-year revenues. This value (−29.64) indicates that for every one-unit increase in the importance rating for this aspect, one-year revenues decrease by about $30. In effect, if physical enjoyment is an important reason for visiting the center for a member, he or she ultimately seems to spend less money. AFC managers may need to put some thought into what this means for the organization.

As a final note to our discussion of regression, we should point out that regression is a robust analytic tool that can also be used when one or more independent variables are categorical as opposed to continuous variables. You can learn more about this—and many other multivariate analysis techniques—by reading a good multivariate statistics text. We hope, however, that you now have a better understanding of the value of analyzing variables in combination.

14 The Research Report

POLL QUESTION:

Sometimes managers prefer having less information than more information.

STRONGLY DISAGREE 1 ○ 2 ○ 3 ○ 4 ○ 5 ○ STRONGLY AGREE

Learning Objectives

1. Discuss three writing standards that a report should meet if it is to communicate effectively with readers.
2. Outline the main elements that make up a standard research report.
3. Explain the kind of information contained in the executive summary.
4. Discuss two fundamental rules for making good oral presentations.
5. List some of the different kinds of charts that can be used in presenting study results.

INTRODUCTION

It doesn't help much to conduct a near flawless research project if you can't communicate the research results. Creating an effective report, whether written or oral, is a challenging process that takes more effort than you probably think. But you have to put in the time to get it right, because the project is a failure if you can't communicate the results effectively.

You will almost always be expected to prepare a written research report. And most of the time, you'll also be expected to present an oral report as well. These reports have a huge impact on whether the information generated by the research is actually used. This makes sense when you consider that the reports are all that most executives—the people who needed answers in the first place and who can make decisions based on the results—will see of the project. A solid written report or presentation sends an important signal about the likely quality of the overall project.

In this chapter, we will offer some simple guidelines for developing successful research reports. We start with written reports and then give some suggestions to help develop an oral presentation. Finally, we'll describe some different kinds of charts that might be useful for communicating the results of the research project.

THE WRITTEN RESEARCH REPORT

Share prices for Apple, Inc., dropped three percent during a period in December 2006 after reports started surfacing in the media about a sharp drop in revenues from the iTunes music download service offered by

© DAVID YOUNG-WOLFF/PHOTOEDIT

the company. An article in Britain's *The Register*, for example, described iTunes monthly revenues as "collapsing" by 65 percent since January of that year, citing a marketing research report prepared by Forrester Research.

It turns out that media members had misunderstood data in the report released by Forrester Research. What the study actually revealed was a leveling off of iTunes downloads, certainly nothing coming close to a collapse in sales. Not surprisingly, with its market value on the line, Forrester received a call from a "clearly upset" Apple, and analysts quickly set the record straight.[1]

As this example illustrates, only one thing really matters with written research reports—how well they communicate with the reader. Research reports must be tailor-made for their readers, paying attention to their technical sophistication, their interest in the subject area, the circumstances under which they will read the report, and how they are likely to use it. Take the time to make the report understandable to your readers.

Sometimes managers prefer having less information than more information. They only want the results, not a discussion of how the results were obtained or any conclusions or recommendations. Other executives prefer just the opposite. They not only want a discussion of the results, but also detailed information on how the results were obtained as well as your conclusions, reasoning, and recommendations. In a nutshell, your audience determines the type of report, and you need to learn the specific preferences of your audience.

Research Report Writing Standards

To communicate effectively, a written report must be complete, accurate, and clear.[2]

Completeness

A report is **complete** when it provides all the information readers need in language they understand. This means that you must continually ask whether every question in the original assignment has been addressed. An incomplete report probably means that you'll soon be writing supplementary reports, which are annoying and potentially deadly to your credibility as a researcher.

completeness
The degree to which the report provides all the information readers need in language they understand.

When it comes to completeness, there's a bit of a paradox. A written report must be complete, without being *too* complete. You need to include all relevant information—but if you include too much information, the report quickly becomes less usable (see the section on clarity). You certainly don't want to force the reader to sift through page after page of nonessential results looking for the things that really matter. The trick is in determining what really matters and what ought to be included in appendices to the report or left out entirely. This isn't always easy. Think carefully about the reader.

Accuracy

Imagine that you've done an amazing job of collecting and analyzing data that are perfectly appropriate for making a key decision, but you hurried as you prepared the research report and made mistakes. **Accuracy** in report development is another important consideration. Exhibit 14.1 illustrates some examples of sources of inaccuracy in report writing.

accuracy
The degree to which the reasoning in the report is logical and the information correct.

Problems with accuracy are hard to correct after the written report has been distributed. As a result, it's a really, *really* good idea to ask several people to review the report for accuracy before it's sent to managers. And, much like a pretest of a survey, it wouldn't hurt to have a manager review a preliminary version of the written report.

Clarity

Clarity of writing is one of the most difficult standards to achieve. Clarity comes from clear and logical thinking and precision

clarity
The degree to which the phrasing in the report is precise.

FAST FACT:
WILLIAMS COLLEGE
IN WILLIAMSTOWN, MASSACHUSETTS, HAS THE HIGHEST RATE OF STUDENTS WHO GRADUATE IN FOUR YEARS: **93%**.

© PALTO/SHUTTERSTOCK.COM

EXHIBIT 14.1

Some Examples of Sources of Inaccuracy in Report Writing

A. SIMPLE ERRORS IN ADDITION OR SUBTRACTION

"In the United States, 14 percent of the population has an elementary school education or less, 51 percent has attended or graduated from high school, and 16 percent has attended college."

An oversight such as this (14 + 51 + 16 does not equal 100%) can easily be corrected by the author, but not so easily by the reader, because he or she may not know whether one or more of the percentage values is incorrect or whether a category might have been left out of the tally.

B. CONFUSION BETWEEN PERCENTAGES AND PERCENTAGE POINTS

The company's profits as a percentage of sales were 6.0 percent in 2000 and 8.0 percent in 2005. Therefore, they increased only 2.0 percent in five years. In this example, the increase is 2.0 percentage points, or 33 percent.

C. INACCURACY CAUSED BY GRAMMATICAL ERRORS

The reduction in the government's price supports for dairy products has reduced farm income $600 million to $800 million per year.

To express a range of reduction, the author should have written, "The reduction in the government's price supports for dairy products has reduced farm income $600–$800 million per year."

D. CONFUSED TERMINOLOGY RESULTING IN FAULTY CONCLUSIONS

The Jones' annual household income increased from $15,000 in 1979 to $45,000 in 2009, thereby tripling the family's purchasing power.

Although the Jones' annual household income may have tripled in 30 years, the family's purchasing power certainly did not, as the cost of living, as measured by the consumer price index, more than tripled in the same period.

of expression. When the underlying logic is fuzzy or the language imprecise, readers won't understand what they've read. If they have to guess what you meant, bad things can happen. Achieving clarity, however, requires effort.

The first, and most important, rule is that the report be well organized. For this to happen, you must first clarify for yourself the purpose of your report and how you intend to accomplish writing it. Make an outline of your major points. Put the points in logical order and place the supporting details in their proper position. Tell the reader what you are going to cover in the report and then do what you said you were going to do.

When it comes to the actual writing of the report, you should use short paragraphs and short sentences. Don't be evasive or ambiguous; once you decide what you want to say, come right out and say it. Choose your words carefully, making them as precise and understandable as possible.

Don't expect your first draft to be satisfactory. First drafts are *never* good enough. Expect to rewrite—or at least severely edit—the written research report several times. When rewriting, attempt to reduce the length by half. That forces you to simplify and remove the clutter. It also forces you to think about every word and its purpose, to evaluate whether each word is helping you say what you want to say. Good reports tend to be concise.

Research Report Outline

Research reports can be organized in a variety of ways. In this section, we'll offer some advice about the key components that need to be in the report, regardless of the specific way that you choose to organize them. Using a good outline can help you achieve clarity, accuracy, and completeness in your report. Don't forget that the report format should be guided by the nature and needs of your audience. As a result, the general format presented in Exhibit 14.2 should be considered flexible.

Title Page The title page shows the subject/title of the report; the name of the organization, department, or individual for whom the report was written; the name of the organization, department, or individual submitting it; and the date. It is especially important to include the name and contact information of the researcher responsible for the project.

EXHIBIT 14.2

Written Research Report Outline

(A) Title page

(B) Table of contents

(C) Executive summary

(D) Introduction

(E) Method

(F) Results
- **a.** Limitations

(G) Conclusions and recommendations

(H) Appendices
- **a.** Copies of data collection forms
- **b.** Data collection forms with univariate results
- **c.** Codebook
- **d.** Technical appendix (if necessary)
- **e.** Exhibits not included in the body (if necessary)
- **f.** Data file for archival storage
- **g.** Bibliography

Table of Contents. The table of contents lists the headings and subheadings of the report, with page references. The table of contents will also typically include tables and figures and the pages on which they may be found. For most reports, exhibits will be labeled as either tables or figures, with maps, diagrams, and charts falling into the latter category.

Executive Summary. This might surprise you, but the executive summary is the most important part of the report, because this is the only part that many executives will read. So, it needs to contain the most essential information in the report. A good strategy when writing the executive summary is to think about what you would most want to communicate about the project if you only had 60 seconds to do so. The executive summary should be no more than one page long.

The summary begins with a statement of who authorized the research and the specific research problems or hypotheses that guided it. Next comes a brief statement about how the data were collected, including the response rate. The most important results obtained in the study are included next, often in "bullet" format, followed by conclusions (and maybe recommendations, depending upon what managers want to see). Invest the time necessary to produce a strong executive summary.

Introduction The introduction provides the background information readers need to appreciate the discussion in the remainder of the report. A little bit of background about the nature of the issue being studied is a good idea. The introduction should always state the specific research problems being addressed by the research (and include hypotheses where appropriate). In addition, this is the best place to define unfamiliar terms or terms that are used in a specific way in the report. For instance, in a study of market penetration of a new product, the introduction might define the market and name the products and companies considered "competitors" in calculating the new product's market share.

Method The methods section is one of the most difficult sections of the report to write. You face a real dilemma here. You need to give enough information so that readers can appreciate the research design, data collection methods, sampling procedures, and analysis techniques that were used—but you don't want to bore or overwhelm the reader. Technical jargon should *not* be used, because many of your readers won't understand it (nor should they be expected to).

Readers must be told whether the design was exploratory, descriptive, or causal (or some combination). They should also be told why the particular design was chosen and what its merits are in terms of the problem at hand. If your project involved multiple stages (e.g., both exploratory and descriptive research), you should present the method and results of the stages sequentially (i.e., discuss the exploratory stage and its results first, followed by the descriptive stage). In some ways, your methods section is a summary—enough detail, but not too much—of the research proposal we discussed in Chapter 2. Readers should also be told whether the results are based on secondary or primary data. If primary, are they based on observation or questionnaires? And, if the latter, how were the questionnaires administered (online, in person, mail, e-mail, telephone)?

Sampling can be a technical subject, but you need to convey how it was approached. If it's particularly complicated, you should place the details in a technical appendix. At a minimum, you need to include the following aspects of the sampling plan in the methods section: (1) explicit population definition, including unit of analysis (e.g., individuals, households, businesses); (2) sampling frame and its source; (3) type of sample drawn; (4) size of sample; and (5) response rate.

Results

The results section presents the findings of the study in some detail, often including supporting tables and figures. This section usually makes up the bulk of the report. The results need to address the specific research problems posed and must be presented with some logical structure. Results that are interesting but irrelevant in terms of the specific research problems should be omitted. A word of advice: Very few managers have any interest in seeing computer output or page after page of charts and tables. It is crucial that you think about how to best organize and present your research findings.

One effective approach is to organize the results section around the questions to be answered by the research. There are typically one or two key issues that are central to the manager's decision problem. Organize the results to provide information and answers to these issues. For example, if target market awareness is a central issue, then present the results for the questions used to assess awareness (e.g., overall recall, recognition, location recall) in a single section. If you have useful breakdowns on these variables (perhaps by gender or zip code or some other relevant variable), present these results in the same section. If another issue driving the research was target market perceptions of the company, organize these results in another section.

Tables and figures are sometimes more effective than plain text for communicating results. Note something, though. Tables, charts, and exhibits of other kinds can't replace text completely. You'll need to explain what the tables and charts mean. Still, clients will expect to see keys points illustrated clearly. Tables and charts that appear in this section of the report should each be easy to understand and focused around a single issue. More complex exhibits should appear in the technical appendix. And please note that not every result requires a table or chart. Tables are often the better choice for presenting results, compared with charts. It's often smart to use charts only for those really important findings that need extra emphasis, because having too many of them can quickly become a distraction. We'll have more to say on this later in the chapter.

It is impossible to conduct a "perfect" study, because every study has limitations. As the researcher, you know what the limitations are, and it is in your better interest to point them out to the reader (many of them are beyond your control). Stating the limitations allows you to discuss whether, and by how much, the limitations might bias the results. So, after you've provided the results, include a short section that highlights any limitations that need to be mentioned.

Conclusions and Recommendations

The results lead to the conclusions and recommendations. Conclusions are based on interpretation of the results; recommendations are suggestions as to appropriate future action. There should be a conclusion for each of the research problems that motivated the study. One good strategy is to link research problems and conclusions so closely that the reader—after reviewing the research problems—can turn directly to the conclusions to find a specific conclusion for each objective. If the study does not provide enough evidence to draw a conclusion about a research problem, you need to make that clear.

Researchers' recommendations should follow the conclusions. With strategy-oriented research, recommendations should be straightforward; after all, the whole point of the project was to make a decision. Recommendations are less straightforward—and probably more important—with

FAST FACT:

9% OF MOBILE TELEPHONE USERS HAVE AN APP FOR TRACKING OR MANAGING THEIR HEALTH.

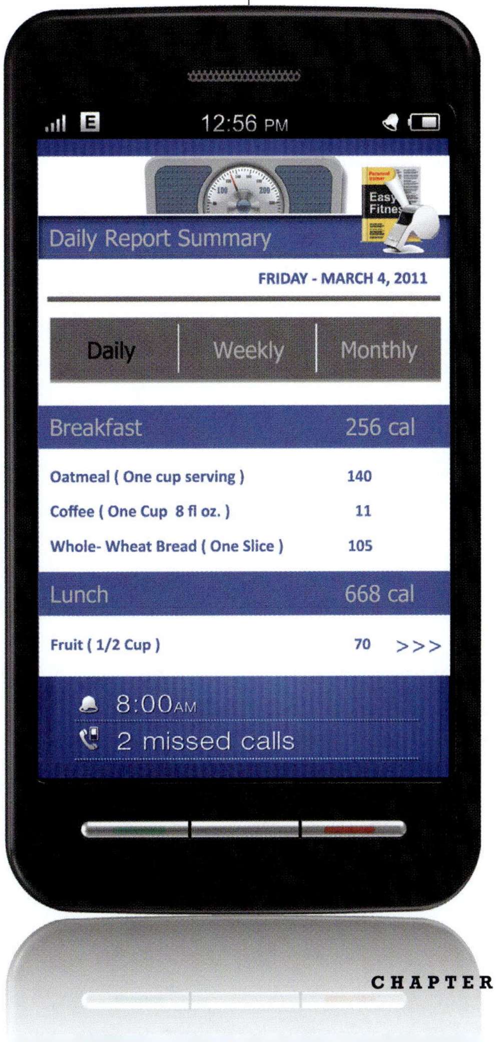

discovery-oriented research. You've collected information and now have some answers; how should the manager use this information? Note, however, that some managers may not want you to offer recommendations. Others will, because they recognize that you're the one who is closest to the research (and results) and they'll value your input.

Appendices The appendices to the report contain material that is too complex, too detailed, too specialized, or not absolutely necessary for the text. The appendices will typically include a copy of the questionnaire or observation form used to collect the data. If there are more detailed calculations for such things as sample size justification or test statistics, these will often appear in a technical appendix. It's also a good idea to compute univariate results for each of the measures in the study and include them on a second copy of the data collection form. That way, if all else fails, a manager can at least get an overall look at how respondents answered the questions. And be sure to include a bibliography if you've used references in the body of the report.

The research report will probably be the only document that eventually remains of the research project. As a result, it serves an important archival function. In addition to the copy of the data collection form, we suggest that you also include a copy of the codebook along with the actual data file containing the raw data of the project. This usually means including the electronic data file in some form. Some researchers also like to include a printout of the raw data. With the data collection form, the codebook, and the data file, any competent researcher ought to be able to recreate your results—or conduct additional analyses. Remember that your current project might become a useful piece of secondary data for some later project.

THE ORAL RESEARCH PRESENTATION

In addition to the written report, most marketing research investigations require one or more oral reports. Often, clients or managers want progress reports during the course of the project. Almost always, they require a formal oral report at the conclusion of the study. As with the written research report, you need to realize that many listeners won't be in a position to truly understand the technical aspects of your research and as a result may not be able to accurately judge its quality. They can, however, judge whether you present the research in a professional, confidence-inspiring manner or in a disorganized, uninformed one. A quality presentation can disguise poor research to some extent, but quality research cannot improve a poor presentation. Exhibit 14.3 contains some excellent ideas about becoming an effective presenter.

A QUALITY PRESENTATION CAN DISGUISE POOR RESEARCH TO SOME EXTENT, BUT QUALITY RESEARCH CANNOT IMPROVE A POOR PRESENTATION.

Preparing the Oral Report

Preparing a successful oral report requires advance knowledge of the audience. What is their technical level of sophistication? What is their involvement in the project? Their interest? You may want to present more detailed reports to those who are deeply involved in the project or who have a high level of technical sophistication. In general, though, it is better to have too little technical detail rather than too much. Executives want to hear and see what the information means to them as managers of marketing activities. What do the data suggest with respect to marketing actions? They

© ALEX JAMES BRAMWELL/SHUTTERSTOCK.COM

EXHIBIT 14.3

OPEN UP! Exceptional Presentation Skills

OPEN UP! is an acronym representing the six characteristics shared by exceptional presenters. The secret is not just knowing the characteristics, but understanding how to incorporate them into your presentation style.

THE EXCEPTIONAL PRESENTER IS:

Organized Exceptional presenters take charge! They look poised and polished. They sound prepared. You get the sense that they are not there to waste time. Their goal is not to overwhelm, but to inform, persuade, influence, entertain, or enlighten. Their message is well structured and clearly defined.

Passionate Exceptional presenters exude enthusiasm and conviction. If the presenter doesn't look and sound passionate about his or her topic, why would anyone else be passionate about it? Exceptional presenters speak from the heart and leave no doubt as to where they stand. Their energy is persuasive and contagious.

Engaging Exceptional presenters do everything in their power to engage each audience member. They build rapport quickly and involve the audience early and often. If you want their respect, you must first connect.

Natural Exceptional presenters have a natural style. Their delivery has a conversational feel. Natural presenters make it look easy. They appear comfortable with any audience. A presenter who appears natural appears confident.

AS AN EXCEPTIONAL PRESENTER, YOU MUST:

Understand Your Audience Exceptional presenters learn as much as they can about their audience before presenting to them. The more they know about the audience, the easier it will be to connect and engage.

Practice Those who practice improve. Those who don't, don't. Exceptional skills must become second nature. Practice is the most important part of the improvement process. If your delivery skills are second nature, they will not fail under pressure.

Source: Excerpted from Timothy J. Koegel, *The Exceptional Presenter* (Austin, TX: Greenleaf Book Group Press, 2007), pp. 4–5.

can ask for the necessary clarification with respect to the technical details if they want it.

Researchers must also decide in advance how the presentation will be organized. There are two popular forms of organization. Both begin by stating the general purpose of the study and the specific research problems that were addressed. They differ, however, with respect to when the conclusions are introduced. In the more common structure, you state the conclusions after you have presented the results, the evidence supporting the conclusions. This allows you to build a logical case in sequential fashion.

The other approach is to present conclusions immediately after you have stated the research problems. This is an immediate attention-grabber, especially if the conclusions are surprising. It not only gets managers to think about what actions the results suggest but also causes them to pay close attention to the evidence supporting the conclusions.

A third important aspect of preparing the oral report is the development of effective visual aids. Even if you can avoid the technical aspects of the research in your presentation, it is all but impossible to communicate results without the use of tables and figures. Most oral presentations make use of computer presentation software, such as Microsoft's PowerPoint or Apple's Keynote. Presentation software allows the relatively easy preparation of many different, high-quality kinds of exhibits ranging from definitions, to bulleted lists, to maps, to various types of charts. Presentation software also allows the use of special effects such as the addition of sound or video in the presentation or the use of animation, fading, dissolving, progressively adding or deleting items in an exhibit, all of which can also create some desired emphasis. Exhibit 14.4 offers some advice for preparing effective presentations.

Another advantage of preparing the report using computer presentation software is that it can easily be distributed electronically to the appropriate managers. By not being stuck in a file drawer, the research report is more likely to contribute to the company's key learnings or accumulated knowledge about some product or issue.

Regardless of how the visuals are prepared or which types are used, it is important to make sure they can be read by everyone in the room. We have endured far too many presentations in which the words are too small or are so close in color to the slide background that they can't be read. It is also important that visuals be kept simple so that they can be understood at a glance.

EXHIBIT 14.4

Ten Tips for Preparing Effective Presentation Slides

- **Keep them simple.** Present one point per slide, with as few words and lines as possible.
- **Use lots of slides as you talk,** rather than lots of talk per slide. Less is more when you are speaking.
- **Aim for one minute per slide,** then move on. Visuals should make their impact quickly.
- **Highlight and emphasize significant points,** using bullets, font sizes or styles, color, or by some other means.
- **Make the slides easy to read.** Use large, legible fonts. Limit fonts to one or two different ones and no more than three sizes. Make certain that the color of the text or exhibits shows up well against the background color.
- **Be careful with the use of color.** Color can add interest and emphasis; it can also distract the audience if not used carefully. Plan your color scheme and use it faithfully throughout.
- **Be careful with the use of slide backgrounds.** A consistent background (figure, logo, etc.) can help the visual display, but not if it gets in the way of communicating the content of the slide.
- **Build complex thoughts sequentially.** If you have a complicated concept to communicate, start with the ground level and use three or four slides to complete the picture.
- **Prepare copies of slides.** Hand them to the audience before or after your presentation. If people have to take notes, they won't be watching or listening closely.
- **Number the slides or pages in the handout.** You will have a better reference for discussion or a question-and-answer period.

Delivering the Oral Report

You probably already know that speaking in front of people is quite stressful for most people. We've experienced that fear too, whether teaching a new group of students for the first time, speaking at church, giving speeches, making research presentations, or on other occasions. Delivering an oral marketing research report is no different; it can be an anxious process, especially for researchers with little experience. It turns out, however, that most of the fear can be eliminated with a little preparation prior to the presentation. You're still likely to experience a little anxiety, but that's OK—if you feel no stress at all, it probably means that you aren't taking it seriously and may be about to embarrass yourself.

There are two fundamental rules for delivering good oral presentations. Carefully following these rules will also alleviate the fear of speaking in front of people for most people. Here's the first rule: ***Know your stuff.*** It's amazing how much fear is caused by uncertainty. In an oral presentation of a marketing research project, there are many potential sources of uncertainty: the nature of the problem, the processes involved with data collection, what the results really mean, whether decision makers want recommendations in addition to conclusions, what objectives need to be accomplished in the oral report, and so on. If you know what you're talking about, it's much easier to stand up and tell your audience what they need to know. And don't forget to practice. Presenting an oral report without practicing it, maybe several times, is foolhardy; you're asking for trouble.

The second rule for delivering a quality presentation is: ***Know your audience.*** The audience is likely to be composed of marketing managers, other executives, or others. You need to know your audience at the group and individual levels. If possible, find out in advance who will be attending the oral presentation. Always keep in mind the purpose of the research and the general answers that your overall audience is interested in learning. And you'll also need to understand the level of technical sophistication of the overall audience. For example, if most people listening to you would understand the notions of sampling error or statistical significance, then feel free to talk about these issues if needed.

There are a few other things to keep in mind about the oral presentation. Honor the time limit set for the meeting; use no more than half of the time for the formal presentation, saving the rest for questions

FAST FACT:

SOUTHERN METHODIST UNIVERSITY WON **26%** OF ITS FOOTBALL GAMES IN THE 20 YEARS FOLLOWING THE NCAA'S ONLY ISSUANCE OF THE **"DEATH PENALTY."**

and answers. But be careful not to rush the presentation of the information contained in the visuals. Remember, the audience is seeing them for the first time. Order your presentation in such a way that there is enough time to both present and discuss the most critical findings.

One of the unique benefits of the oral presentation is that it allows interaction. The question-and-answer period may be the most important part of your presentation. It allows you to clear up any confusion that may have arisen during your talk, emphasize points that deserve special attention, and get a feeling for the issues that are of particular concern to your audience.

Finally, it's *always* wise to get into the presentation room well before the actual presentation. This allows you to get a feel for the room and to make absolutely certain that the presentation equipment and software are working correctly. Nothing kills a great presentation faster than technical problems.

GRAPHIC PRESENTATION OF THE RESULTS

The old adage that a picture is worth a thousand words is also true for marketing research reports and presentations, provided that you do it right. Sometimes, though, the graphics can get in the way of effective communication. An inappropriate, inaccurate, or poorly designed chart can easily cause confusion or be misinterpreted. In this section, we briefly review some of the most popular forms of charts.

To be effective, you have to do more than simply convert a set of numbers into a chart. Instead, an illustration must give your audience—whether they are reading a report or watching an oral presentation—an accurate understanding of comparisons or relationships that they'd have to hunt through the numbers to get otherwise. If you do it right, a chart will allow greater understanding more quickly, more forcefully, more completely, and more accurately than could be done in any other way.

Graphic presentation isn't the only way to present quantitative information, nor is it always the best. Sometimes text and tables are more effective. Over the years, we've seen lots of beginning researchers get a little bit carried away with charts—and we understand why (check out the "Chart Builder" function in SPSS). But not every result needs to be illustrated graphically. In fact, tables are often more than enough to effectively present results from a project.

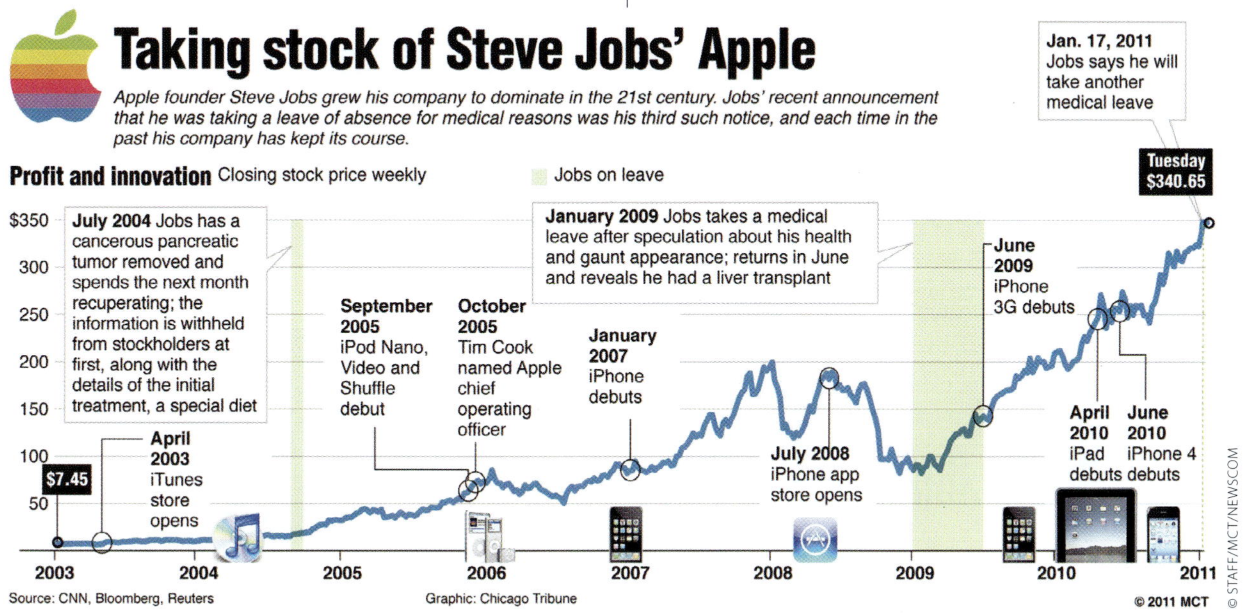

Graphics should be used *only* to illustrate key findings and when they allow insights into data that might not be seen otherwise. If you use too many charts, you'll dilute the value of the really important ones.

To help demonstrate different types of charts, we pulled 12 years' worth of personal consumption expenditures (see Exhibit 14.5) from a government report. We'll use these data for most of the examples in this section.

EXHIBIT 14.5

Personal Consumption Expenditures for a Recent 12-Year Period (billions of dollars)

Year	Total Personal Consumption Expenditures	Durable Goods	Nondurable Goods	Services
Year 1	$3,659.3	$480.3	$1,193.7	$1,983.3
Year 2	3,887.7	446.1	1,251.5	2,190.1
Year 3	4,095.8	480.4	1,290.7	2,324.7
Year 4	4,378.2	538.0	1,339.2	2,501.0
Year 5	4,628.4	591.5	1,394.3	2,642.7
Year 6	4,957.7	608.5	1,475.8	2,873.4
Year 7	5,207.6	634.5	1,534.7	3,038.4
Year 8	5,433.7	657.4	1,619.9	3,156.7
Year 9	5,856.0	693.2	1,708.5	3,454.3
Year 10	6,246.5	755.9	1,830.1	3,660.5
Year 11	6,683.7	803.9	1,972.9	3,906.9
Year 12	6,987.0	835.9	2,041.3	4,109.9

Pie Chart

A **pie chart** is simply a circle divided into sections, with each of the sections representing a portion of the total. Because the sections are presented as part of a whole, pie charts are really effective for depicting relative size. Exhibit 14.6, for instance, shows the breakdown of personal consumption expenditures by major category for a particular year (Year 12). The conclusion is obvious. Expenditures for services account for the largest proportion of total consumption expenditures.

pie chart
A circle representing a total quantity and divided into sectors, with each sector showing the size of the segment in relation to that total.

EXHIBIT 14.6

Pie Chart: Personal Consumption Expenditures by Major Category (One Year)

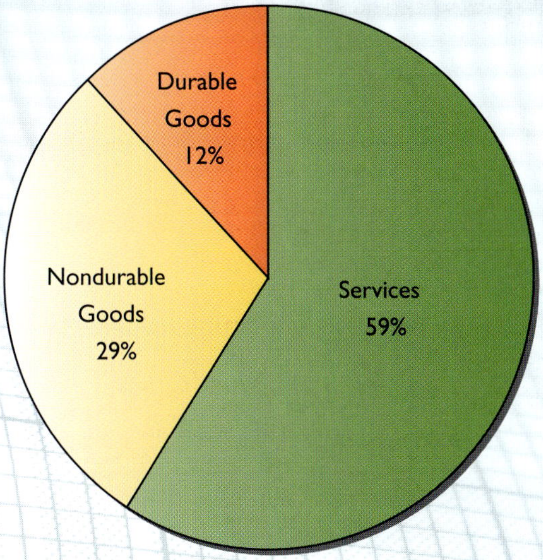

Exhibit 14.6 has three slices, and it's easy to interpret. If the variable you want to display contains more than about five or six levels (i.e., slices), however, the pie chart can quickly become confusing and ineffective, and a different type of chart (or maybe just a nice table) should be used. The sections of a pie chart normally are organized clockwise in decreasing order of size—be sure to include the exact percentages (but remember, no decimal places) on the chart.

Line Chart

The **line chart** is a two-dimensional chart that is particularly useful in depicting relationships over time. For example, Exhibit 14.7 has the same information about personal expenditures for Year 12 as the pie chart in Exhibit 14.6—but it also contains information for the other 11 years as well.

line chart
A two-dimensional chart with the *x*-axis representing one variable (typically time) and the *y*-axis representing another variable.

The line chart is probably used even more often than the pie chart. The *x*-axis normally represents time, and the *y*-axis represents values of the variable or variables. When more than one variable is presented, use different colors or types of lines (dots and dashes in various combinations) to represent the different variables. Also, be sure to identify the different variables, using a key, or legend.

Stratum Chart

The **stratum chart** serves in some ways as a dynamic pie chart, in that it can be used to show relative emphasis by sector (e.g., quantity consumed by user class) and change in relative emphasis over time. The stratum chart consists of a set of line charts whose quantities are grouped together (or a total that is broken into its components). It is also called a *stacked line chart*. For example, Exhibit 14.8 again shows personal

stratum chart
A set of line charts in which quantities are aggregated or a total is disaggregated so that the distance between two lines represents the amount of some variable.

EXHIBIT 14.7

Line Chart: Personal Consumption Expenditures by Major Category (12 Years)

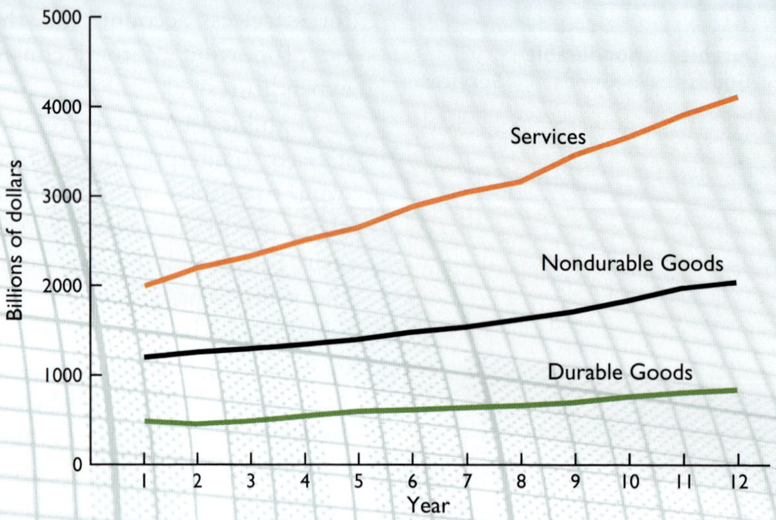

EXHIBIT 14.8

Stratum Chart: Personal Consumption Expenditures by Major Category (12 Years)

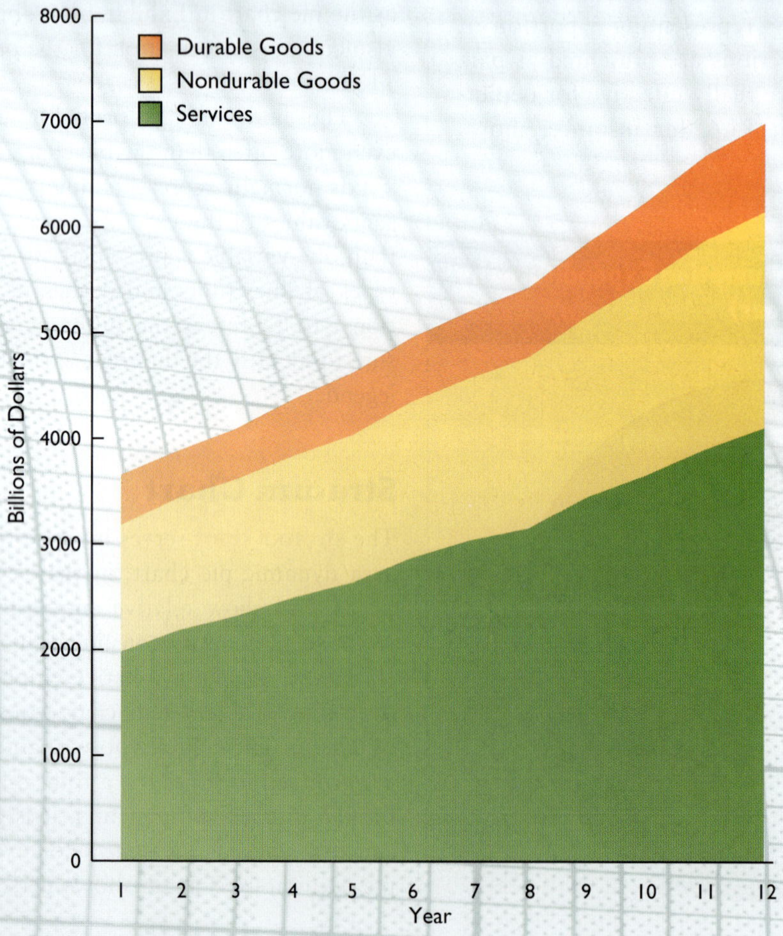

EXHIBIT 14.9

Bar Chart: Personal Consumption Expenditures by Major Category (Year 12)

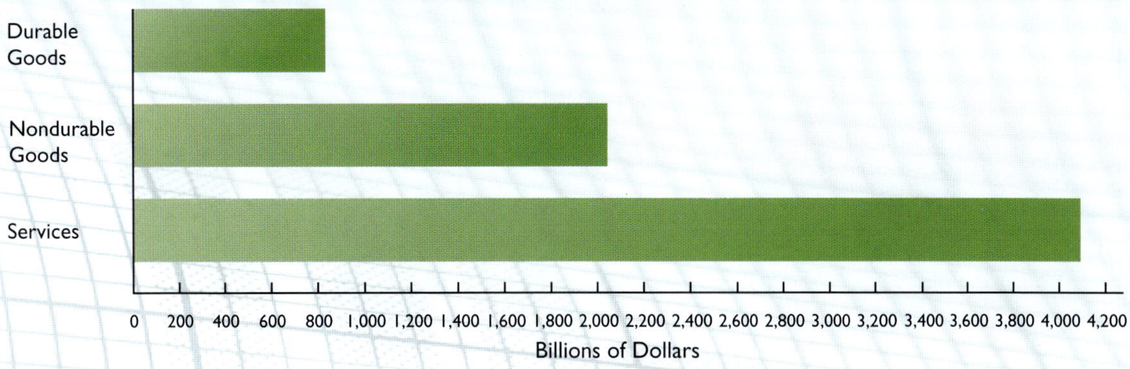

consumption expenditures by category for the 12-year period. The lowest line shows the expenditures just for services; the second lowest line shows the total expenditures for services plus nondurable goods; the top line shows the total of all three expenditures. We would need multiple pie charts (one for each year) to capture the same information, and the message wouldn't be as obvious.

The x-axis typically represents time in the stratum chart, and the y-axis again captures the value of the variables. As with the pie chart, be careful not to use a stratum chart for variables that include too many components.

Bar Chart

The **bar chart** is a widely used chart that can take several different forms. Exhibit 14.9, for example, is a simple bar chart that shows personal consumption expenditures by major category at a single point in time. This is pretty much the same information as shown in the earlier pie chart (Exhibit 14.6), but it's a little more revealing because it offers information about the size of the expenditures by category. Bar charts can be drawn either vertically or horizontally (see Exhibit 14.9), but if you're going to show change in a variable over time, standard procedure is to use a vertical chart and to track time along the horizontal axis.

bar chart
A chart in which the relative lengths of the bars show relative amounts of variables or objects.

Bar Chart Variations

Bar charts are flexible and can be used in many ways. One variation is to convert them to **pictograms**. Instead of using the length of the bar to capture quantity, amounts are shown by piles of dollars for income, pictures of cars for automobile production, people in a row for population, and so on. Pictograms can be a really effective communication tool. Be careful, however, because they can easily mislead an audience. Exhibit 14.10 shows two different pictograms, both of which are supposed to communicate the same doubling of corporate taxes paid by a company from one year to the next. For some reason, the top chart makes the tax burden seem much greater, don't you think? The proper form for the pictogram is the bottom version. Be especially careful when reading pictograms because it's easy to be led to the wrong conclusion (which is exactly what people who practice advocacy research are hoping).

pictograms
A bar chart in which pictures represent amounts—for example, piles of dollars for income, pictures of cars for automobile production, people in a row for population.

Another variation of the bar chart—the *grouped-bar chart*—can be used to capture the change in two or more series through time. Exhibit 14.11, for example, shows the change in consumption expenditures by the three major categories across the 12-year period. There is also a bar chart equivalent to the stratum chart—the *stacked-bar chart*. Its construction

EXHIBIT 14.10

Two Versions of a Pictogram

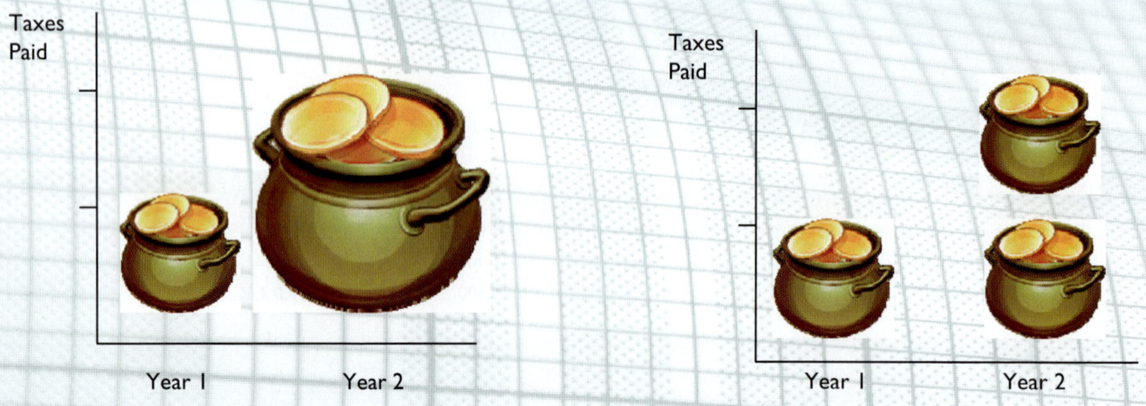

EXHIBIT 14.11

Grouped-Bar Chart: Personal Consumption Expenditures by Major Category

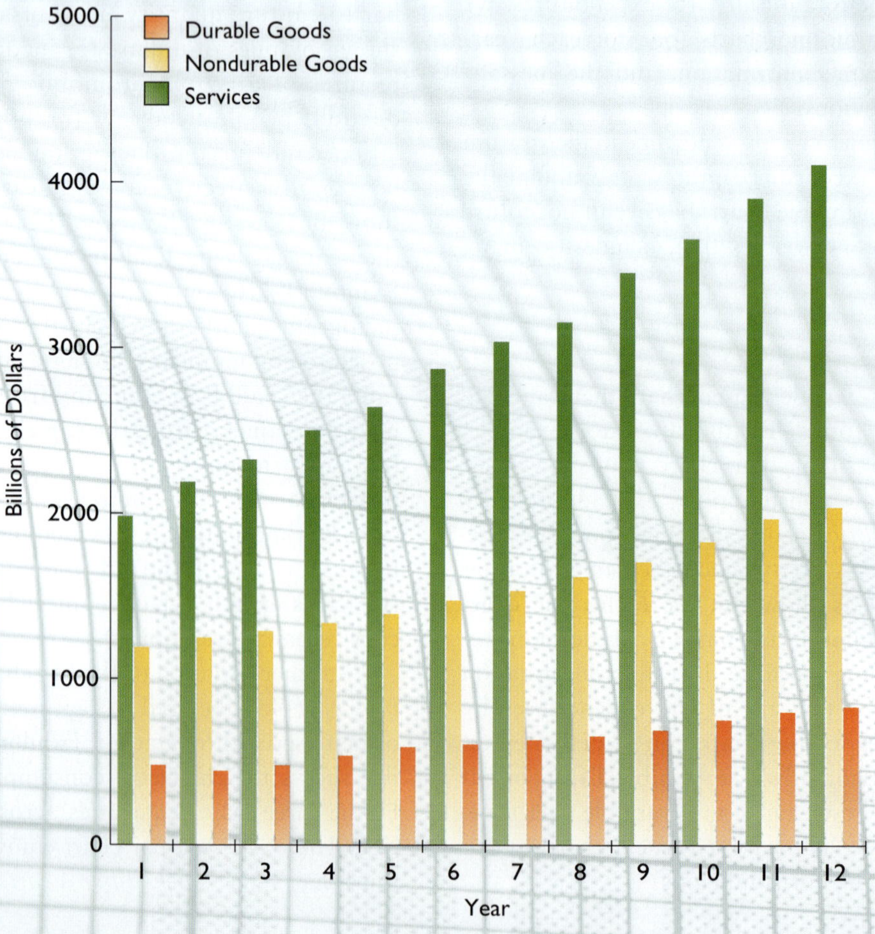

EXHIBIT 14.12

Stacked-Bar Chart: Personal Consumption Expenditures by Major Category

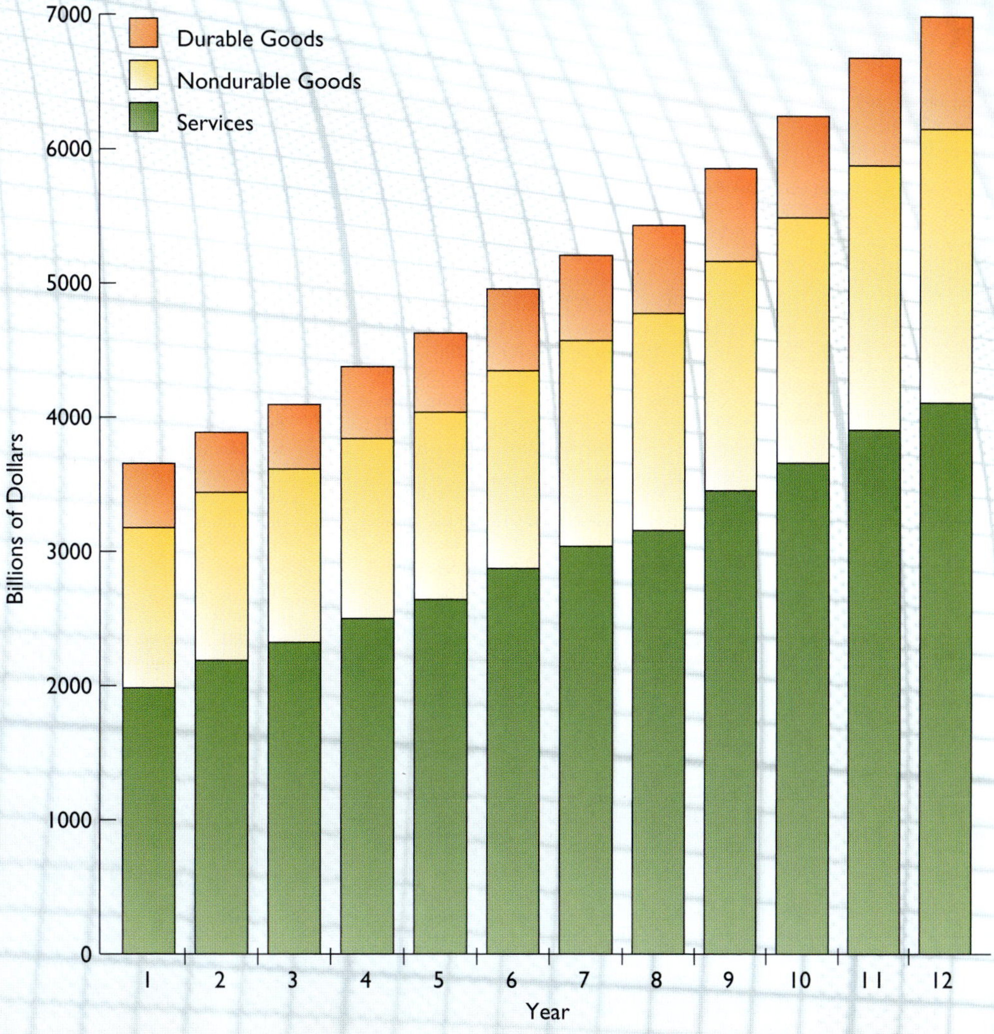

and interpretation are similar to those for the stratum chart. Exhibit 14.12, for example, is a stacked-bar chart of personal consumption expenditures by major category. It shows both total and relative expenditures through time, and it makes use of distinctive color for each component.

ACCORDING TO MOBILE APP MAKER MUSIC WITHME, THE AVERAGE ITUNES LIBRARY HAS 5,409 SONGS OF WHICH **4,195** (78%) HAVE **NEVER BEEN PLAYED.**

Endnotes

CHAPTER 1

1. Marc Gunther, "Best Buy Wants Your Electronic Junk," *Fortune* (December 1, 2009), accessed July 15, 2010, from http://money.cnn.com/2009/11/30/technology/best_buy_recycling.fortune/index.htm.
2. "McDonald's Still Hungry for U.K. Growth," *The Independent* (June 10, 2010), accessed July 12, 2010, from www.businessweek.com/globalbiz/content/jun2010/gb20100610_557814.htm; "How McDonald's Conquered the UK," *Marketing*, accessed July 24, 2008, from www.brandrepublic.com/.
3. Lawrence C. Lockley, "History and Development of Marketing Research," Section 1, p. 4, in Robert Ferber, ed., *Handbook of Marketing Research*, Copyright © 1974 by McGraw-Hill, 1974. Used with permission of McGraw-Hill Book Company.
4. "Women in China: The Next Emerging Market for Brands: MEC Research Decodes Untapped 542 'Lower Tier Cities' for Brands," accessed July 12, 2010, from www.wpp.com.
5. Jack Honomichl, "Honomichl Top 50," *Marketing News*, June 30, 2010, accessed July 13, 2010, from www.marketingpower.com/ResourceLibrary/Publications/ MarketingNews/2010/6_30_10.
6. Chad Terhune, "Into the Fryer: How Coke Officials Beefed Up Results of Marketing Test; Consultant Gave Kids' Clubs Cash to Buy Value Meals in Burger King Promotion; Wiring $9,000 for Whoppers," *The Wall Street Journal*, August 20, 2003, p. A1, accessed June 14, 2005, via ProQuest (www.proquest.com).

CHAPTER 2

1. Frederick Allen, *Secret Formula* (New York: Harper Collins, 1994).
2. Ibid. p. 401.
3. Jeff Ousborne, "The 25 Dumbest Business Decisions of All Time," *MBA Jungle* 1, May 2001, pp. 64–70.
4. Zachary Wilson, "Coca-Cola's 100-Flavor Interactive Freestyle Soda Fountain in Action," Fast Company, accessed September 15, 2010, from www.fastcompany.com/blog/zachary-wilson/and-how/coca-cola-gives-ten-times-choices-freestyle.
5. "The Coca-Cola Company Invites Consumers to Experience 'Freestyle,'" accessed September 15, 2010, from www.thecoca-colacompany.com/presscenter/nr_20090428_freestyle.html.
6. Marie Moody, "How to Profit from Complaints," *Fortune Small Business* (December 24, 2009), accessed July 15, 2010, from http://money.cnn.com/2009/12/23/smallbusiness/profiting_from_customer_complaints.fsb/index.htm.

CHAPTER 3

1. Steven P. Galante, "More Firms Quiz Customers for Clues About Competition," *The Wall Street Journal*, March 3, 1986, p. 17. See also Thomas Legare, "Acting on Customer Feedback," *Marketing Research: A Magazine of Management & Applications* 8, Spring 1996, pp. 46–51.
2. "Online Extra: Targeting the *Universal American Kid," BusinessWeek online*, June 7, 2004, accessed August 10, 2008, from www.businessweek.com.
3. *"VISA: Using S*trategy-Oriented Research to Select a New Brand Mark," in G. A. Churchill Jr., T. J. Brown, and T. A. Suter, *Basic Marketing Research*, 7th ed. (Mason, OH: South Western Cengage Learning, 2010), pp. 62–64.
4. Daniel Gross, "Lies, Damn Lies, and Focus Groups," *Slate*, posted October 10, 2003, accessed August 10, 2008, from http://slate.msn.com.
5. Matthew Boyle, "Carbonated Yogurt: Sizzle or Fizzle?" *Fortune online*, September 18, 2007, accessed August 10, 2008, from http://money.cnn.com/.
6. This quotation is credited to Dev Patnaik. See Philip Hodgson, "Focus Groups: Is Consumer Research Losing Its Focus?" *User focus*, June 1, 2004, accessed August 10, 2008, from www.userfocus.co.uk.
7. "Online Extra: Targeting the Universal American Kid," *Business Week online*, June 7, 2004, accessed August 10, 2008, from www.businessweek.com.
8. Bruce Horovitz, "Marketers Take a Close Look at Your Daily Routines," *USA Today* (April 30, 2007).
9. Scion Case Study accessed August 5, 2008, from www.nielsenbuzzmetrics.com/files/uploaded/NBZM_Scion_Case_Study.pdf.
10. Charles M. Brooks, Patrick J. Kaufmann, and Donald R. Lichtenstein, "Trip Chaining Behavior in Multi-Destination Shopping Trips: A Field Experiment and Laboratory Replication," *Journal of Retailing* 84, no.1 (2008), pp. 29–38.
11. "McDonalds Rolls out Coffee Bar Buildout Concept at Select Restaurants in Southwest," *Financial Wire*, July 9, 2008, accessed July 11, 2008, via Pro-Quest (www.proquest.com).
12. Robert Walker, "Working with Marketing Research: A Message to Marketers," *Quirk's*, October 2001, accessed July 11, 2008, from www.quirks.com; "Test Marketing: What's in Store," *Sales and Marketing Management* 128, March 15,1982, pp. 57–85. See also Richard Gibson, "Pinning Down Costs of Product Introductions," *The Wall Street Journal*, November 26, 1990, p. B1.
13. Gabriele Stern, "GM Expands Its Experiment to Improve Cadillac's Distribution, Cut Inefficiency," *The Wall Street Journal*, February 8, 1995, p. A12.
14. Vanessa O'Connell, "Altria Drops New Filter Cigarettes in Strategic Setback," *The Wall Street Journal*, June 23, 2008, accessed July 11, 2008, via ProQuest (www.proquest.com).
15. Hanah Cho, "Baltimore a Valuable Test Market for Chick-fil-A," *The Baltimore Sun*, July 25, 2010, accessed July 26, 2010, from http://articles.baltimoresun.com; Natalie Zmuda and Emily BrysonYork, "McD's Tries to Slake Consumer Thirst for Wider Choice of Drinks," *Advertising Age*, June 9,2008, accessed July 11, 2008, via EbscoHost (www.ebscohost.com); "Rite Aid Caters to Spanish-Language Customers," *DSN Retailing Today*, March 28, 2005, accessed June 23, 2005, via ProQuest (www.proquest.com).
16. Don A. Wright, "The Perfect Place for a Test Market," *The Business Journal*, May 21, 2001, p. 12.
17. "IRI Behaviorscan Testing," accessed July 26, 2010, from www.symphonyiri.com; Peter S. Fader, Bruce G. S. Hardie, Robert Stevens, and Jim Findley, "Forecasting New Product Sales in a Controlled Test Market Environment," accessed June 23, 2005, from the Wharton College of Business's Marketing Web site, www.marketing.wharton.upenn.edu. See also the 10-K SEC filing by Information Resources, Inc., March 27, 2003, accessed July 2, 2008, from http://edgar-online.com.
18. "Nielsen's Forecasting Solutions for the Sales & Marketing Planning Process," (February 5, 2009), accessed July 26, 2010, from http://en-us.nielsen.com.
19. Julie S. Wherry, "Simulated Test Marketing: Its Evolution and Current State in the Industry," June 2006, MBA thesis, MIT Sloan School of Management, accessed July 23, 2008, from http://dspace.mit.edu/bitstream/1721.1/37225/1/85813336.pdf; Jim Miller and Sheila Lundy, "Test Marketing Plugs into the Internet," *Consumer Insight*, Spring 2002, pp. 20–23.

CHAPTER 4

1. "Renovating Home Depot," *Fortune* (August 31, 2009), pp. 45–50.
2. Phaedra Hise, "Grandma Got Run Over by Bad Research," *Inc.*, January 1998, accessed September 13, 2008, from www.inc.com/magazine/19980101/851.html.
3. Wally Wood, "Targeting: It's in the Cards," *Marketing & Media Decisions*, September 1988, pp. 121–122.
4. Eldon Y. Li, Raymond McLeod, Jr., and John C. Rogers, "Marketing Information Systems in *Fortune* 500 Companies: A Longitudinal Analysis of 1980, 1990, and 2000," *Information & Management* 38, 2001, pp. 307–322.
5. Irem Radzik, Sprint's Journey to Success with Real-Time Data Integration, September 21, 2010, accessed December 8, 2010, from http://blogs.oracle.com/dataintegration/2010/09/sprints_journey_to_success_wit.html.
6. For more information, see Berend Wierenga and Gerrit H. Van Bruggen, "Developing a Customized Decision-Support System for Brand Managers," *Interfaces*, May–June 2001, pp. S128–S145; S. Kanungo, S. Sharma, and P. K. Jain, "Evaluation of a Decision Support System for Credit Management Decisions," *Decision Support Systems* 30, 2001, pp. 419–436; R. Jeffrey Thieme, Michael Song, and

Roger J. Calantone, "Artificial Neural Network Decision Support Systems for New Product Development Project Selection," *Journal of Marketing Research,* November 2000, pp. 499–507; and Jehoshua Eliashberg, Jedid-Jah Jonker, Mohanbir S.Sawhney, and Berend Wierenga, "MOVIEMOD: An Implementable Decision-Support System for Prerelease Market Evaluation of Motion Pictures," *Marketing Science,* Summer 2000, pp. 226–243.
7. Robert P. Schumaker, Osama K. Solieman, Hsinchun Chen, Sports Data Mining, Springer 2010.
8. The exhibit and surrounding discussion are adapted from David W. Stewart and Michael A. Kamins, *Secondary Research: Information Sources and Methods,* 2nd ed. (Thousand Oaks, Calif.: Sage Publications, 1993).
9. See *Starch Readership Report: Scope, Method, and Use* (Mamaroneck, NY: Starch INRA Hooper, undated).
10. Information accessed in part July 28, 2010, from the Experian Simmons Website, www.smrb.com.
11. Information accessed July 28, 2010, from the GfK MRI Web site, www.gfkmri.com.

CHAPTER 5

1. See, for example, Jerry W. Grizzle, Alex R. Zablah, Tom J. Brown, John C. Mowen, and James M. Lee, "Employee Customer Orientation in Context: How the Environment Moderates the Influence of Customer Orientation on Performance Outcomes," *Journal of Applied Psychology*, September 2009, 94(5), 1227–1242.
2. "Frito-Lay Profiles Salty Snack Consumers," *Supermarket News*, March 18, 1996, p. 39.
3. "The GenWorld Teen Study," Energy BBDO (undated report, data collected in 2005), accessed July 29, 2010, from www.businessfordiplomaticaction.org/learn/articles/genworld_leave_behind.pdf.
4. Albert C. Bemmaor, "Predicting Behavior from Intention-to-Buy Measures: The Parametric Case," *Journal of Marketing Research* 32, May 1995, pp. 176–191; William J. Infosino, "Forecasting New Product Sales from Likelihood of Purchase Ratings," *Marketing Science* 5, Fall 1986, p. 375.
5. Paco Underhill, *Why We Buy: The Science of Shopping* (New York: Touchstone, 2000), p. 18.
6. Krispy Kreme example (dated December 2002), accessed July 21, 2005, from the Williams Inference Center Website, www.williamsinference.com; Barbara Whitaker, "Yes, There Is a Job That Pays You to Shop," *The New York Times,* March 13, 2005, accessed November 17, 2008, via ProQuest (www.proquest.com).
7. "Undercover Shoppers Find It Increasingly Difficult for Children to Buy M-Rated Games," May 8, 2008, accessed August 20, 2008, from www.ftc.gov/opa/2008/05/secretshop.shtm.
8. Nicholas Varchaver, "Scanning the Globe," *Fortune,* May 31, 2004, pp. 144–156.

CHAPTER 6

1. Michael W. Link and Robert W. Oldendick, "Call Screening: Is It Really a Problem for Survey Research?" *Public Opinion Quarterly* 63, Winter 1999, pp. 577–-589.
2. Michael Conklin, "What Impact Do 'Bad Respondents' Have on Business Decisions?" MarketTools White Paper (November 2008).

CHAPTER 7

1. Peter D. Bennett, ed., *Dictionary of Marketing Terms,* 2nd ed. (Chicago: American Marketing Association, 1995), p. 173.
2. The scale was first proposed by Rensis Likert, "A Technique for the Measurement of Attitudes," *Archives of Psychology* 140, 1932.
3. Charles E. Osgood, George J. Suci, and Percy H. Tannenbaum, *The Measurement of Meaning* (Champaign: University of Illinois Press, 1957).
4. Jon A. Krosnick et al., "The Impact of 'No Opinion' Response Options on Data Quality: Nonattitude Reduction or an Invitation to Satisfice?" *Public Opinion Quarterly* 66, Fall 2002, pp. 371–403, accessed July 15, 2004, via Pro-Quest (www. proquest.com).

CHAPTER 8

1. This procedure is adapted from one suggested by Arthur Kornhauser and Paul B. Sheatsley, "Questionnaire Construction and Interview Procedure," in Claire Selltiz, Lawrence S. Wrightsman, and Stuart W. Cook, *Research Methods in Social Relations,* 3rd ed. (New York: Holt, Rinehart and Winston, 1976), pp. 541–573.
2. Sam Gill, "How Do You Stand on Sin?" *Tide* 21, March 14, 1947, p. 72.
3. E. Noelle-Neumann, "Wanted: Rules for Wording Structural Questionnaires," *Public Opinion Quarterly* 34, Summer 1970, p. 200; Philip Gendall and Janet Hoek, "A Question of Wording," *Marketing Bulletin* 1, May 1990, pp. 25–36.

CHAPTER 9

1. Jack Neff, "P&G Enlists 13-Year-Olds in Summer Intern Jobs," *Advertising Age, June* 28, 1999, p. 20.

CHAPTER 10

1. Leslie Kish, Survey Sampling (New York John Wiley, 1995). Chapter 13, "Biases and Nonsampling Errors," is particularly recommended for discussion of the errors arising from nonobservation.
2. W. Edwards Deming, "On a Probability Mechanism to Attain an Economic Balance between the Resultant Error of Response and the Bias of Nonresponse," *Journal of the American Statistical Association* 48, December 1953, pp. 766–767. See also Benjamin Lipstein, "In Defense of Small Samples," *Journal of Advertising Research* 15, February 1975, pp. 33–40; William C. Dunkelburg and George S. Day, "Nonresponse Bias and Callbacks in Sample Surveys," *Journal of Marketing Research* 10, May 1973, pp. 160–168; Lorna Opatow, "Some Thoughts about How Interview Attempts Affect Survey Results," *Journal of Advertising Research* 31, February/March 1991, pp. RC6–RC9.
3. Ronald M. Weiers, *Marketing Research,* 2nd ed. (Englewood Cliffs, N.J.: Prentice Hall, 1988), pp. 213–217.
4. Brian Tarran, "Respondent Engagement and Survey Length: The Long and the Short of It," *Research*, April 7, 2010, accessed December 23, 2010, from www.research-live.com/news/news-headlines/respondent-engagement-and-survey-length-the-long-and-the-short-of-it/4002430.article.

CHAPTER 11

1. Art Shulman, "War Stories: True-Life Tales in Marketing Research," *Quirk's Marketing Research Review,* December 1998, p. 16.
2. "The Gallup Panel," accessed June 27, 2008, from www.gallup.com.

CHAPTER 12

1. See the classic book by Hans Zeisel, *Say It with Figures,* 5th ed. (New York: Harper and Row, 1968), pp. 16–17, for conditions that would support reporting percentages with decimal-place accuracy.
2. Earlier, we referred to this range as the precision range. After data have been collected and analyzed, it is more appropriate to refer to this range as a confidence interval, because the range itself, which represents the margin of sampling error, is established for a given level of confidence. If we change the level of confidence, the confidence interval itself will also change.
3. See the classic book by Darrell Huff, *How to Lie with Statistics* (New York: Norton, 1954).
4. Robert J. Lavidge, "How to Keep Well-Intentioned Research from Misleading New-Product Planners," *Marketing News* 18, January 6, 1984, p. 8.
5. In our discussion of testing for statistical significance we assume the use of two-tailed tests in all cases because it eases the presentation of the material and because two-tailed tests are commonly used in practice. More information about the use of one- versus two-tailed tests of statistical significance can be found in any basic statistics text.
6. The term "degrees of freedom" refers to the number of things that can vary independently, and for the chi-square test, degrees of freedom is one less than the number of categories. If we know the total number of respondents and the number of respondents in five of the six categories of education level, the number of respondents in the

remaining education category is fixed and cannot vary independently.

CHAPTER 13

1. Actually, there are several assumptions that have to be met to ensure that it's appropriate to use the sample results to draw inferences about the population (this is true of most statistical techniques), but those go well beyond the scope of this book. Many statistics books—and books specifically about regression analysis—are available if you want more information. The good news is that regression is a robust technique that works fairly well even if some of the assumptions aren't fully met.

CHAPTER 14

1. Andrew Orlowski, "iTunes Sales 'Collapsing,'" *The Register,* accessed December 4, 2008, from www.theregister.co.uk/2006/12/11/digital_downloads_flatline/; Antone Gonsalves, "Research Firm Clarifies: iTunes Sales Are Not Collapsing," *InformationWeek,* accessed August 29, 2008, from www.informationweek.com.
2. William J. Gallagher, *Report Writing for Management* (Reading, Mass.: Addison-Wesley, 1969), p. 78. Much of this introductory section is also based on this excellent book. See also Pnenna Sageev, *Helping Researchers Write, So Managers Can Understand* (Columbus, Ohio: Batelle Press, 1995).

FAST FACTS

CHAPTER 1

Nielsen's Three Screen Report, Vol. 8, 1st Quarter 2010, accessed September 15, 2010, from www.nielsen.com/us/en/insights/reports-downloads/2010/three-screen-report-q1-2010.html.

CHAPTER 2

Kathryn Rem, "Grocery Stores Say Refrigerated Dog Food is a Big Seller," February 18, 2009, The State Journal-Register, accessed September 15, 2010, from www.sj-r.com/features/x426331710/Kathryn-Rem-Grocery-stores-say-refrigerated-dog-food-is-a-big-seller.

Ben Parr, "The First Thing Young Women Do in the Morning: Check Facebook," July 7, 2010, Mashable, accessed September 15, 2010, from http://mashable.com/2010/07/07/oxygen-facebook-study/.

Bruce Feiler, "Married, but Sleeping Alone," New York Times, July 23, 2010, accessed June 7, 2011 at http://www.nytimes.com/2010/07/25/fashion/25FamilyMatters.html?_r=1&src=me.

CHAPTER 3

"Record Surge in Positive Ratings of Auto Industry," August 23, 2010, accessed September 15, 2010, from www.gallup.com/poll/142409/record-surge-positive-ratings-auto-industry.aspx.

D'Vera Cohn and Gretchen Livingston, "Childlessness Up Among All Women; Down Among Women with Advanced Degrees," June 25, 2010, accessed September 15, 2010, from http://pewsocialtrends.org/2010/06/25/childlessness-up-among-all-women-down-among-women-with-advanced-degrees/.

Tudor-Locke, Catrine, William D. Johnson, and Peter T. Katzmarzyk (2010), "Frequently Reported Activities by Intensity for U.S. Adults: The American Time Use Survey," *American Journal of Preventive Medicine*, 39 (Issue 4/October), 13–20.

"The NPD Group Reports Nearly 9 in 10 Makeup Users Are Using Makeup Containing Skincare Benefits, While Overall Makeup Usage is Down," August 17, 2010, accessed September 15, 2010, from www.npd.com/press/releases/press_100817.html.

CHAPTER 4

"True Loves Be Warned: Despite Weak Economic Picture PNC Christmas Price Index Jumps a Staggering 9.2 Percent," November 29, 2010, accessed November 29, 2010, from http://pnc.mediaroom.com/index.php?s=43&item=756.

Noreen O'Leary and Todd Wasserman, "Old Spice Campaign Smells Like a Sales Success, Too," July 25, 2010, accessed March 9, 2011, from www.adweek.com/news/advertising-branding/old-spice-campaign-smells-sales-success-too-107588.

"Google share of searches at 72 percent for May 2010," June 21, 2010, accessed November 29, 2010, from www.hitwise.com/us/press-center/press-releases/google-searches-may-10/.

CHAPTER 5

"Gartner: Growing percentage choosing social networking over e-mail as primary communication vehicle," accessed December 22, 2010, from http://reliableplant.com/Read/27477/Gartner-social-networking-email.

Eric A. Hanushek, Paul E. Peterson, and Ludger Woessmann, "Teaching Math to the Talented," accessed December 22, 2010, from http://educationnext.org/teaching-math-to-the-talented/.

Tony Santaella, "2010 SC Scrooges & Angels List for Charities Released," accessed December 22, 2010, from www.wltx.com/news/story.aspx?storyid=107683&catid=2.

Helen Chernikoff, "Exclusive: Online shoppers click on coupons, don't buy," accessed December 22, 2010, from www.reuters.com/article/2010/11/17/us-usa-retail-holiday-coupons-idUSTRE6AG4H520101117.

"Chart: Percentage of U.S. adults who smoke," accessed December 22, 2010, from www.latimes.com/news/nationworld/nation/wire/la-sci-cigarette-packages-g,0,387868.graphic.

CHAPTER 6

"Tis the Season to Work—New Survey From Xobni Shows Most Americans Will Be Doing Work Email During Thanksgiving and Other Holidays This Season," November 23, 2010, accessed December 22, 2010, from www.prnewswire.com/news-releases/tis-the-season-to-work—new-survey-from-xobni-shows-most-americans-will-be-doing-work-email-during-thanksgiving-and-other-holidays-this-season-110113154.html.

"Primary Laws and Fine Levels Are Associated with Increases in Seat Belt Use, 1997–2008," November 2010, accessed December 22, 2010, from www.nhtsa.gov/staticfiles/traffic_tech/TT400.pdf.

"Most popular US travel websites—December 18 2010," accessed December 22, 2010, from www.tnooz.com/2010/12/21/data/most-popular-us-travel-websites-december-18-2010/.

comScore Media Metrix, "Twitter.com Top 10 Global Markets by Percent Reach," July 2010, accessed December 22, 2010, from www.comscoredatamine.com/wp-content/uploads/2010/09/Twitter-Mult-Market2.jpg.

Centers for Disease Control, "CDC: Oklahomans Detect Cancer In Late Stages," November 25, 2010, accessed December 22, 2010, from www.ktul.com/Global/story.asp?S=13567707.

CHAPTER 7

"Percentage of e-mails with infected attachments doubled in the third quarter," accessed December 29, 2010, from http://freshfinancialnews.com/itc/percentage-of-e-mails-with-infected-attachments-doubled-in-the-third-quarter.html.

Morpace, "Facebook's Impact on Retailers," provided to eMarketer, "Brand Interactions on Social Networks," April 1, 2010, accessed December 22, 2010, from www.emarketer.com/Report.aspx?code=emarketer_2000694.

CHAPTER 8

Borislav Agapiev, "What percentage of the web does Google index, and how has it changed over time?" November 18, 2010, accessed December 22, 2010, from www.quora.com/What-percentage-of-the-web-does-Google-index-and-how-has-it-changed-over-time.

Susan Donaldson James, "Four Out of Five Recent Presidents Are Southpaws," February 22, 2008, accessed December 22, 2010, from http://abcnews.go.com/Politics/Vote2008/Story?id=4326568&page=1.

P.K. Daniel, "A whopping 83 percent of teen girls play sports," August 19, 2008, accessed December 22, 2010, from www.signonsandiego.com/uniontrib/20080819/news_7s19gal.html.
U.S. Census Bureau American FactFinder, accessed December 22, 2010, from http://factfinder.census.gov/servlet/QTTable?_bm=y&-geo_id=01000US&-qr_name=DEC_2000_SF3_U_QTP20&-ds_name=DEC_2000_SF3_U&-redoLog=false.

CHAPTER 9

Mary Madden and Lee Rainie, "Adults and Cell Phone Distractions," June 18, 2010, accessed December 23, 2010, from www.pewinternet.org/Reports/2010/Cell-Phone-Distractions.aspx.
Amanda Lenhart, Sousan Arafeh, Aaron Smith, and Alexandra Macgill, "Writing, Technology and Teens," April 24, 2008, accessed December 23, 2010, from www.pewinternet.org/Reports/2008/Writing-Technology-and-Teens.aspx.
Leah Finnegan, "6.7% Of World Has College Degree," May 19, 2010, accessed December 23, 2010, from www.huffingtonpost.com/2010/05/19/percent-of-world-with-col_n_581807.html.
Leah Goldman, "The 20 Countries With The Highest Percentage Of Female Entrepreneurs," November 26, 2010, accessed December 23, 2010, from www.businessinsider.com/women-in-business-2010-11.

CHAPTER 10

Richard Webster, "School Crime and Safety 2010: Report," November 26, 2010, accessed December 23, 2010, from www.examiner.com/education-headlines-in-baltimore/school-crime-and-safety-2010-report.
Robert Longley, "Lifetime Earnings Soar with Education," February 13, 2010, accessed December 23, 2010, from http://usgovinfo.about.com/od/moneymatters/a/edandearnings.htm.
Lee Rainie and Kathryn Zickuhr, "Video calling and video chat," October 13, 2010, accessed December 23, 2010, from www.pewinternet.org/Reports/2010/Video-chat.aspx.
Joseph A. Giannone, "Mom and pop investors get the cold shoulder: study," November 26, 2010, accessed December 23, 2010, from www.reuters.com/article/2010/11/26/us-brokers-smallinvestors-idUSTRE6AM69Y20101126.
"Up To Half Of Americans Recycle 'All The Time'," March 23, 2008, accessed December 23, 2010, from www.environmentalleader.com/2008/03/23/up-to-half-of-americans-recycle-all-the-time/?graph=full.
"Global Trends in Healthy Eating," August 30, 2010, accessed December 23, 2010, from http://blog.nielsen.com/nielsenwire/consumer/global-trends-in-healthy-eating/.

CHAPTER 11

Christina Warren, "An In-Depth Look at How People Are Using the iPad," July 8, 2010, accessed September 5, 2010, from http://mashable.com/2010/07/08/ipad-usage-report/.
"Percentage of deaths linked to distracted driving remains steady," September 20, 2010, accessed September 23, 2010, from http://articles.cnn.com/2010-09-20/us/distracted.driving.report_1_texting-driver-distraction-traffic-fatalities?_s=PM:US.
Allen Barra, "Why Heisman Winners Are NFL Also-Rans," December 14, 2009, accessed September 5, 2010, from www.bloomberg.com/apps/news?pid=newsarchive&sid=acSp9te15aq0.
Aaron Smith and Le Rainie, "8% of online Americans use Twitter," December 9, 2010, accessed December 31, 2010, from www.pewinternet.org/Reports/2010/Twitter-Update-2010.aspx.

CHAPTER 12

Edward Moyer, "Black Friday sees online spending rise," November 27, 2010, accessed December 31, 2010, from http://news.cnet.com/8301-1023_3-20023923-93.html.
"Best Colleges 2011," accessed December 31, 2010, from http://colleges.usnews.rankingsandreviews.com/best-colleges/lowest-acceptance-rate.
"M-rated video games sales jump in United States," December 19, 2010, accessed December 31, 2010, from http://articles.sfgate.com/2010-12-19/business/25209029_1_roth-ira-wealthy-taxpayers-regular-individual-retirement-account.
"Gartner Says Worldwide Mobile Application Store Revenue Forecast to Surpass $15 Billion in 2011," January 26, 2011, accessed June 7, 2011 at http://www.gartner.com/it/page.jsp?id=1529214.

CHAPTER 13

Kathryn Zickuhr and Aaron Smith, "4% of online Americans use location-based services," November 4, 2010, accessed December 31, 2010, from www.pewinternet.org/Reports/2010/Location-based-services.aspx.
Angela Greiling Keane and Jeff Green, "Obama Bolsters U.S. Hybrid Automobile Sales in Waning Consumer Market," November 22, 2010, accessed December 31, 2010, from www.bloomberg.com/news/2010-11-23/obama-bolsters-u-s-hybrid-auto-sales-in-waning-consumer-market.html.
Erica Ogg, "Netbook, laptop sales growth biggest in 8 years," May 25, 2010, accessed December 31, 2010, from http://news.cnet.com/8301-31021_3-20005908-260.html.

CHAPTER 14

"Best Colleges 2011," accessed December 31, 2010, from http://colleges.usnews.rankingsandreviews.com/best-colleges/highest-grad-rate.
Susannah Fox, "Mobile Health 2010," October 19, 2010, accessed December 31, 2010, from www.pewinternet.org/Reports/2010/Mobile-Health-2010.aspx.
Jordan Hofeditz, "Death Penalty killed football, saved SMU," December 5, 2009, accessed December 31, 2010, from www.smudailycampus.com/2.6641/death-penalty-killed-football-saved-smu-1.960307.
Jason Hiner, "Average iTunes user only listens to 19% of music library," June 6, 2011, accessed June 7, 2011 at http://www.techrepublic.com/blog/hiner/average-itunes-user-only-listens-to-19-of-music-library/8485.

Index

J

K

L

M

N

O

S

T

U

V

W

Z

Andersen Ross/Getty Images

LEARN YOUR WAY!

SHE DID

We know that no two students are alike. You come from different walks of life and with many different preferences. You need to study just about anytime and anywhere. **MR** was developed to help you learn Marketing Research in a way that works for you.

Not only is the format fresh and contemporary, it's also concise and focused. And, **MR** is loaded with a variety of study tools, like in-text review cards, printable flash cards, and more.

Go to CourseMate for MR to find plenty of resources to help you study—no matter what learning style you like best! Access at www.cengagebrain.com.

1 CHAPTER IN REVIEW

Marketing Research: From Data to Information to Action

CHAPTER OUTLINE

I. Introduction
II. The Problem: Marketers Need Information
III. Who Does Marketing Research?
  A. Producers of Products and Services
  B. Advertising Agencies
  C. Marketing Research Companies
IV. Why Study Marketing Research?
V. The Marketing Research Process
VI. Marketing Research Ethics

POWERPOINT HIGHLIGHTS

Slide 6
Distinction between Data and Information

Slide 7
Definition of Marketing Research

Slide 14
Stages in the Research Process

Slide 15
Marketing Research Ethics Discussion

LEARNING OBJECTIVES

Learning Objective 1

Define marketing research.

Marketing research is the function that links the consumer to the marketer through information. The information is used to identify and define marketing problems; generate, refine, and evaluate marketing actions; monitor marketing performance; and improve understanding of marketing as a process.

Learning Objective 2

Discuss different kinds of organizations that conduct marketing research.

Producers of products and services often have marketing research departments and gather information relevant to the particular products and services they produce and the industry in which they operate. Advertising agencies often conduct research, primarily to test advertising and measure its effectiveness. Marketing research companies are in business to conduct research; some focus on very specific topics or aspects of the research process, whereas others are more general in focus.

Learning Objective 3

List three reasons for studying marketing research.

(1) Some students pursue careers in marketing research; (2) almost everyone is a consumer of marketing research in one way or another and needs to be able to know how to evaluate the likely validity of the research; and (3) managers must understand what marketing research can and cannot do, as well as what is involved in the process of conducting research.

Learning Objective 4

Discuss why researchers should care about marketing research ethics.

Marketing research ethics are the principles, values, and standards of conduct followed by marketing researchers. The goal of any marketing research project should be to uncover the truth about the topic of interest, not to produce a result that the researcher or managers want to see. Researchers must behave ethically because their jobs depend upon the trust and goodwill of research participants.

KEY TERMS

marketing research p. 4
research process p. 8
marketing research ethics p. 10
advocacy research p. 11
sugging p. 11

POSSIBLE STUDENT CHALLENGES ANSWERS

1. List at least two different kinds of firms that conduct marketing research. Be specific. Give an example of the primary types of research done by each.

- Producers of Products and Services. Example: Target does store image research
- Advertising Agencies. Example: Market potential of a proposed new product

2. Specify some useful sources of marketing research information for the following situation.

Whitney Vance, editor of the local newspaper, is concerned that subscription rates and advertising revenues for the print version of her newspaper continue to decline. Where might she obtain information about the following?

a. Trends and print subscription rates within the print newspaper industry
   - Newspaper Association of America (www.naa.org) follows the industry as an industry association. This would be a form of secondary research.

b. Customer satisfaction of current print subscribers
   - Ms. Vance would do well to conduct primary research via personal interviews.

c. Customer satisfaction of past print subscribers
   - Ms. Vance would again do well to conduct primary research. In this instance, a Web-based survey might be more appropriate.

3. For which of the following businesses is marketing research relevant?

a. A local dog groomer
b. The regional office of a national bank
c. A national chain restaurant
d. An international automobile manufacturer

For the businesses for which you indicated marketing research is relevant, give an example of the type of research each might find useful.

- Marketing research is relevant for all these firms. Both primary and secondary data would be useful. For example, a local dog groomer might interview dog owners regarding their grooming needs, whereas a national chain restaurant might secure trade association data from Nation's Restaurant News (www.nrn.com).

TEACHING TIP

Fast Facts, available throughout the text, are designed to enhance the consumption of marketing research. Also, Tracy Suter provides new, timely fast facts on Twitter at @TracySuter.

An interesting aspect of these fast facts is that they can be used multiple ways to spark class discussion. First, referring to the first Fast Fact, if 53 percent of U.S. households have HDTVs, what does this mean for manufacturers and retailers? What are the marketing implications? This makes for a very nice product life cycle or diffusion of innovation discussion. The marketing implication of this fact is that HDTVs are maturity stage products (product life cycle) being purchased by late-majority consumers (diffusion of innovation/categories of adopters). Second, encourage students to update this fact. This was true in 2010; what is it today? This motivates secondary data search. Third, what types of Fast Facts are interesting to students? Perhaps they are not interested in HDTVs. What topics are of interest? Encourage them to bring their own Fast Facts to class on topics of more interest to them. If they have Twitter accounts, encourage them to send the facts to @TracySuter as they discover them.

2 CHAPTER IN REVIEW

The Research Question: Formulation of the Problem

CHAPTER OUTLINE

I. Introduction
II. Problem Formulation
   A. Problems versus Opportunities
III. The Problem Formulation Process
   A. Step 1: Meet with Client
      1. Planned Change versus Unplanned Change
   B. Step 2: Clarify the Problem/Opportunity
   C. Step 3: State the Manager's Decision Problem
   D. Step 4: Develop Possible Research Problems
   E. Step 5: Select Research Problem(s) to Be Addressed
   F. Step 6: Prepare Research Request Agreement
IV. The Research Proposal
   A. Problem Definition and Background
   B. Research Design and Data Sources
   C. Sampling Plan
   D. Data Collection Forms
   E. Analysis
   F. Time Schedule
   G. Personnel Requirements and Cost Estimate
   H. Appendices

POWERPOINT HIGHLIGHTS

Slide 5
Problems versus Opportunities

Slide 7
The Problem Formulation Process

Slide 15
The Problem Formulation Process (Example of Discovery-Oriented Decision and Research Problems)

Slide 16
The Problem Formulation Process (Example of Strategy-Oriented Decision and Research Problems)

Slide 18
The Problem Formulation Process (Selection of Research Problems to Be Addressed)

LEARNING OBJECTIVES

Learning Objective 1

Specify the key steps in problem formulation.

The six key steps are (1) meet with client, (2) clarify the problem/opportunity, (3) state the manager's decision problem, (4) develop full range of possible research problems, (5) select research problem(s), and (6) prepare and submit a research request agreement.

Learning Objective 2

Distinguish between two types of decision problems.

A decision problem is the basic problem or opportunity facing the manager. Discovery-oriented decision problems typically ask "What?" or "Why?" and generate information that can be used by managers to make important decisions. Strategy-oriented decision problems are usually directed at "how" planned change should be implemented and focus on making decisions.

Learning Objective 3

Distinguish between a decision problem and a research problem.

A decision problem is the problem as seen by managers. Research problems restate the decision problem in research terms, from the researcher's perspective.

Learning Objective 4

Describe the research request agreement.

The research request agreement summarizes the problem formulation process in written form and is submitted to managers for approval. It includes the following sections: origin, decision problem, research problem(s), use, targets and their subgroups, and logistics.

Learning Objective 5

Outline the various elements of the research proposal.

Most research proposals contain the following elements: problem definition and background, research design and data sources, sampling plan, data collection forms, analysis, time schedule, personnel requirements and cost estimate, and appendices.

KEY TERMS

normal thinking p. 17

decision problem p. 17

discovery-oriented decision problem p. 18

strategy-oriented decision problem p. 18

research problem p. 19

research request agreement p. 21

research proposal p. 24

request for proposal (RFP) p. 24

POSSIBLE STUDENT CHALLENGES ANSWERS

1. Are the following decision problems discovery oriented or strategy oriented?

a. Why have sales of my brand decreased?
   - Discovery-oriented

b. What pricing strategy should I choose for my new product?
   - Discovery-oriented

c. How can I increase in-store promotion of existing products?
   - Strategy-oriented

d. Should I change the sales-force compensation package?
   - Discovery-oriented

2. Identity at least one possible research problem for each of the above-mentioned decision problems.

- a. Investigate current customer satisfaction with the brand.
- b. Measure customer's willingness-to-pay thresholds.
- c. Investigate effectiveness of different in-store promotions.
- d. Determine employee response to different compensation packages.

3. Convert Figure 2.1 to a series of decision and research problems. Hint: the orange diamond and yellow rectangles can be different types of decision problems.

- See Teaching Tip below.

TEACHING TIP

It is our experience that students, especially undergraduates, tend to look at many marketing problems as awareness problems. They use phrases like "they need to get their name out there" or "consumers are not aware of the product or service the firm provides." The implication is if consumers knew, surely they would buy. Perhaps what they really mean are they themselves are not aware so others must not be either.

Use Figure 2.1, in conjunction with Student Challenge Question 3, to consider the role of customer awareness as one of many possible issues that might relate a manager's decision problem to a researcher's research problems. The overarching issue might be lagging revenue. This could be converted to a discovery-oriented decision problem "Why are store revenues so low?" The next layer of Figure 2.1—number of clients times spend per client—could be converted to strategy-oriented decision problems like "How can we increase the number of clients we serve?" and "How can we increase client spending on our products or services?" The blue boxes in Figure 2.1 can now be expressed as research problems: "Determine customer awareness," "Investigate effectiveness of free samples on customer trial," "Measure customer likelihood of repeat business," and "Investigate current customer's spend per visit." This approach is intended to enhance the understanding of the discovery-versus-strategy-oriented decision problems and the relationship between decision and research problems.

3 CHAPTER IN REVIEW

Exploratory, Descriptive, and Causal Research Designs

CHAPTER OUTLINE

I. Introduction
II. Types of Research Design
III. Exploratory Research
    A. Types of Exploratory Research
        1. Literature Search
        2. Depth Interviews
        3. Focus Groups
            a. The Role of the Moderator
            b. The Dark Side of Focus Groups
        4. Case Analyses
            a. Benchmarking
            b. Ethnography
IV. Descriptive Research Designs
    A. The Importance of Dummy Tables
    B. Two Types of Descriptive Studies
        1. Longitudinal Analysis: Consumer Panels
        2. Cross-Sectional Analysis: Sample Survey
V. Causal Research Designs
    A. Concept of Causality
    B. Experiments as Causal Research
VI. Market Testing
    A. Key Issues in Market Testing
        1. Cost
        2. Time
        3. Control
    B. Types of Test Markets
        1. Comparing the Three Types of Test Markets

POWERPOINT HIGHLIGHTS

Slide 6
Types of Research Design: *CSI* Version

Slide 7
Types of Research Design

Slide 9
Exploratory Research Examples

LEARNING OBJECTIVES

Learning Objective 1

Describe the major emphasis of each of the three basic types of research design.

The major emphasis in exploratory research is on the discovery of ideas and insights. Descriptive research is typically concerned with determining the frequency with which something occurs or the relationship between variables. A causal research design is concerned with determining cause-and-effect relationships.

Learning Objective 2

Describe the key characteristics and basic uses of exploratory research.

Exploratory studies are typically small scale and are very flexible; anything goes. Exploratory research is useful for helping define the problem, developing hypotheses, or gaining familiarity with a problem or opportunity. In general, exploratory research is appropriate for any problem about which little is known. The output from exploratory research is ideas and insights, not answers.

Learning Objective 3

Discuss the various types of exploratory research and describe each.

Common types of exploratory research include literature searches, depth interviews, focus groups, and case analyses. Literature searches involve reviewing conceptual and trade literature, or other published information. Depth interviews attempt to tap the knowledge and experience of those familiar with the general subject being investigated. Focus groups involve a discussion among a small number of individuals, normally eight to 12, simultaneously. With case analyses, researchers study selected cases of the phenomenon under investigation; ethnographic research is a popular example.

Learning Objective 4

Discuss the difference between cross-sectional and longitudinal descriptive research designs.

A cross-sectional design involves researching a sample of elements from the population of interest at a single point in time. Various characteristics of the elements are measured once. Longitudinal studies involve panels of people or other entities whose responses are measured repeatedly over a span of time.

Learning Objective 5

Explain the difference between a continuous panel and a discontinuous panel.

In a continuous panel, a fixed sample of subjects is measured repeatedly with respect to the same type of information. In a discontinuous panel, a sample of elements is still selected and maintained, but the information collected from the members varies with the project.

Learning Objective 6

Clarify the difference between laboratory experiments and field experiments.

Laboratory experiments differ from field experiments primarily in terms of environment. The researcher creates a setting for a laboratory experiment; a field experiment is

Slide 14
Descriptive Research

Slide 15
Causal Research

Slide 18
Experiments as Causal Research (Both definitions and examples)

KEY TERMS

exploratory research p. 27
descriptive research p. 27
causal research p. 27
hypothesis p. 28
literature search p. 29
depth interview p. 30
focus group p. 30
moderator p. 30
moderator's guidebook p. 31
case analysis p. 31
benchmarking p. 32
ethnography p. 32
dummy table p. 34
cross-sectional study p. 35
longitudinal study p. 35
continuous panel p. 35
discontinuous panel p. 35
sample survey p. 36
experiment p. 37
laboratory experiment p. 37
field experiment p. 38
market testing (test marketing) p. 38
standard test market p. 40
controlled test market p. 40
simulated test market (STM) p. 40

conducted in a natural setting. Both types, however, involve control and manipulation of one or more presumed causal factors.

Learning Objective 7

Distinguish among a standard test market, a controlled test market, and a simulated test market.

In a standard test market, companies sell the product through their normal distribution channels in certain test market cities. In a controlled test market, the entire program is conducted by an outside service. The service pays retailers for shelf space and therefore can guarantee distribution. In a simulated test market, information typically is fed into a computer model that then makes projections about the likely level of sales for the product in the market.

POSSIBLE STUDENT CHALLENGES ANSWERS

1. **For the situation described below, which type of research design is most appropriate? Why?**

   The management team at World of Wonder Video Games strongly suspects that the company's current advertising campaign is not achieving its stated goal of raising consumer awareness of the company's name to a 75 percent recognition level in the target market. The team has decided to commission a research project to test the effectiveness of the various ads in the current campaign.

   - Descriptive—awareness (recognition) can be determined by the frequency with which it occurs in the target market.

2. **Follow the example of Exhibit 3.3 to make your own dummy tables. The first table is formatted for you. Use local restaurants from your community and gender as the variable categories. Format the second using household income and local recreational event locations as the variable categories. For household income, use Under $20,000, $20,000–$39,999, $40,000–$59,999, $60,000–$79,999, $80,000–$99,999, and Over $100,000 as the categories. Select four local recreational event locations to complete the table.**

Dummy Table: Local Restaurant Preference by Gender

	Local Restaurant Preference			
Gender	**Broken Egg Cafe**	**Duffy's**	**Ted's**	**Total**
Female	XX%	XX%	XX%	100%
Male	XX%	XX%	XX%	100%

(Sample size = XX)

TEACHING TIP

Market testing fascinates students. They may not be overly interested in completing survey questions, but they enjoy knowing about a new product being tested.

Tell them Procter & Gamble is in talks with major fashion houses like Tommy Hilfiger and Calvin Klein to test market the idea of cologne-scented laundry detergents. Think Tide scented with Eternity by Calvin Klein. (We don't know this to be true. In fact, it probably isn't true because we made it up.) Would it be better to use a standard, controlled, or simulated test market to determine whether consumers would be receptive to these types of laundry detergents? The tendency will likely be toward standard test markets due to their "real-world," field-based approach plus the favorable external validity and prediction accuracy; however, simulated test markets have more advantages across other important categories (see Exhibit 3.5 for review).

4 CHAPTER IN REVIEW

Collecting Secondary Data from Inside and Outside the Organization

CHAPTER OUTLINE

I. Introduction
II. Advantages and Disadvantages of Secondary Data
III. Internal Secondary Data
  A. Decision Support Systems
    1. Components of Decision Support Systems
IV. External Secondary Data
  A. Searching for Published External Secondary Data
  B. Using Standardized Marketing Information Services
    1. Profiling Customers
    2. Measuring Product Sales and Market Share
      a. (Online) Diary Panels
      b. Scanners
    3. Measuring Advertising Exposure and Effectiveness
      a. Television and Radio
      b. Print Media
      c. Internet
      d. Multimedia Services

POWERPOINT HIGHLIGHTS

Slide 5
Secondary versus Primary Data

Slide 6
Advantages and Disadvantages of Secondary Data

Slide 8
Internal versus External Data

Slide 9
Decision Support Systems (DSS)

Slide 13
External Secondary Data

LEARNING OBJECTIVES

Learning Objective 1

Explain the difference between primary and secondary data.

Primary data are originated by the researcher for the purpose of the investigation at hand, to answer a specific question related to a specific business decision. Secondary data are statistics not gathered for the immediate study, but for some other purpose.

Learning Objective 2

Cite two advantages offered by secondary data.

The most significant advantages offered by secondary data are time savings and money savings for the researcher.

Learning Objective 3

Explain the difference between internal and external secondary data.

Internal data are those found within the organization for which the research is being done; external data are those obtained from outside sources.

Learning Objective 4

Define what is meant by a decision support system (DSS).

A decision support system is designed to help managers make better decisions. A DSS includes a data system that includes internally as well as externally generated data, a model system with analytic techniques for working with the data, and a dialog system that allows managers to develop and access customized information.

Learning Objective 5

List three common uses of the information supplied by standardized marketing information services.

The information supplied by standardized marketing information services is commonly used to (1) profile customers, (2) measure product sales and market share, and (3) measure advertising exposure and effectiveness.

POSSIBLE STUDENT CHALLENGES ANSWERS

1. **List some major secondary sources of information for the following situations:**
   a. **The marketing research manager of a national soft-drink manufacturer has to prepare a comprehensive report on the soft-drink industry.**
      - The soft drink industry: National Licensed Beverage Association Industry Directory, Washington, D.C.; *National Soft Drink Bottlers Directory*, WMD Publications, New York; *Beverages*, All American Publishers Service, Inc., Illinois; *Beverage World*, Keller Publishing Corporation, New York; *Beverage Retailer Weekly*, New York; *Food Beverage Service Handbook*, Air Publishing Company, Inc., Connecticut, 1970; *Annual Survey of Manufacturers*, U.S. Bureau of the Census, Washington D.C.; *Almanac of Business and Industrial Financial Ratios*; Prentice Hall, Inc., New Jersey.

KEY TERMS

secondary data p. 43
primary data p. 43
primary source p. 45
secondary source p. 45
decision support system (DSS) p. 46
expert system p. 47
data mining p. 47
geodemography p. 50
scanner p. 51
single-source data p. 52
people meter p. 52

b. Owning a grocery store has been Mrs. Smith's dream, and she finally decides to make it a reality. The first step she wishes to take is to collect information on the grocery business in her hometown.

- The grocery business: *Progressive Grocer's Annual Report of the Grocery Trade*, New York; *Grocery Store Fact Book*, Fairchild Publications, Inc., New York; *Current Business Reports: Weekly Retail Sales Report, Advance Monthly Retail Sales Report, Monthly Retail Trade Report*, and *Annual Retail Trade Report*, U.S. Bureau of the Census, Washington, D.C.; *Grocery Bulletin Buying Guide and Directory*, California; *Thomas Grocery Register*, New York; *Progressive Grocer's Marketing Guide Book*, New York; *Grocery Bulletin*, Bulletin Enterprises, Inc., California; *Grocery Products and Promotion News*, Product Promotion Publications, California; *Progressive Grocer*, Progressive Grocer Publishing Company, New York.

2. Using the current U.S. Statistical Abstract (www.census.gov/compendia/statab/), answer the following questions:

a. Which metropolitan statistical area in the United States has the largest population?

- New York–Northern New Jersey–Long Island, NY–NJ–PA (2009) www.census.gov/compendia/statab/2011/tables/11s0020.pdf

b. What is the population of this metropolitan area?

- 19,070,000 (2009) www.census.gov/compendia/statab/2011/tables/11s0020.pdf

c. What is the median age of the U.S. population?

- 36.8 years (2009) www.census.gov/compendia/statab/2011/tables/11s0007.pdf

3. Something interesting is happening regarding the data contained in Exhibit 4.5. From June 2010 to March 2011, Facebook moved from third place behind Google and Yahoo! to second, behind only Google in terms of the Top Web Brands. Complete the comparison table below with the most recent data to see whether Facebook has passed Google for first place. Facebook was already well ahead in time per person, but the ranking is based on unique audience metrics.

June 2010 Rank*	Brand	Unique Audience (000)	Time per Person (hh:mm:ss)	Rank (Current Date)	Brand	Unique Audience (000)	Time per Person (hh:mm:ss)
1	Google	152,494	1:13:01	1			
2	Yahoo!	132,412	2:11:10	2			
3	Facebook	127,011	6:02:59	3			

**Source:* The Nielsen Company, accessed July 28, 2010, from http://blog.nielsen.com/nielsenwire/online_mobile/june-2010-top-online-sites-and-brands-in-the-u-s/.

TEACHING TIP

Exhibit 4.2 discusses the ever-expanding reach of data mining. Amazon.com does it. Apple's iTunes does it. Even Netflix and eHarmony employ data mining. One of the newer entrants is Hunch. Billed as a personal recommendation engine, Hunch starts with a long list of questions (THAY, or Teach Hutch About You), then mines this data to recommend—well, anything. It also has a social media component by allowing users to follow other users. If you and/or the students are so inclined, build Hunch profiles or at least review THAY questions to see how this sort of data becomes a personalized recommendation *or* read the Hunch blog (http://blog.hunch.com/) to see how Hunch is mining the data currently available from users.

5 CHAPTER IN REVIEW

Collecting Primary Data by Observation

CHAPTER OUTLINE

I. Introduction

II. Types of Primary Data

- A. Demographic/Socioeconomic Characteristics
- B. Personality/Lifestyle Characteristics
- C. Attitudes
- D. Awareness/Knowledge
- E. Intentions
- F. Motivation
- G. Behavior

III. Two Methods of Obtaining Primary Data

- A. Versatility
- B. Speed and Cost
- C. Objectivity and Accuracy

IV. Observation Research

- A. Structured versus Unstructured Observation
- B. Disguised versus Undisguised Observation
- C. Natural versus Contrived Setting for Observation
- D. Human versus Mechanical Observation
  1. Using Mechanical Observation in Advertising Tests

POWERPOINT HIGHLIGHTS

Slide 5
Types of Primary Data

Slide 9
Methods of Obtaining Primary Data

Slide 11
Decisions for Collecting Primary Data (Structured vs. Unstructured Observation)

LEARNING OBJECTIVES

Learning Objective 1

List the seven kinds of primary data about individuals that interest marketers.

Marketers often measure (1) demographic/socioeconomic characteristics, (2) personality/lifestyle characteristics, (3) attitudes, (4) awareness/knowledge, (5) intentions, (6) motivation, and (7) behavior.

Learning Objective 2

Describe the two basic means of obtaining primary data.

The two basic means of obtaining primary data are communication and observation. Communication involves questioning respondents to secure the desired information, using a data collection instrument called a questionnaire. Observation involves scrutinizing the situation of interest and recording the relevant facts, actions, or behaviors.

Learning Objective 3

State the specific advantages of each method of data collection.

In general, the communication method of data collection has the advantages of versatility, speed, and cost, whereas observation data are typically more objective and accurate.

Learning Objective 4

List the important considerations in the use of observational methods of data collection.

Observational data may be gathered using structured or unstructured methods that are either disguised or undisguised. The observations may be made in a contrived or a natural setting and may be secured by a human or an electrical/mechanical observer.

Learning Objective 5

Cite the main reason researchers may choose to disguise the presence of an observer in a study.

Most often, an observer's presence is disguised in order to control the tendency of people to behave differently when they know their actions are being watched.

Learning Objective 6

Explain the advantages and disadvantages of conducting an observational experiment in a laboratory setting.

The advantage of a laboratory environment is that researchers are better able to control outside influences that might affect the observed behavior. The disadvantage of the laboratory setting is that the contrived setting itself may cause differences in behavior. A contrived setting, however, usually speeds the data collection process, results in lower cost research, and allows the use of more objective measurements.

Learning Objective 7

Discuss four types of mechanical observational research.

Response latency is the amount of time a respondent deliberates before answering a question. Because response time seems to be directly related to the respondent's uncertainty in the answer, it assists in assessing the individual's strength of preference when choosing among alternatives.

A *galvanometer* measures changes in the electrical resistance of the skin associated with the tiny traces of sweat that comes with emotional arousal; in marketing research, the stimulus is often specific advertising copy. *Voice-pitch analysis* examines changes in the relative vibration frequency of the human voice that accompany emotional arousal. The amount an individual is affected by a stimulus question can be measured by comparing the person's abnormal frequency to his or her normal frequency. *Eye tracker cameras* are used by researchers to study a subject's eye movements while he or she is reading advertising copy. The visual record produced can allow researchers to determine the part of the ad the subject noticed first, how long his or her eyes lingered on a particular item, and whether the subject read all the copy or only part of it.

KEY TERMS

personality p. 56
attitude p. 57
awareness/knowledge p. 57
intentions p. 58
motive p. 59
behavior p. 60
communication p. 60
observation p. 60
structured observation p. 64
unstructured observation p. 64
undisguised observation p. 65
disguised observation p. 65
natural setting p. 65
contrived setting p. 65
human observation p. 66
electrical or mechanical observation p. 66
response latency p. 66
galvanometer p. 67
voice-pitch analysis p. 67
eye tracker camera p. 67

POSSIBLE STUDENT CHALLENGES ANSWERS

1. Be a mystery shopper and assess the service provided to customers at the checkout counter at a grocery store in your area. Complete the following structured observation table:

Store:	**Date:**	
Location:	**Time:**	
Too few checkout counters	Yes	No
Long wait in line	Yes	No
Cashier: Quick and efficient	Yes	No
Cashier: Prices well recorded	Yes	No
Cashier: Friendly and pleasant	Yes	No
Purchases packed quickly	Yes	No
Purchases packed poorly	Yes	No
Bags carried to car	Yes	No
Bags provided were flimsy	Yes	No
Bags provided were attractive	Yes	No
Other facts		

2. If you were the product manager of a leading brand of toothpaste, how would each of the following help you do your job?

a. Observational studies in a retail store

b. Observational studies in a consumer's home

- An observational study can lead to many insights into the consumer decision-making and consumption processes. An observer can determine how much thought goes into the purchase, the effect of displays, the effect of coupons, and many other aspects of consumer interaction with the environment. All of this information would help the product manager assess the importance of product attributes and elements of the marketing mix.

TEACHING TIP

One of the key sentences in this chapter reads, "Observation research doesn't have to be sophisticated to be effective." We continue by discussing different color promotional flyers for different zip codes, car dealer service areas checking radio dials for future advertising, and scuffmarks on a museum floor as a measure of popularity. Applying this same concept, what would be the pros and cons of the on-campus cafeteria or food court tracking the food purchases of students via their student IDs? The types and quantities of food purchases could be matched to the demographics of the student. Would this be a good use of observational research? Tesco, the British grocery chain discussed in this chapter, has used a very similar approach via its Clubcard program.

6 CHAPTER IN REVIEW

Collecting Primary Data by Communication

CHAPTER OUTLINE

I. Introduction
II. Structured versus Unstructured Communication
III. Disguised versus Undisguised Communication
  A. The Ethics of Disguise
IV. Methods of Administering Questionnaires
  A. Personal Interviews
    1. Sampling Control
    2. Information Control
    3. Administrative Control
  B. Telephone Interviews
    1. Sampling Control
    2. Information Control
    3. Administrative Control
  C. Mail Questionnaires
    1. Sampling Control
    2. Information Control
    3. Administrative Control
  D. Internet-Based Questionnaires
    1. Sampling Control
    2. Information Control
    3. Administrative Control
  E. Comparing Methods of Administering Questionnaires
    1. Combining Administration Methods

POWERPOINT HIGHLIGHTS

Slide 8
Methods of Administering Questionnaires

Slide 9
Methods of Administering Questionnaires (cont.)

Slide 15
Percent of Marketing Research Revenue by Major Communication Methods

LEARNING OBJECTIVES

Learning Objective 1

Explain the concept of *structure* as it relates to questionnaires.

The degree of structure in a questionnaire is the degree of standardization imposed on it. In a highly structured questionnaire, the questions to be asked and the responses permitted by the subjects are completely predetermined. In a questionnaire with less structure, the response categories are not provided; sometimes even the questions can vary.

Learning Objective 2

Cite the drawbacks of using high degrees of structure.

Fixed-alternative questions may force a subject to respond to a question on which he doesn't really have an opinion. They may also add error if none of the response categories fits the respondent's answer.

Learning Objective 3

Explain what is meant by *disguise* in a questionnaire context.

The amount of disguise in a questionnaire is the amount of knowledge hidden from the respondent as to the purpose and/or sponsor of the study. An undisguised questionnaire makes the purpose of the research obvious by the questions posed; a disguised questionnaire attempts to hide the purpose of the study.

Learning Objective 4

Differentiate among the main methods of administering questionnaires.

Personal interviews imply a direct face-to-face conversation between the interviewer and the respondent, as opposed to *telephone interviews*. In both types, the interviewer asks the questions and records the respondents' answers either while the interview is in progress or immediately afterward. *Mail questionnaires* are sent to designated respondents with an accompanying cover letter. The respondents complete the questionnaire at their leisure and mail their replies back to the research organization. *Internet-based questionnaires* involve surveys that are completed by respondents via the Web.

Learning Objective 5

Discuss three important aspects used to compare the four different methods of administering questionnaires.

Sampling control concerns the ability to identify, reach, and receive answers from population members. Information control involves the amount, type, and quality of information that can be retrieved from respondents. Administrative control is concerned with the degree of quality control possible and time and cost requirements.

POSSIBLE STUDENT CHALLENGES ANSWERS

1. Suppose you were asked to design an appropriate communication method to find out students' feelings and opinions about the various food services available on campus.

a. What degree of structure would be appropriate? Justify your choice.

KEY TERMS

structure p. 69
fixed-alternative question p. 69
open-ended question p. 70
disguise p. 70
debriefing p. 72
personal interview p. 72
mall intercept p. 73
telephone p. 74
random-digit dialing (RDD) p. 75
computer-assisted interviewing (CAI) p. 75
mail questionnaire p. 76
Internet-based questionnaire p. 78

b. What degree of disguise would be appropriate? Justify your choice.

- a. & b. The structured undisguised questionnaire is suggested for the following reasons:
  - Because food service available on campus is an issue that students probably hold a clear opinion about
  - Ease of administration, tabulation, and analysis
  - Reliability of responses

  In order to decrease the loss of validity, it might be useful to include a "no opinion" category for the fixed alternatives and to include some open-ended questions to allow accurate expression of opinions. Because the issue is not a highly sensitive one, disguised questionnaires are not necessary.

c. What method of administration would be appropriate? Justify your choice.

- An Internet-based questionnaire is recommended for the following reasons:
  - The sampling frame is the student population, thus a good e-mail list should be available from the registrar's office or information technology. If it cannot be secured, the student telephone directory can probably be used. This would minimize sampling biases and would allow for a representative sample.
  - If the university conducts the study, the problem of securing cooperation will be minimized.
  - The information to be collected pertains to an issue that students have clear opinions about. This rules out the necessity of probing and personal interviewing.
  - The likely length of the questionnaire argues against telephone interviews.
  - Internet-based questionnaires would probably be very inexpensive to administer.

  Although personal interviews might be suggested, it should be noted that this would be a waste of resources because the nature of the information desired and sample lend themselves well to an Internet-based questionnaire.

2. What method of gathering data would you use in each of the following situations? Justify your choice.

a. Administration of a questionnaire to determine the number of people who listened to the "100 Top Country Tunes in 2010," a program that aired on December 31, 2010.

- In this situation, speed of response is crucial and a telephone survey is appropriate. The questionnaire would be short, further justifying the use of this method.

b. Administration of a questionnaire by a national manufacturer of microwave ovens in order to test people's attitudes toward a new model.

- In this situation, the questionnaire would be lengthy and could involve specific technical information that lends itself to the personal interview method. Due to the nature of the data, mail surveys may lead to misinterpretations. The amount of data to be collected precludes the use of a telephone survey.

c. Administration of a questionnaire by a local dry cleaner who wants to determine customers' satisfaction with a recent discount promotion.

- In this situation, cost would probably be an important factor, so a mail survey is suggested. Speed is also relatively important, though, and a case could be made for a telephone survey.

TEACHING TIP

Exhibit 6.2 indicates that 2007 was the year cellular service surpassed wireline, or landline, service in terms of monthly personal consumption expenditures for telephone service per household. In April 2011, the Centers for Disease Control (CDC), in partnership with Prevention's National Center for Health Statistics, reported that the percentage of U.S. wireless-only homes has doubled in three years. This data could indicate a significant widening of the expenditure gap. At present, about 27 percent of U.S. homes had only a wireless phone. Moreover, 44 percent of 18- to 30-year-olds are wireless only. Review the CDC report, found at www.cdc.gov/nchs/data/nhsr/nhsr039.pdf, with the class for more interesting insights.

7 CHAPTER IN REVIEW

Asking Good Questions

CHAPTER OUTLINE

I. Introduction

II. Scales of Measurement

- A. Nominal Scale
- B. Ordinal Scale
- C. Interval Scale
- D. Ratio Scale

III. Measuring Attitudes and Other Unobservable Concepts

- A. Itemized-Ratings Scale
  1. Summated-Ratings (Likert) Scale
  2. Semantic-Differential Scale
  3. Other Itemized-Ratings Scales
- B. Graphic-Ratings Scales
- C. Comparative-Ratings Scale

IV. Other Considerations in Designing Scales

- A. Number of Items in a Scale
- B. Number of Scale Positions
- C. Including a "Don't Know" or "Not Applicable" Response Category

V. Establishing the Validity and Reliability of Measures

- A. Reliability

POWERPOINT HIGHLIGHTS

Slide 5
Scales of Measurement

Slide 10
Interval versus Ratio Scales

Slide 11
Ordinal versus Ratio Scales

Slide 14
Summated-Rating (Likert) Scales

Slide 15
Semantic-Differential Scales

Slide 20
Reliability versus Validity

LEARNING OBJECTIVES

Learning Objective 1

Define the term *measurement* as it is used in marketing research.

Measurement consists of rules for assigning numbers to objects in such a way as to represent quantities of attributes.

Learning Objective 2

List the four scales (levels) of measurement.

The four scales of measurement are nominal, ordinal, interval, and ratio scales.

Learning Objective 3

Name some widely used attitude scaling techniques in marketing research.

The summated-ratings scale and the semantic-differential scale are the most widely used attitude scaling techniques in marketing research.

Learning Objective 4

List some other key decisions to be made when designing scales.

Other key considerations include whether to use a global or a composite scale, how many scale positions to use (and whether to use an even number or an odd number of scale positions), and whether to include a "don't know" response category.

Learning Objective 5

Explain the concept of validity as it relates to measuring instruments.

Any scale or other measurement instrument that actually measures what it was intended to measure is said to have validity. As systematic and/or random error increases, the validity of a measure decreases. A valid measure must be reliable, but a reliable measure isn't always valid.

POSSIBLE STUDENT CHALLENGES ANSWERS

1. Identify the type of scale (nominal, ordinal, interval, ratio) being used in each of the following questions. Justify your answer.

a. During which season of the year were you born?

winter spring summer fall

- Nominal—The measurement identifies or categorizes the seasons.

b. What is your total household income? ________________

- Ratio—Income has a natural zero and equal intervals.

c. Which are your three most preferred brands of cigarettes? Rank them from 1 to 3 according to your preference, with 1 as most preferred.

Marlboro	Newport	Benson and Hedges
Salem	Camel	Merit

- Ordinal—The measurement indicates rank position, but nothing is said about the difference in preference between the brands.

KEY TERMS

measurement p. 83
nominal scale p. 84
ordinal scale p. 86
interval scale p. 87
ratio scale p. 87
self-report p. 88
itemized-ratings scale p. 89
summated-ratings scale p. 89
semantic-differential scale p. 90
snake diagram p. 91
graphic-ratings scale p. 91
comparative-ratings scale p. 92
constant-sum method p. 92
global measure p. 92
composite measure p. 93
systematic error p. 94
random error p. 94
validity p. 95
reliability p. 95

d. How much time do you spend traveling to school every day?

under 5 minutes | 5–10 minutes | 11–15 minutes
16–20 minutes | 30 minutes and over

- Ordinal—Even though number of minutes has a natural zero and could be measured using a ratio scale, in this case it is being measured in categories. If students argue for an interval scale, point out that the intervals are not equal (e.g., "30 minutes and over").

e. How satisfied are you with Newsweek magazine?

very satisfied | satisfied | neither satisfied nor dissatisfied
dissatisfied | very dissatisfied

- Interval or ordinal—Some would argue that the scale is interval because the measurement of this attitude has order properties and equal scale increments of satisfaction are displayed by the descriptors. Others would argue that the scale is only ordinal unless specific steps were taken to make sure the descriptors were interpreted as having equal increments of the property "satisfaction."

f. On average, how many cigarettes do you smoke in a day?

over 1 pack | less than 12 pack | 12 to 1 pack

- Ordinal—As with (d), number of cigarettes has a natural zero and could be measured using a ratio scale but has instead been measured in categories.

g. Which of the following courses have you taken?

marketing research | sales management
advertising management | consumer behavior

- Nominal—The measurement identifies particular courses as having been completed.

h. What is the level of education for the head of household?

some high school | some college
high school graduate | college graduate and/or graduate work

- Ordinal—The measurement of education level indicates rank position but nothing is said about equal intervals. If the question were framed as number of years of schooling completed, then many would interpret that as an interval scale.

TEACHING TIP

Sometimes it is difficult for students to fully comprehend that collecting data at a higher level means that the data can be represented at that level or lower. For instance, data collected with yes/no responses are nominal data, but data collected on a 6-point scale (1 = unfavorable, 6 = favorable) at the interval data level can be represented or categorized as "Yes" or "No" by collapsing the data (1, 2, 3 = "No;" 4, 5, 6 = "Yes"). However, the opposite is not true. A "Yes" response cannot be represented as a 5 on the 6-point scale. To further illustrate this point, look at the 2011 Harris Poll EquiTrend (Brand) Rankings (www.harrisinteractive.com/Insights/EquiTrendRankings.aspx). The data were collected at the interval level but represented at the ordinal level. Being more specific, quality, an important component of Harris's measurement, has characteristically been measured by asking respondents to *rate* brand quality on a 10-point scale (interval data), but the ultimate findings are discussed as *rankings* (ordinal data). In this case, Southwest Airlines *ranked* first among airlines, so it must have received the highest *rating*.

8 CHAPTER IN REVIEW

Designing the Questionnaire

CHAPTER OUTLINE

I. Introduction
   A. Step 1: Specify What Information Will Be Sought
   B. Step 2: Determine Method of Administration
   C. Step 3: Determine Content of Individual Questions
   D. Step 4: Determine Form of Response to Each Question
      1. Open-Ended Questions
      2. Closed-Ended Questions
   E. Step 5: Determine Wording of Each Question
      1. Use Simple Words
      2. Avoid Ambiguous Words and Questions
      3. Avoid Leading Questions
      4. Avoid Unstated Alternatives
      5. Avoid Assumed Consequences
      6. Avoid Generalizations and Estimates
      7. Avoid Double-Barreled Questions
   F. Step 6: Determine Question Sequence
      1. Use Simple and Interesting Opening Questions
      2. Use Funnel Approach
      3. Design Branching Questions with Care
      4. Ask for Classification Information Last
      5. Place Difficult or Sensitive Questions Late in the Questionnaire
   G. Step 7: Determine Physical Characteristics of Questionnaire
   H. Step 8: Develop Recruiting Message or Script
   I. Step 9: Reexamine Steps 1-8 and Revise If Necessary
   J. Step 10: Pretest Questionnaire and Revise If Necessary

LEARNING OBJECTIVES

Learning Objective 1

Cite some of the techniques researchers use to secure respondents' cooperation in answering sensitive questions.

When asking sensitive questions, researchers may find it helpful to (1) guarantee respondent anonymity or confidentiality; (2) make use of a counter-biasing statement; (3) phrase the question in terms of others and how they might feel or act; (4) put sensitive questions near the end; (5) use categories or ranges rather than specific numbers; and/or (6) use the randomized-response model.

Learning Objective 2

List some of the primary rules researchers should keep in mind in trying to develop bias-free questions.

Among the rules of thumb that researchers should keep in mind in developing bias-free questions are (1) use simple words, (2) avoid ambiguous words and questions, (3) avoid leading questions, (4) avoid unstated alternatives, (5) avoid assumed consequences, (6) avoid generalizations and estimates, and (7) avoid double-barreled questions.

Learning Objective 3

Explain what the funnel approach to question sequencing is.

The funnel approach to question sequencing gets its name from its shape, starting with broad questions and progressively narrowing down the scope. This is important for question sequencing because asking for specific information early in a questionnaire will often influence respondents' answers to later questions, a source of error known as question order bias.

Learning Objective 4

Explain the difference between basic information and classification information, and tell which should be asked first in a questionnaire.

Basic information refers to the subject of the study; classification information refers to the other data we collect to classify respondents for analysis. The proper questionnaire sequence is to present questions securing basic information first and those seeking classification information last.

Learning Objective 5

Explain the role of pretesting in the questionnaire development process.

Questionnaire pretesting is the final step in the questionnaire development process. It is the last chance that the researcher has to ensure that the data collection form is working properly prior to data collection; pretesting must not be overlooked.

POWERPOINT HIGHLIGHTS

Slide 5
Procedure for Developing a Questionnaire

Slide 8
Determine Wording of Each Question (Avoid Assumed Consequences)

Slide 10
Determine Question Sequence (Funnel Approach)

Slide 13
Determine Physical Characteristics of Questionnaire

KEY TERMS

filter question p. 98
response order bias p. 102
split-ballot technique p. 102
leading question p. 103
unstated alternative p. 105
assumed consequence p. 105
double-barreled question p. 106
funnel approach p. 106
question order bias p. 107
branching p. 107
pretest p. 109

POSSIBLE STUDENT CHALLENGES ANSWER

Use the Questionnaire Preparation Checklist to prepare a questionnaire about student and faculty attitudes and use of technology in the university classroom.

- See the Teaching Tip below for a possible approach to providing an example

TEACHING TIP

During the Fall 2010 semester, Tracy Suter participated in an Oklahoma State University pilot study that assessed the use of Apple iPads in the Marketing Research course. In this context, iPads were used primarily as a field research tool, where students designed questionnaires, administered them, and shared results with classmates entirely on the iPad. There are many examples of technology use in the classroom, from clickers, to teaching in computer labs, to allowing students to use laptops and smartphones. If you would like to see the pre- and post-pilot questionnaires used to assess the iPad or the study results, please contact Tracy directly at tracy.suter@okstate.edu or via Twitter @TracySuter.

9 CHAPTER IN REVIEW

Developing the Sampling Plan

CHAPTER OUTLINE

I. Introduction
II. Defining the Target Population
  A. Parameters versus Statistics
III. Identifying the Sampling Frame
IV. Selecting a Sampling Procedure
  A. Nonprobability Samples
    1. Convenience Samples
    2. Judgment Samples
    3. Quota Samples
  B. Probability Samples
    1. Simple Random Samples
    2. Systematic Samples
    3. Stratified Samples
    4. Cluster Samples
V. Determining How Big a Sample You Need
  A. Basic Considerations in Determining Sample Size
  B. Multiple Estimates in a Single Project
  C. Population Size and Sample Size
  D. Other Approaches to Determining Sample Size

POWERPOINT HIGHLIGHTS

Slide 5
Procedure for Drawing a Sample

Slide 9
Define the Target Market

Slide 13
Select a Sampling Procedure

Slide 22
Select a Sampling Procedure (focus on generalizability)

Slide 24
Determine the Sample Size

LEARNING OBJECTIVES

Learning Objective 1
Explain the difference between a parameter and a statistic.

A parameter is a characteristic of the population; if it were possible to take measures from all population members without error, we could arrive at the true value of a parameter. A statistic is a characteristic or measure of a sample; statistics are used to estimate population parameters.

Learning Objective 2
Explain the difference between a probability sample and a nonprobability sample.

In a probability sample, each member of the target population has a known, nonzero chance of being included in the sample. The chances of each member of the target population being included in the sample may not be equal, but everyone has a known probability of inclusion. With nonprobability samples, on the other hand, there is no way of estimating the probability that any population element will be included in the sample. Thus, there is no way of ensuring that the sample is representative of the target population. All nonprobability samples rely on personal judgment at some point in the sample-selection process.

Learning Objective 3
List the primary types of nonprobability samples.

The primary types of nonprobability samples include convenience samples, judgment samples (including snowball samples), and quota samples.

Learning Objective 4
List the primary types of probability samples.

The primary types of probability samples include simple random samples, systematic samples, stratified samples, and cluster samples (including area samples).

Learning Objective 5
Discuss the concept of total sampling elements (TSE).

Because it is common that information cannot be collected from or about all elements chosen for a sample (due to bad contact information, refusal to participate, inability to reach the respondent, and so on), it is usually necessary to draw a larger number of sample elements in order to ultimately achieve the desired sample size. This larger number of elements is known as total sampling elements.

Learning Objective 6
Cite three factors that influence the necessary sample size.

When estimating a sample size, researchers must consider (1) how precise the estimate must be, (2) the degree of confidence that the population parameter falls within the precision interval, and (3) how much variation there is on the parameter of interest in the population.

Learning Objective 7
Explain the relationship between population size and sample size.

In most instances, the size of the population has no direct effect on the size of the sample. The exception is when the sample size will comprise more than 5 to 10 percent of the population; in this case the finite population correction factor will be employed, resulting in a smaller required sample size.

KEY TERMS

census p. 113
sample p. 113
population p. 114
parameter p. 114
statistic p. 115
sampling error p. 115
sampling frame p. 115
nonprobability sample p. 116
convenience sample p. 116
judgment sample p. 117
snowball sample p. 117
quota sample p. 117
probability sample p. 118
simple random sample p. 118
systematic sample p. 118
sampling interval p. 118
total sampling elements (TSE) p. 119
stratified sample p. 120
cluster sample p. 120
area sample p. 121
precision p. 122
confidence p. 122

TEACHING TIP

Walking down the street and passing out surveys to unknown people "at random" is "random" in the everyday sense, but not random in the scientific sampling sense. To achieve random samples, each unit included in the population has a known and equal chance of being selected for the sample. To demonstrate this, make each unit included in the population milk chocolate (formerly known as Plain) M&Ms instead of people. According to M&M/Mars, the population proportions of milk chocolate M&Ms are as follows: 24 percent blue, 20 percent orange, 16 percent green, 14 percent yellow, 13 percent brown, and 13 percent red. If you were to buy a 1.69 oz. (47.9 g) bag of M&Ms at random as a sample, the sample proportions should match the population proportions, right? Have each student try it and see. They can select any bag "at random," but it is very unlikely that their "random" sample will match the M&M/Mars population.

POSSIBLE STUDENT CHALLENGES ANSWERS

1. For each of the following situations, identify the appropriate target population and sampling frame.

a. A local chapter of the American Lung Association wants to test the effectiveness of a brochure entitled "12 Reasons for Not Smoking" in the city of St. Paul, Minnesota.

- The population could be defined as all persons 12 years of age or older in the city of St. Paul, Minnesota. The sampling frame could be the city directory (e.g., R. L. Polk's city directory), which would provide a list of addresses from which samples of dwelling units could be developed.

b. A large wholesaler dealing in household appliances in the city of New York wants to evaluate dealer reaction to a new discount policy.

- The population could be defined as all retailers that sell household appliances in the city of New York. The sampling frame might be the telephone book Yellow Pages. Alternatively, there might be an association of appliance dealers. If so, the membership roster could serve as the sampling frame.

c. A local department store wants to assess the satisfaction with a new credit policy offered to charge account customers.

- The population could be defined as all persons 18 years of age or older in the particular town or city, or alternatively it could be defined simply as current charge account customers. The sampling frame could be the city directory, which would provide a list of addresses from which samples of dwellings can be developed. If the focus were current charge account customers, then the list of the store's credit customers would serve as the sampling frame.

2. Management decided to conduct a study to determine people's attitudes toward the particular activities that were available at a popular tourist resort. A request was deposited in each hotel room of the two major hotels in the resort, indicating the nature of the study and encouraging customers to participate. The customers were requested to report to a separate desk located in the lobby of the hotels. Personal interviews, lasting 20 minutes, were conducted at this desk.

a. What type of sampling method was used?

- The method employed by the management of the tourist resort is that of convenience sampling, as volunteers were asked to come forward.

b. Critically evaluate the method used.

- Convenience samples may or may not be representative. In this case, volunteers might possess the characteristics of being helpful and kind and might provide a biased or favorable view of the actual situation. Alternatively, a random sample of hotel rooms could have been selected and questionnaires could have been left in the room for the respondents to complete. This, of course, could produce a problem in nonresponse bias because some guests would probably not complete the questionnaire. An alternative strategy would be to select the rooms randomly and attempt to conduct personal interviews with the guests in them.

10 CHAPTER IN REVIEW

Data Collection: Enhancing Response Rates while Limiting Errors

CHAPTER OUTLINE

I. Introduction
II. Types of Error
  A. Sampling Error
  B. Noncoverage Error
  C. Nonresponse Error
  D. Response Error
  E. Office Error
  F. Total Error Is the Key
III. Calculating Response Rates
  A. Web-based and Mail Surveys
  B. Telephone Surveys (No Eligibility Requirement)
  C. Telephone Surveys (With Eligibility Requirement)
  D. Other Methods of Data Collection
IV. Improving Response Rates
  A. Survey Length
  B. Guarantee of Confidentiality or Anonymity
  C. Interviewer Characteristics and Training
  D. Personalization
  E. Response Incentives
  F. Follow-Up Surveys

POWERPOINT HIGHLIGHTS

Slide 7
Types of Error

Slide 8
Sampling Error

Slide 10
Nonsampling Error

Slide 16
Calculating Response Rates

Slide 22
Improving Response Rates

LEARNING OBJECTIVES

Learning Objective 1
Describe the five types of error that can enter a study.

There are five basic types of errors: sampling error, noncoverage errors, nonresponse errors, response errors, and office errors. Sampling error is simply the difference between the sample results and what is true for the population. Noncoverage errors occur because part of the population of interest was not included in the sampling frame. Nonresponse errors are possible when some elements designated for inclusion in the sample did not respond and were systematically different from those who did respond on key characteristics. Response errors occur because inaccurate information was secured from the sample elements. Office errors occur when errors are introduced in the processing of the data or in reporting the findings.

Learning Objective 2
Give the general definition for response rate.

Response rate is defined as the number of completed interviews with responding units divided by the number of eligible responding units in the sample.

Learning Objective 3
Discuss several ways in which response rates might be improved.

There are several approaches for improving response rates, including making the data collection instrument and procedure as interesting and as short as possible, guaranteeing confidentiality or anonymity to respondents, carefully choosing and training interviewers, personalizing data collection forms as much as possible, providing incentives, and sending follow-up surveys.

POSSIBLE STUDENT CHALLENGES ANSWERS

1. The placement office at a university has hired you to assist it in determining the size of starting salaries and the range of salary offers received by graduating seniors. The placement office has always gathered some information in this regard in that historically some seniors have come in to report the name of the company for which they are going to work and the amount of their starting salary. The office feels that these statistics may be biased, and thus it wishes to approach the whole task more systematically. This is why it has hired your expertise to determine what the situation was with respect to last year's graduating seniors.

a. Describe how you would select a sample of respondents to answer the question of starting salaries. Why would you use this particular sample?

- There is one condition that should make the sampling in this case much simpler than it is in many applied problems—there should be a relatively accurate, up-to-date list of population elements. As a matter of course, universities attempt to keep track of the names, addresses, and other demographic information of their graduating seniors. Thus, it seems possible that this roster could be used to select the sample. This, then, begs the question of what type of sample should be selected. Because it is likely that there exist systematic differences in starting salaries by major, a stratified sample may be appropriate. The population of graduating seniors could be sorted into subgroups by major and a random sample taken from each subgroup. Although we might wish to canvass all graduating seniors, it would be better, if the budget is limited, to sample the various subgroups. The smaller sample size would allow more follow-up to reduce nonsampling errors.

KEY TERMS

noncoverage error p. 126
nonresponse error p. 126
refusals p. 127
not-at-homes p. 127
response error p. 128
office error p. 129
response rate p. 130

b. What types of nonsampling errors might you expect to encounter with your approach, and how would you control for them?

- The analyst should expect to wrestle with all of the common types of nonsampling errors. Noncoverage errors due to sampling frame inadequacies could be expected to be less troublesome than in many problems, but they should be by no means eliminated. The roster of graduating seniors will not be completely accurate. This means that some of the questionnaires will be sent to incorrect addresses. The burden on the researcher here is to follow up on those questionnaires and by process of follow-up (e.g., through the student's parents) ascertain the correct address.

  Nonresponse errors could also be expected to occur. Some students might inadvertently not answer, for example, because they misplaced the questionnaire, whereas others might be reluctant to answer because they are embarrassed by the size of their starting salary or feel perhaps it is none of the university's business. The inadvertent nonresponses could be handled by follow-up, but the refusals would require more delicate follow-up. One would have to take the time to convince these subjects of the need and value of the study. This might require some long-distance phone calls, or perhaps it could be handled in a mail follow-up.

  Response errors could also be expected to result, in that it is highly unlikely that all of the information that is collected will be completely accurate. The longer the interval between the time the students graduated and the time the study is conducted, the greater the likelihood of natural forgetting. Motivated forgetting, if the starting salary was low, might also be expected to occur. Respondents should also be expected to make themselves "look good." Thus, any rounding that occurs in the starting salaries might be expected to be upward rounding. These types of response errors could be difficult to deal with. One can make a case for accuracy in the cover letter and can guarantee anonymity, but the number the respondent puts in the salary box is pretty much up to him or her.

  Errors can also arise when processing the data. This is one reason why, if computers will be employed for the analysis, the data should always be verified. One should also generate frequency distributions to determine whether any of the salaries are out of line with the rest and perhaps should be double-checked, or else treated as a special case.

2. A large furniture store located in a city in the southwestern United States was interested in determining how households living in and around the city viewed the image of the store. Store managers hired a local market research company to collect data. The researchers drew a systematic sample of 2,500 names from the local telephone directory and set out to conduct telephone interviews. At the conclusion of the data collection phase of the project, the researchers recorded 1,223 completed interviews, 598 not-at-homes, 427 refusals, and 252 nonworking telephone numbers. Calculate the response rate on the project.

- In this situation, there is no eligibility requirement, and the "regular" response rate for telephone interviews is used:

$$RR = \frac{1223}{1223 + 427 + 598} = 54\%$$

  Note that the number of nonworking numbers is *not* included in the calculation.

TEACHING TIP

Many students do not initially think about the possibilities of error in a research project. It might take a little background work, but this point can be demonstrated fairly simply. Administratively obtain the standardized test scores (i.e., SAT or ACT) and overall GPAs of the students in the class through campus systems; then aggregate for means scores and GPAs for the class in total. Ask the students to self-report the same and aggregate their self-reports. The likelihood is at least one person will either (1) fail to remember their exact scores, (2) purposefully misrepresent them (upward or downward), or (3) purposefully avoid answering the question. Thus, the two sets of aggregated scores would be different. The conclusion: Error is common in any research context.

11 CHAPTER IN REVIEW

Data Preparation for Analysis

CHAPTER OUTLINE

POWERPOINT HIGHLIGHTS

Slides 7–8
Coding (Closed-Ended Items)

Slides 9–10
Coding (Open-Ended Items)

Slide 12
Building the Data File (Codebook Example)

Slide 13
Cleaning the Data

Slide 14
Handling Missing Data

LEARNING OBJECTIVES

Learning Objective 1

Explain the purpose of the editing process.

The purpose of editing is to inspect, and correct if possible, any mistakes in the raw data. During the editing process, you must make certain that open-ended responses use consistent units, decide what to do about cases with incomplete answers, identify obviously wrong answers, and make judgment calls about answers that reflect a lack of interest.

Learning Objective 2

Define what coding is.

Coding is the technical procedure by which data are categorized. Through coding, the raw data are transformed into symbols—usually numerals—that may be analyzed by computer.

Learning Objective 3

Describe the kinds of information contained in a codebook.

The codebook contains the general instructions indicating how each item of data was coded. It contains the variable names, location of each variable in the data file, a description of how each variable is coded, and an explanation of how missing data are treated in the data file.

Learning Objective 4

Describe common methods for cleaning the data file.

Blunders may be located by examining frequency distributions for all variables to identify obviously incorrect codings, by sampling records from the data file and comparing them with the original questionnaires, or by using double-entry of data in which data are entered into two separate data files and then compared for discrepancies. Optical scanning can also be used to help create data files with fewer errors.

Learning Objective 5

Discuss options for dealing with missing data in analyses.

Several options exist, including (1) eliminating the case with missing information from all analyses, (2) eliminating the case with missing information from only analyses using variables with missing information, (3) substituting values for the missing items, and (4) contacting the respondent again.

KEY TERMS

editing p. 137
coding p. 138
codebook p. 141
blunder p. 144
double-entry p. 144
optical scanning p. 144
item nonresponse p. 145

POSSIBLE STUDENT CHALLENGE ANSWER

Compare the codebook for the Avery Fitness Center questionnaire (Exhibit 11.3) to the actual Avery Fitness Center questionnaire (Exhibit 11.2). Write the variable names used in the codebook on the quesionnaire itself. For instance, Q1 has five "check all that apply" options, so the first five variables in the codebook after ID relate to Q1. As such, you would write "WEIGHT" next to Weight Training, "CLASSES" next to classes, and so forth. Do this throughout the entire questionnaire all the way to the "STATUS" variable. Next, recognize that some questions, like Q3, have one variable associated with it but multiple response options. Use the far right-hand column of the codebook to write the associated number for each word or phrase on the questionnaire. For Q3, you would write "DAYPART" next to the question *and* write "1" next to morning, "2" next to afternoon, and "3" next to evening. Continue this pattern, where appropriate, to the end.

- The second half of this exercise applies to DAYPART, GENDER, EDUCAT, and INCOME.

TEACHING TIP

It bears noting that many of the topics discussed in this chapter are more intensive for personal interview, telephone, and mail questionnaire data. Internet-based questionnaires require these issues be handled a bit differently. For instance, if respondents are essentially doing the data entry as they answer the Internet-based questions, the data entry steps are largely or entirely eliminated. To demonstrate this point, ask students to combine administrative methods. Have students ask half of a respondent pool to complete a paper-based questionnaire while the other half completes a Web-based questionnaire consisting of all the same questions.

PROCEDURE FOR DEVELOPING A QUESTIONNAIRE

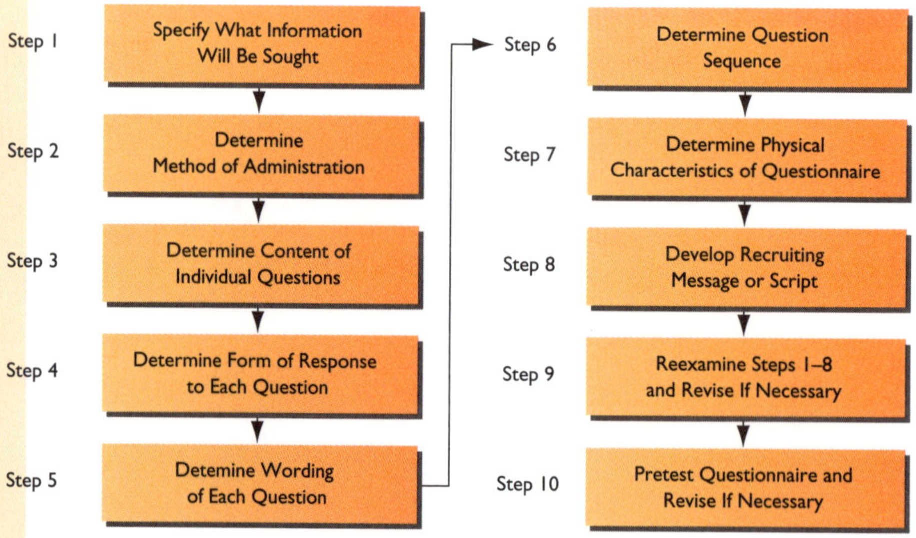

12 CHAPTER IN REVIEW

Analysis & Interpretation: Individual Variables Independently

CHAPTER OUTLINE

I. Introduction

II. The Avery Fitness Center (AFC) Project

III. Basic Univariate Statistics: Categorical Measures

- A. Frequency Analysis
  - 1. About Percentages
- B. Other Uses for Frequencies
- C. Confidence Intervals for Proportions
  - 1. A Word of Caution

IV. Basic Univariate Statistics: Continuous Measures

- A. Descriptive Statistics
- B. Converting Continuous Measures to Categorical Measures
- C. Confidence Intervals for Means

V. Hypothesis Testing

- A. Null and Alternative Hypotheses
- B. Hypothesis Testing in Practice

VI. Testing Hypotheses About Individual Variables

- A. Testing Statistical Significance with Categorical Variables
- B. Testing Statistical Significance with Continuous Variables

POWERPOINT HIGHLIGHTS

Slide 6
Basic Univariate Statistics: Categorical Measures

Slide 10
Confidence Intervals for Proportions

Slide 12
Basic Univariate Statistics: Continuous Measures

Slide 14
Basic Univariate Statistics: Continuous Measures (Two-Box Technique)

Slide 15
Confidence Intervals for Means

LEARNING OBJECTIVES

Learning Objective 1

Distinguish between univariate and multivariate analyses.

Univariate analyses are conducted on individual variables; multivariate analyses involve multiple variables.

Learning Objective 2

Describe frequency analysis.

A frequency analysis is a univariate technique that involves counting the number of responses that fall into various response categories.

Learning Objective 3

Describe descriptive statistics.

Descriptive statistics describe the distribution of responses on a variable. The most commonly used descriptive statistics for continuous measures (interval- or ratio-level measures) are the mean, or arithmetic average, and the standard deviation. The mean is a measure of central tendency; the standard deviation provides a measure of the dispersion of responses.

Learning Objective 4

Discuss confidence intervals for proportions and means.

The confidence interval is the range within which the population parameter (the true proportion or mean) is likely to fall, with a given level of confidence (usually 95% confidence). The confidence interval is equal to the sample statistic plus or minus estimated sampling error.

Learning Objective 5

Overview the basic purpose of hypothesis testing.

Hypothesis tests are conducted to determine whether a result from a sample is likely to apply to the population from which the sample was drawn. In general, researchers want to reject the null hypothesis and tentatively accept the alternative hypothesis that a result is true for the population.

KEY TERMS

POSSIBLE STUDENT CHALLENGES ANSWERS

Download the Avery Fitness Center data from the Web site (www.cengagebrain.com), and replicate the exhibits in this chapter. Note: the two-box results exhibit is produced by the researcher, not the analytical software of choice (i.e., SPSS). The researcher condenses statistical software output to arrive at such an exhibit.

- Universities maintain a lot of different versions of SPSS, so menu selection may vary slightly. The "Working with SPSS" card should offer generally reliable guidance. Most of the exhibits in this chapter can be replicated with the Analyze > Descriptive Statistics > Frequences menu selections or the Analyze > Descriptive Statistics > Descriptives approach.

TEACHING TIP

Our tendency is to think about SPSS as the statistical package for analyzing marketing research data, but we recognize that the availability of SPSS varies. With that in mind, many simple statistical procedures can be completed in Excel, an application in the Microsoft Office suite of productivity software. Take Exhibit 12.1, for instance; a COUNTIF function for 1 (Male) and then another for 2 (Female) should provide the same results as SPSS. A similar approach could be followed for Exhibit 12.2. Variables like age (Exhibit 12.4) make Excel more cumbersome as there is so much variability in the data. Although Excel can replicate the SPSS output, SPSS and other statistical software applications were designed for the task.

13 CHAPTER IN REVIEW

Analysis & Interpretation: Multiple Variables Simultaneously

CHAPTER OUTLINE

I. Introduction

II. Cross Tabulation

III. Independent Samples *T*-Test for Means

IV. Paired Sample *T*-Test for Means

V. Pearson Product-Moment Correlation Coefficient

  A. Caution in the Interpretation of Correlations

VI. Regression Analysis

POWERPOINT HIGHLIGHTS

Slide 6
Why Conduct Multivariate Analysis?

Slide 8
Cross Tabulation

Slide 14
Analyses Involving Categorical and Continuous Measures

Slide 19
Analyses Involving Continuous Measures

LEARNING OBJECTIVES

Learning Objective 1

Discuss why a researcher might conduct a multivariate analysis.

Multivariate analysis often provides a much deeper understanding of the data. Univariate analyses produce broad, overall results. Multivariate analyses look for differences across groups or associations among variables.

Learning Objective 2

Explain the purpose and importance of cross tabulation.

Cross tabulation is the most commonly used multivariate technique. Its purpose is to study the relationships among and between categorical variables.

Learning Objective 3

Describe a technique for comparing groups on a continuous dependent variable.

When comparing two groups, the independent samples *t*-test is used to determine whether the mean score on the dependent variable for one group is significantly different from the mean score for the second group.

Learning Objective 4

Explain the difference between an independent sample *t*-test for means and a paired sample *t*-test for means.

In the independent samples *t*-test, mean scores on the dependent variable are compared for different groups of respondents. In a paired sample *t*-test, mean scores on two different variables (measured on similar scales) are compared across a single group (i.e., all respondents provide scores on both variables).

Learning Objective 5

Discuss the Pearson product-moment correlation coefficient.

The Pearson product-moment correlation coefficient assesses the degree of linear association between two continuous variables.

Learning Objective 6

Discuss a technique for examining the influence of one or more predictor variables on an outcome variable.

With regression analysis, a mathematical equation is derived that relates a dependent variable to one or more independent, or predictor, variables. The predictor variables can be either categorical or continuous.

KEY TERMS

cross tabulation p. 162

Pearson chi-square (χ^2) test of independence p. 163

Cramer's *V* p. 164

independent samples *t*-test p. 164

paired sample *t*-test p. 166

Pearson product-moment correlation coefficient p. 167

regression analysis p. 169

coefficient of multiple determination (R^2) p. 170

POSSIBLE STUDENT CHALLENGES ANSWERS

1. Do men or women use Avery Fitness Center more in the morning? Use a cross-tabulation analysis to answer this question and complete the table below. (*Hint:* the key variables are DAYPART and GENDER, and a cross-tabulation analysis is a Descriptive Statistics technique in SPSS.) Exhibit 13.2 is a cross-tabulation analysis of two other variables from the same data set.

Part of the Day Normally Visiting AFC by Gender Cross Tabulation (Percentages in Parentheses)

Part of the Day	Male	Female	Total
Morning	30 (20%)	123 (80%)	153 (100%)
Afternoon	12 (28%)	31 (72%)	43 (100%)
Evening	0 (0%)	10 (100%)	10 (100%)
Total	42 (20%)	164 (80%)	206 (100%)

- Clearly, women use Avery Fitness Center more in the morning than men do. When testing for statistical significance, the story is less clear. The Pearson chi-square value is 4.116 on 2 degrees of freedom (df), and the associated *p*-value is 0.128. For most statistical purposes *p*-values have to be under 0.05 in order for a result to be "statistically significant." Because that is not the case here, gender and part of the day normally visiting AFC are unrelated in the population, and we cannot reject the null hypothesis of independence.

2. A well-known athletic shoe manufacturer developed a mobile telephone app to monitor various financial markets. In the app, as a market indicator (like the Dow Jones Industrial Average) went up, athletic male and female models would add layers of the company's athletic apparel. In contrast, when the market went down, the models would "lose their shirts" in the market. Explain the relationship between financial market indicators and model clothing in Pearson product-moment correlation coefficient terms for this PG (i.e., no nudity) app.

- First, the well-known athletic shoe manufacturer was Puma. Second, the app was made for the iPhone, but at last check the app was no longer available in Apple's App Store or on Puma's Web site. Third, Puma was capitalizing on a direct or positive correlation in that as the Dow went up, number of clothing items went up; and as the down went down, the number of clothing items went down. Rest assured, models never got to a state of complete undress. Puma makes athletic undergarments, too. An alternative explanation that may surface is that as the market went up, amount of visible skin went down. The contrast would certainly be that as the market decreased, the amount of visible skin increased. This would be a negative or inverse correlation. The first explanation is expected; the second explanation is viable. Each is an analysis involving continuous measures. Moreover, this is an opportunity to reiterate that Dow Jones did not cause the app models to change their dressing behavior. These activities were related for the purposes of the app.

TEACHING TIP

Frequently remind students to be very careful with their language when discussing statistical results. Many of the techniques discussed in this chapter allow a researcher to calculate a measure of confidence. For instance, Exhibit 13.6 produces a strong positive correlation between age and revenues with a 0.000 *p*-, or significance, value. Clearly the significance level is below 0.05 (95% confidence), even below 0.01 (99% confidence), but a *p*-value of 0.000 does not indicate 100 percent confidence. Remind students that a statistical software program does not eliminate the potential for error in the overall study or individual results like those present in this correlation matrix.

14 CHAPTER IN REVIEW

The Research Report

CHAPTER OUTLINE

I. Introduction
II. The Written Research Report
  A. Research Report Writing Standards
    1. Completeness
    2. Accuracy
    3. Clarity
  B. Research Report Outline
    1. Title Page
    2. Table of Contents
    3. Executive Summary
    4. Introduction
    5. Method
    6. Results
    7. Conclusions and Recommendations
    8. Appendices
III. The Oral Research Presentation
  A. Preparing the Oral Report
  B. Delivering the Oral Report
IV. Graphic Presentation of the Results
  A. Pie Chart
  B. Line Chart
  C. Stratum Chart
  D. Bar Chart
    1. Bar Chart Variations

POWERPOINT HIGHLIGHTS

Slide 6
Written Research Report

Slide 8
Written Research Report: Executive Summary

Slide 9
Written Research Report: Conclusions versus Recommendations

Slide 10
The Oral Research Presentation

LEARNING OBJECTIVES

Learning Objective 1

Discuss three writing standards that a report should meet if it is to communicate effectively with readers.

A solid research report should meet the standards of completeness (everything important has been included in as concise a manner as possible), accuracy (no mistakes have been made), and clarity (the intended meaning can be clearly understood by the reader).

Learning Objective 2

Outline the main elements that make up a standard research report.

A standard report generally contains the following elements: title page, table of contents, executive summary, introduction, method, results, conclusions and recommendations, and appendices.

Learning Objective 3

Explain the kind of information contained in the executive summary.

A good executive summary gives the most important points of the report, especially focusing on key results, conclusions, and recommendations.

Learning Objective 4

Discuss two fundamental rules for making good oral presentations.

When presenting oral reports the two fundamental rules are (1) know your stuff and (2) know your audience.

Learning Objective 5

List some of the different kinds of charts that can be used in presenting study results.

A number of different charts can be used. Some of these include (1) pie charts, (2) line charts, (3) stratum charts, (4) bar charts, (5) pictograms, (6) grouped-bar charts, and (7) stacked-bar charts.

POSSIBLE STUDENT CHALLENGES ANSWERS

1. **In presenting a report to a group of grocery store managers, a researcher stated the following: "The data from the judgment sample of 10 grocery stores were analyzed, and the results show that the 95 percent confidence interval for average annual sales in the population of grocery stores is $1,000,000 +/− $150,000."**
   a. As far as the audience is concerned, what is wrong with this statement?
      - The statement does not properly take into account the audience's level of technical sophistication. Results of a study must be presented with the technical

KEY TERMS

completeness p. 174
accuracy p. 174
clarity p. 174
pie chart p. 183
line chart p. 183
stratum chart p. 183
bar chart p. 185
pictogram p. 185

competence of the audience in mind. Moreover, because a judgment sample was used, the calculation of confidence intervals in the usual sense is incorrect.

b. Rewrite the statement. Be sure to include all the relevant information while correcting the problem.

- "In a judgment sample, the elements are purposely picked. The 10 grocery stores we selected were chosen because we believed they would provide a representative estimate of average annual sales in this area. After analyzing the results, we are reasonably confident that the average of annual sales for all the grocery stores in this area is between $850,000 and $1,150,000."

2. Your marketing research firm is preparing the final written report on a research project commissioned by a major manufacturer of lawn mowers. One objective of the project was to investigate seasonal variations in sales, both on an aggregate basis and by each of the company's sales regions individually. Your client is particularly interested in the width of the range between maximum and minimum seasonal sales. Exhibit 1 was submitted by one of your junior analysts. Critique the table and prepare a revision suitable for inclusion in your report.

EXHIBIT 1

Seasonal Sales Variation

	Sales in Thousands of Dollars			
Sales Region	**Spring**	**Summer**	**Fall**	**Winter**
Northeast	120.10	140.59	50.90	30.00
East-central	118.80	142.70	61.70	25.20
Southeast	142.00	151.80	134.20	100.10
Midwest	100.20	139.42	42.90	20.00
South-central	80.77	101.00	90.42	78.20
Plains	95.60	120.60	38.50	19.90
Southwest	105.40	110.50	101.60	92.10
Pacific	180.70	202.41	171.54	145.60

- Exhibit 1 can be faulted on a number of points. Among these are:
  1. Aggregate figures are not furnished.
  2. No indication of the range between maximum and minimum seasonal sales is given.
  3. The order of the sales regions is not in tune with the purpose of the table. They are ordered geographically when ordering by magnitude of seasonal range would be more appropriate.
  4. The table is cluttered by the use of too many decimal places.

TEACHING TIP

Even marketing students have a fear of public speaking. The reality is presenting an oral/verbal report presentation is critical, especially if managers are not technically sophisticated or well trained in the research process. One of our colleagues took an interesting approach recently. He had students video-record their presentations and show them in class as opposed to having them present in class. There are a variety of benefits to this approach, not the least of which is having a verbal presentation that can be given to the client for reviewing at a later time.

Qualtrics Research Suite

Quickstart Guide

Create an Account

To sign up for a Qualtrics account with your Cengage Access code:

1. Go to http://qualtrics.com/cengage
2. Click on the red **Free Account** button.
3. Enter your email address and desired password. Click **Get Started**.
4. On next page, enter in your name (optional) and phone number (optional). Click **Finish**.
5. On the final page, enter the access code found in your textbook and click **Go**.
6. A verification email will be sent to your email address with instructions on how to verify your account. After verifying your account, you will be able to log in at Qualtrics.com.

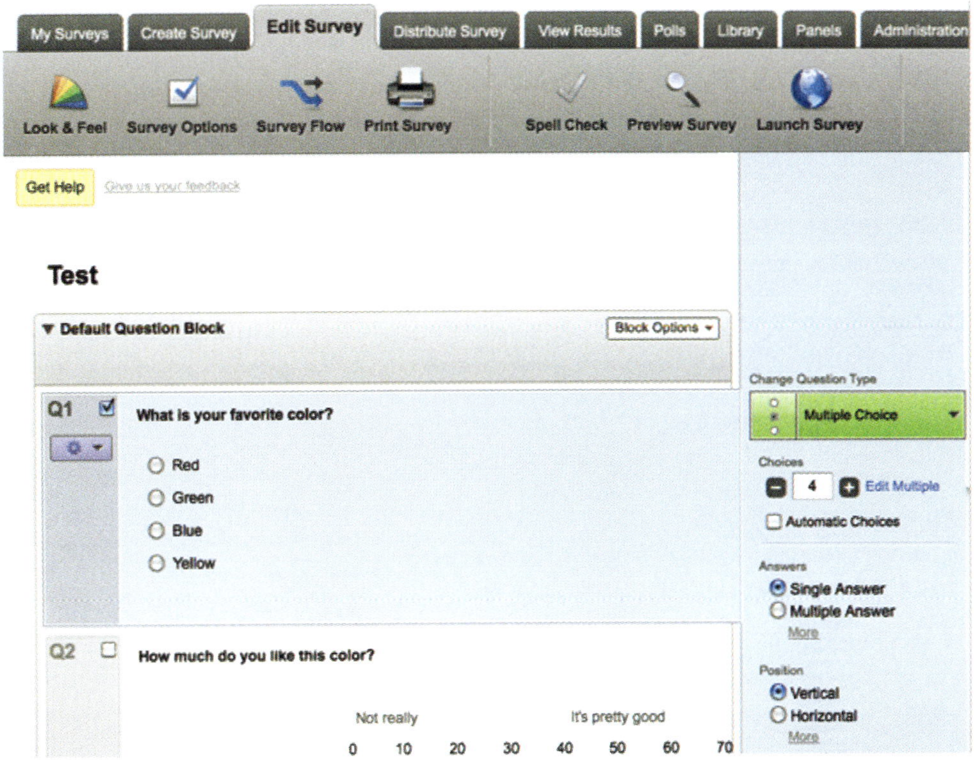

Surveys

Create a New Survey

1. Click **Create Survey**.
2. Select **Quick Survey Builder** to create a blank survey.
3. Enter a Survey Name and click **Create Survey**.
4. Create questions by clicking **Create a new question**.
5. Change the question type by clicking the green **Question Type** button in the question options pane.
6. Edit the question and answer text in the large, central question box.
7. Create more questions by clicking the above and below each question.

Autosave

Qualtrics automatically saves your survey while you work on it. Some dialog boxes will have Save buttons when necessary.

Apply Skip Logic

1. Select a question.
2. Click the **Advanced Question Options** button and select **Add Skip Logic**.
3. Complete the logic statement.
4. Click **Done** to apply the logic.

Display Logic

1. Select a question.
2. Click the **Advanced Question Options** button and select **Add Display Logic**.
3. Complete the logic statement.
4. Add additional conditions by clicking the button.
5. Click **Save** to apply the logic.

Change the Look

1. From the gray navigation bar, click **Look & Feel**. The Look & Feel dialog box will appear.
2. You may adjust:
   - The Survey Header and Footer.
   - The Next and Previous button text.
   - Change the Survey Skin.

Include a Progress Bar

In the Look & Feel dialog box, a progress bar may be inserted by selecting an option from the drop-down menu.

Validation

1. Select a question.
2. In the question options pane, find the Validation heading. Check the **Force Response** box to require a response to the question. Select **Request Response** to prompt the user to answer the question but not require a response before advancing.

Survey Flow

In the Survey Flow dialog box, you can insert blocks of questions and other advanced elements like the Randomizer, Branching Elements, Authenticator and End of Survey elements.

1. Click on the **Edit Survey** tab.
2. Select the **Survey Flow** icon from the gray navigation bar.

Survey Options

Before sending out a survey, be sure to check over the Survey Options. These can be accessed by clicking on the **Survey Options** button. Some important options to review are:

- Prevent Ballot Box Stuffing.
- Partial completion time.
- Survey expiration dates.

Block Options

Add a Question Block

1. While editing a survey, click on **Advanced Options** on the gray navigation bar.
2. Select **Add Block**.

Randomization

Blocks, questions and answer choices can all be randomized. (See *Survey Flow* to randomize question blocks.)

Answer Randomization

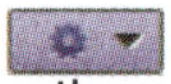

1. Select a question and click on the **Advanced Question Options** button.
2. Choose **Randomization...**
3. Choose a randomization option from the list. Click **Save**.

Question Randomization

1. To randomize questions, select **Block Options** at the beginning of the block.
2. Select **Question Randomization.**
3. Choose a randomization option from the list. Click **Save**.

Distribution

Activate your survey by clicking the gray box next to your survey name on the **My Surveys** tab. Choose one of the distribution options below.

Anonymous Survey Link

1. Click on the **Distribute Survey** tab.
2. Click on the **Survey Link** button in the gray navigation bar.
3. Copy and Paste the link to distribute the survey.

Email a Survey

1. Click on the **Distribute Survey** tab.
2. Select the **Email Survey** button from the gray navigation bar.
4. Enter the recipient information and pick a send time. You may also select a panel (See *Create a Panel* below.)
5. Edit the email message and subject. (See *Enter Piped Text* below.)
6. Click **Schedule Mailing** at the bottom of the page.

Create a Panel

1. Click on the **Panels** tab and click on **Create New Panel**.
2. Name the panel and click **Create**.
3. Choose **Import From a File**.
4. Download the **Example** document provided and format your contacts as shown in the example.
5. Save the file as **.csv** and upload it into your panel by going back to **Import From a File**.

Piped Text

1. To enter the recipient's name or other information in the survey mailer, select the **Piped Text** icon.
2. In the dropdown menu, select a category.
3. Select **Panel Field** to insert the recipient's name, if necessary.
4. Click the appropriate panel field.

Piped text can also be inserted into question text by clicking on the blue **Piped Text** tab above a text box.

Results

To view your results, click on the **View Results** tab in the gray navigation bar.

View Reports

1. To view a report of your data with graphs and statistics tables, click on the **View Reports** button.
2. Click on the **Initial Report**.
3. Click on the list of questions to the left to navigate through them.
4. Add a graph to a page by clicking on **Insert Graph** in the upper right hand corner of the page.
5. Filter by a subgroup by selecting **Add a Subgroup to This Report**. Use the dropdown menus to set conditions on which a filter will be applied.

Individual Responses

1. Click on the **Responses** button.
2. Under the **Recorded Response** tab, click on the **Response ID** to view an individual report.
3. Delete responses by checking the responses you want to delete and then click **Delete** at the top of the list.
4. View responses in progress by clicking on the **Responses in Progress** tab.

Download Data

1. To download your data into Excel or SPSS, select the **Download Data** button.
2. Click on the **CSV** link to download a file compatible with Excel. The SPSS file download is located beneath the CSV.
3. The options at the top of the page let you:
   - Select individual questions you would like to download.
   - Download data as values or labels.
   - Set a time range.

Add a Trigger

1. Under the **Edit Survey** tab, click on **Advanced Options** in the gray navigation bar on the right.
2. Choose **Triggers** and select **Email Trigger**.
3. Click **Add a Condition** at the top of the dialogue box.
4. Build the logic condition to trigger the email.
5. Modify the email address, the subject, and the survey message. Choose whether a response report will be included below the message body.
6. Click **Save Triggers**.

Collaboration

Share a Survey

1. From the **My Surveys** page, click the **Collaborate** icon in the **Tasks** column.
2. Enter your collaborator's user name or email address and click **Add**.
3. Modify the permissions assigned to your collaborator. Click **Details** for more options
4. Click **Save**.

Question Types

Constant Sum - Respondents enter numeric answers or percentages for each statement to total a number you define.
Text/Graphic - Displays instructions or consent information - no answer choices.
Matrix Table - A list of statements with a uniform Likert scale formatted in a table. You can use radio buttons, check boxes or text-entry fields.
Multiple Choice - A question type with multiple answer choices a respondent may select.
Text Entry - Allows for open-ended text responses.
Rank Order - The respondent ranks items in order of preference.
Slider - The respondent can click or drag to a spot on a scale to designate a value.
Pick, Group, and Rank - Items in a list can be dragged into and ranked in pre-defined or user-defined groups.
Timing - Tracks how much time a respondent spends on the active page.
Side by Side - Allows different question types to be placed in a table next to each other.

Questions?

Qualtrics University Help Site:
http://www.qualtrics.com/university